Friends and Citizens

Friends and Citizens

Essays in Honor of Wilson Carey McWilliams

Edited by
Peter Dennis Bathory and Nancy L. Schwartz

ROWMAN & LITTLEFIELD PUBLISHERS, INC.
Lanham • Boulder • New York • Oxford

ROWMAN & LITTLEFIELD PUBLISHERS, INC.

Published in the United States of America
by Rowman & Littlefield Publishers, Inc.
4720 Boston Way, Lanham, Maryland 20706
http://www.rowmanlittlefield.com

12 Hid's Copse Road
Cumnor Hill, Oxford OX2 9JJ, England

British Library Cataloguing in Publication Information Available

Library of Congress Cataloging-in-Publication Data

Friends and citizens : essays in honor of Wilson Carey McWilliams / edited by
Peter Dennis Bathory and Nancy L. Schwartz.
    p. cm.
    Includes bibliographical references and index.
    ISBN 0-8476-9746-0 (cloth : alk. paper)
       1. Political culture—United States. 2. Friendship—United States.
  3. Citizenship—United States. 4. Communitarianism—United States.
  5. Democracy—United States. I. McWilliams, Wilson C. II. Bathory, Peter
Dennis. III. Schwartz, Nancy Lynn, 1946– .
  JK1726.F685   2000
  320—dc21   00-025893

Printed in the United States of America

♾™ The paper used in this publication meets the minimum requirements
of American National Standard for Information Sciences—Permanence of
Paper for Printed Library Materials, ANSI/NISO Z39.48-1992.

Contents

Preface

Peter Dennis Bathory and Nancy L. Schwartz

When we began this project with a letter to prospective authors—colleagues, teachers, students, and friends of Wilson Carey McWilliams—we quoted from an essay in which he concluded, "Democracy is for friends and citizens, not masters and slaves."[1] As is so often the case with Carey, a commonplace assertion quickly becomes much more, as he reminds us that "The ultimate ground for democratic ideas of equality and the highest limitation on democracy's excesses both derive from a universe in which humanity is at home, my dignity is guaranteed by the majesty of the law I obey, and perhaps even by 'those who have no memorial' who do not pass from memory" (101). Fittingly, that essay was published in 1980 during the American bicentennial celebrations, in a volume entitled *How Democratic Is the Constitution?* "Most Americans," he had begun, "would agree that the Constitution has become more democratic with time." Ever the contrarian, Carey argued that the Constitution has not necessarily become more democratic; the extension of the franchise, the direct election of senators, and other procedural measures are democratic in only limited ways. Democracy is not defined solely by "voting by majority rule." He relied, he said, "on an older, more comprehensive understanding that makes citizenship, rather than voting, the defining quality of democracy" (79).

The essays in the present volume remind us of this important observation. The lessons we have all learned from our friend through his writing (from *The Idea of Fraternity in America* [1973] to *Beyond the Politics of Disappointment?* [2000]), through his speaking (formal lectures, public speeches, and long conversations), and through his constancy and loyalty are all reflected in *Friends and Citizens*.

vii

Friendship is much more than an abstraction or something paired with citizenship in order to make democracy work. It has its own worth for Carey, both in the persons of his many friends and as painstakingly set out in *The Idea of Fraternity*, and is implicit in other works, including the essay in *How Democratic Is the Constitution?* Friendship is a relation of mutual affection and knowledge that seeks to share the best with one's friend. The danger of modern America, Carey teaches us, is that "democracy has few footholds." "The citizen finds little in public life to elevate the spirit or support dignity"; indeed, a citizen "finds much that damages both." In the process, friendship must suffer as well, for it becomes merely private, not without value but without excellence. Excellence demands that others, publicly chosen and politically engaged, not "retreat into the solitude of [one's] own heart" (100). Carey recoils against such a retreat even in his most pessimistic and solitary moments. We retreat from public life and political commitment at our peril. Why? Because, in essential ways, "politics frees us," he tells us (83).

"Autonomy is possible for human beings only as parts of wholes in which our 'partiality' and the things to which we are partial are realized as secondary, though important." This ancient understanding is one that Carey will repeat again and again. It is an understanding that forges the strongest links between friendship and citizenship. Indeed, for us, it is this link between citizenship and friendship that is most remarkable in his writing, teaching, and public life. "The polis allows me to find friends," he contends, looking to the ancients for counsel, "who choose me (as I choose them) because they like me, not my genealogy" (83). The city provides the space for people to act as citizens and to choose friends. The "freedom" of democratic politics arises as it empowers citizens and teaches the importance of self-rule.

"The excellent or complete human being," he writes, "is the end for which the city exists." Such a human being would recognize a "debt to the city and know that freedom involves obligations" (83). Friendship becomes a reward of freedom and a solace for the hard work of living up to democratic obligations. We understand, Carey suggests, that even as a democrat, one never really "lives as one likes," at least not in the contemporary, individualist sense of that phrase. The individualist, "preferring to be free from all rule . . . supports democracy," he warns, "from weakness and lack of spirit, but he is not a democrat" (82). For the individualist, friendship is weakened as much as citizenship, since interest is his guiding spirit. Partiality tied to interest is his defining characteristic. Such individuals, by choosing to be separated from politics and instead driven by self-interest, are prone to be suspicious or manipulative of friends.

Democracy, for Carey, requires community, civic dignity, and religion. His pessimism about the health of American democracy does not, however, negate his admiration for democracy's history in America, the glimpses of full citizens now and then, nor his hopes for the American experiment. The themes of the essays here, beginning with an essay on Genesis, echo both the hopes and fears of Carey—his faith and his prophecy. Citizenship is complex and requires much of us, since civic dignity is threatened by technology and globalization. The concluding essays on citizenship celebrate the many forms of governance—ancient and modern—that Carey has taught us about. Yet friendship must be part of all this; without it, community is hollow, and civic dignity absent. The possibility of friendship depends in part on overcoming pride or, at least, facing its temptations and coming to terms with the limitations of humanity. The essays of the first section discuss friendship as a link between the first things of religion—the nature of humans and their deity—and the world of politics. The second section, on citizenship, completes the whole.

The work of teaching is always about these themes, for Carey. Whether he confronts them head on, in his lectures on "American Political Thought" and "Religion and Politics" or via his wonderful lectures on the Greeks, the themes recur. The enterprise of theory and theorizing is brought to life for undergraduates. Speaking of Aeschylus or Plato, he moves deftly to the decline of the American jury system, to issues of gender, or to piety and impiety in ancient Greece and contemporary America. He breathes life into ancient texts with examples from contemporary American life and he breathes a vital ancient breath into the decaying culture of democracy in America.

Theory, Carey reminds his students, teaches us to distrust appearances, to understand that the data of our culture(s) is not that of simple sensory perception but rather the result of constructs we receive and create to organize the complexity presented by our senses. At the same time, theory teaches us to be wary of those very constructs that help us arrange, order, and interpret data. Indeed, theory's main task is to question those categories even as it understands their necessity. This, however, makes the task of theorizing potentially dangerous, even subversive. Theory asks us to question the commonplace and, therefore, to call into question that which gives order to our lives. Political philosophy involves, Carey says, a kind of madness as it calls the commonplaces of social order into question. Political philosophers are in turn shameless as they ask us to think and rethink the unthinkable. But, if political philosophy is dangerous, if it can produce a treacherous Alcibiades, then what are we to conclude? Not, he insists, that theory is to be avoided, but rather that its risks be acknowledged and its benefits highlighted.

An early exercise in Carey's lectures about the nature of theory makes the point. He has written about Mark Twain since his chapter on Twain in *The Idea of Fraternity*. Returning to Twain in recent years, he has discovered a short piece, "A Fable," [2] in which Twain speaks of the nature of a text. Those students not already captured by the Greeks' sacred voyage of *theoria* and contemporary political problems are now given an alternative route to the challenge faced by the theorist. In his "Fable," Twain tells of an artist who was disappointed with a small and "very beautiful picture" he had painted and so placed it in front of a mirror, which "doubles the distance and softens it," and makes it "twice as lovely as it was before." The story of the picture is, Twain says, told to the animals in the woods by the "housecat, who was greatly admired by them because he was so learned, and so refined and civilized, and so polite and so well-bred, and could tell them so much which they didn't know before, and were not certain about afterward."

Anyone in the class who knows or, through Carey's prompting, remembers any of Twain's writings is immediately intrigued. Who is this critic and what will he say? First, the cat must define a picture, then a mirror. A picture, says the cat, is "wonderfully flat, marvelously flat, enchantingly flat and elegant and oh so beautiful." The animals want to know what makes it beautiful, and the cat responds, "The look of it." A mirror, says the cat, "is a hole in the wall, and there you see the picture, and it is so dainty and charming and ethereal and inspiring in its unimaginable beauty that your head turns round and round and you almost swoon with ecstasy." All of this has excited the other animals but the "ass" began to doubt what he heard. Why should something so beautiful have emerged now, for "there never had been anything as beautiful as this before," he thought. So, the ass determined to view this wonderful sight. He went with the cat to see the picture, but not knowing where to stand, he stood between the picture and the mirror. "The result was that the picture had no chance and didn't show up," says Twain. All that the ass saw was himself, and, so, he reported: "The cat lied. There was nothing in that hole but an ass. There wasn't a sign of a flat thing visible. It was a handsome ass, and friendly, but just an ass and nothing more." And so it was with the other animals who repeated the ass's "mistake" and saw themselves in the mirror. The cat, they concluded, had lied to them. But the cat, having observed all of the animals, was not deterred by their anger at him and the "moral and mental blindness" of which he was accused. Instead, the cat offers the following moral: "You can find in a text whatever you bring, if you will stand between it and the mirror of your imagination. You may not see your ears, but they will be there." The adventure of reading political theory depends upon "what" you see, upon your imagination, and upon what you hear, but you must "listen" with great care. The careful student is in turn ready to begin to read, to listen to the text as Carey has compelled most of them to listen to him.

Carey begins his introductory course, "American Politics: Public and Private," with lectures on Aristotle. Again the breath goes both ways, between ancient and modern. So it is also for his world outside the classroom—engaged in university life since the University of California at Berkeley, then at Oberlin and Brooklyn Colleges, and now at Rutgers, the State University of New Jersey. Outside the academy, he has been Democratic Party chair for the borough of Flemington, New Jersey, an elder in his church, vice president of the Institute for the Study of Civic Values, and a member of the Hunterdon County Historical Society. Carey is a friend and citizen in ways the ancients wrote about.

This Festschrift attempts to mark, if not capture, his qualities. Throughout his work he stresses the passionate nature of men and women, our need for connection and for limits. Connections can be to other people, to the city, and to God. Limits are not only constraints but also qualities of internal mastery and harmony—self-rule. Constraints come from laws and customs that encourage civic virtue; more significantly, they come from political experience, its joys and responsibilities. These points and their relation to politics can perhaps be set out in propositional form, yet beyond such propositions lie the tension and grace of Carey's writing style: his wit, his eye for paradox, his ear for contradiction and hypocrisy, his elusiveness, his judgment, and his forgiveness. Using language skillfully, he becomes a great teacher of moral and civic life.

NOTES

1. Wilson Carey McWilliams, "Democracy and the Citizen: Community, Dignity, and the Crisis of Contemporary Politics in America," in *How Democratic Is the Constitution?* ed. Robert A. Goldwin and William A. Schambra (Washington, D.C.: American Enterprise Institute, 1980), 101.

2. Mark Twain, "A Fable," in *The Complete Short Stories of Mark Twain*, ed. Charles Nieder (New York: Hanover House, 1957), 597–99.

Acknowledgments

We would like to thank Frances Warren, coordinator of the College of Social Studies at Wesleyan University, and Jonathan McFall, graduate student in political science at Rutgers University, for their work on this manuscript. Their great skill and good spirits were invaluable. We are indebted to Stephen Wrinn, our editor at Rowman & Littlefield, for his enthusiasm and faith in this Festschrift, which he, Mary Carpenter, and Mary C. Hack shepherded to completion. We are grateful to Richard Rose for his fine photograph of Carey. And we thank Nancy R. McWilliams for her kindness and encouragement over the years.

Introduction: What Wilson Carey McWilliams Saw in America

Patrick J. Deneen and Joseph Romance

Admirers of G. K. Chesterton will recognize an echo to the title of Chesterton's masterful 1921 essay about his travels in the New World, "What I Saw in America." Upon Chesterton's arrival in America, he was presented with a series of questions by customs officials ranging from "Are you an anarchist?" to "Are you a polygamist?" (to which he wished to answer in the latter case, "no such luck"). To the question, "Are you in favor of subverting the government of the United States by force?" Chesterton boldly replied, "I prefer to answer that question at the end of my tour and not the beginning."[1] Wilson Carey McWilliams—known to nearly everyone simply as Carey—has been answering that and many other questions about America throughout his splendid journey. Only rarely has America produced such a great critic and such a great lover of his country, and with boundless joy many of us have had the privilege to accompany Carey and learn from his keen vision. We are lucky that he did not have a better fastball, for baseball's loss was our gain. However, Carey has brought to the study of politics the artfulness of a pitcher able to paint the corners of the plate at will.

Political theory was not Carey's first academic love. Having returned from military service in Germany, Carey originally intended to study international relations upon entering graduate school at Berkeley. He wrote his master's thesis on Hans Morgenthau and Reinhold Niebuhr, and he would always keep a Machiavellian concern for political consequences in his work. Prompted by one of his international relations professors, he enrolled in a political theory course taught by Sheldon Wolin. There was no sudden conversion, "only the slow, soft charm of Wolin's lecturing," and soon those charms and the undeniable appeal of theory taught by one

1

of its greatest lovers forever captured Carey's heart and imagination. As Carey describes it, Wolin made theory marvelous and mysterious, timeless and timely. "A secular agora, Wolin's classroom was also part sanctuary, a place where politics took on grace and mystery."[2]

His turning toward political theory was completed not solely within the classroom, but characteristically confirmed during an encounter in the world of politics. He locates this "turning point of his life" as having occurred during a meeting with Governor-elect Pat Brown immediately after his election in 1958.[3] As Carey tells it:

> After the election, we had a dinner for Pat with a bunch of intellectuals who had supported him. A sociologist was sitting next to Brown, talking about the election. Finally, Brown turned to him and said, "Professor, what I want to know is, why is it every time I talk to a social scientist, he tells me how to get elected. God damn it—I know how to get elected. I have just won the Governorship of this State by a million votes. What I want to know from social-scientists is now that I am elected, what in God's name do I do?"[4]

The political theory to which Carey has devoted himself always takes as its touchstone this question posed by Governor Brown, never seeking to abandon the pressing questions of contemporary political life in the effort to construct a perfect, if abstract, philosophical system. Carey shares Aristotle's view that the study of politics is "the master science," the one discipline that encompasses all disciplines by describing the manner and reasons for which humans pursue certain goods either in concert or individually. For Carey, the study of politics serves to illuminate moral choices—answers to the question "what in God's name are we to do?"—that must nevertheless always be attentive to the effects of those choices on one's fellow citizens and the world. Political science, in this older sense of the word, is never at war with political theory.

To our knowledge, Carey has many intellectual heroes, ranging from older thinkers—Sophocles, Plato, Aristotle, John Calvin, and the Anti-Federalists, Nathaniel Hawthorne, and Henry Adams—to more recent commentators on the American scene—Leo Strauss, Bertrand de Jouvenel, Sheldon Wolin, John Schaar, Ralph Ellison, James Baldwin, and Kurt Vonnegut. However, his two intellectual passions are Alexis de Tocqueville and Mark Twain. They form an interesting pair. One is a "furriner" (to use Carey's Twain-inspired term for non-Americans), a deeply serious student of America, and a Catholic; the other a consummate American—simultaneously a westerner, a southerner, a Midwesterner, and New Englander—a comic, a critic, a traveler, a storyteller, and a Calvinist. Each is a uniquely superb reader of the American mind. We have heard Carey say that Tocqueville is the only thinker who, in his view, is "just plain right" in every instance about America. Carey describes Twain, whom he often and lovingly quotes, as the greatest teacher about America to Americans in the mass setting that Tocqueville envisaged. One might venture to say that Carey combines the best of the two, providing Tocquevillian insights with a Twainian sense of humor.

Both are teachers of what Carey views as the central truth about America: America is a land with a divided soul, born of conflicting ortho- doxies rooted, on the one hand, in Enlightenment liberalism, and on the other in the "culture, in institutions, festivals, tales and songs of love and glory . . . and preeminently, in religion" derived from the Old World.[5] The former, eternally hostile to the latter, teaches Americans to cherish their liberties, to pursue self-interest in both material and moral matters as long as no one is visibly damaged in the pursuit. The latter, a fainter and of- ten attenuated voice, serves as a corrective to the excesses of modern lib- eralism, reminding us of our limits and our obligations, of the possibility for a common good. This older tradition is more demanding, at times calling upon citizens to deny their most obvious self-interest—often cen- tered on the body—in order to comprehend a broader and more long- term, even generational idea of the good. Because it competes against a liberal tradition that sees interest narrowly, that proposes gratification more quickly and more easily, the prospects of America's "alternative tra- dition" have grown ever dimmer as materialism and short-term thinking prevail.

In order to see and hear this subdued and older tradition in America, one has to have a certain resistance to philosophical abstraction, even at times a willfully non- or anti-academic disposition. Above all, one needs to be sensitive to the comic and the tragic manifestations of America's other tradition, mindful of the laughter and tears that give to it its imme- diate force and power. Since this tradition erupts in curious places, one has to be willing to search everywhere it might appear, but especially in the language of the sermon, poetry, fiction, comedy, even popular media. Carey is uniquely sensitive to all these voices, having written and lectured on the ancient playwrights, America's novelists, and finding in films such as *Casablanca* and *E.T.* enduring lessons about sacrifice and the importance of homecoming.[6]

Carey is keenly attentive to the voices in this alternative tradition that seek to teach most widely and engagingly, and comedy is especially a source and means for teaching modern democracies. Mark Twain is the consummate educator of a large-scale democracy, since comedy appeals widely, subtly erodes pretensions and dashes prevailing assumptions, and teaches mostly through indirection often without the overt awareness of the audience.[7] Twain is very funny even as he instructs. Carey is also very funny, and to the same end: stories and jokes often teach fundamental lessons in ways that are both more intimate and more memorable. Like Twain, for example, Carey appreciates exercise: Twain praised exercise often, relating that he exercised frequently by carrying the coffins of friends who died exercising. The joke amuses, but the lesson persists: modernity often bribes our rightful fear of death by justifying ambiguous practices and technologies, apparent advances that in turn massage our desire for longevity, for life. But the offer of life itself does not address the deeper and more difficult question—one reminiscent of Governor Brown's—of "why?" and "to what end?" Technologies such as the locomotive and the telegraph—John Dewey's favorite examples of the benefits of progress—tell us nothing about where we should be going and what needs to be said.[8] Carey likes to relate the response of Henry David Thoreau, who, when told that a magnetic telegraph connected Maine and Texas, remarked: "[B]ut Maine and Texas, it may be, have nothing to communicate." As Carey has observed, "[T]echnology and skill create a demand for their own use, and can easily define rather than serve human purposes."[9]

Technology is a special case, since it affords the illusion of progress and advancement that in turn contributes to dangerous confidence, even hubris, among its users and too easily obfuscates the lessons of the past. One of Carey's favorite books, and one that unerringly explores this dynamic, is Twain's *A Connecticut Yankee in King Arthur's Court.* Twain rightly expects his audience immediately to identify with Hank Morgan, the ingenious Yankee, who is transported back to Arthur's court and gleefully exposes the superstitions and foibles of that era. Yet, by the end of the novel, when Hank Morgan has slaughtered hundreds of knights using the superior technology of the nineteenth century (by means of a Gatling gun, at which point we recall that he was transported to the past during a break from his job at the Colt firearms plant), our former easy identification with Morgan results in a shattering of our own confidence in progress and technology. We are shown that potential for human cruelty always remains, but that the absence of the restraints of older traditions and the ease of technology magnify the results of that cruelty.[10]

Carey observes that the philosophy of antiquity and religious thought is pervaded with mysteries, whereas modern thought attempts to dispel mystery through uncovering, disclosing, even torturing nature.[11] If the ancients appeal to nature as a standard—here Aristotle comes to mind—the fact that the defining aspect of human nature is our capacity as "political animals" suggests the extent to which "nature" remains an obscure and elusive goal. The investigation of standards provided by nature can only occur cooperatively, within political settings, and only imperfectly since human communities, and humanity itself, are never perfectible. By contrast, modernity inaugurates the quest to dissolve all mysteries by asserting that nature is now "hostile rather than mysterious, and that enmity drives individuals back to the self as the only safe ground of knowledge."[12] If older traditions suggested that the great mysteries of human existence required fellowship and politics for their partial solution, modernity—perhaps captured most ably by Descartes's image of an "evil genius" who deceives—drives us farther into "the solitude of our own hearts" in the face of hostile humanity and nature.[13]

Despite claims to transparency, democracy is in fact the regime based on the greatest mystery of all: equality. As Carey likes to point out, equality is the least self-evident proposition ever set forth. What is self-evident is difference: we are each endowed with different appearances, histories, talents, tastes, and desires. Postmodernism, obsessed by *"différence,"* belabors the obvious naggingly.[14] To perceive any kind of equality underlying all these apparent differences requires great mental effort that finally points us toward philosophy, that is, toward the whole that makes singular the many manifestations of humanity. There is no moment in democratic practice where this form of equality is better revealed than on election day, the moment when Americans simultaneously act as "rulers" and "ruled" in turn, when presidents and janitors enter a polling place to cast one vote, declaring with utter simplicity the equal dignity of all citizens. This mystery of equality is captured with appropriate reverence in the image of the shrouded voting booth. As Carey relates, it is an almost mystical place, evinced by one of his great-aunts who "believed that God would guide her hand when she marked her ballot, and He surely did, since she always voted the straight Democratic ticket."[15]

Like his aunt, Carey believes that transformative events are at work in any election. One of his important contributions to the discipline of political science has been a series of essays chronicling the significance of recent electoral contests.[16] While pundits and campaign consultants tend to see in elections nothing more than conflicting personalities and competing campaign tactics, and mainstream political scientists manipulate dry statistics endlessly, Carey seeks to elucidate "the meaning of the election" in order to remind us that Americans are also engaged in a long-term debate about the most fundamental choices. If his recent work highlights the word *disappointment*, he is not given to despair. He hears in recent elections—in the rhetoric of the campaigns, through the decisions and attitudes of voters, and by means of the words and actions of various candidates—echoes of America's noble traditions: a sense of equality, a commitment to community, and a belief in human dignity. With a theorist's inner eye, Carey searches beneath the superficial images of partisanship to detect the nearly imperceptible gestures of political nobility that go unnoticed in an age increasingly dominated by television. He reminds us, for example, that more important than the visible bitterness that accompanied Ted Kennedy's handshake with Jimmy Carter at the 1980 Democratic convention was the fact that he shook hands in the first place, subordinating a deeply personal crusade to the demands of party. In such moments, Carey hears echoes of that second voice of American politics. If its melody is fainter, as the siren song of individualism drowns the voices that seek to unite where so much of modern politics tends to divide, Carey teases out the strains of equality and mutual obligation that can still be heard among the cacophony of political sounds.

The great mystery of democratic equality, and the Herculean philosophic effort involved in conceiving equality, finally makes civic education the inescapable feature of a healthy democratic regime. Civic education, or education in the ways of the *city* (*civitas* or *polis*), necessarily involves tempering the claims of partisan interest—without altogether denying the demands of the body and those one loves—for the sake of an overarching conception of equal worth and common good. As Aristotle observed, unless democracies impart an understanding of democratic rule as necessarily involving self-rule, that is, the need to reproach one's own ambitions and interests out of respect for a greater common good, then the likely result of democratic life aimed at individual satisfaction will be the belief that it is best not to be ruled at all, but to "live as one wants."[17] When democracy is dominated by individuals in pursuit of their own self-interest narrowly understood, the demands of politics become an obstacle and the private sphere gains prominence in relation. However, because in mass society the private sphere allows us little recourse for expression except as consumers or as insignificant statistics in public opinion polls, and because large-scale government arises in part as a response to the problems of mass society, the inevitable logic of a self-interested polity is the loss of public dignity.[18]

Carey has argued that there are few sources of dignity in modernity, and what few sources remain are under constant fire since they often brazenly go against the prevailing strain of individualism in the American tradition. One of these sources is association, embodied especially in political parties. Tocqueville taught that associations were vital to making American democracy work and, although he faulted parties, in mass society they present one of the most important and inclusive civil associations. The weakening of political parties as mediating institutions is a *leitmotiv* of Carey's writings, and an abiding concern in his own noble attempts to help Democrats recapture the governance of Hunterdon County—futilely, it seems—and, with greater success, in his hometown of Flemington. Political parties remind citizens of their need for others and the needs for political sacrifice; a two-party system demands that individual citizens and interest groups compromise for the good of the party in order to win.[19] In forging an alliance in order to win elections, the idea of political equality is reinforced in subtle ways. It is not an equality achieved by stripping away all that is central to a person's background and self-definition, but one that seeks to come to terms with difference through a civility that nevertheless does not deny profound divisions, even antipathies. As Carey writes of his own partisan wearing of the orange tie on St. Patrick's Day: "[C]ivility does not require that I adopt your manners, your creed, or your costume. It does demand the empathic effort to understand you and your ways as you understand them yourself. Civility, like equality, is the sameness of spirit that does not require us to deny our differences. In fact, when civility is strongest, we can argue with some heat. . . . Only diplomats are always polite; a political society requires some heat."[20]

If political parties have the ability to draw us outside our narrow interests by means of "empathic effort," hence affording dignity to those who find fellowship and belonging in the midst of many others, the second great source of dignity in modern America—religion—has a similar effect but a different goal. It points us beyond elections and partisanship, even beyond politics to some extent, to the divine source of human dignity and equality that finally serves as a firm buttress against the indignities of modern politics. In this regard, Carey follows the teaching of Tocqueville, who wrote that

> every religion places the object of man's desires outside and beyond worldly goods and naturally lifts the soul into regions far above the realm of the senses. Every religion also imposes on each man some obligations toward mankind, to be performed in common with the rest of mankind, and so draws him away, from time to time, from thinking about himself.[21]

While many democratic theorists view democracy as necessarily antithetical to religious teachings, like Tocqueville, Carey views religion as an essential feature of healthy democratic life. For religion helps to temper the worst effects of majority tyranny and private liberty most pervasive in modern democracies by revealing "a law above the will of the majority and a code of morals at odds with calculations of utility," and "commands love and sacrifice, the moral signs of nobility."[22]

Religion, in part, teaches us that man is simultaneously a comic and tragic figure: comic in part because of the hubris of his longings, but tragic too because of the nobility that often accompanies the attempt to fulfill those longings. We gain dignity by our striving, despite our limitations; indeed, the continued effort, if undertaken without hubris, is the source of profound human worth. Twain observed: "man is the creature somewhere between the angels and the French." Recognizing our mixed nature led him to conclude: "I am a great and sublime fool. But then, I am God's fool, and all his works must be contemplated with respect."[23]

Although Carey is deeply interested in strengthening our political and civic institutions, he knows at bottom that we must rely upon individuals to maintain democratic society. As he once observed, "[W]hen institutions fail, political society depends on men, and men are feeble reeds, prone to acquiesce in—if not to commit—iniquity."[24] Thus, the act of teaching takes on vital political significance, because good teachers can make better individuals despite the iniquities of the city and can mitigate the failings of our political system even in the worst of times.

Teaching involves more than simple knowledge of one's own history, of which Carey has an encyclopedic knowledge nevertheless.[25] Experience can be as deceptive a guide as it can be enlightening. Carey likes to relate Mark Twain's observation that

> we should be careful to get out of an experience only the wisdom that is in it and stop there; lest we be like the cat that sits down on a hot stove lid. She will never sit down on a hot stove lid again, and that is well, but also she will never sit on a cold one anymore."[26]

In addition to experience, one needs also reflection, ultimately by means of theory and philosophy, in order to provide the lamp for which experience provides only the mirror.[27] Storytelling can be a fairly unreflective way to relate past experiences if one does not look beyond the surface meaning of the tale, but through training in keen listening or reading, one can tease out lessons and precepts, finding an overarching story on the meaning of those stories. At his best—and he is among the best—Carey is a great teller of stories about stories, revealing the fundamental meaning of jokes, hymns, tales, and poems. Talking about one of his own teachers, Carey has said that the best teachers "are unexcelled in that *good* humor which, confident that our humanity is enough, gently punctuates the pretensions of those who refuse to accept the limits of our estate. . . . And so it is, if we have teachers who are the salt of the earth and give life its savor."[28] Each of us, as rapt students of a great and loving teacher, have savored the rich offerings of—and, appropriately, drunk many libations celebrating—the life and words of Wilson Carey McWilliams.

NOTES

1. G. K. Chesterton, *What I Saw in America*, vol. 21 of *Collected Works* (San Francisco: Ignatius Press, 1990), 39.

2. These sentences are taken from an unpublished essay by Wilson Carey McWilliams recalling his early encounters with Sheldon Wolin. Essay in authors' possession.

3. This makes the "turning point" of Carey's life considerably more recent than that of Mark Twain's, who located his at the moment that Julius Caesar crossed the Rubicon. We suspect, however, that if pressed Carey would, like Twain, point to the moment when Adam and Eve ate from the apple of good and evil in the Garden of Eden. Twain simply claimed he was not being paid enough by *Harper's* to go that far back. See Twain's "The Turning Point of My Life," in *The Complete Essays of Mark Twain*, ed. Charles Neider (New York: Doubleday, 1963).

4. McWilliams, "The Alternative Tradition," speech delivered 25 June 1977. Essay in authors' possession. Carey also admires Bertrand de Jouvenel for making much the same point with his observation that political science is "like a car with taillights into the past, and dashboard lights to help us quantify the present, but no headlights let us see into the future." See McWilliams, foreword to *The Nature of Politics: Selected Essays of Bertrand de Jouvenel*, ed. Dennis Hale and Marc Landy (New York: Schocken Books, 1987).

5. McWilliams, *The Idea of Fraternity in America* (Berkeley and Los Angeles: University of California Press, 1973), 98–99.

6. See McWilliams's essays, "Politics: The Fundamental Things Apply," *Worldview* 23 (October 1980): 2; and "E. T.: A Tale of Two Worlds," *Worldview* 25 (December 1982): 2.

7. See McWilliams's essay, "Poetry, Politics and the Comic Spirit," *PS: Political Science & Politics* 28 (June 1995): 197.

8. John Dewey, *A Common Faith* (New Haven, Conn.: Yale University Press, 1934), 49.

9. McWilliams, *The Undergraduate Learner: Challenges for the Year 2000* (Trenton: New Jersey Department of Higher Education, 1987), 8. See also his essay, "Science and Freedom: America as the Technological Republic," in *Technology in Western Political Thought*, ed. Arthur M. Melzer, Jerry Weinberger, and M. Richard Zinman (Ithaca, N.Y.: Cornell University Press, 1993), 85–108. It should be observed that Carey only recently and reluctantly recognized the inevitability of the computer age. We easily recall seeing Carey pecking away at his manual typewriter well into the '90s, and he only recently assented to the installation of an answering machine in his home.

10. See McWilliams, "Mark Twain's *A Connecticut Yankee*: The Prince and the Public," in *The Elmira Mark Twain Papers* (forthcoming).

11. The image of "torturing" nature comes from Francis Bacon and is cited favorably by John Dewey in *Reconstruction in Philosophy* (New York: New American Library, 1950), 48.

12. McWilliams, "Democracy and Mystery: On Civic Education in America," *Halcyon* 11 (1989): 51, hereafter cited as "Democracy and Mystery."

13. The phrase is drawn from Alexis de Tocqueville, "Of Individualism in Democratic Countries," in *Democracy in America*, vol. 2, bk. 2, chap. 2.

14. On the tensions between democracy and multiculturalism, see McWilliams,

"Democratic Multiculturalism," in *Multiculturalism and American Democracy*, ed. Arthur M. Melzer, Jerry Weinberger, and M. Richard Zinman (Lawrence, Kans.: University of Kansas Press, 1998), 120–29.

15. McWilliams, "Democracy and Mystery," 46.

16. Collected in McWilliams's *The Politics of Disappointment* (Chatham, N.J.: Chatham House Publishers, 1995) and *Beyond the Politics of Disappointment?* (Chatham, N.J.: Chatham House Publishers, 1999).

17. Aristotle, *Politics*, trans. Carnes Lord (Chicago: University of Chicago Press, 1984), bk. 6, chap. 2.

18. See McWilliams, "Democracy and the Citizen: Community, Dignity, and the Crisis of Contemporary Politics in America," in *How Democratic Is the Constitution?* ed. Robert A. Goldwin and William A. Schambra (Washington, D.C.: American Enterprise Institute, 1980) (hereafter cited as "Democracy and the Citizen").

19. See McWilliams, "Parties as Civic Associations," in *Party Renewal in America*, ed. Gerald M. Pomper (New York: Praeger Publishers, 1980), 51–68. See also his essay, "The Antifederalists, Representation, and Party," *Northwestern University Law Review* 85 (1990): 12–38.

20. McWilliams, "The Wearing of Orange," *Worldview* 31 (March 1988): 1.

21. Tocqueville, *Democracy in America*, trans. George Lawrence (1835; reprint, New York: Doubleday Anchor), 444–45.

22. McWilliams, "Democracy and the Citizen," 97.

23. Mark Twain, "The Damned Human Race," in *Letters from the Earth*, ed. Bernard De Voto (New York: Harper & Row, 1962), 182. See Twain, "Letter to William Howells, December 1877," in *Selected Mark Twain–Howells Letters, 1872–1910*, ed. Frederick Anderson, William Gibson, Henry Smith (Cambridge, Mass.: Harvard University Press, 1967), 105.

24. McWilliams, "Civil Disobedience and Contemporary Constitutionalism," *Comparative Politics* 1 (January 1969): 226.

25. One listener to his storytelling once commented that Carey "must either have a very large bookcase or a very battered library card."

26. Mark Twain, *Following the Equator: A Journey Around the World* (1897; reprint, New York: Dover, 1989), 124.

27. McWilliams, "Address of Acceptance of the Witherspoon Award," 15 November 1989, in *New Jersey Humanities* (New Jersey Committee for the Humanities), (Winter 1990): 10.

28. McWilliams, "On Moral Education," *Worldview* 24 (April 1981): 2.

First Things
(The Problem of Human Pride)

1

Political Philosophy's Response to the Challenge of Creation: An Essay in Honor of Wilson Carey McWilliams

Thomas L. Pangle

A distinguishing mark of Carey McWilliams's wide-ranging and fertile scholarship has been his stress on the Bible as a powerfully influential, deeply instructive, and, above all, sharply provocative source of political ideas. In clarifying the precise role played by biblically inspired thinking in the evolution of American political thought, Carey McWilliams has highlighted the invigorating challenges such thinking has posed to, and received from, that secular philosophic rationalism that has been the predominant source and guide of American constitutionalism. He has thereby provided much needed, and often chastening, insight into the deepest and most problematic dialogue underlying our modern civic culture. But he has also and simultaneously, it seems to me, directed and incited his fellow political theorists, schooled in the classics of political philosophy, to reconsider the Bible itself, on the basis of that schooling but with genuinely open minds. He has urged listening to and learning from the Bible in order to keep alive and to participate in the perennial, mutually illuminating, dialogic confrontation between "Jerusalem and Athens"—between the conception of the human condition as guided ultimately by suprarational or even contra-rational revelation; and the alternate view, which looks to reason as our "only Star and compass,"[1] and proceeds to reinterpret or indeed to rewrite even the Scripture accordingly. I judged that I might best honor Carey McWilliams, and at the same time indicate my indebtedness to the impulse communicated through his teaching and example, by presenting him with my own attempt at a clarification of the challenges posed to, and issued by, rationalist political philosophy when it encounters and tries to take seriously the biblical account of Creation and the Fall.

13

APPROACHING THE BIBLE FROM THE PERSPECTIVE
OF POLITICAL PHILOSOPHY

Politics, citizenship, and the proper shaping of civil society surely do not come to sight as the primary themes of the Bible. The very terminology is of Greco-Roman, rather than scriptural, provenance. Yet this first impression is misleading in a crucial respect. From the outset, and above all at the outset, the Bible focuses on and teaches us something of the character of God's rule—or of what may be called, with a pardonable imposition of classical terminology, "God's politics."[2] The Bible thus instructs us in the supreme model, and source of standards, for all just rule and lawful obedience. More specifically, the accounts of Creation and of the Fall help us to begin to understand the character and original aims of Him who is the Giver, through Moses, of those laws that are at the heart of the Bible's teaching on the right way of life for humans on this earth, individually and collectively. Accordingly, an ancient Platonist has not implausibly characterized the scriptural account of Creation as an educative "prelude" to the laws of Moses, intended "to mold beforehand the minds of those who were to use his laws."[3] Considered in this light, that is, as a work of education, civic, and trans-civic, "the Bible begins reasonably"— and not merely in the rather trivial sense that it starts at the beginning of the story that it has to tell. More radically and more fundamentally, the Bible begins at *the* beginning.[4] The opening of Genesis lays the foundation for all that is to follow by elaborating a chronological, causal explanation for all existence as we experience it.

Yet that explanation bifurcates into two different versions, which, if taken literally, are mutually contradictory or at any rate incompatible. According to the first description of Creation, vegetation and all the other animals were created prior to humanity, whose creation, male and female in the image of God (Gen. 1:11–12, 1: 24–29) was the culmination of His work. According to the second telling, at least some vegetation, and most if not all of the animals, were created after Adam, and for the benefit of Adam; while Eve was created from and for Adam, after the animals had proved to be inadequate companions for him (Gen. 2:5–9, 2:18–24). The reasonable beginning thus soon becomes bewildering.[5]

It would appear to be impossible to take absolutely literally the two inconsistent accounts of Creation without falling into contradiction or incoherence. To be sure, it does not necessarily follow that we are not to take the two accounts absolutely literally. For may not the Scripture intend implicitly to warn us, from the beginning, that we cannot avoid contradiction, and thus that we cannot achieve full intelligibility, when speaking or thinking of Creation—of the mystery of Creation?

Yet even if the Bible intends to impress upon us first and foremost this rather forbidding admonition, the Bible may also mean to indicate, as a second and more inviting impression, the somewhat parabolic or allegorical, and hence non-literal, character of its teaching. Perhaps the glaring contradiction illustrates the didactic wisdom of the Bible. The Bible may mean to suggest that the two competing narrations of Creation afford two contrasting but thereby complementary perspectives on the mystery of Creation, precisely when they are not taken strictly literally—and precisely if they are taken as requiring a strenuous effort of interpretative integration by the reader. The first of the two accounts, in order to survey the whole of Creation and to clarify the rank, and indicate the principle of ranking, of all the various kinds of created beings, may suppress other essential and qualifying aspects of Creation—above all the momentous limitations of the creature who is the peak of Creation. The initial abstraction from the deficiencies of the human creature would be then conspicuously corrected in the succeeding, alternative account; but the incompleteness, the need for supplement, of this second rendition is made palpable when it is viewed in contrast with the previous rendition, which teaches, in an unambiguous fashion, divine omnipotence. The surface contradictions between the two narrations of creation may reflect with some exaggeration, and thus help us to recognize, profound tensions within creation. It may well be part of the Bible's educative intention to present us readers with the task of ascending, through sustained reflection, from the surface contradictions between two incomplete presentations toward a properly ambiguous single or whole lesson. It may even be that the human redactors were gripped by the awareness that the ascent leads or points beyond their own, beyond any merely human, understanding.

This interpretive approach, which views the Scripture as self-consciously educative, but not necessarily as entirely comprehended by its human redactors, does not require us to resolve every puzzling feature by finding in it a lesson behind which stands an intelligible authorial intention, though it urges us in the case of each difficulty to strive to do so. We need not, and perhaps should not, ever rule out the possibility that in any particular case, contradiction or other obscurity in Scripture is a manifestation of irresolvable ambiguity or even incoherence caused either by human equivocation or by divine mystery. In other words, this approach does not force upon the Bible a philosophic or strictly rationalist intentionality. And by the same token, as Strauss has shown, we may, in adopting this approach, accept the sensible results, or even some reasonable version of the principles, of modern archaeological "higher criticism," without necessarily siding from the outset with the authority of scientific reason over and against that of faith. "For the Bible does not require us to believe in the miraculous character of events that the Bible does not present as miraculous. God's speaking to men may be described as miraculous, but the Bible does not claim that the putting together of those speeches was done miraculously."[6]

We may grant, then, that each of the two accounts of Creation has a very different "historical source" (the first account is usually ascribed to "P," and the second to "J"); we may grant, further, that each of the two conflicting accounts is itself woven out of manifold pre-existing and disharmonious traditions. Still, whoever put Genesis together in its final form, as we now have it, may nonetheless have discerned, in the manifold traditions, two predominant if contradictory traditions whose conjunction—indeed, whose contradiction, if taken as a provocation to reflection and not as something to be ignored, papered over, or used as a basis for dismissal—provokes a specific line of interpretive reflection and appropriately humble reasoning that leads the attentive reader up a path toward understanding what can be humanly comprehended regarding the mystery of Creation.

THE CREATION OF HEAVEN AND EARTH

In teaching us, at the outset, about the created character of the whole in which we find ourselves, the Bible ignores, or does without, what the Greek philosophers have taught us for centuries to speak of as "nature" (φύσις; *physis*). From the perspective of rational science or philosophy, no feature of the initial Creation account is so unsettling and even threatening; to suppose that one can philosophize while conceding that "it is not nature that brings into being and causes to pass away all things, and that there is then something which comes into being out of nothing or that suddenly disappears into nothing" is to "surrender the city of philosophy while guarding its outworks."[7] For in the light of the biblical teaching of Creation, the objects of science—"nature" as a whole, human "nature," "natural" law, "natural" rights—are so mutable as to afford only a provisional, an incomplete or essentially uncertain, semi-"knowledge," and the philosophic life thus loses, in a decisive sense, both its theoretical and its practical meaningfulness. One must add that we confront here a direct challenge to our liberal democratic political theory, for that foundation is laid in the modern doctrine of immutable natural rights and consequent natural law, and in the modern dedication to the rational Enlightenment of mankind, on the basis and by means of the intelligible lawfulness of things discovered by modern science. Naturally, then, the philosophic godfathers of liberal constitutionalism were compelled to give a radically new reading to the creation account. Our most authoritative political theo-

rist has begun his greatest work by proclaiming as the necessary theological basis of liberal constitutionalism the principle that "the Creation, which
would appear to be an arbitrary act, presupposes rules as invariable as
the fatality of the atheists" (Montesquieu, *Spirit of the Laws*, bk. 1, chap.
1). But if we read the biblical text with candor, we must confess that there
is little there to support such a thesis (and Montesquieu, we may note,
does not even attempt to find any scriptural support for his fundamental
thesis). It is true that the Bible conspicuously employs number without
indicating God's creation of number. It is equally true that the goodness
of Creation seems to be perceived, or discovered, by God rather than
willed or created ("and God saw that the light was good" [Gen. 1:4]).
Above all, one may observe, *pace* Cassuto, that the Hebrew of the opening sentence seems not to convey unambiguously the idea of what philosophers have taught us to think of as "creation *ex nihilo*": at the least,
one would have to remark that the biblical text does not seem to share
the concern for, or to be aware of, what the philosophers are certain is the
importance of settling the question of whether or not God has to work
with, and within the limits of, a matter that he did not create. The biblical text does not seem to address squarely the question of what must be
presupposed when God asks, rhetorically, "Is anything too marvelous for
the power [היפלא] of the Lord?"[8] Yet however grave the questions or
qualifications these observations may suggest,[9] the thrust of the Bible's
message is that heaven and earth, and all they contain, do not constitute
a cosmos, whose character, whose forms or species, are fixed, or whose
roots are invariable elements, or matter, or atoms, or even laws of physics. All such apparently unvarying entities and principles, insofar as they
do exist, are in truth the free, unnecessitated, and hence changeable or
even extinguishable products of a willing, thinking, impassioned, mysterious Being whose perfect existence preceded and was independent of His
Creation—and whose being and consciousness are thus radically unlike
our own (Isa. 40:12–25; Job 38:4 ff.). The Bible will abound with marvels,
portents, or powers (פלא or θαυμάσια) that we are at first inclined to call
miracles, beginning with the greatest miracle, that of Creation. But just as
the Hebrew Bible does not speak of "nature,"[10] so it does not speak of
"miracles." To speak of the "miraculous" implies a natural order that is
somehow suspended or interrupted, and, despite the force of what
Spinoza says, it would seem that the deepest or at any rate the most profoundly challenging (if not univocal) teaching of the Bible is one that seeks
to do without "nature," and hence without "miracles."[11]

While the Hebrew Bible does not refer to nature, it does refer to the
concomitant concept of chance or accident: the Bible quotes certain
Philistine priests and diviners who carry out a test to see if widespread
suffering said to be a providential punishment might not in fact be an

"accident."[12] The outcome of the test confirms that the suffering is providential. The general implication is less clear. Does the Bible leave any room for accident? But if so, would this not entail some limitation on God's power? In order to avoid this, must we not conclude that, just as there is no "natural necessity" in Creation, so there is no "accident"? The same term that is used by the Philistine diviners, and also the narrator of Ruth (2:3), to mean "accident" or "chance" is used by Ecclesiastes (2:14, 15; 3:19; 9:2, 3) to mean God's iron decree.[13]

The Greek philosophers were the first (of whom we have clear records) who attempted to orient human existence by a stable truth of "nature" discoverable by independent reason. They were famous or notorious for appealing to the orderly heavens for the decisive clue as to the character of what they called the "cosmos."[14] The Babylonian sages, of whom we know much less, are portrayed in the Bible as having appealed to the orderly heavens on a very different basis—in the light of the promise or hope that life could somehow be guided by a fatalistic but predictive astrology.[15] Through its treatment of the heavens and the heavenly bodies, the Bible's initial account of Creation makes most evident its implicitly polemical stance toward each of these two very different pretentions to wisdom. The heavens are indeed the first, and arguably the highest,[16] part of Creation mentioned: "In the beginning God created the heavens and the earth." But by putting the heavens first, it would appear that the Bible means to say that the heavens too, even the heavens, are created by God; nothing, not even the visibly highest, is independent of God.[17] What is more, life-giving light and warmth are emphatically not traced to the sun, nor to any heavenly body (cf. Rev. 21:23–26); light exists, day and night follow their order, vegetation flourishes on the earth, well before the creation of the sun.[18] Finally, the second day is conspicuously missing any divine pronouncement that the thing created on that day—the "expanse" between the waters, the expanse which God named "the heavens"—was "good." The demotion of the heavens and the heavenly bodies entails a promotion of the earth and seas: on the third day, in striking contrast to the second day, God twice pronounces his day's work "good." On the fourth day, God finally creates the sun and the moon, "to rule" the day and the night respectively. He calls these creations and the stars that accompany them "good," but only after he has emphasized the service they perform for the beings on earth. The order followed throughout the six days of Creation is, as Strauss ("Jerusalem and Athens," 152–53) has demonstrated, one of a lucid ascent, from the less to the more mutable or versatile or lively. The fixed earth is of higher rank than the empty heavens, but is in turn outranked by vegetation with its movement of growth, then by the heavenly beings that change place according to fixed orbits, and then finally by the unpredictably mobile earthly animals, culminating in man. So, even though the sidereal beings are demoted, their splendor and allure are not denied: "The heavens record the glory of God, the expanse of the sky proclaims His handiwork" (Ps. 19:2; cf. 8:3–6). As we later learn, the worship of the heavenly bodies among the gentiles, after the Fall, is not contrary to the divine plan (cf. Deut. 4:19–20 with 17:3).

Precisely because providence, focused on the earth, excludes both Babylonian-astrological fatalism and Greek-philosophic natural necessity, it entails orderly care. The absence of nature in the account of Creation does not entail the presence, let alone the predominance, of the uncanny, the monstrous, or the chaotic. Indeed, with the exception of the "sea monsters," there is no reference, in the first account of Creation, to any creature unknown to us in common experience.[19] By the same token, the Bible gives no hint of an evolution of the species, of the species known to us, from some strange earlier species of which we have no direct, non-hypothetical knowledge. More generally, the Bible gives no hint of a true or ideal or "noumenal" world somehow behind the world of "mere appearances." The Bible joins Aristotle in teaching that the world familiar to us not only is, but always was (or was from the beginning), *the* world, the only world.

This world, our world, the only world, is the product of divine *will*, not of divine passion that overpowers God or yokes God to another. Creation does not bespeak "Eros, He the most beautiful among the immortal gods, / Liberator of the limbs, Who overwhelms in all gods and humans / the mind and prudent counsel in their breasts" (Hesiod *Theogony* 120–22). God as Creator of the beings is emphatically not a procreator, and the earth and seas, though fertile, are also not procreative: so far are they from being maternal or paternal, they are not even alive. The utterly unerotic character of God and His act of creating is particularly striking if we compare not only Near Eastern cosmogonic accounts but also Greek cosmogony, poetic and philosophic.[20] Humanity, as male and female, is created in the image of God, but the whole context warns us against taking this to mean that eroticism in any form is an aspect of divinity, as the Bible conceives divinity. The Bible's first word on *eros* is a conspicuous silence that rules out divine eroticism and, indeed, one is tempted to add, eroticism altogether, in the form in which it is so powerfully and awesomely invoked by Hesiod. The first commandment God delivers in the Bible, a commandment for the fish and birds, is, "be fruitful and multiply" (Gen. 1:22). God does not multiply. Nothing multiplies, on its own, or without God's commandment. This commandment is then reiterated, not only for or before man and woman but "to them," and is then immediately conjoined with the commandment to subdue the earth and rule over the beasts (Gen. 1:28). Human procreation is thus presented as the consequence of obedience to a positive divine law; procreation does not "come naturally" (accordingly, when Eve bears her first child, she quite properly recognizes that what she has gained is due to the help of the Lord [Gen. 4:1]). And it is noteworthy that the lawful injunction addressed to humans to engage in procreative sexual intercourse is coupled with a commandment to rule or dominate over (רדה) the animal. Sexuality, we may conclude, is that aspect of humanity that is most obviously more akin to the animal than to the divine; sexual congress is that aspect of humanity that is most problematic for, or most qualifying of, man's being in the image of God. Sexual intercourse is commanded and blessed as a means to procreation, not as an end or a pleasure good in itself, or good or necessary for some aspect of companionship; procreation is an activity excluded from the being (one is tempted to say the nature) of the "Lord our God, who is One" (Deut. 6:4). The transcendence of *eros* is a principal feature of the holiness of God the Creator. A qualified transcendence of *eros* will be a principal feature of the holiness that God's elaborate legislation eventually demands from His people.

God's making is deliberate, but, as creative, it is radically unlike human art. Almost as prominent as God's production in the opening verses is God's intrusive activity of separating or distinguishing the created things. Without God, there would be no distinction, no form. Formlessness, fluidity, precedes form: the only element whose character is established at the moment of its creation is water. But prior to any articulation, there is to be light, by which to make discernible even the pre-articulate confusion. God exists prior to light, without need for light, and yet God makes His Creation illuminated and hence intelligible. God is the enshrouded, unilluminable source of the light, of the light that God sees to be good, of the light that illuminates Creation. Yet even light, once created, is in or of itself not distinct from darkness; even this primordial distinction is an effect of the superimposing divine will. According to Isaiah, God creates the darkness—though He does not see it as good, though He associates it with woe.[21] Darkness, it would seem then, is not uncreated or simply given, because darkness, or as God calls it, "Night," presupposes light or "Day," just as light, to become fully manifest, presupposes darkness. Before Creation, we may venture to speculate, God existed in a state prior to darkness as well as to light;[22] unlike His creatures and creation, God's "sight" would seem not to have presupposed light and darkness (cf. Ps. 139:11–12) just as His goodness, unlike the goodness we know, would seem not to have presupposed evil or woe. On the seventh day, God rested, and because He rested, He did not only bless, He declared holy this seventh day. God had not declared holy any of His creation, or any of the previous days—not even the sixth day, on which the creation was completed and seen to be "very good." God, this would seem to suggest, is not merely a creator: He has a distinctive being, a being at rest, that is prior to or that transcends His creating.[23] It is true that we later hear God Himself saying that "on the seventh day He rested, and was refreshed."[24] But it would seem most prudent to avoid taking this as implying that God was in need of recuperation.

God concludes His creating by giving all the vegetation to mankind and to "all" the animals as food; the carnivorous does not seem to be part of God's original, harmonious Creation.[25] If so, this would seem to be one of many reasons why God can survey His Creation as a whole and find it "very good." Yet this emphatic pronouncement draws our attention to the fact that God conspicuously failed to declare, after His creation of man in His image, that man was "good." The silence about the goodness of man casts a faintly ominous shadow over an otherwise perfect picture.

THE KNOWLEDGE OF GOOD AND EVIL

When we look back at the first account of Creation from the perspective afforded by the second account, we can see that God's characterization of the whole of Creation as "very good" was not incompatible with—it would seem even to have presupposed—a silence and hence reservation regarding the goodness of man. For man, male and female, was created in God's image; and this means, as the principle underlying the ordering of the works of Creation suggests, that humanity is characterized above all by radical mutability, by radical (spiritual) freedom. But the goodness of such radical freedom in a creature, we now learn, is inextricably interwoven with that creature's capacity for evil: a human creature's radical freedom entails its following the Creator or the Creator's plan through voluntary obedience, and hence with the possibility or capacity for willful disobedience—and even for the aspiration to some kind of autonomy. The second account of Creation supplements and completes the first by teaching us about the character and the consequences of humanity's radical freedom.

Still, what must be stressed to begin with is that the second account of Creation continues and reinforces the teaching of the first account to the effect that creation, as it left God's hands, was untarnished.[26] Creation as we now know it is the product of a ruinous change due not to God but to man. It is true that God effected most of the change, but He did so in His capacity as judge, as upholder of justice.

Humanity's pollution of God's creation is rendered all the more shocking by virtue of the fact that we now learn how assiduous and complete was God's original provision for mankind. This indeed would seem to be the key to the differences, the apparent inconsistencies, between the two accounts. The first account abstracted somewhat from God's care for

humans and from humanity's dependence on God's care, in order to highlight the preeminent rank of humanity within creation, a rank based on
humanity's relative freedom or godlike independence among the creatures. The second account stresses humanity's relative rank somewhat less
(nothing is said of man being created in the image of God), in order to
bring into relief God's intimate care for needy humanity and the consequent outrageousness of humanity's heedlessness of or ingratitude for that
care.

We now learn that, while humanity—male and female—may have been
created in the image of God on high, the male is created out of the lowly
dust (cf. Gen. 2:7 with 3:19), and the female then out of, and for the sake
of, the male. The sexual differentiation now appears as the primary manifestation of man's human, all-too-human, social interdependency or needi-
ness: God (not Adam) recognized that "the man's being alone is not good."
What man proved to need in order no longer to be alone was not any
animal servant but rather another kind of human, with whom he could
join in a unity of the flesh.[27] Since woman is a human being, this coupling
by no means effaces her need and capacity to deliberate and act as a free
agent, as a being who can profoundly influence and even take the lead
from her partner. Yet it was to the man that God delivered the first momentous commandment, well before woman existed (Gen. 2:16–18 and
3:17): God apparently assigned to Adam the grave responsibility for teaching and thus guiding his companion. God did not, however, announce or
draw Adam's attention to this grave responsibility.

Still, Adam was unquestionably negligent, if not in leaving the woman
alone, then in neglecting to explain to her that the tree whose fruit they
were prohibited from eating was the tree of knowledge of good and evil.
As a consequence, the serpent was able to be the first to call her attention
to that fact and did so in a most dazzling and seductive manner (Gen. 2:17,
3:2–6). He tempted her with the prospect of becoming godlike; he appealed to her pride. But was it pride that motivated her to eat the forbidden fruit? After all, until she tasted the fruit, the Bible stresses, she, like
Adam, did not know shame at her own nakedness. Can a being that has
little sense of shame have much sense of pride? Our first impression is
that the woman succumbed to the temptation because of her childlike
response to the goodness of the tree (for eating), to the beauty of the tree,
and, above all, to the desirability of the tree as a source of wisdom. Wisdom, it would seem, the woman desired for its own sake. She was, for
that moment, what is called in Greek a "philosopher," if in a childlike
sense. But is not the philosopher as such, in the purity of his desire to
know and the purity of his delight in seeing, childlike, not only in his
wayward departure from ancestral authority, but also in the sense that his

concern for knowledge eclipses or subordinates the concerns that other humans regard as most serious (consider Plato *Laws* 820c4–e7, *Euthydemus* 304c6–305b3, and *Timaeus* 22b4–8)? The Bible seems to be aware of the apparent human fascination with knowledge for its own sake; the Scripture suggests that succumbing to this charm is childlike in the sense of being childish, and dangerously so. The woman, like a child playing at the edge of a cliff, seems to have sensed no abyss beneath her. She casually shared the fruit with her man, who, with childlike insouciance, accepted the fruit and ate of it. But then their eyes were opened and both were brought, for the first time, to the shameful self-consciousness of adulthood; then the childish love of wisdom evaporated.

If the woman was childlike in her fascination with the tree, Adam was childlike in his negligence, first of the woman's instruction, and then of the significance of the fruit itself. There seems at first sight to be no suggestion of prideful rebellion in Adam's acceptance of the fruit from his wife. Indeed, one is led to wonder whether Adam had grasped the significance of the divine prohibition. After all, in his ignorance of good and evil, could Adam have understood the evil of disobedience, or of punishment? Could he have interpreted the divine prohibition and threat as anything more than prudent counsel, parental advice? But did Adam even grasp the significance of the harm against which he was being warned— did he comprehend the meaning of death? It seems that at any time during their sojourn in Eden, the pair could have eaten of the unprohibited Tree of Life, thus gaining immortality (Gen. 3:22); they were not so moved. Their not apprehending the significance of death would seem to go with their not being moved to procreate. Only after the Fall does Adam "name his wife Eve, because she was the mother of all the living"; only after the expulsion does Adam "know his wife" so that she conceives (Gen. 3:20, 4:1). In the creation of the woman and in her reception by Adam, there is no reference to her role as partner in procreation, and this silence is underlined by the narrator's striking interruption, which refers to procreation and parenthood in the narrator's own, much later, epoch (Gen. 2:24). It was God, not Adam, who recognized that it was not good for Adam to be alone: Adam seems to have felt no explicit desire for companionship; he seems to have had no conscious awareness of his own loneliness. Was not the situation in Eden prior to the Fall truly infantile in its innocent ignorance? But does this not mean that the pair was immature, incomplete, lacking in full self-consciousness, and therefore without the capacity for true responsibility?[28] Is not the so-called Fall in fact a necessary step on the way to maturity? Is the whole drama not planned and intended by God? For was it not He who created the serpent and allowed or moved it to tempt the utterly naive woman?

These reflections lead one to entertain the hypothesis that the drama of the Fall is in fact nothing more and nothing less than a means of educating, first, Adam and Eve, and then, by way of them, the entire human race, which will subsequently come to hear their story or parable. The lesson would be that humans cannot be fully human, or cannot be complete as images of God, without knowing sin, without knowing good and evil, as opposed to the merely pleasant and unpleasant, and the good and bad (or beneficial and harmful). In order to know sin, creatures (unlike the Creator) must have begun to experience sin as sinners. Shame, guilt, and fear of punishment (as opposed to fear of hurt), are preconditions for aspiration to dignity, that is, to an eligibility, and an awareness of eligibility, for salvation at the hands of a God who is perceived as an awesome though merciful judge and not merely as a benevolent parent or keeper. A true sense of dignity, a true striving after dignity, presupposes a vivid experience of the conflict, uncertain in outcome, between what is tempting, what is seemingly good for us, and what is right. Dignity consists in self-overcoming through obedience to divine commandment or law. Humans may have open to them the destiny of living in ultimate harmony with God, but that ultimate harmony, in order to be fully self-conscious, must be a reconciliation won by a long climb, with God's help, from a prior alienation that is necessarily attendant on the emergence from the cocoon of innocence.

The hypothesis that the Fall is in fact such an education, planned by God from the beginning, not only makes intelligible the presence of the serpent in Eden as an agent of God's benevolent educative drama, it helps us understand, in a manner that does not call into question divine omniscience, how God tolerates what otherwise would seem to be a drastic overturning of His original plan, and why He does not revert to that supposed plan after the Flood. God's abandonment of what is merely an apparent original plan is not a sign of any defect in His true, initially concealed, plan; nor does it imply that God had something to learn, or that He was compelled to revise His original plan in the light of hard-won experience.

But it is difficult to sustain this educative interpretation without very considerable qualifications. The Fall may indeed begin to afford an education, but the lesson is more problematic or less coherent than we have yet allowed. For what we have said fails to explain the single most important feature of the story: the punishment. To the extent that Adam and Eve's misdeed was the result of childish or more than childish ignorance, to the extent that they acted prior to being given the decisive education, their misdeed would seem to deserve no more than a rebuke or punishment suited to innocent children. To be sure, an apparently severe retributive punishment was perhaps in order, to give the "children" a vivid, if benevolently false, experience of consequence, responsibility, and guilt. But the onlooker, and, as the lesson sank in, Adam and Eve, would recognize that whatever the pair suffered as a consequence of their failure to heed the commandment given in Eden was principally a means of helping them (and others) to understand the possibility and danger of future sins, no longer so innocent, attended by future retributive, and not merely or chiefly educative, punishment. Now this is not what is suggested by the lasting severity and the sternly retributive character of the punishments God in fact decrees, first and foremost for the serpent, and then for the man and woman in whose guilt is somehow mysteriously implicated all subsequent serpents, men, and women. If the Fall were simply a rich educational exercise, then the sufferings that burden human existence— woman's pain and danger in childbirth and her subordination to her husband; man's toil over cursed, recalcitrant soil; and, above all, human mortality (Gen. 3:14–19)—would not be the fault of mankind, but would seem to become the unjustified injuries inflicted upon us by a cruel or unintelligibly tyrannical god. The Scripture, on the contrary, teaches that these evils, and other evils yet to come in the story, are the fault of mankind who violated God's authentic original intention and thus brought upon themselves condign punishment.

"But here" (to quote John Locke) "will occur the common objection, that so many stumble at: 'How doth it consist with the justness and goodness of God, that the posterity of Adam should suffer for his sin; the innocent be punished for the guilty?'"—this Adam whom, our liberal political philosopher remarks a bit earlier, "millions had never heard of, and no one authorized to transact for him, or be his representative."[29] To this very grave question, Locke himself offers a response that is rather obviously lame and legalistic, not to say smacking of chicane. He asserts that in fact there was no punishment of any of Adam's heirs involved in the punishment of Adam, because it cannot be called punishment merely to "keep one from what he has no right to"; and "the state of immortality, in paradise, is not due to the posterity of Adam." "Therefore, though all die in Adam," that is, "by reason of his transgression, all men are mortal, and come to die . . . yet none are truly punished, but for their own deeds." Perhaps the gravest of the many difficulties with this Lockean response is that it leaves simply unintelligible, or without any grounds whatsoever, God's inflicting death on, or removing immortality from, all of mankind subsequent to Adam and Eve. We would seem to remain closer to the spirit of Scripture if we begin by recognizing that the Bible does not start from the Lockean individualist premise: the Bible does not conceive of humans as responsible only for those actions of others whom they have "authorized to transact for them" or whom they have formally made their "representatives." The Bible rather conceives of humans as essentially members of their families, as originally parts of the larger whole formed by family kinship, to such a degree that each person is implicated in the deeds of the others, and implicates the others in his deeds. Human beings, in the Biblical perspective, must live with the burden of a responsibility, not only for their own conduct, but also (in some measure) for their ancestors' behavior; they must live in the recognition of the moral consequences of their own behavior, not only for themselves, but for their whole posterity.[30]

The divine punishments that attend the Fall imply then that God holds all men and women, and some non-human beings (for example, the serpent), from the beginning and regardless of their level of sophistication or education, fully responsible for their own, and, to some extent, for their ancestors' and descendants' moral actions. In order to take proper account of the divine punishments, we seem compelled, therefore, to revise many of our first impressions of the condition of Adam and Eve in Eden. For if they in fact disobeyed, they must have been capable of understanding the meaning of disobedience and, hence, of evil prior to their tasting of the tree of knowledge. Their knowledge of evil may have been very incomplete, but it cannot have been nonexistent or even merely incipient. They were never totally innocent. That is, they were never simply ignorant, as very young children may be (Deut. 1:39), of the decisive difference between right and wrong. The serpent appealed to Eve's pride because it discerned that although she lacked shame at her nakedness, she did not totally lack the capacity for pride and envy.[31] Lurking at the heart of Eve's apparently pure delight in the beauty of knowledge was something akin to the serpent's cunning. (Initially, this almost invisible vice is signaled by the Scripture's clever play on the words for "nakedness" and "cunning").[32] Are we not led to surmise that Eve was moved, in her depths, by an incipient longing to usurp the place of God, to become the mistress of her own destiny?[33] Adam's sin is more incomprehensible than Eve's inasmuch as he did not hear, and Eve did not tell him of, the serpent's tempting promises; but in order to render intelligible Adam's sin as a sin, must we not presume that a covert, nascent longing for self-determination and rebellion against God's rule hid itself also beneath Adam's negligence and carelessness? God's original prohibition would then be "meant merely as a medicine to make man's obedience strong, and as a reminder that it was good for man" (St. Augustine, *City of God* 14.15). God, we may suggest, permitted the serpent to tempt Eve because He wanted humans to choose to reject full autonomy, to choose to remain in what would then become a state of purity but not innocence.[34] God wanted His human creatures to advance to a condition of knowledge that represented a deeper, truer awareness of sin than any that can be gained by sinning. In John

Milton's arresting formulation, God wanted Adam and Eve to "know to know no more":

> Not free, what proof could they have giv'n sincere
> Of true allegiance, constant Faith or Love,
> Where only what they needs must do, appear'd,
> Not what they would? what praise could they receive?
> What pleasure I from such obedience paid,
> When Will and Reason (Reason also is choice)
> Useless and vain, of freedom both despoiled,
> Made passive both, had serv'd necessity,
> Not mee. (*Paradise Lost* 4.775, 3.103–11)

This reading does, it is true, diminish the significance of the special or additional knowledge of good and evil that is consequent to the eating of the fruit of the tree of knowledge.[35] The fact that the couple's "eyes were opened" only after they ate the forbidden fruit need not imply that they were previously altogether unaware of the potential for sin, i.e., for defiance of God's ordinance. And accordingly, the excuses that they give to God when he calls them to account sound pathetically hollow; the excuses in fact betray the pair's apprehension of their guilt (Gen. 2:12–13).

What the pair first discover when their eyes are opened by the tasting of the forbidden fruit is their sense of shame at their nakedness: the couple becomes rightly aware, it would seem, of the powerful temptation to further transgression implicit in their sexuality (Gen. 2:7; cf. Ex. 20:23). That awareness expresses itself in the passions of fear and of shame or, more precisely, in a shame-induced fear: "I was afraid because I was naked," says Adam (Gen. 3:10). This passion is not simply or primarily a fear of punishment, but is rather an awareness of actual and potential baseness, of a baseness that makes one deserving of punishment. At the heart of human evil, it would appear, is humanity's refusal to accept its proper rank. On the one hand, man feels the sensual temptation to degrade his holy, and austerely demanding, share in divinity by descending into the lascivious enjoyment of animal sexuality for its own sake; on the other hand, man feels the temptation to ascend, in arrogant revolt against his tutelage to God. The awareness of man's rank amidst these dual and sometimes coincident temptations, the awareness that constitutes the appropriately human, all-too-human, or sinful, knowledge of good and evil is an awareness that expresses itself in the passion of shame.[36] By the same token, the improper awareness, the succumbing to the temptations to violate the true ranking of things, expresses itself in the passions of pride and lust. If the Fall had been avoided, we may venture to surmise, mankind would have felt humility and awe or reverence, but neither pride nor shame, let alone guilt (cf. Fradkin, "God's Politics," 92).

But does this reading not imply the existence of real bounds on God's knowledge and hence His power? Does God not learn as He goes, and is there not implicit in human freedom a grave qualification of God's initial, and therefore perhaps His subsequent, understanding of His creation? Does His wisdom not depend on His gradually coming to know the immutable, uncreated limits to what He can expect or accomplish? This is a question that will recur repeatedly in the biblical narrative, for God is repeatedly said to "change His mind," to "regret," or to "repent" (נחם), to alter His deeds and plans, in response to human actions. Most notable is the "regret" He expresses at His own act of Creation, when He decides to bring the flood that purges creation.[37] It is true that Scripture does twice emphatically declare, through the prophets, that "God is not human, that He would deceive, and He is not the son of man, that He would repent (נחם)" (Num. 23:19; cf. 1 Sam. 15:29). But the utter rejection of the idea of a divine change of mind is, in the first of these declarations, referring to God's unwavering fulfillment of His promises. God might well be understood never to waver from his promises without necessarily being understood never to waver or to change his mind simply. In the second case, the reference is to God's unwavering adherence to the word He has declared to His prophet Samuel. That word is in fact to the effect that God has "regretted" a most important action—His appointment of Saul as king (1 Sam. 15:11, 35). The prophets Isaiah, Jeremiah, Joel, Amos, and Jonah repeatedly teach that God is capable of "repenting" His plans to punish and His plans to reward in the face of actions of contrition or arrogance on the part of His intended subjects.[38] But if we take these teachings literally, can we still do justice to the omnipotence that elevates God radically beyond all created mind and power? Do we leave room for the omnipotence that is the ground of our hopes from His grace and of our fears of His judgment? Is it not more consistent with faith to suppose that God "repents" or "regrets" only figuratively, that He foreknows His apparent "change of mind," perhaps because he knows of an unstated qualification on his first apparently unqualified judgment?[39] And that in the case of the Fall, in particular, He foreknew the outcome? Ought we not to conclude that in this first great case He means to teach us that any and every human, placed in similar circumstances, would similarly choose defiance? Is this not perhaps the most important sense in which we are all implicated in the Fall? And yet: does not such foreknowledge suggest an absolute limit on human capacity and freedom? To such a question Milton's God replies:

> They therefore as to right belong'd,
> So were created, nor can justly accuse
> Thir maker, or thir making, or thir Fate;

As if Predestination over-rul'd
Thir will, dispos'd by Absolute Decree
Or high foreknowledge; they themselves decreed
Thir own revolt, not I: if I foreknew,
Foreknowledge had no influence on their fault,
Which had no less prov'd certain unforeknown.[40]

Yet does not certainty of an outcome imply necessity, thereby foreclosing possibility, and hence, moral freedom? Moreover, if God foreknew the Fall, could He have wisely planned for or intended anything that did not presuppose the Fall? In choosing to create mankind, did He not choose to create beings whom He knew would fall? Could not God have created beings who were *not* so prone to Fall? If He *could* have, is not our proneness to fall in part His responsibility, the product of *His* choice?[41] If He could *not* have created such beings, why not? Is there some fixed limit (in the "nature" of things?) before which even God must bow?[42]

But perhaps we ought to recognize that we are here starting to slip into waters over our heads. As regards the divine mind, its knowledge and its power, we scarcely have direct evidence or experience. Perhaps we ought to limit ourselves to those matters about which we do have direct evidence and experience. We do have such evidence and experience in the matters pertaining to man, pertaining to human action and human understanding, and pertaining to the teachings God addresses to man and hence makes intelligible to man. Let us then leave behind, as an unfathomable mystery, the apparently incoherent coexistence of God's omnipotence (and foreknowledge) with (fully responsible) human choice; let us consider how we are to comprehend, as a choice, the human choice of defiance.

Benedict de Spinoza poses, in this regard, a characteristically unabashed and bracing challenge to the biblical notion of sin and the Fall. To those who "maintain, that the human mind is not produced by natural causes at all, but is the direct creation of God, and is so independent of the rest of things that it has an absolute power to determine itself and use right reason," Spinoza responds:

But experience teaches all too well that it is no more in our power to have a sound mind than to have a sound body. Moreover, since each thing strives as much as it can to preserve its own being, we cannot have the slightest doubt that, if it were as much in our power to live by the precept of reason as it is to be led by blind desire, all men would be guided by reason, and would order their lives wisely; which is very far from being the case. For everyone is captivated by his own pleasure. Nor do theologians dispose of this difficulty by maintaining that the cause of this impotence is the vice or sin which takes its origin from the fall of our first ancestor. For if precisely in the first man there was as much power to stand as to fall, if his mind was

sound and his nature whole, how, with his knowledge and prudence, could
he possibly have fallen? They say that he was deceived by the Devil. Who
was it, in truth, that deceived the Devil himself—who, I ask, made the very
foremost of all intelligent creatures so mindless that he wished to be greater
than God? For surely, if he had a sound mind, he must have been striving
all he could to preserve himself and his own being? Moreover, if the first
man himself was sound in mind and master of his own will, how could he
possibly have allowed himself to be seduced and tricked in his mind? Now
if he had the power to use right reason, he could not have been deceived;
for he must necessarily have been striving as much as he could to preserve
his own being and his own sound mind. But the premise is that he had this
power: therefore it necessarily follows that he must have preserved his
sound mind, and could not have been deceived. This, however, is shown to
be false by the story told about him; and so it must be admitted that the first
man did not have it in his power to use right reason, but, like ourselves, was
subjected to passions.

But that man, like any other individual in nature, strives as much as he
can to preserve his being, no one can deny. In fact, one could only conceive
man to differ from other things in this respect if one assumed that he had
free will. Yet the more free we conceived man to be, the more should we be
compelled to maintain that he must necessarily preserve himself, and be of
sound mind; as everyone who does not confuse freedom with chance
[*contingentia*] will readily grant me. For freedom is virtue or perfection: and
so what betokens weakness in a man cannot be ascribed to his freedom. In
consequence, it is quite impossible to call a man free because he can fail to
exist, or because he can fail to use reason; he can be called free only in so
far as he has the power to exist and act in accordance with the laws of human nature. So the more free we conceive a man to be, the less we can say
that he can fail to use reason, and choose bad in preference to good.[43]

Now on its own terms this objection might seem to be decisive, but the
closer one looks, the more Spinoza's critique seems to rest on assertions
rather than arguments, or the more it seems to assume what is in need of
demonstration. Spinoza's appeal to our "experience" is contradicted by
the experience some have had of the divine call, a call that complements
and completes the universal human experience of the sense of indigna-
tion and moral responsibility or freedom. Now of course Spinoza claims
to demonstrate the self-contradictoriness or unintelligibility of this purported sense of responsibility and freedom. The difficulty in Spinoza's
demonstration is his assumption that freedom or free will means acting
in order to maximize one's own mental and physical security. Why, we
might ask Spinoza, should we assume that there is no conceivable alternative to an intelligent being's acting with a view to its own benefit or
pleasure? Does not the Bible presume, more commonsensically, that an intelligent being acts not only with a view to its own benefit and pleasure,

but also with a view to what is right or noble simply, and that the simply right or noble is not identical with, that it is, in addition, sometimes contrary to, the beneficial or pleasant for oneself? Is not precisely this the significance of the divine commandment, that it calls us to obedience regardless of the (admittedly tempting) real or apparent consequences for our own benefit or pleasure?

It is true that a sanction or punishment is affixed to the commandment, but this does not necessarily imply that we are supposed to obey solely out of fear of punishment or hope of reward. Quite to the contrary. Punishment and reward are understood to be something we deserve. Now what we mean by this deserving would make no sense if our obedience or disobedience were simply a consequence of our ignorance of the punishment. Ignorance and costly mistakes in calculation of our self-interest do not make us deserving of punishment, any more than knowledge and accurately profitable calculation of costs and benefits to ourselves make us deserving of reward. If we deserve punishment, it is because we failed to do what is right, because we consulted exclusively our own pleasure and benefit; the punishment in part deprives us of the profit from our ill-gotten gains. If we deserve reward, it is because we acted according to what was right, regardless or to the neglect of our interest and pleasure; the reward in part compensates us for our noble sacrifice.

Yet if this undercuts Spinoza's challenge to the Bible as he states that challenge, perhaps it does not dispose of all the difficulties implicit in Spinoza's challenge. In the first place, might not Spinoza point out that the biblical context of the Fall (life in Paradise, communing intimately with God) suggests that the Bible itself conceives of the obedience to divine law, away from which Eve and Adam turned, as something supremely good for them? If, in our reply, we forced Spinoza to concede that despite this, the Bible as a whole plainly means, by obedience to God, in part a self-forgetting or self-sacrificing devotion to God, might not Spinoza retort that the Bible remains on this crucial point confused or contradictory? That to make the meaning of obedience to divine law intelligible, one must decide if that obedience is to be understood as ultimately good or as fundamentally not good for the obedient—since it cannot be both at once—and that one must consider whether one can hold to the view that obedience to God's law is fundamentally bad for the obedient? In the second place, must we not concede this much to Spinoza: that there is strong plausibility in his assertion that free action presupposes some kind of rational deliberation, and that every choice by a free agent depends on, and is guided by, some opinion as to what is best—whether we conceive of the best as the most pleasant, or most noble or right (involving the subordination or sacrifice of one's well-being), or most beneficial to oneself?

One might indeed resist such a concession by observing that the essence of will is not deliberation, and subsequent action in accord with what is conceived to be best, but sheer will, as the ungrounded ground: the will is spontaneous, and does not depend on anything prior to the will. To borrow somewhat freely from Moses Maimonides, "the fact that it may will one thing now and another thing tomorrow does not constitute a change in the will's essence and does not call for another cause; just as the fact that the will acts at one time and does not act at another does not constitute a change, or call for another cause" (*Guide of the Perplexed*, 2.18).[44]

But, a Spinozist might well reply, would this not leave the will a manifestation of sheer arbitrariness or chance (*contingentia*), and difficult if not impossible to distinguish from erratic, if vigorous, mindlessness? Would not the will to obey God's commandment be as groundless and senseless as the will to disobey? If Adam and Eve willed in this sense (our Spinozist might complain), it would seem that their "action," whether obedient or disobedient, was more akin to impulse, or to being possessed by impulse, than to self-possessed, perspicacious, and circumspect responsibility. Now, while the Bible leaves us to speculate on the possible motives for Adam's accepting the fruit from Eve, in the case of Eve Scripture surely indicates that she was motivated not by some sort of groundless "decision," but rather by the apparent good and beauty of the tree—as well as by the serpent's questioning of the threatened penalty and by his promise that she might become divine.

If then Eve was motivated by some opinion as to the balance of better and worse entailed in the options of obeying and disobeying, respectively, must we not consider what that opinion and balance could have been? If she was responsible, then she knew it was wrong to eat of the fruit. But since she decided to eat the forbidden fruit in the face of this knowledge, was her decision not based on the opinion, on the apparent knowledge, that the benefit and pleasure outweighed the wrong? But did she not then think it was, on balance, better or preferable to disobey, worse or less preferable to obey? Did she not somehow fail to grasp the fact that the right outweighed, was better than, was preferable to, the pleasant and beneficial? But then is her fault not a result of some kind of confusion, ignorance, or blindness, even if only of a momentary sort?[45]

But no, we may respond: if Eve was criminally responsible, she was not blinded by confusion or ignorance. Let us suppose, then, that on the contrary, Eve was not ignorant or confused as to the priority of the right over the pleasant and the apparently beneficial; let us suppose that she knew not only what was right, but that she saw unmistakably that in case of conflict the right is preferable to the pleasant and beneficial; let us suppose that she made her choice in defiance of what she clearly saw to be best, or preferable. She decided to do what she clearly saw to be the worse, the less preferable, of two options. But if Eve embraced what she clearly knew to be worse, was she not in a condition in which she was driven or gripped or tyrannized by something other than the piloting awareness of what she preferred, of what was choiceworthy or desirable? Is this not an even graver sort of incapacity than the blindness that occurs in choice of the worse based on the mind's misapprehension of it as the better? Is this not the condition of an intelligent being no longer guided by her mind or intelligence, no longer fully in possession of her self? Is she not to an even greater degree a pitiable victim of a kind of terrible debility, rather than the willful deserver of punishment?

The Bible does not raise and probably does not even invite these sorts of questions that we have been compelled by Spinoza's challenge to pursue. Scripture does not try to penetrate the veil that covers responsibility as it comes to sight in our primary experience. As a consequence, the Bible does not need to leave moral responsibility in the very ambiguous light in which Aristotle leaves it (*Nicomachean Ethics* 1114b1–15a3). The Bible remains firmly within the bounds of our common-sense conviction that we and others are capable of a perversely self-conscious embrace of evil, with full awareness of the significance of our acts, and that when we act on this perverse capacity we deserve to suffer, not only the intrinsic ill consequences of our embracing what we see clearly to be bad but, in addition, a penalty that dramatically worsens our already blighted condition.

But this last formulation brings home to us a final troubling question. However we are to understand criminal responsibility, what are the intelligible grounds for the overwhelming conviction that the guilty deserve to suffer for what they have done; and what are the intelligible grounds for the concomitant hope that they—that even we ourselves—will suffer the punishment that they, and we, deserve? For guilt betokens sin or vice. Now sin and vice are either genuinely and severely harmful in the most important respect to the very soul of the criminal; or else they betoken an alienation of the criminal from the source of meaning for him as a being destined to devotion. Why then is it appropriate, why is it sensible, that such a crippled or alienated being receive, in addition to and as a consequence of its corruption or alienation, harm or suffering? Why is it so terribly important for us that to injustice be added extrinsic bad consequences for the perpetrator? Does the biblical account of creation help us at all to answer these two questions?

I believe that the Scripture may give some help, that the Bible may allow us a glimpse of one important part at least of an answer to the second of the two previous questions. A clue may come to sight if we reflect on the more attractive side of the Scripture's teaching on retribution. I have in mind the facet that becomes prominent in the close of the creation account. For of course the biblical God tempers retribution with mercy. While God expelled Adam and Eve from Paradise, and thereby from the possibility of eating the fruit of the tree of life and living forever, He did so not only to punish them, but also to prevent their engaging in further and perhaps worse evil.[46] He did not, in the event, carry out the lawful execution that had been laid down as the retributive penalty ("*on the day* [italics added] of your eating of it, you shall surely die" [Gen. 2:17]). Instead, He clothed the guilty pair and then allowed them to live in tolerable conditions for many centuries. Most important of all, God made Adam and Eve the never-to-be-forgotten parents of the entire human race, a race to whom he subsequently offers final, eternal redemption and salvation. Now to be sure, we must never lose sight of the fact that divine mercy, which the Bible thus exemplifies from the outset, has as its necessary premise guilt, sin, and retributive justice. Divine mercy (in contrast to divine benevolence) is bestowed only on creatures who have justly deserved, and, what is more, who contritely acknowledge that they have justly deserved, the retributive punishment that is nevertheless alleviated as the expression of a love that transcends, and might seem to contradict, even or especially while presupposing, justice. By bringing the guilt and the just deserts of the first humans to the foreground of the self-reflective reader's attention, Genesis brings to the fore the guilt and the just deserts of selfish or self-loving humanity as such. The Scripture thus guides us toward putting the concern for retributive justice in the foreground of our own existence. Inasmuch as we do so, we may understand ourselves to be putting in the background our concern for our own well-being, most obviously because justice, as retributive justice, can be said to be in a decisive sense a threat for all of us as sinners or potential sinners. We thus find ourselves apparently transcending, however belatedly and incompletely, our self-love. In this way, the embrace of holy retributive justice—the confession of our guilt and of our just deserts at the hands of an angry God, even as the premise of our beseeching forgiveness and mercy—may give us the sense of a re-illumination within us of the fact that we were created in the image of the holy God.[47] Through this qualified renewal of our participation in the divine holiness of justice we may recover, in an appropriately chastened manner, our self-exaltation, our sense of divinely endowed worth. These reflections, I think, give us the clue to one important meaning of the biblical teaching to the effect that it is only when, and because, we fervently acknowledge that we do not justly deserve mercy, that we instead deserve punishment, that we can begin fervently to hope for God's eternal mercy.

CONCLUSION

The scriptural account of the beginnings indicates the deeply puzzling character of the principle that lies at the heart of all authentically biblical politics and community, or friendship. The Bible reveals the human condition to be defined by God's call upon each individual to become devoted in love to larger communal wholes that, properly understood, culminate in God's all-embracing creation. God's call to dedication is centered in commandment or law, which, as such, implies that there is something in humanity that is deeply recalcitrant to the call. The human resistance proves from the outset to be so deep as to make obedience appear nigh impossible. Yet disobedience is man's responsibility; it is man's fault; it deserves punishment (though it encounters mercy). How can this be understood, except by recognizing that human contumacy is rooted in self-love, which knowingly resists a call that in fact demands a radical subordination of self and of self-concern? The fact that the refractory are seeking chiefly their own good would appear to be what makes fitting their condign punishment, that is, harm or diminution that is proportionate to their attempted self-promotion. And on the other hand, the self-sacrifice of the obedient is what would appear to make compensatory recognition appropriate for them. Rebellion against divine law would then not be a mistaken or blinded turning away from one's own true good. Yet it is. For the law is issued by a loving God, a God whose care is for the good of each of His creatures and, above all, each of His creatures that are created in His image. How then can knowing obedience, that is, obedience that grasps the meaning of God's love, obedience that grasps the fact that God intends His law to be above all for the good of each and every addressee, possibly comprise a giving up or subordination of self-concern? If God's law intends my good, how can I conform to that intention without intending my good? Is it not through obedience to the law that I would discover my truest self, and richest spiritual good—thus rising above my poor self and merely apparent good? Yet the law calls me not to love myself, but to "love the Lord thy God with all thy heart, and with all thy soul, and with all thy might"—and to love thy neighbor, *and* the stranger, as thyself (Deut. 6:4; Lev. 19:18, 19:34). So, am I finally called to care only for that which is (also) the greatest good for me, or am I not called to care decisively less for myself than for something or someone else? Can I be called to both? How? Or do we here reach the limit of our capacity for the knowledge of good and evil? Is not this limit reached perhaps in every profound investigation of what presents itself as calling to the truly moral or just or noble? Is the Bible perhaps the fullest expression of what every such call implies? A student of the Greek philosophers would wonder how one can guide one's life by that which remains unintelligible or contradictory. But perhaps the striving to do so is the precondition for the hope for the fruit of the tree of life.

> See now, yea see, my friend, and understand;
> And turn aside from the lure of thorns and snares,
> And let not the wisdom of the Greeks beguile thee,
> Which has no fruit, but only flowers—
> Or her fruit is: that the earth was never outstretched,
> Nor the tents of the sky spread out.
> Nor was any beginning to all the work of creation,
> Nor will any end be to the renewal of the months.
> Hark how the words of her wise are confused,
> Built and plastered up on a vain, unstable base;
> And thou wilt come back with a heart stripped empty
> And a mouth full of dross and weeds.
>
> —Jehudah Halevi[48]

NOTES

I wish to thank the Carl Friedrich von Siemens Stiftung in Munich for supporting me during the time when I completed this essay; and the Social Sciences and Humanities Research Council (SSHRC) of Canada, and the Lynde and Harry Bradley Foundation for supporting me during earlier periods of work leading up to this essay.

Citations from primary sources other than Scripture are by standard pagination of original-language editions (Stephenus in the case of Plato, and Bekker for Aristotle) or by book, section, or paragraph numbers of recognized critical editions. All translations from primary sources not written in English are my own. English translations from the Bible are my own, on the basis of the Hebrew text in *Biblia Hebraica Stuttgartensia*, ed. R. Kittel et al., 4th and rev. ed. (Stuttgart: Deutsche Bibelgesellschaft, 1977); and of the Greek text in *Septuaginta, Id est Vetus Testamentum graece iuxta LXX interpretes*, ed. Alfred Rahlfs (Stuttgart: Deutsche Bibelgesellschaft, 1979)—and I have consulted various published translations in my quest for the most literal accuracy consistent with correct English.

1. John Locke, *Two Treatises of Government*, bk. 1, sec. 48.

2. Hillel Fradkin, "God's Politics—Lessons from the Beginning," *This World* 4 (Winter 1983): 86–104. In what follows and in my reading of the Bible generally I have been much assisted by this essay, as well as by Leo Strauss's two studies, "On the Interpretation of Genesis," *L'Homme: Revue française d'anthropologie* 21 (1981): 5–36, and "Jerusalem and Athens: Some Preliminary Reflections," in *Studies in Platonic Political Philosophy* (Chicago: University of Chicago Press, 1983), hereafter cited as "Jerusalem and Athens."

3. Philo of Alexandria, *On the Making of the Cosmos According to Moses*, sec. 2 (the Platonic notion of legal "preludes" [προοίμια] is developed in *Laws* 719b–723d).

4. Strauss, "Jerusalem and Athens," 152.

5. Umberto Cassuto's attempts, in his *Commentary on the Book of Genesis*, trans. Israel Abrahams, 2 vols. (Jerusalem: Magnes Press, Hebrew University, 1961–64) 1:84–96, 101–2, 108, 127–29, to resolve the contradictions are not, I think, entirely successful. His discussion is animated by a laudable respect for the integrity of the text, and his arguments are erudite, ingenious, and often persuasive, but he does not do justice, it seems to me, to the massive and primary impression the two accounts give, of being very different accounts.

6. Strauss, "Jerusalem and Athens," 152; see the passage as a whole (149–52). Compare Cassuto's formulation (*Commentary on Genesis*, 1:12) of what he calls his interpretive "hypothesis": "Particularly in the case of a book like ours, which was not intended for the thinkers and the elect few only, but for the people as a whole, including also its common folk, it was proper that its ideas should be embodied in the language of concrete description. Hence the Torah made use of the concrete traditions that found expression in the 'Wisdom' literature and in the ancient heroic poetry of Israel, and drew from them material for its structure. Choosing only what it deemed worthy, it refined and purified the selected matter, and moulded the entire narrative into a pattern of its own—a pattern befitting its purpose and educational aim." See further Cassuto's elaborations of his "hypothesis" at 1:71–76, and 1:93–94, where he insists in the following words on a sharp distinction between the proper dissection of the text with a view to the divergent traditional sources of its "*content*" and the improper dissection of its "*literary* aspect": "Literary dissection in the divergent ways proposed by the different critics is impossible; for the variegated material deriving from the ancient sagas that the Torah utilized consist not of verses or fragments of verses, but of themes, ideas, narratives. This material, and also its own original contribution, the Torah cast, as it were, into a crucible and fused the whole together, and out of the integrated matter it created a unitary product." For further vigorous discussion and application of the "hypothesis," see 1:56, 185, 189, 190, 193, 266–67, and especially 2:34 and 307 (on the redactor as "no ordinary compiler," "no ordinary editor," "but a writer in the true sense of the word"), as well as 2:38, 142–43, 184–85, 234–36, 269–70, 273, 293–94, 299, 336–38. See also the translation and commentary in Samson Raphael Hirsch, *The Pentateuch*, 2d. ed., trans. Isaac Levy (Gateshead, England: Judaica Press, 1973), 299: the Torah's "goal" is "education of the people of Israel, and to this end it employs traditional material." And Robert Alter's kindred but less homiletic and more emphatically literary approach, *The Art of Biblical Narrative* (New York: Basic, 1981), especially 10, 13–15, 19–20, 24, 34–35, n. 100, 103–4, 132–33, 138, 141–42.

The fundamental difference between Strauss's hermeneutic hypothesis and that of Cassuto is indicated by comparing Cassuto's characterization of the redactor as "the creator of a work of art by his own efforts" (*Commentary on Genesis*, 2:34) with Strauss's contrast between the redactor(s) of the Bible and the Greek poets ("Jerusalem and Athens," 163; see also "On the Interpretation of Genesis," end). Strauss has a much more stringent criterion for what a book in the strict sense is, and for what an author or "poet" in the true sense of the word is; he accordingly denies that the Bible as a whole is a book, and questions whether even the Torah is a book: "[T]he author of a book in the strict sense excludes everything that is not necessary, that does not fulfill a function necessary for the purpose that his book is meant to fulfill. The compilers of the Bible as a whole and of the Torah in particular seem to have followed an entirely different rule. Confronted with a variety of pre-existing holy speeches, which as such had to be treated with the utmost respect, they excluded only what could not by any stretch of the imagination be rendered compatible with the fundamental and authoritative teaching; their very piety, aroused and fostered by the pre-existing holy speeches, led them to make such changes in those holy speeches as they did make."

I must say that it does seem to me that Strauss's formulation here goes too far in his repeated assertion that the compilers "excluded only what could not *by any stretch of the imagination be rendered compatible* with the fundamental and authoritative teaching," or in his conclusion that "their work may then *abound* in contradictions and repetitions that no one ever intended as such," for this would not appear to explain that unity and discriminating carefulness or thoughtfulness which Strauss himself finds in the texts upon which he comments, and in particular in the contradictions and repetitions (italics mine).

7. Cicero, *On Divination* 2.37; comparable in the decisive respect (though of course by no means identical) to the biblical outlook is the view easily accessible to the Greco-Roman philosophers by way of Hesiod's purported revelation from the Muses in *Theogony* 116–17: "Now at the very first, Gaping Emptiness [Chaos] came into being; and after that / Broad-bosomed Earth, a safe seat forever for all / The immortals who possess the peak of snowy Olympus;" as well as by way of utterances such as these of Pindar: "The power of the gods makes a light achievement out of even what surpasses what one would swear or hope possible" (Olympian Ode 13, l. 83); "For from the gods spring [ἔφυν] all the devisings of mortal virtues, and the wise, and the mighty with their hands, and the eloquent" (Pythian Ode 1, ll. 41–42); "To me nothing ever appears to be incredible among the wonders of the accomplishing gods" (Pythian Ode 10, ll. 48–50); "by the power of god, unsullied light can spring forth from dark night, and the pure light of day be hidden by dark cloud" (fragment quoted in Clemens Alexandrinus *Stromata* 5.708).

8. Gen. 18:14; cf. Matt. 19:26, Mark 10:27, Luke 1:37.

9. See Spinoza's exploitation of the difficulties or ambiguities, as a key part of the foundation of his attempted demolition of the authority of the Bible: Carl Gebhardt, "*Tractatus Theologico-Politicus*," in Gebhardt, ed., *Spinoza Opera* (Heidelberg: Carl Winters Universitaets Buchhandlung, 1925), 38–39, 81–82; cf. Strauss's discussion of these passages and their import: "How to Study Spinoza's *Theologico-Political Treatise*," in *Persecution and the Art of Writing* (Glencoe, Ill.: The Free Press, 1952), 198–200.

10. In the New Testament, which has come under a certain influence of Greek philosophy, the word for nature (φύσις) and derivatives is found sixteen times; in the Septuagint, φύσις is found twelve times, all in the Hellenistic books Wisdom of Solomon (7:20, 13:1; 19:20), 3 Maccabees (3:29), and 4 Maccabees (1:20; 5:7, 8, 25; 13:27; 15:13, 25; 16:3).

11. See the O. E. D., s.v. "miracle," no. 1; St. Augustine *Against Faustus the Manichean* 26.3; St. Thomas Aquinas *Summa Theologica* 1a Q. 105 a. 7 and 8;

Spinoza, *Tractatus Theologico-Politicus*, chap. 6, "Of Miracles"; and Strauss, *Natural Right and History* (Chicago: University of Chicago Press, 1953), 81–84, as well as "Jerusalem and Athens," 151. The RSV translates פלא as "miracle" at Ps. 78:12. Consider the lengths to which Philo must go in order to force upon the text of Genesis a version of a Platonic conception of nature: *On the Making of the Cosmos*, secs. 8–9, 24–29.

12. 1 Sam. 6:9; the term (מקרה) is translated in the Septuagint as σύμπτωμα; for the scientific significance of this latter Greek term, cf. Aristotle *On Prophecy in Sleep* 462b27–463a3, and 463b1 ff.; see also *Physics* 199a3–6 and context.

13. See also the use of the verbal root (קרה) at Num. 11:23, Isa. 41:22, Eccles. 9:11, Dan. 10:14; see, similarly, the connotation of the other word for accident (פגע) at 1 Kings 5:18 and Eccles. 9:11 (at both points, the Septuagint uses ἀπάντημα).

14. For the theologico-political issues at stake in the philosophic preoccupation with the stars, see especially Plato *Laws* 885e7–886a8, 886d4–e2, 888e4–890a2, 898d3–899b9, taken together with 966e2–968a1; *Apology of Socrates* 18a7–19d7, 23d2–7, 26d1–e2; Cicero *Tusculan Disputations*, bk. 5, sec. 10; Aristotle *Physics* 196b1–4 and context. For a high expression of the still vigorous, pre-philosophic Greek understanding of the heavens, or more precisely of the "meaning" of a solar eclipse, see the fragment of Pindar's (Ninth) Paean to the Thebans (preserved in Dionysius of Halicarnassus, "On Demosthenes" 7).

15. Dan. 1:20 ff.; Isa. 47:13; Jer. 10:2; cf. 2 Kings. 17:16, 21:3, 23:5.

16. Cf. Ps. 115:16 with Cassuto, *Commentary on Genesis*, 1.21.

17. Jer. 51:15, Ps. 8:4, Neh. 9:6; cf. 1 Kings. 8:27, 2 Chron. 2:5, 6:18.

18. Cassuto observes (*Commentary on Genesis*, 2:101–2) that in the account of the Flood, "The Torah does not refer to the heat of the sun as one of the factors contributing to the evaporation of the waters, although it would have been but logical to mention this detail." In contrast, in the Sumerian myths of the Flood, from which the biblical account may be derived, "stress is laid on the action of the God Samas at the end of the Flood, when he shed his light in the heavens and on the earth."

19. See Strauss "Jerusalem and Athens," 154, and Cassuto, *Commentary on Genesis*, 1:49–50. On the sea monster as "the one exception," see the apt remark by Robert Sacks, "The Lion and the Ass: A Commentary on the Book of Genesis (Chapters 1–10)," *Interpretation: A Journal of Political Philosophy* 8, 2–3 (1980): 43.

20. See notably Hesiod *Theogony* 120 ff.; Parmenides *On Nature*, fragment 13 (Diels-Kranz); John Gardner and John Maier (with the assistance of Richard A. Henshaw), trans., *Gilgamesh, Translated from the Sîn-Leqi-Unninnî Version* (New York: Alfred A. Knopf, 1984), Tablet 1, column 2, ll.16–17, 27–28, 35; column 4, ll. 8ff.; column 3, ll. 8–19. Cf. Henri Frankfurt et al., *Before Philosophy: The Intellectual Adventure of Ancient Man* (Harmondsworth, England: Penguin, 1951), especially chap. 8.

21. Isa. 45:7; cf. the Talmudic Seder Kodashim, Mas. Tamid 32a, secs. 4–5.

22. Contrast however Cassuto, *Commentary on Genesis*, 1:26.

23. Cf. St. Thomas *Summa Theologica* 1a Q. 73 a. 2: "when all things were made He is not said to have rested 'in' His works, as though needing them for His own

happiness, but to have rested 'from' them, as in fact resting in Himself, as He suffices for Himself and fulfills His own desire. And even though from all eternity He rested in Himself, yet the rest in Himself, which He took after He had finished His works, is that rest which belongs to the seventh day. And this, says Augustine, is the meaning of God's resting from His works on that day (*Commentary on Genesis* ad loc., 4)"; see also *Commentary on the Sentences* 2d. 15.3.3.

24. Ex. 31:17; cf. 20:11, and Cassuto, *Commentary on Genesis*, 1:63.

25. See Cassuto, *Commentary on Genesis*, 1:59, who invokes Isa. 11:7 and 65:25 as evidence that in the Messianic era the original vegetarianism of all animate creation will be reestablished. St. Thomas Aquinas characteristically demurs from such a reading, on the grounds that "the nature of animals was not changed by man's sin, as if those whose nature now it is to devour the flesh of others, would then have lived on herbs, as the lion and falcon" (*Summa Theologica* 1a Q. 96 a. 1, Reply Obj. 2).

26. Sacks's attempt ("Commentary on the Book of Genesis [Chapters 1–10]," 37–45) to show that "under the surface" of the first account of creation there is a "deeper sense" teaching that "the most fundamental difficulties lie not in the heart of man, but in the heart of being" I find unconvincing; as Sacks stresses, his specific interpretations of the verses stand or fall by the peculiar, and, it seems to me, unwarranted, construction he puts on the repeated and (for his interpretation) crucial phrase "And it was so" (כ‎ -וַיְהִי‎) at Gen. 1:7, 9, 11, 15, 24, 30.

27. There is no suggestion that what man needed was a city, fellow citizens, or a political community of any kind (contrast Aristotle *Politics* 1252b27–53a39, as well as Thomas Aquinas *Commentary on the Politics of Aristotle* ad loc., sec. 35). Nor is there any indication that friendship with another male—such as David was to have with Jonathan—was what Adam needed. The heterosexual and monogamous couple, constituting the core of the family, is the only form of human society that is explicitly intended by God for man in his pristine condition.

28. John Milton disposes of, and thus highlights, the difficulty by introducing the angel Raphael to instruct Adam: "God to render Man inexcusable sends Raphael to admonish him of his obedience, of his free estate, of his enemy near at hand; who he is, and why his enemy, and whatever else may avail Adam to know" (*Paradise Lost*, bk. 5, "The Argument").

29. John Locke, *The Reasonableness of Christianity, as Delivered in the Scriptures*; the quotations here and in the following sentences are from paragraphs 1, 2, and 6. Contrast St. Augustine *Free Choice of the Will* 3.19 beg., where, confronting essentially the same objection, St. Augustine attributes it to "discontented men ready to blame anything whatsoever—except themselves—for sin."

30. Cf. Ps. 109:10, 12–15; 137:9. Contrast Plato *Laws* 856c9–d2 and Hugo Grotius *On the Laws of War and Peace* 2.21.13.

31. See 1 Timothy 2:13–14, and St. Augustine's interpretation of this passage (*City of God* 14.11, 14.13). St. Thomas Aquinas (*Summa Theologica* 1a Q. 94 a 4, Reply Obj. 1) follows St. Augustine: "Though the woman was deceived before she sinned in deed, still it was not till she had already sinned by interior pride. For Augustine says (*Commentary on Genesis* ad lit. 11.30) that 'the woman could not have believed the words of the serpent, had she not already acquiesced in the love of her own power, and in a presumption of self-conceit.'" Elsewhere

(*Summa Theologica* 2a–2ae Q. 163 a.1, Reply Obj. 4) St. Thomas adds, "this does not mean that pride preceded the promptings of the serpent, but that as soon as the serpent had spoken his words of persuasion, her mind was puffed up, the result being that she believed the demon to have spoken truly." The sin that preceded the eating of the forbidden fruit must have been a mortal and not merely a venial sin, according to St. Thomas (*Summa Theologica* 1a–2ae Q. 89 a. 3; *On Evil* Q. 2 a.8, Reply 1; see also *Summa Theologica*, 2a–2ae Q. 163 a 1 and a. 2, "On the Contrary," and St. Augustine *Commentary on Genesis* 11.5: "We must not suppose that the tempter would have overcome man, unless first of all there had arisen in man's soul a movement of vainglory which should have been checked." Yet compare the Gloss that St. Thomas reports on 1 Tim. 2:14: "Having had no experience of God's severity, it was possible for him to be so mistaken as to think that what he had done was a venial sin" [*Summa Theologica* 1a–2ae Q. 89 a. 3, Obj. 1] and see St. Thomas's curious "Reply." For some clarification, see *Disputed Questions on Truth* Q. 18 a.6, Obj. 11 and Reply).

32. Gen. 2:25–3:1—"Adam and his woman were naked (עֲרוּמִּים) but unashamed. The serpent was cunning (עָרוּם)." Just the omission of a dagesh forte would make the first sentence read: "Adam and his woman were cunning (עֲרוּמִים) but unashamed." Cf. Cassuto (*Commentary on Genesis*, 1:143), commenting on Gen. 3:1: "In order to make the wordplay more apparent, Scripture uses in the previous verse the form עָרוֹם and not עֵירוֹם, which occurs subsequently in verses 7, 10, 11, and it prefers the full to the defective mode of spelling." I have not, however, been able to follow Cassuto's interpretation of this wordplay, when he takes it to support his contention that the serpent is not meant to have here an independent existence, but is "an allegorical allusion to the craftiness to be found in *man himself.*"

33. See St. Thomas *Summa Theologica* 2a–2ae Q. 163 a 2, Obj. 2 and Reply. The link between the philosophic or scientific quest for "nature" and the desire for the fruit of the tree of knowledge of good and evil is brought out in the words of C. S. Lewis's *Queen of Perelandra* (his fictional analogue to the biblical Eve, who differs from Eve in that she resists the devil—with the help, to be sure, of a fallen human): "And why should I desire the Fixed except to be sure—to be able on one day to command where I should be the next and what should happen to me?" See *Perelandra* (New York: Collier-Macmillan, 1965), 208.

34. Compare St. Augustine (*Commentary on Genesis* 11.4): "it seems to me that man would have had no prospect of any special praise, if he were able to lead a good life simply because there was none to persuade him to lead an evil life; since both by nature he had the power, and in his power he had the will, not to consent to the persuader." Yet must we not then add that since God punished the serpent as well, and the serpent's progeny for all time, it would seem that the serpent cannot have been merely an instrument in God's plan? The serpent too, it would seem, was being tested; and if it had not chosen to succumb to the temptations of its own cunning, then some other means of testing Adam and Eve would have to have been awaited or devised.

35. See St. Thomas Aquinas, *Compendium of Theology* 1.188 ("The Tree of Knowledge of Good and Evil"), and the words of C. S. Lewis's *King of Perelandra*, in *Perelandra*, 209: "We have learned of evil, though not as the Evil

One wished us to learn. We have learned better than that, and know it more, for it is waking that understands sleep and not sleep that understands waking. There is an ignorance of evil that comes from being young: there is a darker ignorance that comes from doing it, as men by sleeping lose the knowledge of sleep. You are more ignorant of evil [on earth] now than in the days before your Lord and Lady began to do it." There is, we may note, only an apparent kinship between this denigration of the knowledge actually contained in the fruit of the tree of knowledge, and the denigration, on altogether different grounds, found in Maimonides' *Guide of the Perplexed*, pt. 1, chap. 2. For a further suggestion as to the character of the knowledge mankind might have had, if the temptation to eat of the fruit of the tree of knowledge had been resisted, see the Queen of Perelandra's words in *Perelandra*, 69): "I thought that I was carried in the will of Him I love, but now I see that I walk with it. I thought that the good things He sent me drew me into them as the waves lift the islands; but now I see that it is I who plunge into them with my own arms and legs, as when we go swimming."

36. Contrast Aristotle *Nichomachean Ethics* 1128b10–33.

37. Gen. 6:6–7; see also Ex. 32:14 (for a recent, serious, and honest, if not altogether successful, struggle to make sense of this instance from Exodus, see Aaron Wildavsky, *The Nursing Father: Moses as a Political Leader* [University, Ala.: University of Alabama Press, 1984] 99–106); Judg. 2:18; 2 Sam. 24:16 together with 1 Chron. 21:15; and Ps. 106:45.

38. Isa. 38:1–6 (=2 Kings 20:1–7), Jer. 18:7–10, 26:3, 42: 10; Joel 2:13–14; Amos 7:3, 6; Jonah 3:9, 3:10 and 4:2; see also 1 Kings 21:29; *Midrash Rabbah*, on Gen. 27:4.

39. Compare Grotius *On the Laws of War and Peace* 2.13.3.3–4: "For in reality God does not change His decrees. Nevertheless He is said to change them and to be influenced by repentance as often as He acts otherwise than His words seemed to mean; and this may happen on account of a condition tacitly understood, which has ceased to exist; Jeremiah 18:8. It is possible to find examples in Genesis 20:3, Exodus 22:14, I Kings 21:29, 2 Kings 20:l, Isaiah 38: 1, Jonah 3:5 and 10. In this sense God cannot properly be said even to deceive us, and the word 'to deceive,' which appears in the passage of the Epistle to the Hebrews ordinarily refers to an event which disappoints expectation. This can be seen both in other passages and in Leviticus 6:2, Joshua 24:27, Isaiah 57:11, Hosea 9:2, and Habakkuk 3:17 (add Job 40:28; Hosea 9:2). But this apparent deception occurs most easily in threats, because these confer right upon no one. It appears at times also in promises, when indeed there is a tacit condition secretly present."

But Grotius's grounds for denying such mutability to God are not simply divine omniscience and omnipotence; on the contrary, in a notorious doctrine, Grotius argues that the Bible gives evidence of another kind of limitation on the divine "nature": "the Scriptures teach us that God Himself, who cannot be bound by any established law, would act contrary to His nature if He did not make good His promises." Nehemiah 9:8; Hebrews 6:8, 10:23; 1 Corinthians 1:9, 10:13; 1 Thessalonians 5:24; 2 Thessalonians 3; 2 Timothy 2:13 (so Baldus, *On Digest* 2.14.1). From this it follows that the obligation to perform promises arises from the nature of immutable justice, which in its own fashion is common to God and to all beings possessed of reason" (ibid. 2.11.4.1).

40. *Paradise Lost* 3.111–119; cf. the words of the Mishnah (Pirke Avoth, 3.15): "everything is foreseen, but the right [of choice] is granted, and the world is judged with goodness, and everything is in accordance with the preponderance of [man's] deed[s]."

41. Consider Amos 3:6, and the ambiguous Isa. 54:15–16. C. S. Lewis, we may observe, limits his angels to suggesting that "in the Fallen World He prepared for Himself a body and was united with the Dust and made it glorious for ever. This is the end and final cause of all creating, and the sin whereby it came is called Fortunate." (*Perelandra*, 215).

42. St. Augustine denies that God is incapable of creating free creatures who are sinless; among the angels, Augustine is confident, there are such. But in Augustine's account a limitation of another kind becomes manifest: Augustine's argument justifying God's creation of man as fallible seems to imply that Creation would not be full nor complete without every rank of creature and hence without a fallible free being; the standard for the full goodness or completion of creation appears then to be prior to creation (*On Free Choice of the Will* 3.5).

43. Spinoza, *Tractatus Politicus*, ch. 2, secs. 6–7, in *The Political Works*, ed. and trans. A. G. Wernham (New York: Oxford University Press, 1965), 268–73; I have altered the translation to make it more literal.

44. See Moses Maimonides, *The Guide of the Perplexed*, trans. Pines (Chicago: University of Chicago Press, 1963), 301.

45. Consider Prv 6:32: "He who commits adultery is devoid of sense; he who does it destroys himself."

46. Compare Gen. 3:22 with Fradkin, "God's Politics," 88 and 90. See also 2 Macc. 6:13–16.

47. "And exalted is the Lord of Hosts by just judgment; the Holy God is proved holy by retributive justice" (Isa. 5:16).

48. From "Song IV" in *Three Jewish Philosophers*, ed. Hans Lewis, Alexander Altmann, and Isaak Heineman (New York: Atheneum, 1972), 137.

Friendship and Fraternity
(Overcoming Pride)

2

Friendship and Politics: Ancient and American

Patrick J. Deneen

Fascination with the ancients perseveres unabated. For admirers, the ancient epic poets, the playwrights, and philosophers remind us of half-forgotten truths, teach us alternative ways of viewing politics, and reveal a distinctive approach to human relationships built on assumptions other than those of modern liberalism.[1] As a pre-liberal democracy, the example of Athens especially attracts, not primarily for any positive model it might offer to contemporary popular rule—in fact, most commentators recognize that such examples are limited—but for what ancient understandings of human relationships reveal about contemporary assumptions.[2] The Greeks are simultaneously present yet distant, embedded in Western tradition, but also are a standing accusation against modern faiths.

Contemporary attentiveness to the ancients is praiseworthy, but at times the distinctiveness that we attribute to the ancients serves only to obscure a similarity between ancient political theory and certain contemporary musings by figures in American thought. Overlooked amid the widespread recognition that thinkers as diverse as the Federalists, Walt Whitman, and John Dewey all viewed the Greeks with disapproval, are curiously ancient contentions proffered by sometimes forgotten opponents of America's official theorists—voices whose arguments often did not carry the day in a decisively modernizing America, but whose cautions against contemporary assumptions nevertheless in retrospect startle and continue to resonate.[3] As Wilson Carey McWilliams has observed,

The most perceptive students of American politics have always seen that American culture is deeply dualistic, that the domination of its formal thought by the Enlightenment does not exclude an informal tradition in

47

symbols, rituals, and arts and letters based on very different notions of man and politics.[4]

Preeminent among those "different notions" were beliefs embedded in the religious traditions of America's new immigrants, engendering an outlook that "has seen man and the world as inadequate," and which has "always provided the emotional and symbolic basis for the appeal to fraternity in American politics as an immediate need rather than a distant goal."[5]

A few intellectual archaeologists have noted a certain kindred approach between the ancients and American theorists regarding issues such as the advantages of small regimes, the shortcomings of representation, the limits of individualism, and the need to embrace a tragic vision of human life and capacities.[6] Greek and alternative American visions also intersect in a less-explored arena of human relations, namely, the extent to which ideas and forms of friendship can be said to be compatible with, and even a necessary component of, a healthy political regime. Particularly noteworthy are some remarkable similarities in the attempts by both Aristotle in the fourth century B.C. and several obscure American thinkers at the turn of the twentieth century to redefine friendship neither as purely private or familial relations, nor as cursory relations between sophisticates—both which might be the inclination of contemporary cosmopolitan liberalism—but rather as relations ideally located within a civic context and, in fact, a necessary basis for civic trust and true justice.

An exploration of Aristotle's writings on political friendship hardly merits justification; his musings in the *Nicomachean Ethics* are rightly renowned and lack no shortage of exegeses. The obscurity of the American writers in question—local reformers concerned about the direction of Progressive programs to dismantle political party organizations, unrenowned figures like H. C. Merwin and Mary Kingsbury Simkhovitch—is primarily reflective of the discrete battles in which they were engaged. Yet, encountering their writings can be as startling as reading Aristotle for the first time, revealing not only the extent of underlying liberal assumptions, but perhaps even reminding us quite how jarring Aristotle's words should be for the modern reader. Merwin's and Simkhovitch's prescience about the direction of contemporary liberalism simply astounds, and their cautions remain fresh and relevant. The assumption, however, that Aristotle simply recorded the prevailing opinions about friendship and politics in fourth-century Athens, whereas Merwin and Simkhovitch resisted prevailing American currents, would be mistaken. While philosophic vistas were undoubtedly more expansive while Aristotle wrote, and musings on civic friendship were not largely forestalled by liberal assumptions of human separateness, by no means was Aristotle preaching to the converted. Indeed, the similarity of the respective defenses of civic friendship in the face of resistance are quite remarkable given the vast difference in time, culture, and circumstance separating democratic Athens and republican America. In the final estimation, perhaps the most significant, if not obvious, difference remains that the possibilities for civic friendship were taken more seriously by the ancients than by the moderns, which suggests perhaps an additional reason for the relative prominence and obscurity of the thinkers in question.

FRIENDSHIP AGAINST POLITICS

Regarded through the lens of Aristotle's discussion of friendship in books eight and nine of the *Nicomachean Ethics*, it might be concluded that ancients believed friendship provided the greatest of external goods for the ethical human life, only superseded by the high praise Aristotle reserves for the philosophic life in book ten. However, his famous discussion is less a summary of existing thought about friendship and its relation to life in the polis than a radical reinvention of existing ideas of friendship. Notwithstanding Aristotle's discussion, friendship was never a political solution in any final sense for the ancients, but rather a constant problem. Rather than being seen as providing a foundation of mutual interest among citizens, friendship was more often than not viewed as a potential opponent to civic cohesion.

Among his first words in Sophocles' *Antigone*, Creon declares:

> No less damned is he who puts a friend
> Above his country; I have no good word for him. . . .
> No man who is his country's enemy
> Shall call himself my friend. Of this I am sure—
> Our country is our life; only when she
> Rides safely, have we any friends at all.
> Such is my policy for our common weal.[7]

Creon reveals one of the greatest threats faced by the ancient polis: the extensive presence of extended kinship ties, which existed in profound tension to civic demands—in this case, demonstrated by the obligations of family burial rites claimed by Antigone. Friendship that undermines the bond of the state ultimately undermines the possibility of friendship itself, Creon suggests.

The competition between the demands of the polis and obligations to family elucidates the constant threat to the public order by private forms of primitive friendship, those kinship bonds formed both between blood relationships and within immediate, affective groups. It was rather friendship as a voluntary bond (not the more obligatory blood ties) that was to become an analogy for politics itself as a means of distinguishing between the household and the polis. The ancients sought to preserve a place for friendship in the civic sphere, realizing its creative potential even as they remained fearful of its destructive dangers. As suggested by historian Horst Hutter: "Greek friendship had thus both a creative and destructive impact. In its creative aspect it was seen as supportive of the life of the polis, a thing indispensable to its well-being. . . . In its destructive aspect it was seen as leading to the ruin of states and social institutions like the family."[8] By drawing friendship away from the automatic kinship of similars, and instead introducing sufficient difference between people— a psychic and real distance—it was to be hoped that its passions could at once be mitigated but not entirely eradicated. A form of friendship coextensive with civic ties, based on voluntary commitments, provided a more benign model for political relationships.

However, friendship in this latter form—in its voluntary, and implicitly political incarnation—was not without its own dangers. Friendships formed on a wholly voluntary and consensual basis also threatened the destruction of the city, although from outside the walls of the city rather than from within. An ancient Greek practice among aristocratic families was to form friendships with the leading families of other cities, thereby establishing a network of "guest-friendships" (*xenia-philoi*) whose affections and demands traversed city borders. A notable example of just such a relationship occurs in a scene in the *Iliad* on the battlefield before Troy:

> [Diomedes] drove his spear into the prospering earth, and in winning
> words of friendliness he spoke [to his opponent], Hippolochos. . . .
> "See now, you are my guest-friend [*xeinos*] from far in the time of our fathers.
> Brilliant Oineus once was host to Bellerophontes
> the blameless, in his halls, and twenty days he detained him,
> and these two gave to each other fine gifts in token of friendship. . . .
> Therefore I am your friend and host in the heart of Argos;
> you are mine in Lykia, when I come to your country.
> Let us avoid each other's spears, even in the close fighting.
> There are plenty of Trojans and famed companions in battle for me
> to kill, whom the god sends me, or those I run down with my swift feet,
> many Achaians for you to slaughter, if you can do it.
> But let us exchange our armour, so that others will know
> how we claim to be guests and friends from the days of our fathers."[9]

Although Hippolochos and Diomedes were strangers to one another, their ancestors had formed a ritual friendship that was inherited intact by their progeny. In this case, their ancestral alliance superseded the duties of their opposing political alliances, suggesting the conflict that the polis faced from these networks of *xenia-philoi*.

These "ritual friendships" were products of the Homeric age, antedating the polis in its fifth-century form, and often opposed to the interests of the regime. Guest-friendship was thus of heroic origin, in which the glory of one's friends and oneself was the sole criterion for evaluating the judgments and actions of each constitutive member. In the event of a slight to the honor of one's friend, one was esteemed for exacting revenge, or disgraced for neglecting him. And, when offending one's own country—as was often the case—one's *xenoi* provided a refuge in exile. These friendships then, engaged in almost exclusively by the elite of ancient society, provided a private and even antipolitical basis for relations among and between foreign citizens.

The extent of these alliances and their ambivalent relationship to the polis has been extensively described by Gabriel Herman, who summarizes that

> when during the eighth and seventh centuries B.C. the contours of the city-state were gradually drawn, the ancient world was criss-crossed with an extensive network of personal alliances linking together all sorts of apolitical bodies (households, tribes, bands, etc.). The city framework imposed itself upon it, yet did not dissolve it. And when the city finally became established as the dominant form of organization, dense webs of guest-friendship still stretched beyond its bounds. Overtly or covertly, guest-friendship continued to act as a powerful bond between citizens of different cities and between citizens and members of various apolitical bodies.[10]

In maintaining these bonds within the context of the city-state and continuing to make private standards the sole basis for honorable action, the polis was faced with continuous compromises of its interests, often by its very leaders. The polis, then, increasingly sought to eradicate such betrayal, on the one hand, by subtly altering the *xenoi* relationships of antiquity on behalf of the regime's interests, and, on the other hand, by transforming these formerly honorable actions to a disgraceful status.

Herman describes the transformation of *xenia* relationships, formerly regulated by leading families, to *proxenia* bonds, which were guest-friendships granted to foreign elites by, and on behalf of, the cities themselves. Thus, rather than permitting the citizen to collude with the stranger against the city, the stranger was charged to look after the foreign city's interests from abroad. *Proxenia* was effectively "a communal invention using as a model *xenia*."[11] In a similar fashion by which the polis combated destructive forms of kinship friendship described above, the polis turned ritual friendship against itself—rather than close the borders and entrap its own citizens. Borders, physical and psychological, were strengthened between insiders and outsiders, not solely for protection of the city from outside threat, but perhaps even more to protect from internal sabotage. A remarkable conclusion to be drawn from this strict delineation between citizens and barbarians is that this solution had class overtones, inasmuch as elites were made to conform to norms set down by the polis on behalf of the less mobile citizens who could not profit from such ritual friendships. The polis was able to transform the interests of the powerful elite of ancient Greek society by redirecting the network of relationships toward the common good—by a transformation of ritual friendships into political friendships.

The ancient city, then, was fixed between the two poles of friendship that sought to tear it asunder both from within and without: on the one side, the friendship (or kinship) formed in households and in clans; and from the other pole, those guest-friendships between citizens and foreigners, formed by elites out of private interest. The ancients sought therefore to transcend the former (without denying those affective ties their rightful place within the city's walls) and to transform or wholly forbid the latter.[12] In effect, the ancients sought to transform destructive forms of friendship into constructive civic friendships in order to secure political stability, whereas modern thought would conceptually turn men against each other to that same end.[13] Thus viewed, Aristotle's philosophic rendering of friendship can be seen in a different light, inasmuch as he sought to contravene the politically destructive forms of friendship with a constructive and constitutive theory of friendship that was thereby inseparable from conceptions of the polis and democratic practice itself.

ARISTOTLE ON CIVIC FRIENDSHIP

Aristotle begins his analysis of friendship in the *Nicomachean Ethics* with an astonishing claim: that "if men are friends, there is no need of justice between them; whereas merely to be just is not enough—a feeling of friendship is also necessary."[14] Justice, as conceived in an impersonal, abstract, and even procedural sense, is superfluous between friends because friendship implies by its nature a preexisting proportion and reciprocity. Justice issued through the auspices of laws and courts proves insufficient: such an abstract approach to justice does not appreciate each individual in his or her specificity. Simply considering all humans equal, without a corresponding sense of what is rightly owed each individual given personal knowledge of each person's respective virtues and vices, fails to attain a robust and encompassing justice. Formal justice is not sufficient in civic affairs; what citizens also need is dignity, respect, and recognition as unique individuals—those qualities accorded by friendship. Thus Aristotle concludes: "Indeed, the highest form of justice seems to have a friendly feeling in it" (*NE* 1155a). Justice in its "highest form" considers the particularity of each individual, ceases to be an abstraction, becoming substantive and individuated justice. And as this "friendly feeling" increases throughout a polis, so do manifestations of justice: "It is natural that the claims of justice should increase with the nearness of the friendship, since friendship and justice exist between the same persons and are coextensive in range" (*NE* 1160a).

Aristotle distinguishes between three types of friendship, based respectively on pleasure, utility, and a shared conception of "The Good" (*NE* 1155b). The former pair he treats with suspicion in the *Nicomachean Ethics*, since they are based ultimately on self-interest, and hence such friendship is subject to dissolution if one's attitude toward a specific pleasure or utility might change (*NE* 1156a). On the other hand, friendship based on "The Good" is unchanging and constant, since Aristotle contends that "The Good" is "a permanent quality" (*NE* 1156b). Since an understanding of "The Good" is accessible only to the philosophic few, it would seem that Aristotle immediately undercuts any claims that were previously made for a civic aspect of friendship (*NE* 1156b). Much of the remainder of the *Nicomachean Ethics* is devoted to a discussion of this highest form of friendship in which friends "wish the good of their friend for their friend's sake . . . since they love each other for themselves and not accidentally," as opposed to the two inferior forms, which are suspect "since bad men do not take pleasure in each other, save as they get some advantage from each other" (*NE* 1156b, 1157a).

Aristotle tempers his apparent harsh judgment of imperfect friendship—especially friendship based on utility—in the less-read *Eudemian Ethics*, noting that such friendships are not necessarily entered upon by solely "bad men," but indeed most often by citizens.[15] Arguing here that "the bad cannot agree," and that "when they choose and desire the same things, is something different" from friendship (*EE* 1241a), he instead points to an imperfect form of friendship that involves agreement between decent men. "There is agreement (*homonoia*) when the two parties make the same choice as to who is to rule, who to be ruled. . . . Agreement is the friendship of fellow citizens" (*EE* 1241a). Such friendship is called by Aristotle "civic friendship" (*philia politike*—*EE* 1242a). Echoing the description of human association in *Politics*, Aristotle suggests that the polis arises out of mutual need, and from that need arises a form of friendship based on utility.

Civic friendship has been established mainly in accordance with utility; for men seem to have come together because each is not sufficient for himself, though they would have come together anyhow for the sake of living in company. Only the civic friendship and its parallel corruption are not merely friendships, but the partnership is that of friends; other friendships rest on the relation of superiority. The justice of those belonging to the friendship of those useful to one another is preeminently justice, for it is civic or political justice. (*EE* 1242a; cf. *Politics* 1252a)

Aristotle identifies a deep tension that persists in civic friendships; on the one hand, it is a "necessary" partnership (*EE* 1243a), wedding the equality born of mutual needs with dissimilarities arising from varying interests. Aristotle stresses the equality of this civic friendship especially, then alternatively notes the contractual basis of this partnership predicated on difference. Civic friendship is hardly absent of dissent; indeed, Aristotle contends, it is the kind most subject to "recrimination," since it claims to be based on the moral plane of mutual trust, but nevertheless appeals relentlessly to the utility of each citizen (*EE* 1243a). By the end of his discussion of civic friendship, Aristotle appears to remove from the concept any meaning other than a strictly utilitarian one, noting that "the legal form of useful friendship is free from recrimination. The legal association is dissolved by a money-payment (for it measures equality in money)" (*EE* 1243a). The justice arising from this kind of civic friendship is entirely contractual and fleeting, evoking the justice of the marketplace, in effect describing the hollow relations of strangers, better described as the fleeting contact between buyer and seller.

However, Aristotle also points to a more elevated (if still imperfect) basis for civic friendship, one that aspires to the highest form of friendship and hence moderates the utilitarian interests to which civic friendship might otherwise yield. He notes that "in some countries the law forbids lawsuits for voluntary transactions between those who associate with one another; and such as these have dealings with one another as good and trustworthy men. In this kind of friendship it is uncertain how either will recriminate on the other, seeing that they trust each other not in a limited legal way but on the basis of their characters" (*EE* 1243a). In effect, Aristotle returns here to an understanding of civic friendship in which justice is the outcome as a result of personal knowledge and not legal recourse. Recrimination is replaced by mutual trust and good character. He suggests that the type of relations that exist between citizens will form in accordance with the assumptions of the political system put into place.

While prior to this passage Aristotle appears to exclude the standard of goodness from the friendship based on utility, here he describes how a kind of goodness might be accessible to the more widespread and utilitarian friendship between citizens. Earlier, Aristotle describes a variety of friendship that approaches a kind of "good" distinct from the singular

"Good," and which is not only accessible to a variety of people, but indeed which demands variety for its realization. If "primary friendship" based on shared conception of "The Good" is marked by the like-mindedness of the friends, a moderate form of goodness can be achieved by opposites precisely because their differences can potentially drive them toward "the mean." Aristotle writes that "in a sense the love of the contrary is the love of the good; for the opposites desire one another because of the mean; they desire one another like tallies because thus out of the two arises a single mean. Further, the love is accidentally of the opposite, but per se of the mean, for opposites desire not one another but the mean. For if over-chilled they return to the mean by being warmed, and if over-warmed by being chilled" (*EE* 1239b).

Civic friendship born of mutual understanding of dissimilar citizens may be most necessary in democratic regimes (*NE* 1161b). In *Politics*, Aristotle establishes that "the fundamental principle of the democratic form of constitution is liberty," but from that liberty also arises the great democratic danger, the claim of each man "to live as he likes; for they say that this is the function of liberty, inasmuch as to live not as one likes is the life of a man that is a slave . . . and from it has come the claim not to be governed" (1317a–b).[16] Such men are therefore self-interested or share bonds with other men who are limited to private ends—the equivalent of those bonds of friendship based entirely on utility, hence mistrust. The requisite ethical groundwork of a good and other-regarding democratic citizenry is an education in a civic form of friendship, a somewhat less-lofty goal than friendship based on "The Good," but one accessible to many, and one that may partake of the better elements of the ideal friendship. For "friendship appears to be the bond of the polis; and lawgivers seem to set more store by it than they do by justice, for to promote concord [*homonoia*], which seems akin to friendship, is their chief aim, while faction [*stasis*] which is enmity, is what they are most anxious to banish" (*NE* 1155a). Aristotle adumbrates that in a democracy—whose citizens are to be both equal and free, but not to such an excess that they become either wholly self-regarding or totally self-denying, but concerned for and invested in the good of the whole—there is the greatest need for civic friendship based on the achievement of "the mean."

Moreover, Aristotle's distinction between types of friendship demotes those forms of friendship that could prove most destructive of widespread civic friendship, manifested in his suspicion toward both kinship relations and ritualized or heroic friendship. Aristotle explicitly rejects kinship relationships from qualifying as friendship in its fullest political form: he states that "friendship between relatives and between members of a comradeship may be set apart as being less in nature of partnerships than are the friendships between fellow-citizens . . . since these [latter] seem to be founded as it were on a definite compact" (*NE* 1161b). Aristotle does not deny kinship relationships their rightful place in the polis; however, he does dismiss them as constituting the basis of citizen bonds, thereby rejecting a conception of organic community as a polis.

Aristotle does not presume that the interests of citizens will be identical, or even nearly so. As we have seen, he argues that even friendships not based on a shared and like-minded conception of "The Good" can partake of a kind of moderate goodness arising from the natural inclination and cultivated ability of different people to seek "the mean." Yet, if the intimate family is not to be the model of the polis, neither can the feuding family. Aristotle presumes a certain cultivated willingness among different people to seek a common point of agreement, the possibility of citizens who will not resist the virtues of differing opinion to the point of adamancy. Aristotle suggests that agreement, arising simultaneously from different perspectives that are nevertheless subordinated to a willingness to engage in conversation, is precisely the kind of friendship that will characterize the best relations between citizens. Such friendship is to be distinguished from the automatic similarity of interests that characterize kinship and clannish relations; civic friendship must be the result of an active search for agreement at "the mean."

Similarly, Aristotle does not reject friendship between citizens and foreigners, proposing to close the city gates, but rather places them on a lower footing than civic friendship, since such friendships do not benefit from the frequency of contact and intimacy possible within a civic setting. In the *Eudemian Ethics*, Aristotle stresses the necessity of proximity, arguing that "it is clear that friends ought to live together, that all wish this above all things, and that the happiest and best man tends especially to do so" (*EE* 1245a). Friendship as both voluntary, created, and simultaneously limited to those in one's immediate surroundings are the features of civic friendship, as distinguished from the more destructive forms of friendship.

Thus, imperfect but proper friendship is equated with political relationships, not the pre- or extra-political relations that ever threatened to destroy the polis. Aristotle, through this voluntary and political notion of friendship, sought in part to counteract prevailing forms of friendship. Worth recalling is that the *Nicomachean Ethics* is directed to "gentlemen" (*kaloskagathoi*) who would be most likely to undermine the polis either in clans within the city or through ritual friendships outside the city. In the place of such destructive friendships, Aristotle did not propose to separate people from one another and thereby guarantee political stability, but rather recommended an alternative and explicitly political theory of friendship based on a goal of common good that even citizens motivated by different interests might achieve.

Aristotle harbored no visions about universal fraternity of all human beings. He points to an immutable fact of physical limitations to friendship, both in space, time, and in the human capacity for such intimacy. While friendships based on a shared conception of "The Good" might occur between a few like-minded people in vastly different places (and conceivably different times, when one considers the disembodied love of philosophers), civic friendship is more expansive in number but limited by circumstance. In the *Nicomachean Ethics*, Aristotle delineates the upper limits of such bonds in sheer numerical terms:

> Ten people would not make a city, and with a hundred thousand it is a city no longer; though perhaps the proper size is not a particular number, but any number between certain limits. So also the number of one's friends must be limited, and should perhaps be the largest number with whom one can constantly associate. [*NE* 1170b]

A city is not infinitely expandable, precisely because of limits imposed on creating friendly conditions among its citizens. Aristotle consistently chose to accept the limitations to human affection and identity rather than posit a possible, all-encompassing love for humanity as the end of politics.

FRIENDSHIP IN AMERICA

Given this significant caveat, it seems profoundly unlikely that any conception of civic friendship—and especially one echoing the ancient teachings—could have any application to the American setting. The political philosophy of America was grounded on a daunting physical ambition—"extend the sphere," argued James Madison in *The Federalist Papers* 10, and thereby drain the energy and influence from factions, those virulent associations that proved so destructive to democratic regimes of small, ancient cities.[17] Thus, the Federalists dismissed the desirability of immediate personal bonds having a positive influence on political life, and instead suggested that the likely outcome of the new system would be the forging of a direct link between citizen and the national government without effective mediating institutions and associations.[18]

Among the associations most mistrusted by the Founders were political parties, precisely because they might be able to overcome the limits to affective relations that an expansive nation would present. In his famous "Farewell Address," George Washington warned his fellow Americans that "the common and continual mischiefs of Party are sufficient to make it the interest and duty of a wise People to discourage and restrain it." If not, he went on, the passions of such associations threaten to "agitate the

Community with ill founded jealousies and false alarms, kindle the animosity of one part against another, [and] foment occasionally riot and insurrection."[19]

The mistrust of Enlightenment America for political parties continued unabated through the new century, when the loyalties of new immigrant groups and their clustering in urban centers made possible the dominance of political party machines. For reformers like Herbert Croly, even more worrisome than the corruption and greed of the machine was its appeal not to rationalism and self-interest, but rather its claims to friendship and loyalty that gave precedence to the group over the individual, and to affection over merit. Croly insisted that while political parties had served a valuable function in the past, with the advent of civil service reform and expertise in the national government, there should be no mediating institutions interposed between citizens and the state. He bemoaned the affective influence of parties, which

> demands of [the people] that they act and think in politics not under the influence of their natural class or personal convictions, but according to the necessities of an artificial partisan classification. In this way it demands and obtains for a party *an amount of loyal service and personal sacrifice which a public-spirited democrat should lavish only on the state.*[20]

There was, then, little comprehension among Progressives of the real and potential benefits of the affective appeal of political parties, an oversight—or inability of sight—that, despite the best efforts of reformers, permitted the machine to continue its practices precisely because it held the affection of the people, as the reformers did not.

Nevertheless, as McWilliams has suggested, "perhaps the most significant impact of the machine on American thought came through its influence on the reformers who opposed it."[21] Most consequences of reforms like the Australian ballot and, most especially, the direct primary were unintended, such as the rise of candidate-centered politics involving campaign broadcast spots and sound bites, PAC campaign funding, and special interest politics; but it cannot be said that the destruction of kinship within political parties and affective ties formed between a community and its parties were likewise an accidental result.[22] It is clear throughout the writings of the Progressives that they are distrustful of people held together by irrational impulses."[23] The Progressives, echoing the Founders, preferred a rational citizenry and hoped that affective ties between citizens could be attenuated or rendered powerless.[24]

Missing in this predominant view of party was a conception of political life that included friendship, loyalty, and commitment.[25] A few voices sought to reform existing party organizations not on the basis of undermining friendship and loyalties between members, but indeed by seeking to extend the understanding of limited partisan friendship into a more encompassing civic definition. Moderate reformers like H. C. Merwin and Mary Kingsbury Simkhovitch argued that the urban machine demonstrated how friendship in politics could ennoble the poor in both body and spirit, how commitment could create a stable community of seemingly irreconcilable people, how loyalty could foster public spirit. The worst abuses of party, combined with the strongest arguments by the party's critics, perhaps irrevocably destroyed any defense that could be made on behalf of party based on affective ties. Yet, strikingly, some defense of this concept of party did contribute to the debate, and, though its contributors are largely disregarded, their arguments resound especially among contemporary critics of declining American political participation and weakened associations.[26]

Little is known about essayist, political commentator, historian, and literary critic H. C. Merwin (1853–1929). His essays appeared frequently in the influential *Atlantic Monthly* in the late 1800s and early 1900s, often arguing that the proposed reforms of the day threatened to undermine the valuable political assets of cooperation and loyalty prevalently found among recent immigrant groups.[27] He marvelled at the "deep reservoir of loyalty" among the Irish especially, although he was not prone to over-romanticizing Celtic virtues, noting that "a Celt is notoriously a passionate, impulsive, kindly, unreflecting, brave, nimble-witted man; but he lacks the solidity, the balance, the judgment, the moral staying power of the Anglo-Saxons."[28] This loyalty—directed especially at the Democratic Party in the northeastern urban centers—was for the most part the unquestioning dedication of "good, true men, worthy of better leadership." Nevertheless, he was struck by the consistency of that dedication: "It is a significant fact that the Republican party, with all its wealth and unscrupulousness which characterizes political parties in general, has never been able to break the solid column of the Irish Democrats."[29]

Sympathetic to reform—clearly he agreed with many Progressives about the "unscrupulousness which characterizes parties in general"—Merwin nevertheless realized that reform undertaken without giving countenance to the reservoir of loyalty within immigrant communities would prove destructive. As he described the foundation of that sentiment:

To understand the cohesive strength of Tammany one must understand how Tammany lies in the mind of an ordinary "average" member of the organization. In the first place he glories in its history. He is obliged to admit, of course, that Tweed and his gang were the leaders of Tammany in their day; but so is a Catholic forced to admit that some of the popes were bad men, and in neither case is the former existence of corrupt leaders a sufficient reason for giving up the organization. . . . Meanwhile, Tammany is his party, his church, his club, his totem. To be loyal to something is a necessity of all uncorrupted natures, and especially of the Celtic nature. . . . Tammany, therefore, stands not only for politics, but for society and amusement and fellowship.[30]

Rather than bemoaning this irrational loyalty, he observed that so deep a commitment might suggest a dimension to American political life that would be worth preserving. Those reformers who distrusted the masses, he argued, were blind to their excellent qualities: "[the laboring class] is the only class in the community the individuals in which are willing to sacrifice themselves for the good of the whole."[31] Other reformers, who viewed the city as a business that needed a more efficient managing class, such as Herbert Croly, neglected the role of the citizen in the polity: in this view, "there is no moral obligation upon any citizen to make [the city] better."[32] "The trouble with the reformers," Merwin continues, "is not that [they have] a wrong conception of government, but that [they have] a wrong conception of human nature."[33] Merwin claims that the reforms seek to go against the grain of people's actual inclinations, rather than availing themselves of what he regards as the best aspects of human nature. Merwin concludes that reform should take place, but with a proper end in mind and with an eye to the actuality of the human condition.

> Perhaps we can base [reform] upon certain old qualities in human nature which have accomplished great things in the past; perhaps we can base them upon the feeling of loyalty, upon sympathy, upon that passion for a totem which has moved whole nations, inspired wars, and operated as an immense dynamic force in the history of the world.[34]

This commitment, evinced by the Irish toward their urban machine—a fundamentally corrupt system of government—suggested to Merwin not the need to break that loyalty, but to direct it to better ends. Taking a page from Machiavelli's idea for controlling "Fortune," Merwin compares "this immense force in human nature" to "a mighty river which could be made to turn the wheels of a thousand mills, but which in fact is allowed to find its way, unemployed and unrestrained, to the sea."[35]

The sentiment that a great reservoir of commitment and loyalty was simply being ignored, if not altogether emptied, by the efforts of zealous reformers is echoed in a significant and largely forgotten essay from this period entitled "Friendship and Politics" (1902) by New York City social reformer Mary Kingsbury Simkhovitch (1867–1951). If relatively little is known about Merwin, by contrast Simkhovitch was in her day nearly as renowned in New York City as was Jane Addams in Chicago. An unusually well-educated woman of her time, she studied at Radcliffe College, the University of Berlin, and Columbia University. In 1902, Simkhovitch founded Greenwich House, which became one of the leading settlement houses of its day, forming a vibrant social and cultural center in Greenwich Park. Simkhovitch's efforts on behalf of the industrial poor drew the attention and praise of John Dewey and Eleanor Roosevelt, and among its residents for a time was Frances Perkins, future secretary of labor. Among Simkhovitch's most visible political accomplishments was prevailing upon Secretary of the Interior Harold Ickes to include in the 1933 National Industrial Recovery Act a provision that included support for federal housing in public works projects, as well as assisting in the writing of the Wagner-Steagall Housing Act of 1937.[36]

Simkhovitch, like Merwin, leaves little doubt that reform of existing institutions should occur; she is not prone to the softhearted affection for the glories of the urban machine. However, she severely criticizes the predominant character of reformers, who possess little understanding of the ethnic communities that they seek to reform and have little sympathy for the mutual affection that informs the relationships between these citizens and their leaders. Most reformers, she writes, are like a "foreigner" to immigrants, one entirely "unfamiliar with all those elements that make up the great traditions of party loyalty"—especially friendship. The reformer seeks to impose changes from above without consideration of their effects on existing relationships. As Simkhovitch writes, the reformer

> is working on the people, not with them. He wants them to be different from themselves and more like him. In all this the position of unconscious superiority is alienating in its effect. . . . [Since he] lives in a world of ideas, the people regard his talk, in the picturesque phrase of the Tammany official, as "a whirlwind of words."[37]

Simkhovitch explicitly places her critique within the context of the ancient tradition, one notably sympathetic with the claims of friendship in civic life. "For as we must, with Aristotle, think of politics as the whole conduct of life in the community, we must admit that he is a great political reformer who raises the whole plane of civic life."[38] Like Aristotle, she is critical of contemporary forms of friendship that rise out of kinship and ethnic ties; these undermine a true form of civic friendship as they are subject to corruption by party machines. However, unlike contemporary reformers, Simkhovitch understands the source of this loyalty: the immigrant community is largely poor, undereducated, and dependent on the party machinery to provide jobs and shelter. Like Merwin, she is deeply impressed by the loyalty exhibited by "the city worker"; like Aristotle, she searches for means to transform this powerful relationship into a more civic, outward-looking sentiment rather than seeking its dissolution.

Following Aristotle's attempt to place a true basis of friendship not on kinship, but rather on a more elevated conception of a shared good, Simkhovitch points to two organizations that provide a provide the possibilities of mutual understanding on which a civic form of friendship can be based: the church and public schools. Echoing Aristotle's discussion of the role of a guiding principle in relations between friends, of the church she writes that "even in its narrowest expressions, [it] has something of the universal in it, and some suggestion of the eternal verities of truth and beauty and honor. It means the perpetual presence of moral standards; it is the institutional embodiment of the great ethical imperatives."[39] If the church provides moral guidance and standards to which people might aspire, schools offer the means of achieving a more elevated comprehension of a common good—the "well-being of its component parts," as she writes—and directs a people toward more "civic responsibility." These institutions, unlike reforms that attack the heart of political parties, do not seek to separate people from one another or attenuate the relationships formed out of the needs of immigrants and the kinship of ethnic groups, but rather seek to refine those relations and point them outward toward a more encompassing vision of public good.[40]

Separated by immense distance in space and time, faced with incomparably different political and social settings, thinkers as disparate as Aristotle, Merwin, and Simkhovitch nevertheless share in common the desire to re-form, not diminish, civic friendship. Critical of friendship based on kinship relations that might undermine stable political life, and equally wary of the cosmopolitanism of either "guest-friendships" or Enlightenment dreams of universal fraternity, these thinkers instead tried to transform existing structures of friendship and embed them within a civic context. Significantly, perhaps revealingly, they did not ultimately succeed. The pull of "extended spheres," Macedonian or American, proved and continues to prove daunting to arguments in support of civic friendship. However, faced now, as then, with the twin temptations of bloody ethnic ties or bloodless cosmopolitan relations—what Benjamin R. Barber has characterized as "Jihad vs. McWorld"—it is perhaps worth remembering these distant but similar arguments offered in defense of civic friendship, both ancient and American.[41] It is a project best started as a conversation between citizens who might become friends, rather than one defended by grandiose theoretical designs; one that, to conclude with the prudent words of Wilson Carey McWilliams, "is a difficult, even daunting task requiring sacrifice and patience more than dazzling exploits."[42]

NOTES

1. Harvey Mansfield reminds us of the "untimeliness" of the Greeks in a review of *Athenian Democracy* by Arlene Saxonhouse in *American Political Science Review* 92, no. 2 (1998): 449–450.

2. As expressed in a recent book by Christopher Rocco, "by bringing the theoretical and political power of the classical past 'on stage,' so to speak, [one can] hope to challenge our most deeply held assumptions about the superiority of the present associated with reason, enlightenment, progress, democracy, and so to reveal the exclusions and acts of violence these values often conceal." See Christopher Rocco, *Tragedy and Enlightenment: Athenian Political Thought and the Dilemmas of Modernity* (Berkeley and Los Angeles: University of California Press, 1997), 18.

3. On the Federalists' disapproval of the Greek model, no more famous passage can be pointed to than that in *The Federalist Papers* 55: "In all very numerous assemblies, of whatever character composed, passion never fails to wrest the scepter from reason. Had every Athenian citizen been a Socrates, every Athenian assembly would still have been a mob." See *The Federalist*, ed. Edward Mead Earle. (New York: The Modern Library), 361. Throughout *Leaves of Grass*, Whitman praises America as an exceptional nation, owing no allegiance to the past. See, for example, his untitled poem: "No Homer, Shakespeare, Voltaire / No palaces, King's palaces nor courts / Nor armies on the land, nor navies on the sea, / But countless living equal men / Average free." John Dewey's disagreement with ancient thought is evident throughout his work, especially for the attempt to ascertain "truth" as distinct from "experience." See Dewey, *The Quest for Certainty* (New York: Minton, Balch & Co., 1929), chap. 1.

4. Wilson Carey McWilliams, *The Idea of Fraternity in America* (Berkeley and Los Angeles: University of California Press, 1973), 98.

5. McWilliams, *The Idea of Fraternity in America*, 99–100.

6. See, for example, McWilliams, "Democracy and the Citizen," in *How Democratic Is the Constitution*, ed. Robert A. Goldwin and William A. Schambra (Washington, D.C.: American Enterprise Institute, 1980), in which he compares Aristotelian and American ideas of democracy. For a marvelous exploration of the ancient tragic spirit in contemporary American thought, see J. Peter Euben's analysis of Thomas Pynchon's *The Crying of Lot 49*, in *The Tragedy of Political Theory: The Road Not Taken*. (Princeton, N.J.: Princeton University Press, 1990), chap. 9.

7. Sophocles, *Antigone*, trans. E. F. Watling (New York: Penguin, 1978), 131.

8. Horst Hutter, *Politics as Friendship* (Ontario: Wilfred Laurier University Press, 1978).

9. Homer, *The Iliad*, trans. Richmond Lattimore (Chicago: University of Chicago Press, 1951), 6.215–234.

10. Gabriel Herman, *Ritualised Friendship and the Greek City* (Cambridge: Cambridge University Press, 1987), 6.

11. Ibid., 132, and generally, 130–142.

12. The attempt to avoid extirpation of older claims of blood and nature is portrayed vividly in the interchange between Athene and the Eumenides at the conclusion of *Eumenides*. See *Aeschylus I: Oresteia*, trans. Richmond Lattimore (Chicago: University of Chicago Press, 1953), 794–1047.

13. Stated baldly, Thomas Hobbes's description of the "State of Nature" assumes that the natural condition of humanity is antagonism, and that political society is only entered upon out of fear of the consequences of perpetual conflict. Political life is derived from self-interest, and remains legitimate, only as long as humans can be conceived as fundamentally self–interested and permanently divided. Thomas Hobbes, *Leviathan*, ed. Richard Tuck (Cambridge: Cambridge University Press, 1991), chap. 13.

14. Aristotle, *Nicomachean Ethics*, trans. H. Rockham (Cambridge, Mass.: Harvard University Press, 1934), 1155a. Hereafter, references to the *Nicomachean Ethics* are cited by the abbreviation *NE*.

15. Aristotle, *Eudemian Ethics*, trans. J. Solomon. In *The Complete Works of Aristotle*, vol. 2, ed. Jonathan Barnes (Princeton, N.J.: Princeton University Press, 1984. Hereafter, references to the *Eudemian Ethics* are cited by the abbreviation *EE*.

16. Aristotle, *Politics*, trans. Carnes Lord (Chicago: University of Chicago Press, 1984). For a detailed analysis of Aristotle's view of democracy, see Delba Winthrop, "Aristotle on Participatory Democracy," *Polity* 11 (1978): 151–71.

17. Earle, *Federalist* 61.

18. This sentiment is expressed by Alexander Hamilton in the *The Federalist Papers* 16, in which he writes that "the government of the Union, like that of each State, must be able to address itself immediately to the hopes and fears of individuals." Earle, *Federalist* 99.

19. Cited in Matthew Spalding and Patrick J. Garrity, *A Sacred Union of Citizens: George Washington's Farewell Address and the American Character* (Lanham, Md.: Rowman & Littlefield, 1996), 182. See also their discussion of Washington's experience and views of party and partisanship, 41–42, 71–76. On the Anti-Federalist support for parties, see Wilson Carey McWilliams, "The Antifederalists, Representation, and Party," *Northwestern University Law Review* 85 (1990): 12–38.

20. Herbert Croly, *Progressive Democracy* (New York: Macmillan Co., 1914), 341 (italics added). For a fuller exposition of Croly's views on party, see Austin Ranney, *The Doctrine of Responsible Party Government* (Urbana: University of Illinois Press, 1954), chap. 8.

21. McWilliams, *Fraternity in America*, 502.

22. Even some of these "unintended consequences" were foreseen by perceptive critics at the time, most notably Henry Jones Ford in "The Direct Primary," *North American Review* 190 (1909): 1–121. A more literary rendition of these insidious effects is portrayed in Edwin O'Connor, *The Last Hurrah* (Boston: Little, Brown, 1956).

23. On the Federalists' concern to avoid agitating the populace by minimizing "public passions," see Earle, *Federalist* 49, 329.

24. The mistrust of political parties as fostering irrational commitments and thwarting genuine individuality is a longstanding one. See Gerald M. Pomper,

"The Contribution of Political Parties to American Democracy," in *Party Renewal in America*, ed. Gerald M. Pomper (New York: Praeger, 1981), and McWilliams, "Parties as Civic Associations," in *Party Renewal in America* for a historical perspective. Strikingly, even some "communitarian" theorists are mistrustful of political parties on similar grounds, hence revealing a continuity with Progressivism. See Benjamin R. Barber, "The Undemocratic Party System: Citizenship in an Elite/Mass Society," in *Political Parties in the Eighties*, ed. Robert A. Goldwin (Washington, D.C.: American Enterprise Institute Press, 1980).

25. Joseph Romance reminds us that this conception of parties provided the affective basis for, if not unity, then "tolerable cooperation." Noting that "democracy requires people to talk to each other, to accept the possibility of defeat, and to respect their fellow citizens," he supports a party system that "created something akin to political friendship among citizens." See "Gridlock and Reform," in *A Republic of Parties?* (Lanham, Md.: Rowman & Littlefield, 1998), 55, 71, 64.

26. See, for example, Robert Putnam, "Bowling Alone," *Journal of Democracy* 6 (1995): 65–78, and his recent book *Bowling Alone: The Collapse and Revival of American Community* (New York: Simon & Schuster, 2000).

27. Books published by Merwin include biographies of Thomas Jefferson, Aaron Burr, and Bret Harte. He was also apparently fond of animals, evinced by his books on dogs and horses. In addition to those political essays discussed below, a good example of his political thought can be found in his essay "The People in Government," *Atlantic Monthly* 63 (February 1889): 443–41, which characteristically both defends, and offends, the rudimentary political understanding of the American populace.

28. H. C. Merwin, "The Irish in American Life," *Atlantic Monthly* 77 (March 1896): 287–89.

29. Ibid., 297.

30. H. C. Merwin, "Tammany Hall," *Atlantic Monthly* 73 (February 1894): 243–44.

31. H. C. Merwin, "Tammany Points the Way," *Atlantic Monthly* 74 (November 1894): 683.

32. Ibid., 684.

33. Ibid., 687.

34. Ibid., 685. Merwin here notes that the passions of loyalty and kinship can have negative as well as positive manifestations. The particularistic loyalties of patriotism and civic friendship can indeed be fanned to incite hatred and warfare. Yet, as my colleague Maurizio Viroli points out, the repudiation by the political Left of particularistic commitments like patriotism and civic friendship has left that language almost exclusively in the hands of potential demagogues. He urges us "to avoid useless forays into rationality, remain well attached to the world of passions, and try to shape them through rhetoric and political action. . . . [O]ne must still conduct the intellectual and political fight at the level of passions and interests aiming to transform sordid and ignoble passions, again through rhetoric and political action, into higher and more generous ones that give strength and translate into solidarity with victims of oppression." See *For Love of Country: An Essay on Patriotism and Nationalism* (Oxford: Clarendon Press,

1995), 17. Interestingly, Richard Rorty has recently made a similar argument in *Achieving Our Country* (Cambridge, Mass.: Harvard University Press, 1998), especially chapters 1–2.

35. Merwin, "Tammany Points the Way," 685–86.

36. A wealth of biographical information about Simkhovitch can be found in her autobiography, *Neighborhood: My Story of Greenwich House* (New York: W. W. Norton, 1938), as well as Allen F. Davis, *Spearheads for Reform: The Social Settlements and the Progressive Movement, 1890–1914* (New Brunswick, N.J.: Rutgers University Press, 1984).

37. Mary Kingsbury Simkhovitch, "Friendship and Politics," *Political Science Quarterly* 17, no. 2 (July 1902): 198–99.

38. Ibid., 200.

39. Ibid., 192. Simkhovitch's description of the role of religion in a democratic setting shares the sentiment of Tocqueville's observations that "every religion places the object of man's desires outside and beyond worldly goods and naturally lifts the soul into regions far above the realm of the senses. Every religion also imposes on each man some obligations toward mankind, to be performed in common with the rest of mankind, and so draws him away, from time to time, from thinking about himself." See Alexis de Tocqueville, *Democracy in America*, trans. George Lawrence (New York: Doubleday Anchor), 444–45.

40. Simkhovitch offers a more lengthy version of this argument in her book *The City Worker's World* (New York: Macmillan Co., 1917), chap. 9.

41. Benjamin R. Barber, *Jihad vs. McWorld* (New York: Times Books, 1995).

42. McWilliams, "Democracy and the Citizen," 100.

3

Politics and Friendship in the Adams-Jefferson Correspondence

Jean M. Yarbrough

John Adams and Thomas Jefferson laid the foundation for their extraordinary friendship in 1775 in Philadelphia where the two met for the first time to lead the fight for American independence. A decade later, they were briefly united again in Paris, when Jefferson accepted a congressional commission to join Adams and Benjamin Franklin in negotiating treaties of friendship and commerce for the newly independent United States. After the Constitution was ratified and a new government established, both men returned to Philadelphia to serve in the first Washington administration. Three years later, they came together for the last time when Jefferson was elected vice president in what was to be Adams's unhappy, one-term presidency.

With the exception of these brief periods, however, they spent most of their fifty remaining years apart from each other, mostly in Paris and London, at Monticello and Quincy, and cultivated their friendship through letters. From a late twentieth-century perspective, it might seem these separations would have prevented them from developing the intimacy so necessary for friendship, but the more restrained eighteenth-century sensibilities of Adams and Jefferson could view letters as superior to conversation because the discipline of setting words to paper enabled the writer to probe subjects more deeply.[1] Accordingly, Adams could write to Jefferson from London, "Intimate correspondence with you . . . is one of the most agreeable events of my life."[2] Nor did it prevent them from cultivating those affectionate bonds that Aristotle regards as the distinctive mark of friendship. While such expressions came more easily to Adams, even the more reserved Jefferson was moved to confess, "I am sure that I really know many, many, things, and none more surely than that I love you with all my heart."[3] The result is that, even in an era famous for its epistolary friendships, the Adams-Jefferson correspondence, especially the second phase beginning in 1812, remains the most celebrated exchange in all of American letters.

Part of its appeal is clearly symbolic: the reconciliation of these great political rivals encouraged Union supporters at an especially critical time to hope that Massachusetts Federalists and Virginia Republicans might find a way to resolve their political differences. But there is also the poignant personal drama of two old warriors laying down their arms, and cultivating the kind of philosophic friendship so prized by the ancient moralists they had both studied. As I have argued elsewhere,[4] and will only briefly recapitulate here, much of the charm of the late correspondence lies precisely in this playful treatment of the most serious things, as when Adams writes: "I cannot be serious! I am about to write You, the most frivolous letter, you ever read." And then proceeds to ask Jefferson: "Would you go back to your Cradle and live over again Your 70 years?" Yet as Adams well understands, this "silly" question raises the most profound metaphysical, theological, and moral considerations, to say nothing of "tragedy, comedy, and farce."[5] But, as Adams, quoting Horace, asks in another context: "Ridendo dicere Verum, Quid vetat." ("What forbids a man to speak the truth by joking?")[6]

In still another delightful exchange from the late correspondence, prompted this time by Jefferson's casual remark that of all the passions, only grief seems to serve no good purpose, Adams explores first the uses and then the abuses of grief.[7] And in contrast to the more softhearted Jefferson, Adams insists that grief can contribute to moral growth and the improvement of individual character. Elsewhere, the aging statesmen find themselves in remarkable agreement about the essence of Christianity and in their assessment of different moral codes. Neither has much patience with the paradoxes of Platonic republicanism[8] or Platonic Christianity, with its mystical doctrine of the Three in One. And both reserve special scorn for the Calvinist doctrines of election and predestination as well as the idea of human depravity. But here, too, subtle differences emerge: Jefferson is far more critical of the morality of the Old Testament, while Adams is more respectful of the different ways in which the Gentiles, Jews, and Christians seek to worship God and is more inclined to seek out commonalities among the world's great religions.

Adams's wonderful description of man as the "stareing Animal"[9] suggests why human beings will continue to probe the mysteries and paradoxes of the universe and search with "eager Impatience . . . into Eternity and Infinity, the First Cause and last End of all Things,"[10] even though they can never fully comprehend them. But once again, the two are not quite in agreement. Where Jefferson, in the absence of certain knowledge about the nature of the universe, embraces materialism as an article of faith, Adams remains unsure. However men define the terms, they can never satisfactorily explain how matter by itself can think or spirit alone can act. The only sensible course is resignation, albeit worldly resignation: "Vain man! Mind your own Business! Do no wrong! Do all the good You can! Eat your Canvas back ducks, drink Your burgundy, sleep Your S[i]esta, when necessary, and Trust in God!"[11] What shines through so clearly in these exchanges is the determination of these two old friends to preserve the affectionate bonds upon which both have come to rely in the evening of their lives, and not to permit them to be disturbed by honest disagreements.

POLITICS IN THE ADAMS-JEFFERSON CORRESPONDENCE

The late correspondence is justly praised for its philosophic detachment, and no one who reads the letters can fail to be struck by the dismissive tone both adopt regarding all things political. From his first reply to Adams's "homespun," Jefferson is at pains to impress upon his old friend that he has "taken final leave" of politics.[12] When, early on, Adams tries to revisit the political issues that divided them, Jefferson gently insists that "the renewal of these old discussions would be useless and irksome."[13] And even Adams, by far the more contentious of the two, occasionally confesses that he has grown "weary" of politics.[14]

Yet, despite these disclaimers, it was impossible for these two intensely political creatures to stay away from politics for long. Their friendship, after all, had been founded on the "perfect harmony" of their political principles during the struggle for independence, and if it was to be renewed, the two would have to come to some common understanding on the issues that began to divide them during the partisan struggles of the 1790s and ended in their total estrangement in 1800. The candid airing of their political differences is important, then, not only because it allows them to renew the affectionate bonds upon which they would later build their philosophic friendship, but because it sheds light on some of the most fundamental issues in American politics. It is this relatively neglected political dimension of the correspondence, along with the implications for friendship, that I want to consider here.

Ironically, one reason the Adams-Jefferson correspondence is so illuminating on political matters is that the two statesmen so often disagreed, if not on first principles, then on the science of government. As a result, they were compelled to defend their positions in ways that they did not have to do, or do very often, with more like-minded allies. One need only compare Jefferson's polite silence with his full-throated opposition to

Adams's analysis of aristocracy when Madison asserts that in a republic, it is the few who need protection from the many. But Madison, for all his fear of popular majorities, never suggested a will independent of society, while Adams, who was actually less sympathetic to the claims of the wealthy few, could find no way to control the rich except by institutional arrangements that strained the limits of democratic republicanism. A second reason why the political opinions expressed in the correspondence remain instructive is that Jefferson and Adams did not write for themselves alone. Both men were keenly aware of the immense interest in their correspondence and were desirous of leaving behind a statement of their views, which posterity might judge. Adams, fearing that he would come out the loser, was particularly eager to set the record straight, and Jefferson, magnanimous in what he supposed would be his triumph, encouraged him to do so.[15]

As early as 1787, the lines of disagreement begin to emerge. Exchanging opinions about the proposed Constitution, Jefferson confessed himself "staggered" by the enormity of the changes, and insisted that three or four amendments to the articles were all that was necessary to perfect the fabric of government. More particularly, he objected to the indefinite reeligibility of the executive, judging the office "a bad edition of a Polish king."[16] By contrast, Adams, who analyzed power in terms of the classical distinction between the one, the few, and the many, thought that the Constitution gave too much power to the "aristocracy" in the Senate and left the president too weak to restrain this most dangerous branch. Commenting upon their differences, Adams observed, "You are afraid of the one—I, of the few. . . . You are apprehensive of Monarchy; I, of Aristocracy."[17] Although Jefferson would later accuse Adams of taking the side of the few against the many, the correspondence suggests that Adams's project was actually to restrain the ambition and pride of the few, albeit by strengthening the powers of the one. To this end, Adams considered the separation of executive power from the legislature as the "greatest and most necessary of all Amendments."[18] His is consistently a constitutionalism of powers rather than of rights.

As Adams later reminded the Virginian, it was Jefferson who first encouraged him to take up the question of aristocracy.[19] But when Adams's *Discourses on Davila* finally appeared in 1791, against the backdrop of the French Revolution, Jefferson wrote to Thomas Paine endorsing his "Rights of Man" as an antidote "for the political heresies which have sprung up among us." Embarrassed by the printer's publication of this note without permission, Jefferson hastened to assure Adams that his comments were never intended to be made public and that it was certainly possible for the two of them to differ in their political opinions and remain friends. "That you and I differ in our ideas of the best form of government is well known to us both: but we have differed as friends should do, respecting the purity of each other's motives, and confining our difference of opinion to private conversation."[20] In a remark that would echo through their late correspondence, Adams protested that their differences were not well known to them both. To the best of Adams's recollection, they had "never had a serious conversation together that I can recollect concerning the nature of Government." Their exchanges on politics had so far been "jocular and superficial"; it was now "high time" for them to "come to an explanation with each other."[21] Turning back to his writings, Adams insisted that he never had any intention of trying to introduce a hereditary monarchy or a hereditary aristocracy into the government of the United States or into any individual state. Any such conclusions could only be the result of misunderstanding or, given the atmosphere of ambition and intrigue swirling about the country, deliberate misreading.

Years later, after they had reconciled, Adams would explain that what he was trying to do in the *Defence of the Constitutions of Government of the United States of America 1787–1788* and the *Discourses on Davila* was revive an older form of political science that focused not on abstract principles of political right, but on the art of government and constitutional forms.[22] From the time of Charles II to the beginning of the French Revolution, writers on politics had "not only neglected, but discountenanced and discouraged" the science of politics. "The English Commonwealth, the Fate of Charles 1st, and the military despotism of Cromwell had sickened Mankind with disquisitions on Government to such a degree, that there was scarcely a Man in Europe who had looked into the subject." By reviving the study of constitutional government, and more particularly, the separation of powers and checks and balances, Adams's volumes were not meant to say anything new, but only "what was new to Lock [sic], to Harrington, to Milton, to Hume to Montesquieu to Reauseau [sic], to Turgot, Condorcet, to Rochefaucault, to Price to Franklin and to yourself; and at that time to almost all Europe and America."[23] After independence, Adams turned away from philosophical inquiries into the origin and ends of government, and directed his studies to the science of politics and the distribution of power. Jefferson, by contrast, continued to think in terms of first principles, and indulged his inclination for pushing ideas to their logical conclusions.[24]

The letter endorsing the "Rights of Man" was not the only communication that caused Jefferson embarrassment.[25] In 1801, the newly elected Republican president penned a reckless letter to the English radical, Dr. Joseph Priestley, condemning as "Bigotry in politics and religion," the idea that we should look back to our ancestors for improvement, rather than trust to future progress in politics and morals. Years later, this letter was reprinted in the memoirs of one Theophilus Lindsey, a copy of which reached Adams, who wrote to Jefferson "demanding" an explanation. Once again, Jefferson replied that the letter was a "confidential communication" to a friend, and never intended for the public. He then denied that the accusations were aimed at Adams personally. In Jefferson's retelling, Adams was cited only because he happened to express, "more pithily" than most, Federalist doubts about progress and the improvability of the human mind. Whereas the party of Jefferson insisted that "no definite" limits could be assigned to progress, the "enemies of reform . . . denied improvement, and advocated steady adherence to the principles, practices, and institutions of our fathers, which they represented as the consummation and the *akme* of excellence, beyond which the human mind could never advance." Whether this was an accurate characterization of their differences, Jefferson, flush from Republican victories, left for posterity to judge.[26]

Uncharacteristically, Adams declared he was not "yet ready to return to Politicks," except to reiterate his long-standing belief that, however much the Republicans ridiculed them, checks and balances are the only security for the progress of the mind. And this applied as much to "liberal Christians in London and in Boston," as it did to those defenders of absolute monarchy, Charles I, and Archbishop Laud. "Every species of these Christians would persecute Deists, as soon as either Sect would persecute another, if it had unchecked and unballanced Power . . . Know thyself, human Nature!"[27]

Jefferson's response to all this is curious. For at the same time that he declares himself an Epicurean, who wishes to avoid old political quarrels in the pursuit of tranquillity of mind,[28] he proceeds to launch into a general discussion of the origin of political parties. Moving beyond his initial characterization of the two parties in terms of their belief in progress and the improvability of the human mind, Jefferson now observes that what divides men and what has always divided them into political parties is a disagreement over who should rule, the people or the *aristoi* (the few who are best). Wherever men are free to think and speak, they have sided with the few or the many, and have supported those institutions that strengthen their cause. While these divisions arise in part from honest differences of opinion, Jefferson also insists that they are rooted in nature. What he means by nature, however, are differences in "temper and constitution of mind," which naturally incline men to either the Whigs or the Tories.[29]

In suggesting that political parties are rooted at least in part in personality differences, Jefferson may have been trying to smooth over their disagreements, but how much sense does this argument make, especially with regard to Adams? By his own account, he and Jefferson had stood together for independence, and again, for the Constitution. It was only after the government was established that the two began to disagree, with Jefferson wanting to strengthen the most popular branch, and Adams, the more permanent.[30] Did Adams undergo a personality change? By what process had he been transformed from what Jefferson elsewhere describes as a "healthy, strong, and bold" Whig into a "sickly, weakly, timid" Tory?[31] More importantly, by attempting to explain political opinions partly in terms of temperament, Jefferson seems to undermine the human capacity for deliberation and free choice so fundamental to his republican project. The sage of Monticello would have to think more deeply about the question of nature.

Adams's letter of June 28 crossed Jefferson's in the mail and so did not immediately force a response. In this exchange, Adams returns to "Politicks," and to Jefferson's letter to Priestley accusing him of "bigotry in politics and religion." Adams has finally located his "Address to the Young Men of Philadelphia," and is emboldened to think that if, in the future, people reading their letters will take the trouble to read his speech through, in its entirety, he will be vindicated. For in advising the youth of America to look back to the general principles of their ancestors, Adams makes it clear that he does not mean to bind them to a distant past. The ancestors he has in mind are Thomas Jefferson and John Adams, the two men who did the most to secure American liberty and independence. And the general principles he exhorts them to follow are those of Christianity, shorn of sectarian dogma, and of English and American liberty, in which both parties were united. However much progress men may make in the arts and sciences, and Adams leaves no doubt that progress on these fronts is still possible, even if not unlimited, he insists that the general principles of Christianity as a moral system and Anglo-American liberty are "eternal and immutable," and can never be contradicted or surpassed. No fair-minded reader of the letter can fail to see that these are not the words of a political and religious bigot, but on the contrary, the fundamental ground of the American republic, as Jefferson himself, in less polemical moments, freely acknowledged.[32]

Adams's response paves the way for the most important exchange of political opinions in the correspondence: the place of aristocracy in republican government. Jefferson had introduced the topic by suggesting that party differences can in part be explained by differences in temperament and personality. Citing Jefferson's opinion that "Whig and Torey [sic] belong to Natural History," Adams shifts the emphasis away from personality types toward a discussion of human nature and challenges Jefferson to give an account of himself. "You and I ought not to die, before We have explained ourselves to each other."[33] For Adams, the fundamental difference between the two parties seems to turn on what he considers "the gross[est] Ideology of them all": equality. While nowhere denying the fundamental truth that all men are created equal, in the sense that no man can legitimately rule over another without his consent or deprive him of his inalienable rights, Adams nevertheless insists that "Inequalities of Mind and Body are so established by God Almighty in his constitution of Human Nature that no Art or policy can ever plain [sic] them down to a Level." This was the great error of the French Revolution and, to a lesser extent, of those French sympathizers in America, the members of the Republican Party. Both had viewed the inequalities created by wealth, birth, and beauty as artificial, when, in fact, they are just as natural as talent and virtue. Indeed, Adams asks, "What chance have Talents and Virtues in competition, with Wealth and Birth? And Beauty," when any three of the last can easily dominate one or two of the first? Inequality is "the great Fact in the natural History of Man," and governments must find some way to control its pernicious effects.[34]

Finally, on 28 October 1813, Jefferson responded. Whereas only months earlier, he had argued that political parties have their origins in the question of whether the few or the many should rule, the fearful Tories siding with the few, and the confident Whigs with the many, he now agrees with Adams that there is such a thing as a natural aristocracy and that republics, too, have need of their services. Indeed, so far is Jefferson from his simple distinction between the few and the many that he now regards as the best form of government that which "provides most effectually for a pure selection of these natural aristoi" into political office. The question that divides them now is much narrower: how to select those men of virtue and talent for government offices, while preventing the ascendancy of that "mischievous" element, the artificial aristocracy of wealth and birth? In place of the checks and balances so dear to Adams's heart, Jefferson relies on frequent elections and the good sense of the people to sift out the natural aristocracy from the pseudo-aristoi. While conceding that, "in some instances, wealth may corrupt, and birth blind them," Jefferson remains confident in the capacity of the American people, uncorrupted by the vices of the "Old World," to select men of virtue and talent for political office.

Jefferson may have thought he had explained himself satisfactorily to Adams, but the sage of Quincy was not finished. After "studying" Jefferson's reply, and noting their agreement on the existence of a natural aristocracy (a major concession from Jefferson), he pushed the question further. Was it really so easy to separate the natural from the pseudo-aristocracy; to distinguish "talents" from birth, wealth, or beauty? Were these not also talents "imperiously" bestowed by nature? Take, for example, the Bowdoin family of Massachusetts, "immortalized by a flourishing University founded by the Family," and distinguished by literary, diplomatic, religious, noble, royal, and imperial honors dating to the Crusades. Was this a natural or an artificial aristocracy? Jefferson's distinction was not "well founded." Instead, Adams argued that all these qualities were natural; aristocracies only became artificial when natural aristocrats succeeded in corrupting elections and making their positions hereditary. Indeed, the genesis of all artificial aristocracies and monarchies lay in "the natural Aristocracy of 'Virtues and Talents.'" Thus, even if only the naturally best are chosen, they must be restrained by institutional checks and balances to make sure that they serve the public good rather than their own private or partisan interests. It was not enough to trust frequent elections and the vigilance of the people. For even assuming that there were men distinguished only by their virtues and talents, it was not so clear that the people would always identify them. To drive home this point, Adams reminded his friend of the near election of Aaron Burr in 1800.[35]

By not responding to these questions, Jefferson effectively put an end to one of the most interesting political exchanges of the day. For Adams had finally succeeded in getting Jefferson to reflect more deeply about the all important question of political philosophy: the nature of the best regime. And although Jefferson confessed that they were both too old to change their opinions, the correspondence suggests otherwise. Not only had Adams persuaded Jefferson to call a halt to his partisan polemics (at least with him) concerning the few and the many, but he got him to admit that the best regime is the one that provides for the selection of a certain kind of aristocracy. Left unanswered, however, was Adams's trenchant question: How to separate the natural aristocracy from the pseudo-*aristoi*, or how to ensure that the people are not seduced by "the gaudy trappings of wealth."[36] That there could today be a successful television show called *Lifestyles of the Rich and Famous*, and not *Lifestyles of the Wise and Virtuous*, suggests that the problem remains unresolved.

It is notable, however, that all of these exchanges took place within the first two years after their reconciliation in 1812. It is as if they could not go forward until they had first gone backward and, as Adams insisted, explained themselves to each other. This done, they could jointly take leave of politics and turn their attention to those religious, scientific, and philosophic exchanges for which the correspondence is justly famous. To be sure, the two occasionally returned to political issues, most notably, when Jefferson admitted that Adams's prophecies about the French Revolution had "proved truer" than his own, and that, if anything, even Adams had underestimated the destruction. And Adams, in grateful response, called the letter "one of the most consolatory, I ever received."[37]

But, increasingly, when they mentioned political issues at all, they were more likely to focus on current events on which they largely agreed: the revolutions in South America, events in Europe, Jefferson's plans for elementary and higher education, their distrust of banks, Adams's participation in the Massachusetts Constitutional Convention of 1820, and the election of John Quincy Adams.[38]

Among the political issues of the day, one in particular gave them cause for anxiety, for they both saw instantly that it had the power to tear the Union apart. Adams was the first to raise the delicate matter of the Missouri Compromise, prompting Jefferson to unburden himself as he did to few others. Although the issue in the Missouri Compromise was whether or not Congress had the power to regulate slavery in the territories (a position Jefferson himself embraced in his draft of the Northwest Ordinance), he saw the Missouri question as involving the power of Congress to "regulate the conditions of the inhabitants of the states," and not just the territories, with the very real possibility that Congress would assert a power to declare the slaves free everywhere. Returning to the "wolf by the ears" theme,[39] which pits justice against self-preservation, Jefferson asked Adams: "Are our slaves to be presented with freedom and a dagger?"[40] For he feared that the inevitable consequence of Congress's declaring them free would be civil war, either between the North and the South, or between the South and the slaves, since he believed that the two races could never live together on the same soil in peace and freedom. Faced with this grim choice, Adams chose not to respond to Jefferson's rhetorical question, except to acknowledge that slavery "terrified" him, and only God knew how it would all turn out.

FRIENDSHIP

Not only does the Adams-Jefferson correspondence explore some of the most important issues in American politics, but it teaches us something about friendship in a liberal republic. The friendship between the two men was first formed during their common struggle for liberty and independence. Like all political friendships, the two did not see eye to eye on everything, and as long as their differences remained private, they could continue to maintain amicable relations. But once they began to compete for the highest political honors, where one could triumph only at the expense of the other, it was inevitable that their friendship would suffer.

Still, as the correspondence makes clear, the political differences between them, while real, were not so great that the recollection of their earlier affection and esteem could not in time reconcile them. To be sure, Adams could not "take final leave" of politics without first trying to get Jefferson to explain himself. And we, their heirs, are the beneficiaries of Adams's stubborn resolve. For the Adams-Jefferson correspondence illuminates some of the most fundamental issues in American politics: the connection between first principles and constitutional forms, the origin of political parties, progress and human nature, the place of aristocracy in republican government, the best regime, the significance of the French Revolution, the Missouri Compromise, and slavery. But it is also true that, having reached a certain level of understanding about these questions, the two drifted away from politics and began to cultivate the kind of philosophic friendship for which their education and inclinations had long prepared them.

Among the many things that the Adams-Jefferson letters help us to see is that the liberal republic they labored to create does not, as the classical republics did, elevate politics and political friendship over everything else. Their political order leaves space for noble souls to pursue equal, if not more important, private interests. At the same time, however, looked at in its entirety, the correspondence does not, as the ancient Epicureans did, promote philosophy at the expence of politics and political life. Rather, this wonderful exchange affirms the dignity and moral seriousness of both ways of life and, in so doing, testifies to the truth of Adams's observation that "no effort in favour of Virtue" is ever lost.

NOTES

I would like to thank Richard E. Morgan and Michael P. Zuckert for their helpful comments on an earlier draft.

1. For a discussion of letter writing and friendship, see Andrew Burstein, *The Inner Jefferson: Portrait of a Grieving Optimist* (Charlottesville: University Press of Virginia, 1995), especially chap. 4.

2. John Adams to Thomas Jefferson, 1 March 1787, *The Adams-Jefferson Letters*, ed. Lester J. Cappon (New York: Simon & Schuster, 1971), 175–77. All citations are from this edition.

3. Jefferson to Adams, 15 August 1820, 565–69.

4. Jean M. Yarbrough, *American Virtues: Thomas Jefferson on the Character of a Free People* (Lawrence: University Press of Kansas, 1998), chap. 5.

5. Adams to Jefferson, 2 March 1816, 464–66.

6. Adams to Jefferson, 15 November 1813, 397–402.

7. Jefferson to Adams, 8 April 1816, 466–69; Adams to Jefferson, 6 May 1816, 472–74; Adams to Jefferson, 3 September 1816 487–88; Jefferson to Adams, 14 October 1816, 490–93.

8. By Platonic republicanism, Jefferson seems to mean principally the arguments set forth in book five of Plato's *Republic*. In taking seriously Plato's proposals for the equality of the sexes, the community of wives and children, and the philosopher-king, Jefferson shows no appreciation for philosophic irony. Adams, by contrast, suspects that the *Republic* is a "satire." Jefferson to Adams, 5 July 1814, 430–34; Adams to Jefferson, 16 July 1814, 434–39.

9. Adams to Jefferson, 16 July 1814, 434–39.
10. Adams to Jefferson, 2 March 1816, 464–66.
11. Adams to Jefferson, 26 May 1817, 516–18.
12. Jefferson to Adams, 21 January 1812, 290–92.
13. Jefferson to Adams, 27 June 1813, 335–38.
14. Adams to Jefferson, 10 February 1812, 296–98.
15. Jefferson to Adams, 27 June 1813, 335–38.
16. Jefferson to Adams, 13 November 1787, 211–12.
17. Adams to Jefferson, 5 December 1787, 213.
18. Adams to Jefferson, 1 March 1789, 236–37.
19. Adams to Jefferson, 6 February 1787, 169–70.
20. Jefferson to Adams, 17 July 1791, 245–47.
21. Adams to Jefferson, 29 July 1791, 247–50.
22. On this distinction, see Michael P. Zuckert, *The Natural Rights Republic: Studies in the Foundation of the American Political Tradition* (South Bend, Ind.: University Press of Notre Dame, 1966), 4–8.
23. Adams to Jefferson, 15 July 1813, 357–58; Adams to Jefferson, 16 July 1814, 434–39.
24. This he did most famously in his 1789 exchange with Madison over whether or not the earth belongs only to the living. But some years later, he floated the same idea in capsule form past Adams, with predictable results. Responding to Jefferson's assertion that the rights of one generation "will scarcely" be bound by the "paper transactions" of the past, Adams amended the sentence to read "the Rights of one Generation of Men must still depend, in some degree," on constitutions and laws made by previous generations. And, in a reprise of Madison's argument, Adams observed that obedience to the social contract and the laws "becomes a national Habit and they cannot be changed but by Revolutions which are costly things. Men will be too economical of the Blood and Property to have Recourse to them very frequently." Jefferson to Adams, 25 April 1794, 253–54, and Adams to Jefferson, 11 May 1794, 254–55.
25. Later on, Adams too would have cause for embarrassment, when a letter he wrote against Jefferson's reelection in 1804 appeared in print. But Jefferson, in a magnanimous gesture, refused to take it personally or let it poison "a friendship co-eval with our government." Jefferson to Adams, 12 October 1823, 599–601. And see Adams's happy response in Adams to Jefferson, 10 November 1823, 601–2.
26. Adams to Jefferson, 29 May 1813, 325–26; 10 June 1813, 326–27; 14 June 1813, 329–30: Jefferson to Adams, 15 June 1813, 331–33.
27. Adams to Jefferson, 25 June 1813, 333–35; Adams to Jefferson, 30 June 1813, 346–48, where Adams, invoking Machiavelli, observes that all parties employ terror and stir up discord in order to preserve their power and privileges; and, on the tendency of the Democrats to distort and ridicule Adams's arguments for their own political advantage, Adams to Jefferson, 9 July 1813, 350–52.
28. See especially Adams's sardonic response to Jefferson's Epicureanism: "I have no doubt You was [sic] fast asleep in philosophical Tranquillity, when ten thousand People, and perhaps many more, were parading the streets of Phila-

delphia," in opposition to Adams's policies. Adams to Jefferson, 30 June 1813 346–48.

29. Jefferson to Adams, 27 June 1813, 335–38.

30. Cf. Adams, who maintains that the first time the two disagreed "on any material Question" was the French Revolution. Adams to Jefferson, 13 July 1813, 354–56.

31. Jefferson to Marquis de Lafayette, 23 November 1823.

32. See especially, Wilson Carey McWilliams, "The Bible in the American Political Tradition," *Religion and Politics*, ed. Myron J. Aronoff (New Brunswick, N.J.: Transaction Books, 1984), 11–45.

33. Adams to Jefferson, 15 July 1813, 357–58.

34. Adams to Jefferson, 13 July 1813, 354–56; Adams to Jefferson, [14?] August 1813, 365–66; Adams to Jefferson, 2 September 1813, 370–72.

35. Adams to Jefferson, 15 November 1813, 397–402; Adams to Jefferson, 19 December 1813, 406–9.

36. Years later, both would return obliquely to these same themes, with Jefferson criticizing the mixed republic of Rome, and insisting that "no government can continue good but under the control of the people," and Adams, turning his thoughts to the bank question and wondering how to prevent virtue from degenerating into vice. "Will you tell me how to prevent riches from becoming the effects of temperance and industry? Will you tell me how to prevent riches from producing luxury? Will you tell me how to prevent luxury from producing effeminacy intoxication extravagance Vice and folly?" But neither could answer the other's questions.

37. Jefferson to Adams, 11 January 1816, 458–61; Adams to Jefferson, 2 February 1816, 461–63. Nevertheless, Jefferson's concession did not prevent Adams three years later from endorsing the authenticity of the Mecklenburg Declaration of Independence, purportedly written in 1775. Still obviously smarting from the glory Jefferson received as the author of the Declaration of Independence, Adams let out as his opinion that "the Genuine sense of America at that Moment was never so well expressed before nor since." When Jefferson offered convincing arguments that the document was in fact spurious, Adams conceded the point to him, but insisted to others that it was genuine.

38. But in the same year that Jefferson congratulated Adams on the election of his son, he discussed with Madison the advisability of publishing his "Solemn Protest" against President Adams's support for internal improvements.

39. Jefferson to John Holmes, 22 April 1820, where Jefferson, commenting on the general problem of slavery, observes: "[W]e have the wolf by the ears, and we can neither hold him nor safely let him go. Justice is in one scale and self-preservation in the other."

40. Jefferson to Adams, 22 January 1821, 569–70.

4

Politics and Friendship: Martin Van Buren and Andrew Jackson

Marc Landy

Republican government confronts a conundrum. It is, quintessentially, government by discussion and yet, at crucial moments, talk must give way to action.[1] The greatest of our presidents were indeed fine talkers, but if those fine words had not translated into decisive action, the "house divided" would have stood and there would have been plenty to fear beside "fear itself." Recent incumbents of the presidential office have made it all too clear that a fine line divides the "bully pulpit" from just plain bull. And yet, decisiveness is a principle that coexists uneasily with republican rule. Harry Truman's endearing remark "the buck stops here" has chilling anti-republican implications. If one individual is so unambiguously in charge, how can he possibly be held to the collective and collegial strictures that form the core of republicanism? Whatever their differences, both the defenders of the Constitution and their Anti-Federalist opponents agreed upon the need for a government in which power was shared among the branches and from which monarchy was precluded. The party of Thomas Jefferson and James Madison, formed only a few years after the passage of the Constitution, named itself "Democratic-Republican" to trumpet its opposition to the Federalist regime, which it thought had already veered perilously in the direction of the "Monocrats."

Andrew Jackson was nothing if not decisive. As a leader of the Tennessee militia, he quelled a troop mutiny by aiming his musket at the mutineers and swearing to kill the first soldier who turned toward home.[2] His all-too-frequent duels indicated an almost compulsive preference for action over words. As president, he acted decisively to prevent disunion and to destroy "the Monster Bank." His enemies called him "King Andrew" and, while unfair, the charge was not so very wide off the mark. He was by temperament closer to Napoleon and other famous "men on horse-back" than to the sober and judicious founders of the American Republic (Alexander Hamilton aside). He relished the awesome responsibilities of military command and chafed at the Byzantine tergiversations of republican politics. His popularity was the result of military victory, not political accomplishment.

But Jackson's presidential legacy was not one of impulsive action nor authoritarian usurpation. The regime he bequeathed was more strongly and deeply republican than the one he inherited. The great threats to the integrity of the Union posed by South Carolina's Nullification Ordinance and to the democratic character of the regime posed by Biddle's bank were quelled. Among his predecessors, only George Washington was as successful in combining executive authority and republican restraint.[3] The burden of this essay is to explain why Jackson the insubordinate Indian fighter became Jackson the republican chief executive. The answer lies in the discipline imposed upon Jackson by the political party he came to lead.[4] But Jackson did not rise to political prominence as a creature of that party. Accepting that discipline involved a self-conscious decision on his part. The source of that epochal choice lay in the unlikely friendship forged between the crusty general and the chief organizer of that party, the slick political operative, Martin Van Buren.

JACKSON

The prognosis for the Jackson presidency seemed particularly bleak because his presidential ambition had been fueled by the combustible mix of popular adulation and smoldering resentment. He had received the most electoral votes in the 1824 presidential election but had been deprived of victory by a "corrupt bargain" between John Adams and Henry Clay. Because no candidate had obtained an electoral vote majority, the election was decided by the House of Representatives. Clay, the Speaker of the House, had thrown his support to Adams, and was subsequently named secretary of state in the Adams administration. Had a deal been struck? Probably. Was the bargain corrupt? Not by the standards of the Constitution, which allowed the House to choose from among the three leading electoral vote getters. As the Founders well knew, it is the very nature of legislatures to come to decision through the striking of bargains. Labeling this deal as corrupt reveals more about Jackson's sense of entitlement to rule than it does about the merits of the case.

Jackson was bold even to the point of recklessness. His resentments regularly threatened to overwhelm his good sense. He was so honor-bound that he provoked and prolonged feuds that threatened to topple his presidency and to end his life. He suffered recurrent illness and debilitating pain from the bullets lodged in his body, which he received in his many duels.

As George Dangerfield described him:

> His civilian career . . . resolved itself into the typical progression of a frontier arriviste. Horse coper, lawyer, politician, judge, enterpriser—by these rungs the general had ascended to the position of slave holder and country gentleman. There was little to set him apart from the rest, except a passionate idiosyncrasy, a conviction that he was always right, which, enforced by an imaginative temperament and a fierce will, transformed him into the most generous of friends and the most remorseless of enemies. . . . At the root of his social being lay the simple ethic he had once expounded for the instruction of a refractory Spanish official: "An eye for an Eye, Toothe for Toothe, and Scalp for Scalp."[5]

Like Washington and Jefferson, Jackson was the most popular man in America when he assumed the presidency. But the source of his popularity was not such as to inspire confidence in his capacity for republican leadership. It was not just that he was a military figure. After all, Washington had also been a general. But Washington was a political general. Like Dwight Eisenhower, his great military achievement was to maintain cohesion and stability of his troops in the face of powerful centrifugal political forces. Washington's army won the Revolutionary War not by dint of great military exploits but simply by enduring. Jackson, like General George Patton, was a warrior. His victory at New Orleans was the first truly decisive battle in American history. It forced the British to give up the dream of reannexing the United States, which neither the end of the Revolutionary War nor the War of 1812 proper had completely extinguished. Jackson's strategic and tactical skills are open to question, but none can doubt his pugnacity and courage. He never shirked a fight.

Washington proved his republican credentials by quelling the mutiny at Newburgh and resisting all attempts to make him king. Jackson did not demonstrate the same clear deference to republican authority. He conquered Florida in the face of what was at best ambiguous instructions from his commander in chief and clearly exceeded his authority in carrying out the summary execution of two British subjects. Jackson's Florida adventure illustrates his recklessness as well as the nature of his immense political appeal.

Spanish occupation of Florida was a particular sore spot with southerners and westerners because of the Spanish willingness to give sanctuary to marauding Indians, most notably the Seminoles. In December 1818, Jackson, general of the southern division of the United States

Army, was ordered by the secretary of war, John C. Calhoun, to lead an expedition against the Seminoles with permission to cross over into Florida in pursuit of them.[6] Jackson had earlier inspired the fear and enmity of the Spanish as a result of his seizure of Pensacola just prior to the Battle of New Orleans in 1815. Designating him to lead the expedition appears to have been a purposeful provocation of the Spanish. Perhaps the hope was that they would choose to abandon Florida rather than contend with so dangerous a presence in their midst. But there is no clear evidence demonstrating that Calhoun either expected or wanted Jackson to gain the territory by conquest.

Despite the lack of a clear order to do so, Jackson impulsively determined to expand his attack on the Seminoles into a full-fledged invasion and conquest of the entire Spanish colony. In less than three months Jackson gained all of Florida, deposed the Spanish government, appointed members of his staff to serve as civil and military governor and collector of revenue, and executed two British subjects whom he accused of aiding the Seminoles. This last act was particularly dubious, involving as it did the trial of the two by an American court convened on what was still legally Spanish soil. As Dangerfield aptly puts it: "the fact that he had now seriously wounded the sensibilities of two empires bothered him not at all."[7]

Whatever encouragement President James Monroe may have initially given Jackson, he was now deeply frightened by the potentially damaging diplomatic ramifications of these acts. He sought advice from his cabinet but the cabinet was deeply divided. Two of its presidential aspirants, Secretary of the Treasury William H. Crawford and Secretary of War Calhoun sought to discredit Jackson lest he become a new and dangerous rival. For similar reasons, Henry Clay tried to convince Congress to pass a resolution condemning this "Napoleonic" usurpation of civil authority. The resolution died.[8] Clay's failure to rouse Congress attests to the great popular groundswell of support for Jackson's actions, however insubordinate they may have been.

The potentially dangerous controversy that Jackson had sparked with the Spanish was smoothed over by the skilled diplomacy of Secretary of State John Quincy Adams, who was the only cabinet member to steadfastly support him. He wielded "Old Hickory" like a club against the Spanish, hinting at an American willingness to let him loose on further military adventures—against Cuba or Texas, perhaps—unless Spain agreed to sell Florida to the United States and recognize the United States' claim to all territory above a line running north of Texas along the forty-second parallel and extending all the way to the Pacific Ocean. Adams deftly exploited Jackson's recklessness to gain a continent.

William Ward retells a perhaps apocryphal story about Jackson's reaction to the controversy that roiled over his Florida conquest.

> Adams had defended him (Jackson) on the high ground of international law as expounded by Grotius, Pufendorf, and Vattel. Jackson's response was, "D__n Grotius, d__n Pufendorf, d__n Vattel—this is a mere matter between Jim Monroe and myself![9]

As the originator of the story, Henry Wise commented, "Jackson made law, Adams quoted it." It was this insouciance, this disrespect for form and love of action that so endeared Jackson to the public. One imagines that had he been Prince of the Danes, Claudius' reign would have been considerably foreshortened.

PARTY

Why did Jackson not turn out to be Napoleon or Cromwell? The short answer is: party. As James Ceaser has so brilliantly described, Martin Van Buren, a key Jackson supporter in the 1828 election, reinvented the party of "Old Republicans," later to be called the Democrats, to keep Jackson's potentially demagogic ambition in check.[10]

These "Old Republicans" harked back to the glory days of 1800, and sought to restore the limits on government and the democratic élan associated with that great victory. Like Thomas Jefferson, they too sought to overthrow "monocracy." According to an article by Michael Wallace:

> The origin of the two great political parties which have divided the country from the adoption of the Constitution to the present day ... are ... mainly to be ascribed to the struggle between the two opposing principles that have been in active operation in this country from the closing scenes of the revolutionary war to the present day—the one seeking to absorb as far as practicable, all power from its legitimate sources, and to condense in a single head. The other, an antagonist principle, laboring as assiduously to resist the encroachments and limit the extent of executive authority. . . . The former is essentially the monarchical, the latter the democratical spirit of society.[11]

But Van Buren differed from Jefferson in seeing the threat of autocracy as a general and not a partisan problem.[12] It was not only Federalist mobocrats who would abuse the power of the presidency: the Republicans would likewise suffer autocratic temptations. Nor could the checks and balances provided by the Constitution be exclusively relied on. They had not prevented the direct appeal by presidential candidates to voters and therefore they permitted the sort of plebiscitary politics that could over-whelm formal constitutional constraints. To buttress the Constitution required subjecting the president to the collective restraint and discipline that only party could impose. Jackson was the first presidential aspirant who had both the great popular appeal and the apparent lack of principled commitment characteristic of the demagogue. The Herculean effort that Van Buren expended in organizing Democratic Party support for Jackson's candidacy in 1828 was geared both to win the race and to throw the blanket of party loyalty over this unpredictable and potentially dangerous political steed.

VAN BUREN

Martin Van Buren was, in many ways, Jackson's opposite. Unlike Jackson, who was tall and gaunt, Van Buren's stature was unprepossessing. His entire life had been devoted to politics. Although he had been extraordinarily successful at gaining and wielding office, this very success was often held against him. The adjectives *clever, wily,* and *manipulative* clung to him like a snug waistcoat. Jackson was nicknamed "Old Hickory," a tribute to his strong unbending character. Van Buren was dubbed "the Magician" and "the Sly Fox." Whereas Jackson was known to be decisive to the point of rashness, Van Buren was accused of being indecisive to the point of duplicity. Van Buren himself recounts a story circulated by his opponents.

A bet was offered by one partisan to another that the latter could not put to me a question on any subject to which he would receive a definitive answer. . . . [T]he question was asked whether I concurred in the general opinion that the sun rose in the East; my answer having been that *I presumed the fact was according to the common impression, but as I invariable(sic) slept until after sunrise I could not speak from my own knowledge."*[13]

The story was told to Van Buren by a newspaper editor who had heard it from people who believed it to be true.[14]

Although Van Buren bitterly chafed at what he felt to be this unfair assessment of his character, he also recognized that he could not completely alter it. He was old enough to have encountered many of the founding generation of American political leaders and wise enough to sense that he lacked their gravitas. Among his contemporaries: Daniel Webster was more eloquent; Calhoun more articulate; Clinton more visionary; and Jackson more noble. From his early encounters with Aaron Burr, and especially from his recurring battles with De Witt Clinton, Van

Buren recognized that he would never be preeminent in a politics based on personality. But his great cunning and his organizational talents could enable him to compete in the less theatrical, more deliberative game of party politics. He could and would accept the limits imposed by the collective nature of party rule because those same constraints would also be placed on his rivals who were less well suited to endure them. Much as his view of party was geared to check Jackson's ambition, it was also geared to serve his.

THE ELECTION OF 1828

The party organization that Van Buren created in New York would serve as the model for what he sought to create on the national level. Its central feature was the caucus. All important policy and personnel decisions were made collectively via the party caucus. To remain in good standing with the party a member had to adhere by the caucus decisions. Loyalty and discipline therefore came to be treated as the greatest political virtues. This might even involve sacrificing other cherished principles and voluntarily relinquishing one's post in government if that were the will of the caucus. As New York Democrat and presidential aspirant William Marcy instructed newspaper publisher T. W. Flagg, party loyalty would even dictate abandoning a superior candidate to support an inferior one if that were the will of the caucus.

> An opposition to a candidate which is abstractly right may be politically wrong. . . . The example of opposing a candidate nominated by political friends is bad not only as to its effects on the pending election but as to others that are to succeed it. An opposition upon the ground of principle will be used to authorize an opposition on the ground of caprice.[15]

Van Buren would have preferred to support a more tractable candidate than Jackson in 1828. Although generally supportive of the strict constructionist views of the "Old Republicans," Jackson harbored the antipartisan animus characteristic of both the founding generation of American public men and their immediate successors. In a letter to President Monroe regarding appointments to the cabinet, Jackson wrote: "[N]ow is the time to exterminate that monster called party spirit."[16] Such views made him a very hard sell even to Van Buren's closest political friends. Robert Remini quotes one stalwart of the radical cause as saying: "Nothing can be gained therefore in principle by turning out Adams and electing Jackson."[17] But Van Buren had no good option. Crawford, a more conventional "Old Republican" whom he had backed in 1824, was in poor health. Jackson, whose popularity had only increased due to the "corrupt bargain" and Adams's executive ineptitude, was a very strong candidate with or without "Old Republican" support. Worst of all, Jackson had already been endorsed by Van Buren's New York nemesis, De Witt Clinton. If Van Buren and his allies did not jump on board, a Jackson victory would cede control of their political base to their partisan enemy.

Therefore, Van Buren felt he had little choice but to gamble that Jackson could be made tractable through the vehicle of party. He got to know Jackson when they briefly served together in the Senate and he had formed a favorable impression of "Old Hickory." When, at the very beginning of the Adams administration, his old ally William Smith of South Carolina inquired about Jackson's electability and political reliability, Van Buren responded:

> By adding the General's personal popularity to the strength of the old Republican party which still acted together . . . we might . . . compete successfully with the power and patronage of the Administration, then in the zenith of its prosperity; that we had abundant evidence that the General was at an earlier period well grounded in the principles of our party, and that we must trust to good fortune and *to the effects of favorable associations for the removal of the rust they had contracted, in his case, by a protracted non-user,* and the prejudicial effects in that regard of his military life.[18]

By "favorable associations," Van Buren meant regular and frequent contact with his party allies. Only by coming to experience and appreciate the collaborative dimension of political life could Jackson overcome the "prejudicial effects . . . of his military life." It is unclear to what extent Jackson had modified his extreme antipartisanship prior to 1828. But, at a minimum, his defeat in 1824 showed him that mass popular appeal alone could not guarantee electoral victory. He needed a national political organization. Having observed that Van Buren's organizational skills had brought Crawford, blind and virtually on his deathbed, to the brink of victory, Jackson determined that the New Yorker was the one best suited to put such a successful electoral force together.

Van Buren aggressively recruited "Old Republicans" from Virginia, North Carolina, and Georgia, as well as from his native New York, to combine with Jackson's formidable strength in Tennessee and Pennsylvania. Well before the actual election, a national network anchored by a renewed New York–Virginia alliance had come into being. It was conscious of itself as a new party whose devotion to Jackson was real but, for the most part, secondary to its devotion to the "Old Republican" principles of 1800. Due in large measure to the diligent work of these party builders, Jackson won a decisive victory over Adams, winning all the western states, all the southern states except Maryland where he split the electoral vote virtually in half, and Pennsylvania as well.[19] Adams triumphed only in New England and New Jersey. Van Buren scored a personal triumph in New York. Despite its proximity to Massachusetts and its large population of immigrant New Englanders, Jackson carried New York by a slim margin.

FRIENDSHIP

Although Jackson had pledged to abide by "Old Republican" principles once in office, that pledge was obviously unenforceable.[20] Indeed, his initial cabinet appointments were made without close consultation with party leaders and were viewed by them as very disappointing. So aggrieved was Van Buren by the appointment of Samuel Swartwout to the highly prized post of collector of the Port of New York, he seriously considered resigning his own appointment as secretary of state. After much soul searching, he decided to stay because he did not believe that Jackson's egregious personnel decisions stemmed from any deep character flaw, and therefore the best hope for his party lay in the "favorable association" he would only be able to cultivate were he to remain in his post.[21]

Van Buren assiduously courted Jackson. They went on horseback rides together almost daily, during which they discussed the full gamut of political questions facing the administration. But even such close and amiable personal contact by itself would not have been sufficient for Van Buren to alter the views of a man as set in his ways and as long in the tooth as Jackson. It took a crisis to unsettle Jackson sufficiently to enable Van Buren to convert him to party ways. That crisis was the so-called Eaton Affair, a scandal that dominated life in Washington for the first two years of Jackson's presidency. What this imbroglio permitted Van Buren to teach the general was that in civilian life the nearest approximation of his cherished martial virtues were to be found in party, or at least in the sort of party that Van Buren was putting together.

John Eaton was a close friend and confidant of Jackson's from Tennessee. He had been one of the leading promoters of Jackson's candidacy and a trusted lieutenant during the campaign. It was unthinkable to the new incumbent not to reward Eaton for his loyalty and energy on Jackson's behalf, and so he appointed Eaton to the post of secretary of war. Eaton had recently married a widow, Peggy O'Neale Timberlake, the daughter of William O'Neale, the proprietor of a Washington boarding house where he was a frequent guest. Her reputation was unfortunately not of the best. She was accused of engaging in flirtations, and more, with her father's customers, particularly Eaton. As her notoriety increased, the Washington gossip mills worked overtime producing a multitude of allegations against her, including the charge of an adulterous liaison with Eaton prior to her first husband's death. Polite society in Washington did not receive her, and the wives of various newly appointed cabinet members made clear that they would follow those unwritten but nonetheless binding dictates.

The snubbing of Mrs. Eaton touched off a chord of anger in Jackson that cannot be fully explained simply by the discourtesy it represented. Jackson and his wife Rachel had suffered a similar fate in the wake of their unconventional courtship and subsequent marriage. Criticism of his behavior towards Rachel while she was still married to another had resurfaced during the recent campaign.[22] Rachel's recent death served only to fuel Jackson's determination to see that his official family did right by this other maligned lady. Jackson bent every effort to defend Peggy Eaton's honor. During the first two years of his presidency, close to half of Jackson's letters were devoted either to the affair itself or to his growing hostility toward Calhoun that it fueled. The president conducted his own intensive investigation of the charges against her and collected documentary evidence rebutting or at least casting doubt on them. Never before or since has a sitting president become so obsessively involved in the defense of a subordinate.

Although Jackson publicly declared Peggy to be "chaste as a virgin," this was obviously the one thing about her that he was least in a position to know for sure. What he did know firsthand was the character of each of the three principals—John Eaton, Peggy Eaton, and her first husband John Timberlake. Jackson, too, had dined at the O'Neales'. He was fond of Peggy. He also knew Timberlake to be a scoundrel. As a naval purser, Peggy's first husband had become involved in a variety of scandals and disastrous business decisions. At the time of his death, perhaps by suicide, he had not seen Peggy in four years. John Eaton was a close friend and patron of Timberlake and they remained on good terms throughout Timberlake's life. Indeed, Eaton was a great benefactor to the O'Neale family. When Peggy's father was forced to declare bankruptcy, Eaton bought the inn from the bank and then resold it on terms that were very favorable to the O'Neales.

Jackson knew that during Timberlake's long absence, Peggy was frequently in Eaton's company. If she was not his mistress, then there was clearly no reason for her to be ostracized. But, if she were his mistress, then he was indeed doing a far nobler thing by honoring their union through matrimony than he would have done by deserting her when his growing political prominence caused her to become an inconvenience. Whatever role personal pique and stubbornness may have played in

Jackson's defense of the Eatons, his moral understanding of the situation was far subtler and deeper than that of their critics. The "high minded independence and virtue," which Calhoun ascribed to the "the ladies of Washington" for snubbing Peggy Eaton, was neither independent nor virtuous.[23] As Jackson's exhaustive research demonstrated, no one really knew whether or not Peggy Eaton was promiscuous. It was not virtue that the Washington ladies were demonstrating, but a Whiggish propriety. This principled but unsentimental view is precisely what Van Buren propounds in his autobiography.

> Major Eaton was a man of moderate intellectual capacities, but justly distinguished for the kindness, generosity, and unobtrusiveness of his disposition and demeanor. If he had done the wrong before his marriage which was imputed to him [he] had also done all that a man could do to remedy the evil and there was no reason even to suspect that the life of the lady after marriage was not, in that respect at least, free from reproach.[24]

Van Buren was the only member of the cabinet to ostentatiously manifest his loyalty to Jackson regarding this delicate matter. Even Jackson's own nephew, his private secretary and namesake Andrew Jackson Donelson, following the dictate of polite society, split with him over the Eaton Affair. By contrast, Van Buren invited the Eatons to his parties and found various ways to express his solicitude for the embattled couple. As a result, he rose in Jackson's esteem to a level beyond that of a political ally or confidant. Jackson determined that Van Buren would be his successor. In order to answer the question of why Van Buren the partisan was so much more trustworthy than the "statesmen" in his cabinet, or even members of his own family, Jackson was forced to reconsider his understanding of what partisanship meant. Woodrow Wilson quoted Jackson as saying that if he were a politician, he would be a New York politician.[25] Disreputable though it might be, Van Buren's political machine embodied the principles of inclusiveness and loyalty, which Jackson cherished far more than mere propriety.

Van Buren also provided the means for extricating Jackson from the political embarrassment brought on by the Eaton imbroglio. On the one hand, the president could no longer coexist with the anti-Eaton cabinet members. On the other, it would be unseemly to force them to resign over what was, after all, a private matter. To break the logjam, Van Buren offered to resign. By accepting Van Buren's resignation, and soliciting Eaton's as well, Jackson could force the entire cabinet to resign without making it appear that Peggy Eaton was the cause. Jackson argued that accepting the departure of those two destroyed the delicate political balance that his original cabinet appointments represented. To reestablish that balance required him to recruit a whole new cabinet from scratch. On those grounds Jackson obtained the resignations of the rest of the cabinet, except from the postmaster general. He replaced the cabinet with one that was much more clearly a creature of the nascent party that he and Van Buren were in the process of fashioning. Van Buren's departure from the cabinet did not diminish Jackson's zeal to make him president. He broached the idea of making Van Buren his running mate in 1832 and then resigning in Van Buren's favor shortly after the commencement of his second term.[26] Although Van Buren disabused him of that plan, the general remained determined to promote the New Yorker to the presidency. Because he feared that Van Buren lacked the political strength to win on his own in 1832, he decided, despite his failing health, to run for reelection and serve out his full second term with Van Buren as his vice president. Recognizing that such a move would make the New Yorker the inevitable party choice in 1836, Van Buren's designation as running mate was opposed by many prominent Jackson loyalists. Jackson countered this opposition by calling for the choice to be made at a party convention, knowing that his own vociferous support of Van Buren would carry the day with the party rank and file.

The anti-Jackson forces in the Senate proceeded to make Jackson's choice of Van Buren far more palatable to the Jacksonian party. Half the Senate voted to oppose Van Buren's appointment as minister to England. This enabled the Senate president, Vice President Calhoun, to cast the deciding vote against it. Thus for a brief but critical moment, the master political manipulator, Van Buren, was cast in the unlikely role of martyr. Opposition to him as the anointed successor melted away.

True to Jackson's plan, Van Buren succeeded him as president in 1836. Although he failed in gaining reelection in 1840, Jackson and Van Buren's combined twelve years in power were enough to forge a partisan entity of sufficient mettle to survive in opposition. Indeed, from the perspective of creating a party system, even Van Buren's defeat was salubrious. To defeat the Democrats, the foes of Van Buren had to move beyond the antipartisan rhetoric of the earlier Jacksonian opposition to forge a real political party of their own. Now there were two entities committed to the idea of party competition, both having abandoned the "party to end party" illusion to which both the Federalists and the Democratic-Republicans had succumbed. This institutionalized the two-party system that dominated American politics throughout the nineteenth and twentieth centuries and that, albeit in desiccated form, continues to play a critical part in American political life. Thus, Peggy Eaton served as midwife for the birth of a new and powerful political movement, and for the first democratic party system as well.

NULLIFICATION

Like any real friendship, the one between Van Buren and Jackson was based not only on mutual respect but on mutual instruction as well. Jackson imbibed Van Buren's teaching about the value of party but he had an equally important political lesson to teach his friend. For all its virtues, the Democratic Party as conceived by Van Buren was radically incomplete. It rested on a North–South alliance, which in turn was based on mutual hostility to the federal government and little else. It reflected the weakness that had characterized the "Old Republicans" since the salad days of 1798. Their fear of centralized domination was so great that they had never been willing to fully repudiate the nullification principle expounded in Jefferson's original draft of the Kentucky resolution. Although they had organized on a national scale, they had not fully committed to the national idea.[27] No wonder they were initially immobilized by South Carolina's Nullification Ordinance of 1832, which claimed that a state could render any federal law null and void within its own borders. By contrast, Jackson's response to nullification was immediate. His commitment to federal supremacy was unequivocal. He showed his party brethren how to uphold a national vision without sacrificing their commitments to liberty and localism. More than two decades before Lincoln, he made clear that "liberty" and "union" were inseparable principles.

The battle over nullification was presaged at a dinner that the would-be nullifiers staged for the ostensible purpose of celebrating Thomas Jefferson's birthday. By so doing, the nullifiers hoped to claim the hallowed name of Jefferson and "the principles of '98" for their cause.[28] A series of toasts, offered by leading nullifiers, were designed both to praise Jefferson and Virginia and to draw parallels between Jefferson's courageous fight against the Alien and Sedition Acts and their own refusal to abide by the "Tariff of Abominations." Jackson had supported this tariff as a compromise between the high tariff demands of certain northern and western states and the low tariff demands of the South. Indicating his implacable opposition to the tariff and his support for its nullification within the borders of his state, Senator Robert Hayne of South Carolina toasted "The Union of the States, and the Sovereignty of the States." Jackson's ensuing toast was characteristically firm, terse, and unequivocal: "Our Federal Union: it must be preserved." Although Van Buren claims in his autobiography that he and Jackson orchestrated their toasts, his bore the marks of one who was not entirely sure that the sun rose in the east: "Mutual forbearance and reciprocal concessions; thro' their agency the Union was established—the patriotic spirit from which they emanated will forever sustain it."[29]

Jackson was no fan of high tariffs. From the beginning of the controversy he signaled his willingness to mollify the nullifiers by seeking to lower the tariffs that they were claiming the right to nullify. There was, therefore, something peculiarly ostentatious in the manner he adopted for dealing with the nullification threat. In his memorable Nullification Proclamation, he declared South Carolina's action to be "incompatible with the existence of the Union, contradicted expressly by the letter of the Constitution, unauthorized by its spirit, inconsistent with every principle on which it was founded, and destructive of the great object for which it was formed."[30]

He expressly denied the Jeffersonian notion that the Union is merely a product of an agreement between the states and of which they are the sole constituents. He claimed that the Union actually predates the Constitution and was formed as a result of the joint decision to declare independence of Great Britain and to fight for that independence as a nation, not a coalition of states.

Under the royal Government we had no separate character; our opposition to its oppressions began as united colonies. We were the United States under the Confederation, and the name was perpetuated and the Union rendered more perfect by the Federal Constitution. In none of these stages did we consider ourselves in any other light than as forming one nation.[31]

Even the Articles of Confederation, despite their woeful lack of enforcement power, required that every state must abide by the determinations of Congress on all questions, which by that confederation should be submitted to Congress. The Constitution was created "to form a more perfect union," remedying the defects of the articles by creating such crucial implementation mechanisms as a judiciary and a means for collecting revenue.

Directly contradicting Jefferson, Jackson claimed that "the people of the United States formed the Constitution. . . . Not only did they establish the federal government but they are its citizens."[32]

The right to make treaties, declare war, levy taxes, exercise exclusive judicial and legislative powers, were all functions of sovereign power. The states, then, for all these important purposes were no longer sovereign. The allegiance of their citizens was transferred, in the first instance, to the government of the United States; they became American citizens and owed obedience to the Constitution of the United Sates and to laws made in conformity with the powers it vested in Congress.[33]

Ever the strict constructionist, Jackson was at pains to show that the tariff power is among the powers expressly delegated to Congress by the Constitution. "The Constitution has given, expressly, to Congress the right of raising revenue and of determining the sum the public exigencies will require."[34] Since Congress had this power, it was entitled to discretion in applying it. Reasonable people could differ about whether or not it had exercised its power wisely in setting tariff rates as it did, but no reasonable person could claim that its use of that power was unconstitutional.

Presaging Lincoln's later defense of the Constitution, Jackson went beyond rational–legal argument to declare that "The Constitution is still the object of our reverence. The sages whose memory will always be reverenced have given us a practical and, as they hoped, a permanent constitutional compact."[35] Perhaps nothing so demonstrates Jackson's determination to foster such devotion as his willingness to invoke the name of Washington, "the Father of his Country," in support of it.[36] Such an encomium was a bitter pill indeed to be swallowed by the devout "Old Republican" who, as a young congressman, had been one of only a few members of the House to vote against a congressionally drafted tribute to Washington issued in the wake of the "Farewell Address."[37]

The final pages of the Nullification Proclamation contain a hymn to the glories of the American nation-state that verges on the Whitmanesque. In it, Jackson implores South Carolinians to:

> Consider the Government, uniting in one bond of common interest and general protection so many different States, giving to all their inhabitants the proud title of American citizen, protecting their commerce, securing their literature and their arts, facilitating their intercommunication, defending their frontiers and making their name respected in the remotest parts of the earth. Consider the extent of its territory, its increasing and happy population, its advance in arts which render life agreeable and the sciences which elevate the mind. See education spreading the lights of religion, morality and general information into every cottage in this wide extent of our Territories and states. Behold it as the asylum where the wretched and the oppressed find a refuge and support. Look on this picture of happiness and honor and say, we too are citizens of America.[38]

Jackson hardly needed to indulge in such a rhetorical outpouring if all he had wanted to do was mollify South Carolina. But Jackson had more than tariffs, or John C. Calhoun, on his mind. Although the specific threat posed by the Nullification Ordinance could have been defused through compromise, to do so immediately would be to lose a crucial opportunity to educate his friends, Van Buren among them. His opponents Daniel Webster and John Quincy Adams already understood the need to preserve federal supremacy. It was the disciples of Jefferson, susceptible to the nullification contagion spread by his Kentucky resolution, who needed to improve their constitutional understanding. Jackson's deepest purpose in issuing the proclamation was to teach Van Buren and other Democrats how to combine their zeal for limited government with an equally strong attachment to the Union.

NOTES

1. On the problem of execution, see Harvey Mansfield Jr., *Taming the Prince: The Ambivalence of Modern Executive Power* (Baltimore, Md.: Johns Hopkins University Press, 1989).

2. Robert V. Remini, *The Life of Andrew Jackson* (New York: Penguin, 1988), 75.

3. See Marc Landy and Sidney Milkis, *Presidential Greatness* (forthcoming).

4. See James Ceaser, *Presidential Selection: Theory and Development* (Princeton, N.J.: Princeton University Press, 1979), and Richard Hofstadter, *The Idea of a Party System* (Berkeley and Los Angeles: University of California Press, 1969). On the development of the American party system from its origins in the early 1790s, see especially William Nisbet Chambers' essay in *The First Party System: Federalists and Republicans*, ed. William Nisbet Chambers (New York: Wiley, 1972); Noble Cunningham, *The Jeffersonian Republicans* (Chapel Hill, N.C.: University of North Carolina Press, 1957); Joseph Charles, *The Origins of the American Party System: Three Essays* (Williamsburg, Va.: The Institute of Early American History and Culture, 1956); and *The American Party Systems: Stages of Political Development*, ed. Walter Dean Burnham and William and Nisbet Chambers (New York: Oxford University Press, 1975), 289.

5. George Dangerfield, *The Era of Good Feelings* (New York: Harcourt, Brace, 1952), 123.

6. Remini, *Life of Andrew Jackson* 117.

7. Dangerfield, *Era of Good Feelings*, 135.

8. Remini, *Life of Andrew Jackson*, 126.

9. Ibid., 63.

10. Ceaser, *Presidential Selection,* 123–69

11. Quoted in Michael Wallace, "Changing Concepts of Party in the United States: New York, 1815–1828," *The American Historical Review* 24, no. 2 (December 1968): 483.

12. Ceaser, *Presidential Selection*, 135.

13. Martin Van Buren, *The Autobiography of Martin Van Buren*, ed. John C. Fitzpatrick (New York: August M. Kelley, 1969), 199 (italics mine). The story is recounted in Marvin Myers, *The Jacksonian Persuasion*, (New York: Vintage Books, 1960), 144–45.

14. Van Buren, *Autobiography*, 199.

15. Wallace, "Changing Concepts of Party," 467.

16. Ibid. 476.

17. Robert V. Remini, *The Election of Andrew Jackson*, (Philadelphia: J. B. Lippincott, 1963), 48.

18. Van Buren, *Autobiography*, 198 (italics added).

19. Ibid., 187.

20. Remini, *The Election of Andrew Jackson*, 57.

21. Van Buren, *Autobiography*, 267–68.

22. Donald B. Cole, *The Presidency of Andrew Jackson* (Lawrence: University Press of Kansas, 1993), 35.

23. Marszalek, *The Petticoat Affair: Manner, Sex, and Mutiny in Andrew Jackson's White House* (New York: Free Press, 1997), 196.

24. Van Buren, *Autobiography*, 352.

25. Woodrow Wilson, *Division and Reunion* (New York: Longmans. 1916), 32.

26. Van Buren, *Autobiography*, 506–7.

27. I take this term from Sam Beer, "The National Idea in American Politics," a lecture delivered to the faculty and officers of Boston College, 21 April 1982. See also his seminal book, *To Make a Nation* (Cambridge, Mass.: Harvard University Press, 1993), especially 1–26.

28. Van Buren, *Autobiography*, 413.

29. Freehling, *Prelude to Civil War Nullification Controversy in South Carolina, 1816–1836* (New York: Harper & Row, 1966) 261–3, and Van Buren, *Autobiography*, 416.

30. James D. Richardson, ed., *Messages and Papers of the Presidents*, vol. 3, (New York: Bureau of National Literature and Art, 1907), 1216 (hereafter cited as *MPP*).

31. *MPP*, 1216.

32. *MPP*, 1211.

33. *MPP*, 1213.

34. Ibid.

35. *MPP*, 1208.

36. Ibid.

37. Remini, *Life of Andrew Jackson*, 36.

38. *MPP*, 1217.

5

Seeing Differently and Seeing Further: Rousseau and Tocqueville

Tracy B. Strong

Briefly put—Alas!—this will for a long time be kept silent about: What will not (henceforth) be built any more, cannot be built any more is—a society in the old sense of that word. To build this everything is lacking, above all the material. *All of us are no longer material for a society*; this is a truth for which the time has come.

—Friedrich Nietzsche[1]

"He shall be taught," said I, "by my life and by my death that the world is a sad one for he who shrinks from its sober duties. My experience shall warn him to adopt some great and serious aim, such as manhood will cling to, that he may not feel himself, too late, a cumberer of this overladen earth, but a man among men. I will beseech him not to follow an eccentric path, nor, by stepping aside from the highway of human affairs, to relinquish his claim upon human sympathy. And often, as a text of deep and varied meaning, I will remind him that he is an American."

—Nathaniel Hawthorne, "Fragments from the Journal of a Solitary Man"

Sixteen out of the twenty chapters of Wilson Carey McWilliams's *The Idea of Fraternity in America* carry epigraphs from Alexis de Tocqueville's *Democracy in America*.[2] Of the others, two are from the Old Testament, one is from G. K. Chesterton, and one, on the "Ambiguous Ideal," carries citations from the songs "America the Beautiful" and "If I Had a Hammer." That of the epilogue is from Robert Frost and warns the reader against the straightness of political categories: "I was never a radical when young / For fear it would make me conservative when old."

The warning is apposite, for the subject matter of the book is not one that has been the subject of most political theory. The central concerns in political theory since the French Revolution have been liberty and equality and their relationship. It might thus be surprising that McWilliams has chosen Tocqueville to set the tone for his chapters, for their subject—the idea of fraternity—seems to be in tension with the world Tocqueville teaches us to grasp. Fraternity is rather, in appearance at least, the field planted by Jean-Jacques Rousseau.[3] It would thus appear natural to investigate the relations and differences between Tocqueville and Rousseau, in order better to grasp the overall project of McWilliams's book.

Of the three slogans of the French Revolution, one might most naturally associate Tocqueville with liberty, Rousseau with fraternity, and see the two sharing a common concern over equality. And there is clearly some accuracy to this.[4] And yet this approach will miss concerns that are common in the understandings of modern politics, as well as obscure important differences in their approaches to political theory as an activity. In any case, that there exists a relation between Tocqueville and Rousseau, and that Tocqueville learned from reading Rousseau, has been accepted by some, at least, for some time. Tocqueville tells us as much. However, his gnomic letter to his close friend Kergorlay relating that each day he spends some time with Pascal, Montesquieu, and Rousseau[5] gives us little indication as to what that relationship actually might be. Indeed, all aspects of this claim have been challenged.[6] Tocqueville, in fact, rarely mentions Rousseau explicitly. In his *Souvenirs*, he suggests somewhat cattily that Louis-Phillipe's style was "some Jean Jacques spiffed up by a XIXth century chef."[7] We will thus not learn much about Tocqueville's relation to Rousseau by examining what he actually said about Jean-Jacques. (And, likewise, we will not learn much about his relation to Pascal, nor to Montesquieu, by examining his explicit comments.)[8] This is not accidental.

I want to ask three questions, mainly of these two Frenchmen, questions that their thought, taken together, requires. First, what conditions shape the possibilities of politics in the modern age? Second, given these conditions, what are the possibilities of a truly human politics, that is, of a politics that does not dehumanize? And, given answers to these first two questions, the last question is: "How is it possible to write political theory in the present age?"

WHAT SHAPES MODERN POLITICS?

Neither Tocqueville nor Rousseau can easily be caught within the divisions central to much contemporary political thought. In 1819, Benjamin Constant announced (or re-announced) the difference between ancient and modern liberty.[9] For the ancients, liberty was the sharing in and of power among the citizens; for the moderns, it was the guarantees accorded private actions by political institutions. This dichotomy, so central to modern liberalism, is accepted neither by Tocqueville nor by Rousseau. Rather, they share with McWilliams the conviction that the place of politics in human life is "to bind together public things and private men."[10] Additionally, both men accept modernity and its open understanding of the self; both see political activity as central to the preservation of a human existence in modern times.

My intentions here also rest on a conviction that standard modern categories that might be applied to each of these men—obvious ones would be "democratic" and "aristocratic"—are, while occasionally superficially true, obfuscatory. Nor is it accurate to oppose a supposed single-purposed, one-will society in Rousseau to a benevolent pluralism in Tocqueville. Such distinctions, I shall argue, hide the degree to which both Rousseau and Tocqueville share the conviction that the problem for political theory is not just in being right about "laws as they are and men as they might be" (Rousseau's phrase at the beginning of *The Social Contract*), but in enabling the audience for political theory to be right about laws and men. Rousseau and Tocqueville are thus centrally concerned with the possibilities of citizenship in the modern age, in a time when the distinctions— both the differences and the honors—that citizenship brings seem thin. As my understanding of Rousseau has been elaborated elsewhere, I will in part, but not only, repeat those arguments.[11] I come back to Tocqueville after nothing more than an occasional visit and tip of the cap over the last thirty years.

Any consideration of the relation between Rousseau and Tocqueville must start with the picture of humans in modern society given in the *Discourse on the Origins of Inequality* and compare it to that of the democratic man in *Democracy in America*. These are the books in which each author sets out his understanding of the dangers and potential strengths of modern politics. Neither work is precisely historical. Rather each author asks "How is society possible?"[12] Such a question is kin to a Kantian transcendental deduction: it does not ask how did society come about, but "what has to be the case for there to be what we call society?"

To answer this question one must imagine what would be the case were there not to be society. This is typically the function of the device of the "state of nature," which, while implicit in the biblical narrative of humanity, becomes central to political theory from at least the time of Thomas Hobbes. Here, at first glance, there would seem to be a major difference between Rousseau and Tocqueville, for the former speaks famously of a state of nature and the latter does not. One must, however, move carefully: Rousseau differs greatly from both Hobbes and John Locke. Pierre Manent, for instance, in his book *Tocqueville and the Nature of Democracy*, appears to contrast Tocqueville with Rousseau, or at least with a frequent reading of Rousseau. A non-Tocquevillian view of politics, Manent notes, rests on the notion of a "social state of nature, constituted by equal and independent individuals such that the society that they are forming could only truly be said to be founded on the simultaneous consent of all."[13]

If Manent thinks that this view applies to Rousseau, he is, I think, mistaken, for Rousseau does not have such a view. For Rousseau, in the state of nature, humans beings are essentially (that is, in their essence, ontologically) without qualities. In nature, he says, humans are *nuls*.[14] In the *Second Discourse*, Rousseau sums up his discussion of the state of nature as follows (in language that Voltaire annotated as that of a "very bad novel"):

> Let us conclude that, wandering in the forests without industry, without speech, without settled abode, without war, and without ties, without any need of others of his kind and without any desire to harm them, perhaps even without ever recognizing any one of them individually, subject to few passions and self-sufficient, centuries went by in all the crudeness of the first ages: the species had already grown old and man remained ever a child.[15]

Eight times "without": the human is literally no-thing in the state of nature. The few passions one has do not become—are not—anything, as these beings have no time frame.[16] If it is the case that human beings in a state of nature are in fact undefined—that it is the nature of being human not to be defined—then it follows that any qualities that human beings may have are particular ones, i.e., ones acquired historically, or, more accurately, ones whose acquisition makes up what history is.[17]

This means that human beings are naturally not any thing. So to be a human being in society means that one must not take as given, as natural, any quality that comes from the relations that make up that particular society. Being human means (at least) not to be any*thing* but simply to be. This presumably means that any encounter between two human beings in the state of nature cannot be understood as the encounter of anything other than that of beings.

Assuming this is so, Rousseau has two related problems. He needs first to account for the fact that there is some difference between a human being's relation to another human being and his relationship to anything else that is—be it tree, rock, or dog. Secondly, he needs to account for the fact and possibility that there be a society that is that of human beings. If he is, as he famously writes, to take "humans as they are and laws as they might be," that means the humans have first to be taken as not having qualities.[18] How then to have a society of *human* beings?

The answer to both of these questions comes in his discussion of one of the few capacities that beings in the state of nature have—pity. For

Rousseau, pity is the capacity—not the same as a quality—that human beings have to recognize another as being like them, and not like a rock or a tree or a dog. For Rousseau, it is the case that human beings will, unless they are protecting some acquired characteristics (Marx will call such self-protection "ideology," Freud, "neurosis"), respond to other human beings as beings of their own kind in a manner in which they will not respond to rocks and trees. He calls this response pity, or in a slightly more elaborated version in the *Émile*, conscience. Pity thus makes it possible that there be society based on human commonalty.

Why is pity important for Rousseau? Why, despite his attempt to disqualify, as it were, beings in the state of nature from any claim to definition, does he retain the notion of pity? Pity does double work for Rousseau. The first task derives from the relationship that exists naturally between sentient beings. That I respond differently when I see an ax sink into a human being than when I see it sink into a tree is not something that needs explanation for Rousseau, but rather acknowledgment.[19] That my response when I see an ax sink into a dog has more to do with my response when I see it sink into a human than when I see it fell a tree has something to do with the fact that dogs are more like me than are trees. The similarity comes from the perception that the dog suffers more in the manner that humans do then do trees.[20]

However, pity is not limited to this reaction. Pity, especially in the form of conscience, which he elaborates in the *Émile*, carries with it a moment of finding oneself in another, acknowledging that other (who can suffer) is like me. He does so because he must have a term to account for the fact that human society is composed, or can be composed, of humans (and not of inner tubes, dolphins, porcupines, and pin cushions). Pity is for Rousseau what makes it actual that one human recognize another being as like oneself, as, that is, human. It is thus not a quality that can be produced by argument—one cannot say "you should have this feeling." It is beneath assessment, part of assessing itself.

Pity is thus what makes commonalty possible: the capacity of recognizing oneself in another. This actuality is for Rousseau constitutive of the human realm: it is only in such acknowledgment that one is human. All *human* beings thus manifest it, insofar as they act like human beings. It follows that often one is not human: as when one is a king, or a bourgeois, or a slave, or the gentleman whom Locke sought to produce through his education (these are all Rousseau's examples). There are a hundred reasons why humans may deny their humanity common to others—we are ever fragile—but such reasons always serve to protect a status, a condition of life—in brief, to protect inequality.[21]

Being human, or more accurately being as human, is therefore for Rousseau a state that has no particular quality in and of itself. Humanness is constituted when and by the acknowledgment of another as a being exactly the same as oneself and is constituted only in that by which I am exactly the same as you, and you as me. I call this commonalty, and not community or Gemeinschaft, and I might have called it fraternity, as does McWilliams.[22] Rousseau's claim, his teaching, is that only when differences between you and me are established in the recognition of this commonalty will those differences not define us in terms of the other. A society is truly human for Rousseau when it rests on the fact or, more accurately, the possibility that I will respond to you as myself, my self understood here as that me that is the same as you. (We are thus in some complex relationship to the Aristotelian realm of friendship, where the friend is "another I".) It means that the presence of another human being requires something of me in a way that the presence of a cat or tree does not. I am, in Ralph Waldo Emerson's word, "provoked"—called out—by the other.[23]

Where does Tocqueville stand on such matters? In the second volume of Democracy in America, Tocqueville adduces the case of Mme de Sévigné.[24] In a passage that calls to mind the torture and execution of regicide Damiens at the beginning of Foucault's Discipline and Punish,[25] Tocqueville quotes the French noblewoman in a nonchalant, joking, and apparently completely unpitying description of the breaking and quartering of a violinist who had opposed a suddenly imposed heavy tax. He suggests that in Europe the sentiment of pity is new—whereas in America it is, as it were, a natural part of human life.

One might conclude here that Tocqueville is historical in his sense of human nature, whereas Rousseau finds it fixed. This conclusion is too easy. I have already argued that whatever nature be in Rousseau, it has no content but is understood merely as the form in which can occur the acknowledgment of one being by another. The difference between Rousseau and Tocqueville cannot therefore be one of static versus dynamic.

The point can be clarified by examining what Tocqueville thinks to be the relationship between America and Europe. When Tocqueville speaks of democracy, he means not so much a particular institutional form of government but a style of social relationship in which each individual finds himself to be of the same moral worth as any other.[26] In the first paragraph of Democracy in America, Tocqueville calls this "l'égalité des conditions." Here, condition means social station or standing as a particular kind of being—a word that one might easily be tempted (and not completely incorrectly so) to translate as class.[27] (One can, however, refer, as have authors from Pascal to André Malraux, to la condition humaine.) Tocqueville holds that this condition is best examined in America where it exists in a relatively pure state; he also is convinced that it will be the future of the human world, as Europe is advancing every day closer and closer to this condition. In relation to the *égalité des conditions*, one cannot correctly think of the relation between America and Europe as that of different historical conditions, for America is already where Europe has not yet arrived. In fact, he thinks of America as "born from chance"—hardly an historical appreciation.[28] America functions, rather, as a kind of ideal type by which one may make sense of what is happening and will happen in Europe.

Tocqueville is not some kind of watered-down G. W. F. Hegel. While it is true that over time he expects *l'égalité des conditions* to become the most salient fact about the human world, it is already with us in America. Thus, human affairs are not running in some kind of dialectical progression toward the end of history: one can be born equal; one can also become so. Both are possible in this day and age.[29] It is not clear what *becoming equal* actually means. Even more importantly, one must determine what the equality of human conditions actually implies in terms of what *being human* can mean.

It follows from this that Mme de Sévigné's unpitying report of the torture and execution of the hapless violinist does not necessarily imply that she is at some earlier psychosocial stage of development; it implies rather that her attitude is consequent to a society that does not display *l'égalité des conditions*. If this were to change (as Tocqueville knows that it will), then pity will become possible.

Keeping in mind what Rousseau says about pity, we can now ask what qualities Tocqueville ascribes to the sentiment. One of the consequences of the pity that characterizes democratic ages is that "each can ascertain in a moment the feelings of others: he glances quickly at himself and that is enough. . . . It makes no difference if it is a matter of friend or enemy: imagination immediately puts him in their place."[30] To see oneself in someone else's place is the strange ecstasy natural to a democratic society. This is not precisely the "disordered self" that Peter Lawler so interestingly analyzes.[31] It is rather a self that finds its humanity to be the same in its own self and in another self. Insofar as I am a human, and insofar as my actions are human actions, they are, for Rousseau, the same actions as yours. Not all my actions are human actions: this is only a problem when they keep me from the possibility of acting in a manner that is human. (Thus, the general will is my will, as it is yours, and is general by virtue of its object, not its ubiquity.) What then does it mean when Tocqueville says that when I see another I see myself, and likewise when I see myself, I see another? To further explore this, let us look at what Tocqueville says about the poetry of democratic societies.

Tocqueville notes that America has not yet found a great poet, but that he is sure that it will as soon as it comes to terms with what must be the subject matter of its poetry. (One should note here that by poetry Tocqueville means artistic representation, or rather presentation, in general. He includes painting, for instance.) Tocqueville argues that there will be democratic poetry when poets recognize and acknowledge that what democracy makes available is the human species as and in itself.

> In democratic ages, the extreme mobility of people and their impatient desires lead them to move from one place to another without pause, and the inhabitants of different countries mix together, see each other, listen to each other. It is not only the members of the same nation who come to resemble each other; nations assimilate themselves one to another and all together they constitute for the eye of the spectator only a vast democracy of which each citizen is a people."[32]

Tocqueville's discussion goes on to suggest that it is only in a democratic society that "one can form a picture . . . in which a nation counts as a single citizen." Thus, he concludes, *"for the first time this places in clear daylight the figure of the human species* [italics added]."[33]

Democratic poetry, it would appear, makes available the understanding of the human that Rousseau sought in the (de)construction of the state of nature. What, one might ask, does it mean to see the world as a democratic poet would see it? For Tocqueville, several matters are involved here. The first is the very possibility of the continuation of poetry as a human activity in a new age. "The spread of equality of the earth," he writes, "dries up the old springs of poetry. We must try to show how other springs are revealed." Some of these new sources will have to do with what the democracy of belief has done to that which can serve as subject for poetry. Importantly, poetry is, as Tocqueville continues, the depiction and portrayal of the "ideal."[34] Poetry, he continues, presents to the spirit a "superior image." In aristocratic and past times, the vision of the poet was directed, as it were, upwards, but now "doubt brings . . . the imagination of [democratic] poets back to earth and closes them into the visible and real world."[35] Democracy thus allows, although it does not require, a new focus—for poetry, for politics. This focus will be this earth, the human itself. Whereas in aristocratic societies past, individuals are idealized as the exaltation of the present, in democratic ones no "individual in particular can be subject for portrayal."[36] Thus: "I am convinced that, in the end, democracy turns the imagination away from all that is external to humans, to fix it only on the human."[37]

The ideal of democratic society is the human, understood by Tocqueville (as by Rousseau) as that which is the same in me as it is in you. The subject of poetry in democratic societies is not the superior man, nor nature; it is certainly not community, and not even properly the depiction of the self. What does it give its reader?

> In democratic societies, where all are very small (*très petits*) and much alike, each, in considering himself, sees at that moment all the others.[38]

I think Tocqueville means here exactly what he says. It is not that I see a great community in the vista of democratic poetry but that I see, as I see myself, every other as myself. This is not identity but commonalty as a topic. This vision holds that from the point of view of democratic politics (and poetry) anything that can happen to anyone can happen to me. Anything that anyone can be, I can be. In principle at least, no identity is foreclosed on the basis of race, color, creed, ethnicity, gender—anything.[39] And likewise, no identity of self can claim any privilege over any other. We *are* nothing. In fact, Tocqueville is careful to say, this is a historically notable achievement (or will be when Walt Whitman starts publishing) for "the most profound and greatest geniuses of Greece and Rome never arrived at this idea, at once so general and so simple, of the likeness of human beings and the equal right to liberty that each of them brings by birth."[40] Democratic poetry thus introduces an idea that Tocqueville finds to be at least on a par with and probably greater than anything achieved by Plato, Aristotle, or Cicero. Democracy makes the human possible. He writes: "All that has to do with the existence of the human species taken as a whole, to its vicissitudes, its future, becomes a very productive (*féconde*) mine for poetry."[41]

Tocqueville goes on to argue that precisely the quality of democratic societies focusing on "the human species itself" produces a transformation in the status of religion. Although religious faith is often precarious in democratic societies (in part because the belief in intermediary powers such as saints, priests, cardinals, and popes is weakened), humans become increasingly disposed to develop a more extensive idea of the divinity itself, as coextensive with all that exitsts, for now the entire human species appears to be following the same path. Tocqueville here anticipates Emerson's recovery and sacramentalization of the ordinary. Emerson writes: "Other world! there is no other world. God is one and omnipresent; here or nowhere is the whole fact."[42]

It is the case, then, that both Tocqueville and Rousseau have a conception of the human as that which is the common share to all human beings. For Tocqueville, insofar as a democratic society is capable of idealization, it will focus on the human. For Rousseau, insofar as human beings act like human beings, their actions will rest upon the acknowledgment of the commonalty of each human being. For both, the human is a condition that is prior to all definition of self: it is in fact that which resists definition as limiting and as engendering a false concrete.

Both writers have an understanding of what it means to have a society in which the human would be immanent. Neither, however, thinks that a society that rests on the human would be stable. Human beings do not live in the human. Or, more precisely, the manner in which they live tends to hide, forget, or abandon the human. Rousseau traces the accidental but essentially unavoidable rise of inequalities. Tocqueville remarks upon the "love of material enjoyments, the idea of the better, competition, the immediate charm of success," and calls them the spurs that prod each individual along a particular path.[43] Why is it that living in and with the human is so difficult?

Let us look first at Rousseau. History—that is, the sense that persons have of having been and of going to be—is for Rousseau the history of inequality. Inequality, for Rousseau, is the particular definition of the self by reference to differences between oneself and another. Rousseau lays out the dynamic of this process quite clearly in the second part of *Discourse on Inequality*. Those who have, trick those who do not have into formalizing their relationships, or rely on the gullibility of the have-nots to achieve that end. This effectuates the establishment of law and right of property: the world now knows rich and poor. This in turn is followed by institution of magistracy, and rich and poor now take shape as the strong and the weak. Finally, strength is transformed into arbitrary power: master and slave. This last is the "ultimate degree of inequality": Rousseau refers to it as a second state of nature, as all have become the same, but are not in any way *human* beings. Society rests on an illusion: the only question will be what illusion it rests on.[44] Thus, that which defines humans as persons, but not as human, is historically acquired.

Compare to Tocqueville. In a number of places, he is struck by the unsettled quality of America:[45]

An American takes up, leaves and takes up again ten situations over the courses of his life; he changes without stopping his place of abode and constantly creates new places to live. Less than any other man of the world is he afraid to risk an acquired fortune, for he knows how easily he may a acquire a new one. In fact, change appears to him to be the natural human state. And how could it be otherwise? All is in ceaseless motion around him: laws, opinions, public figures (*fonctionnaires*), fortunes; the earth itself changes appearance every day. In the middle of this universal movement, the American would not know how to be still.[46]

An entire chapter of the second volume of *Democracy in America* is entitled "Why there is so much Disquiet among Americans in the Midst of

Prosperity," in which he ascribes that disquiet to the "constant strife between the desires inspired by equality and the means it supplies to satisfy them."[47]

Here the analysis is very close to that of *Second Discourse*. The constant
motion of Americans is a consequence (but is it the only possible one?)
to what I might call (with apologies) their ontic motility. For Rousseau,
after a set of circumstances that were not necessary but which, because
of their contingency (*"des faits qui pouvaient être ou ne pas être"*) have become universal, human beings came to judge and understand themselves
in relation to their *amour propre*. That is, what each thinks him or herself
to be and to be worth is consequent to judgments that compare one to
another. For Rousseau, such a state, that of inequality, is contrary to that
which is human, for it avoids the manner in which each is the same as
the other. Rather it focuses on the fact that some will have more and some
less. What is important here, and most often missed in understandings
of Rousseau, is that we can only have a sense of inequality if we have or
retain some sense of our equality in the human. The realm of inequality
rests, therefore, upon the presumption that such a state of affairs is unjust. And this must carry always the sense that it can be legitimately rectified. To deny that injustice can and should be rectified is, for Rousseau,
to deny the human in ourselves, something which he came to think characterized most of his age. In the first line of *Rêveries*, he will announce
himself as the only human on earth; *Confessions* is a portrait of not so much
of him as of the human, of which he is, he says, the only publicly available exemplar.[48]

In Rousseau, modern humans are distinguished by two characteristics.
First, they are in constant motion. In modern society, individuals live not
as themselves. "The citizen, always active, sweats, scurries, constantly
agonizes in search of still more strenuous occupations: he works to his
death, even rushes towards it to be in a position to live. . . . The sociable
man, always outside himself, only knows how to live in the opinion of
others, and, so to speak, derives the sentiment of his own existence solely
from their judgment."[49]

Secondly, political relations between modern humans tend to reduce
themselves to relations of force and domination. Rousseau's description
of the modern man is remarkably similar to that of Tocqueville. It is true
that his tone is different: the difference comes from the fact that Rousseau
writes of these beings as already enmeshed in power relations—we are
at the third stage of the second part of the development of inequality. For
Rousseau, the point of *Second Discourse* is to trace out the developments
of modernity to which a society of *The Social Contract* will have to respond,
specifically the tendency of modernity to engender tyranny.

Here is the last stage of inequality, and the ultimate point which closes the circle and meets the point from which we set out: Here all private individuals again become equal, because they are nothing. . . . Here everything reverts to the sole law of the stronger and consequently to a new state of nature.[50]

Tocqueville, on the other hand, writes when the possibility of tyranny is visible but not yet actual. He notes, in an extension of his discussion of mobility, that "when any nation has, in a short period of time, changed leaders, opinions and laws, those who make up that nation end by acquiring a taste for movement and by becoming accustomed to change made rapid by the help of force. They thus naturally develop disdain for forms (*les formes*) of which they each day see the impotence, and they only endure with impatience the rule of law (*l'empire de la règle*) from which one has withdrawn so many times."[51] Tocqueville has, in other words, identified in America a situation where two possible tracks are visible, to him at least. In fact, after the chapter on democratic poetry, there follows one on theater, one on historians, and another on public speaking—all forms of rhetoric in a democratic society. With that he ends the first part of the second volume and turns to a consideration of the dangers of what he calls "individualism" and the possibility that in democratic societies this individualism will be combated through free institutions.[52] (Here it is worth noting that Tocqueville criticized his translator Reeve for making the English translation of *Democracy in America* sound too critical of democracy.)[53]

For both thinkers, the consequence of this restlessness (and also the premise for free institutions) is that each become nothing. As Emerson remarked: "Things are in the saddle and ride mankind." Humans have no definition of their own at all.

To designate Rousseau as a proponent of equality is, then, to miss the point. Equality is being like something else. But Rousseau is not here distressed that one be like someone else—being like is not what pertains to the *moi commun*. He is concerned with the way in which one is exactly like another, the way and the extent to which I find you in me as me, and me in you as you. Rousseau is not a proponent of equality but a theorist of commonality and of freedom. He is quite clear (see the end of the *Discourse on the Origin of Inequality*) that human beings can be equal without being free. Freedom is made possible by, and requires the acknowledgment of, our commonalty and the institutions appropriate to that commonalty.

Rousseau uses the word "common" to refer to a human context and "general" to refer to a political one. By both usages, he means the way and the extent to which I am exactly like you. Having something in common is thus sharing the ordinary, the vulgar. Thus, the general will can refer only to that which is exactly the same for me as it is for you. Anything that differentiates us is not a proper matter for the general will—it is not of the *moi commun*, which is the you that is me and the me that is you. (We might think of this as the grammar of the language of the human.) But that differentiation, it is important to realize, can only take place, only be a differentiation, if there exists a ground of and in the common. Any differentiation that does not retain and embody the common will produce inequality, the opposite of which for Rousseau is not equality but commonalty. (In this sense, Rousseau is not an egalitarian.) It will also, as Rousseau is at pains to show in *Second Discourse*, culminate in the dehumanizing of humans, that is, as existing only in and as their acquired qualities, thus as nonbeings. Humans are then in a perverse sense equal again, but it is an equality to which they have no access.

Nor is Tocqueville a proponent of equality. He wants to deal with it, for equality is (increasingly) given.[54] The analysis of equality as equality (in Tocqueville) is clearly related to that which one finds in Rousseau. "Equality places humans the one side by side with the other, without a common tie that might hold them. Despotism raises barriers between them and separates them. It disposes them not to think of those who are like them and makes a sort of public virtue of indifference. Despotism, dangerous at all times, is thus particularly to be feared in democratic centuries."[55]

What is key here is that the development of inequality leads to all becoming nothing in face of tyranny. There is thus no practical political contradiction between Rousseau's picture of the evolution of society and that in Tocqueville. For both, the political problem consists in determining what path might be taken from equality.

WHAT MIGHT BE DONE ABOUT MODERN POLITICS?

Is a human politics possible on the basis of the acceptance of these conditions? Any vision of human beings that rests on such an acceptance will, of necessity, have a politics characterized by three qualities. First, no human being can be understood as privileged in his or her access to the most important things, be these God, power, or knowledge. Secondly, whatever quality is required for someone to be a participant in the political realm must be, in principle, available to all. It is not the case that this implies that character or ideas of the good are irrelevant (as later liberalism, for example, Rawls would argue), but that to the degree that such ideas came into play, all persons have to be capable of them. Lastly, such a vision of human beings implies that the status of government is always contingent and can rest on no natural or necessary human quality.[56]

What would such a politics entail? Can one find it in Rousseau and Tocqueville? What is given up and what gained? To make this matter clearer, I would like here to engage in a short excursus to a solution that has been offered—both in the nineteenth century and in the present—in order to contrast it, partially, with those of Tocqueville and Rousseau.

For both Rousseau and Tocqueville, the human is defined as the acknowledgment of the manner in which I am exactly the same as you. Suppose we ask what may be the claim that the political realm might have on our lives.[57] Such a question is at the heart of the philosophy of one American who thought deeply about these questions during Tocqueville's time: Ralph Waldo Emerson.[58] Politics is, as all have known since Plato, the realm of appearance, of surface and outline. Emerson's writings seek— they can be read as seeking—to make us transparent to the claims of politics, that is, to have us live in the political realm but not be of it.[59] Transparency of the self is necessary to democratic politics, in this view, if we are not to be caught in outline, made into a cartoon. Democratic politics is thus the politics that allows the most motility to the self.

In his great essay "Experience" and elsewhere, Emerson addresses the appeals of community,[60] aware that these appeals are most often the stuff of the Cave, what Emerson calls in the poem epigraph to "Experience," the "lords of life." He counterposes to this temptation the vision of this passage from "New England Reformers":

> The world is awakening to the idea of union, and these experiments show what it is thinking of. It is and will be magic. . . . But this union must be inward, and not one of covenants, and is to be reached by a reverse of the methods they [the New England Reformers] use. *The union is only perfect, when all uniters are isolated* [italics added]. It is the union of friends who live in different streets or towns.[61]

Or, I might add, coasts and countries. In "Experience," Emerson refers to this as "Consanguinity." Nothing could be less spatially situated than this. Emerson's vision of union is not and cannot be spatial, for space is what causes our vision to rest on surfaces and outlines. He seeks to ensure that our non-definition, which he, like Rousseau and Tocqueville, understands as necessary to our humanness, remains immaculate. I find much attractive here in Emerson; but there are prices to pay, and perhaps not only personal ones.

To be in the same space as someone is to be near that person, to have a share with him, to have the everyday, the ordinary in common with him. What is it to be near to someone, to share with someone? Martin Heidegger remarks in "The Thing" that "the frantic abolition of all distances brings no nearness; for nearness does not consist in the shortness of distance."[62] In "Self-Reliance," Emerson, like Hawthorne in *The House of the Seven Gables*, attacks traveling, calling it a "fool's paradise." The reasons are, however, different. Hawthorne thought travel often to be an attempt at escaping the space of our home.[63] For Emerson, the danger with traveling is that it leads us to bring things back, to imitate, to quote others.[64] The reason this is bad, presumably, is that no imitator can be a genius, and genius is the tonic of the essay.

> To believe in your own thought, to believe that what is true for you in your private heart is true for all—that is genius.[65]

In *The American Scholar*, Emerson calls genius "the sound estate of everyman."[66] Genius is the basis for the democratic polity as Emerson envisages it. Hegel, whom Emerson surely had in mind here, caught this well. In a passage that partially echoes in "Self-Reliance" and "New England Reformers," Hegel wrote in *The Phenomenology of Spirit*:

> It is the moral genius which knows the inner voice of what it immediately knows to be a divine voice; and since, in knowing this, it has an equally immediate knowledge of existence, it is the divine creative power which in its Notion possesses the spontaneity of life. Equally it is its own self divine worship, for its action is the contemplation of its own divinity. This solitary divine worship is at the same time essentially the divine worship of a community.[67]

This passage is from the section "The Beautiful Soul" and calls to mind Tocqueville's discussion of poetry in a democratic society. As is known, Hegel goes on to suggest that in this state one is assured of always being right without regard to what one is right about. The "beautiful soul" cannot externalize itself and endure existence.

Such a soul thus has no need to exist in space, that is, to exist in a world where one is necessarily caught by the sight of others. In some awful way it is parasitical. (Rousseau knew this, as I have argued, and made it the basis of both the awful realm of inequality and the society of the social contract.) But Hegel's critique of the limitations of the beautiful soul does not completely capture the Emersonian notion of genius. Emerson's notion—and thus possibly the self of democratic poetry—is both subject and not subject to Hegel's critique.

Clearly, genius as Emerson understands it would be impossible unless I know that I am not alone in the world. How then does Emerson's genius know that? One answer is that she or he lets himself or herself be known. But how might this happen? The Emersonian answer is in the notion of provocation. In the "Divinity School Address," he writes:

Truly it is not instruction but provocation that I can receive from another soul. What he announces I must find true in me, or wholly reject."[68]

Does commonalty threaten Emerson here? When I find myself in you and you in me, surely reciprocal acknowledgment cannot be far behind. In Hegel, the spirit will move on to embodiment. It is, however, essential to Emerson that no self-reliant person so provoked—so revealed—be caught unthinkingly twice in the same self. This is why "Experience" is intended as the cure to the danger of permanence, of a self-imitation that will destroy the genius of democracy and the democratic geniuses. In "Experience":

> Our love of the real draws us to permanence, but health of the body consists in circulation, and sanity of mind in variety or facility of association. We need change of objects. Dedication to one thought is quickly odious.[69]

This, for Emerson, is the demand of honesty, and, explicitly, not that of morality.[70] This is Emerson at his most radical: life is a miracle, has no memory—"I am ready to die out of nature and be born again into this new yet unapproachable America I have found in the West." For Emerson, this provides a way of being American that is constantly that of genius.

Can we, can one—who can—live like this? To what dangers does it open America? Emerson continues: "It is very unhappy, but too late to be helped, the discovery we have made that we exist" (presumably as Americans). Emerson calls this discovery "the Fall." The reason it is unhappy is that such a self will combine the worst of all worlds. The "Fallen American Self" will be without moral restraint ("Civilized in externals but a savage at heart," says Melville in *Israel Potter*), but self-certain of a given identity. There is, I believe, even in Emerson a recognition of the lack of restraint built into the democratic genius. "Where do we find ourselves?": the opening line of "Experience"—a dangerous answer is given after "the Fall" and given in action.

Emerson would have us not discover that we exist. He aims and hopes to counter the dangers of what Tocqueville calls individualism by ensuring that each of us never becomes dedicated to any one thing. He insists upon and even intensifies the motility that characterizes democratic man—he is as aware as Tocqueville and Rousseau of the temptation to be some thing, any thing. As Nietzsche wrote at the very end of the *Genealogy of Morals*: "One would rather will the void than be void of will."

Emerson is worried that we will be tempted to find ourselves and thus lose our humanness. Where do Rousseau and Tocqueville stand on this? Rousseau's answer to the question of where human beings might find themselves is given in *The Social Contract* and *Émile*.[71] There, society is based on the premise of the existence of modern human beings—that is, ones with the experience of inequality and indeed ones to whom the extremes of inequality have returned the recognition of the qualitative nullity. (There is at least a half-truth to the 1871 Commune chorus: "*Nous ne sommes rien, nous serons tout.*") The entire text of the first three books of *Social Contract* is a determination of what institutions can be built upon the sole acknowledgment of the way in which I am the same as you. The last book is an analysis of the way the passage of time affects such institutions and what may be done about time.

Tocqueville's answer to the question of where we find ourselves—if one can imagine this question to be his—must be "in America." And like Rousseau, that which makes a polity what it is, here makes America American, is the development of its free institutions. Tocqueville dedicates an entire chapter to these. He admires especially the way in which American institutions give the citizen something of his own to be concerned with—that they are parochial rather than global. Americans, he says flatly, "have fought the individualism that equality gives rise to by freedom, and they have conquered it."[72]

But this is not the vision of institutions as transmitters and aggregators of revealed preferences, adequate in and of themselves, in the manner of the "new institutionalism" of contemporary American political science. What Tocqueville likes is the quality of relations between human beings that these institutions make possible. Consider the following passages:

> From the moment that common matters are treated in common, each person perceives that he is not as independent of those like him as he first thought. . . . It thus happens that one thinks of those like oneself by ambition and that often one finds it in some manner in one's interest to forget oneself . . . American legislators . . . thought it proper to give a political life to each portion of the territory, so as to multiply to infinity, for the citizens, the opportunities to act together (*ensemble*), and to make them feel every day that they are dependent the one on the other. . . . The free institutions which the inhabitants of the United States have, and the political rights of which they make so much use, recall without ceasing, and in a thousand ways, to each citizen, that he lives with others (*en société*).[73]

The freedom of American institutions then consists in the fact that they require that each acknowledge and recognize that he or she lives with others. Tocqueville does not like these institutions for reasons that are Mandevilleian or those typically thought to be Madisonian.[74] This is not pluralism. Nor is this Constantian public/private. Instead, the institutions counter the despotic track that equality of conditions opens up, life in what Michael Walzer once called "a society of strangers."[75] They make it possible to avoid what Robert Frost lamented some hundred years later: "All they maintain the path for is the comfort / Of visiting with the equally bewildered. / Nearer in plight their neighbors are than distance."[76]

For Tocqueville, the genius of American political institutions is that they permit and require a sacramental reaffirmation that I and Other are one.

WHAT IS THE ROLE, THEN, OF THE POLITICAL THEORIST?

Frost continues the poem cited above with the worry that "I fear they shall never know where they are." It seems to me clear from the above that one cannot convince someone of his commonalty with someone else. Like McWilliams's fraternity, it is to be chosen when come upon. But then, why write political theory? I wish to claim that part of the enterprise of political theory in the contemporary world (including at least those who have a call upon our attention) is the recognition that no writer can claim privilege over his or her material. I mean that the appeal to a standard or positions transcending the human world is, in all cases, illegitimate. This does not imply that there are no universals—it means only that they do not have the character of being transcendental. Take for instance the most central of Tocqueville's convictions, that of the gradual development of equality. This is a "providential fact [and thus has its] principal qualities: it is universal, it is lasting, it escapes every day from human abilities; all occurrences, as well as all humans, assist in its development." Tocqueville avers that he writes these lines in "a sort of religious terror." [77] It is "a sort" because it comes from experience and not from hearing God speak. Tocqueville indicates that he has had no more need to hear God on this matter than he would have had had he been observing the movement of the stars.

This matter is all the more difficult for Tocqueville as his concern (as had been Machiavelli's)[78] is with "new objects." Tocqueville writes: "One must not forget either that the author who wishes to make himself understood is obliged to push each of his ideas to their theoretical consequences, often to the limits of the wrong and the impracticable; for if it is sometimes necessary to set oneself apart from the rule of logic in ones [sic] actions, one would not do the same in speech (*dans les discours*), and a person finds almost as much difficulties in being without consequence in what he says as he usually encounters in having a consequence to his acts." [79]

If I read this correctly, Tocqueville is saying that his writing endeavors to be without consequences, that is, to present itself as science, as the way that the world is. In an address to the *Académie des sciences morales et politiques*, he sees the role of the scientist as teaching "the most appropriate laws for the permanent and general condition of humankind."[80] This, however, he firmly rests in the world of ideas and therefore finds science inappropriate for "the mob, which only obeys the logic of their passions." Tocqueville's writing does not and cannot influence the way the world is— that is left to "the art of government." The distinction rests on the deep, deep gulf that Tocqueville found between the rational and the emotional.[81] This was not something that set easily with him, but it was, he thought, inevitable. In 1843, lamenting his lack of political influence, he writes to his friend Kergorlay:

> Like all complex ideas, mine cannot be understood but through the study of a large number of particular facts and will never penetrate deeply into the mob. It is not of a sort to seize or passionately engage a large number of men, not to serve as a visible goal for the efforts of some political party.[82]

Here Rousseau conceives of his authorial presence differently. He responds directly to the central fact of modernity—that what is lacking for a just world cannot be given didactically to others. If a human politics in our times rests upon the possibility of the acknowledgment of the common, it then rests on what Rousseau called sentiment. It relies on a quality that humans must acknowledge, but which they cannot be taught. Rousseau hoped to exercise this quality by being convincing, as he put it, "without persuading." Most of the time, therefore, Rousseau eschews what might be called argument in the presentation of his teaching. His writings are filled with images so striking that one cannot but react to them.[83] As noted above, the whole of *Confessions* is to present a "portrait of the human" (not precisely of himself) such that readers can see what a world in which humans lived was like. Hence, Rousseau thinks of himself not as the last man, but as the only human: there is a sense in which he hopes, as *Dialogues* make evident, that a human world may be reborn from the acknowledgment of his presence in it.[84] What Rousseau is after is, he is convinced, so close to every eye that all (almost all) deny seeing it. He writes to make the human evident, available, and to make persons incapable of refusing its acknowledgment. He writes as the last and first of humankind; he sees differently.

Tocqueville, as he himself says, sees further. He does not have that passionate sense of separateness; rather he cultivates, as the tone of *Souvenirs* makes clear, a pathos of noble distance. In a marginal annotation to *Souvenirs*, he writes that "[t]he only true portraits are those made not to be shown."[85] Tocqueville writes as he does so as to create in his readers the sense that equality is inevitable, in the way that the will of God is and was inevitable. His is not a fatalistic acceptance of an inevitable process but a desire to show that process in such a way that humans will accept it *as if it were* fated. He wants to convince humans that the progressive development of equality has the quality of being a divine command. He writes:

> If long observations and sincere reflection bring the men of our times to admit that the gradual and progressive development of equality is at once the past and future of their history, this discovery will of itself give to this development the sacred quality of the will of the lord and master (*du souverain maître*). To wish to stop democracy will thus appear to be to struggle against God Himself, and it will only be left to countries to accommodate themselves to the social state that Providence imposes on them.[86]

This is not a claim that God has willed equality, nor that God governs human affairs. It is a claim that if we think that Providence shapes human affairs, we will deal with them better. And the writing of his books is designed to reflect that claim.

Is the distance achieved in Tocqueville's approach to writing political theory adequate to the circumstances he depicts? I am not talking here about Tocqueville's *parti pris* vis-à-vis the categories that he picks to analyze, say, France in 1848.[87] Rather, and for instance: just before the June Days (22 to 26 June 1848), Tocqueville has dinner in Paris at the home of Richard Milnes, Lord Houghton. Milnes was a member of the British Parliament. Among the guests was Georges Sand, next to whom Tocqueville was seated. Tocqueville records:

> I had strong prejudices against Madame Sand, for I detest women who write, especially those who disguise the weaknesses of their sex in some system, rather than interesting us by making us see them as they actually are; despite this, I liked her (*elle me plut*). [There follow comments about her appearance, mainly critical.] We spoke for an hour about what was going on (*des affaires publiques*); one could speak of nothing else at that time. Besides, Madame Sand was then a sort of political personage (*homme politique*); what she said on the subject struck me sharply; it was the first time that I had entered into a direct and friendly relation with a person who could and did tell me what was going on in the camp of our adversaries. The sides did not know each other. . . . Madame Sand gave me a very detailed portrait of the state of the workers of Paris. . . . I thought her picture overloaded and it was not: that which followed showed this clearly.[88]

What is striking here is not so much the attitude toward "women who write," but the fact that Tocqueville has a distance on his opponents that keeps him from acknowledging them. They are like strangers to him: and being like strangers, the risk will be that he finds nothing of himself in common with them. It clearly never occurred to him to go to the streets and ask his facts from those on the other side of the barricades. His distance keeps him from seeing them. For instance:

It was then that I saw appear and take his turn at the podium a man whom I only saw that day, but the memory of whom has always filled me with disgust and horror; he had haggard and withered cheeks, white lips, the appearance of being sick, mean and filthy; his body seemed mildewed; he wore no visible linen and an old black smock was pasted on his slender and emaciated arms and legs. He seems to have lived in the sewer and to have just left it. I was told that it was Blanqui.[89]

This Blanqui is the brother of Adolphe Blanqui, an economist and member of the *Institut*, whom Tocqueville refers to as his *"confrère."*[90] Could one say that this is what Tocqueville told himself in order not to see the brother of his brother in this state? Perhaps, but he wrote it down. Brothers do not write on brothers. The distance that Tocqueville achieves is consequent, I think, to the privilege that his science gave him. Rousseau, I think, rather sought to avoid such privilege. Perhaps the duality of these understandings form the basis of what McWilliams has called "the ambiguous ideal" of fraternity—in America, in any place we find ourselves.

NOTES

1. Friedrich Nietzche, *The Gay Science* (New York: Vintage, 1974), sec. 356 (emphasis in original).
2. Wilson Carey McWilliams, *The Idea of Fraternity in America* (Berkeley and Los Angeles: University of California Press, 1973).
3. Indeed, Tocqueville himself seems to indicate that Rousseau, and the reality and ideal of fraternity, was but a late addition to the increasingly heady mixture of the French Revolution. In *The European Revolution*, he avers that at the start of the revolution, one heard mainly Montesquieu cited, whereas at the end, "no one [was] but Rousseau."
4. For the view that Tocqueville intends his work as a correction to excesses (against liberalism) in Rousseau, see Sanford Lakoff, "Liberty, Equality, Democracy: Tocqueville's Response to Rousseau," in *Life, Liberties and the Public Good: New Essays in Political Theory for Maurice Cranston*, ed. George Feaver and Frederick Rosen (Basingstoke, England: Macmillan, 1987), 101–21.
5. Alexis de Tocqueville, letter to Kergorlay, 10 November 1836, *Oeuvres, Papiers correspondance*, ed. J. P. Mayer (Paris: Gallimard, 1951), 10:148. This letter is not included in Roger Boesche's excellent edition of the letters, *Selected Letters on Politics and Society*, ed. Roger Boesche (Berkeley and Los Angeles: University of California Press, 1985) (hereafter cited as *SL*).
6. The various interpretations that have been given are well set out in the notes to Peter Augustine Lawler's important book, *The Restless Mind: Alexis de*

Tocqueville on the Origin and Perpetuation of Human Liberty (Lanham, Md.: Rowman and Littlefield, 1993), hereafter cited as *Restless Mind*. I came upon Lawler's book when I had written about half of this essay. I have tried to overlap as little as possible (albeit, I recognize, inadequately) with his impressive treatment of the topics here addressed. Lawler argues that democratic society produces an incoherent soul, and that this is possibly a good thing in that it allows democratic citizens the possiblity of encountering the meaninglessness of life, and opens the door to the diversions from such an encounter that are necessary. Tocqueville, Lawler argues, shares much of this soul and the need for these diversions. He chooses to divert himself to politics. Americans, most of the time, have taken as their diversion the pursuit of materialism. This is regrettable, although rarely dangerous; importantly, it is not necessary. The strongest claim of Tocqueville's indebtedness to Rousseau is made by John Koritansky, *Alexis de Tocqueville and the New Science of Politics: An Interpretation of Democracy in America* (Durham, N.C.: Carolina Academic Press, 1986).

7. "*du Jean-Jacques retouché par une cuisinière du XIXième siècle.*" See Tocqueville, *Souvenirs* (Paris: Gallimard, 1942), 29, hereafter cited as *S*.

8. Lawler has done an excellent job of tracing the importance of Pascal in Tocqueville. He downplays, properly I think, the actual importance of Montesquieu (cf. con. Jean-Claude Lamberti, *Tocqueville et les deux "Démocraties"* [Paris: PUF, 1983]). There is no doubt that Tocqueville has Montesquieuian categories in mind when doing the preparatory work for *De la démocratie en Amérique*—his notebooks are full of them. But when he proclaims, "The government that is called mixed has always seemed to me a chimera," and attributes this to the fact that each society has a *principe*—presumably a different investigation than that of the *esprit* of laws—he is clearly on non-Montesquieuian grounds. See Tocqueville, *De la démocratie en Amerique, Oeuvres*, ed. André Jardin, with an introduction by Jean-Claude Lamberti (Paris: Gallimard, 1992), 2:289, hereafter cited as *DA*.

9. Benjamin Constant, "*De la liberté des anciens et des modernes*," in *Oeuvres*, ed. Alfred Rowlin (Paris: Gallimard, 1964). The best and most sympathetic exposition of this argument can be found in Stephen Holmes, *Benjamin Constant and the Making of Modern Liberalism* (New Haven, Conn.: Yale University Press, 1984).

10. McWilliams, *The Idea of Fraternity in America*, 499.

11. Tracy B. Strong, *Jean Jacques Rousseau. The Politics of the Ordinary* (Thousand Oaks, Calif.: SAGE, 1994).

12. I take the question from Georg Simmel's classic essay "How is Society Possible?" in *Philosophy of the Social Sciences*, ed. Maurice Natanson (New York: Random House, 1963).

13. Pierre Manent, *Tocqueville and the Nature of Democracy* (Lanham, Md.: Rowman and Littlefield, 1996), 65.

14. Jean-Jacques Rousseau, "Lettre à de Beaumont," in *Oeuvres Complètes en cinq volumes* (Paris: Gallimard, 1965), 4:936, hereafter cited as *OC*.

15. Rousseau, *Discourse on the Origins of Inequality* 1, *OC*, iii, 160–61, hereafter cited as *DOI*.

16. Can one call them human? Yes, in the way that one can call a fetus human. Can one call them persons? No, in the way that one cannot call a fetus a person.

17. *Amour de soi* (self-love) is the quality that leads one to want to continue alive; pity is the fact that when one sees another human being (indeed, any being that can suffer), one recognizes that being as like oneself.

18. Lest my "humans" (for *hommes*) be taken as a surfeit of political correctness, let me point out that *homme* in French derives ultimately from the Sanskrit word for earth and signifies beings of this world as opposed to gods. So also human, but not "man." See the discussion in Strong, *Jean-Jacques Rousseau and the Politics of the Ordinary*, and Emile Benveniste, *Le vocabulaire des institutions indo-européens*, (Paris: Minuit, 1969), 2:180.

19. I take the term from Stanley Cavell. See, inter alia, "Knowing and Acknowledging," in his *Must We Mean What We Say?* (New York: Scribner's, 1969). See the comments in Hilary Putnam, *Renewing Philosophy* (Cambridge, Mass.: Harvard University Press, 1992) 177–78.

20. But humans are not the same as dogs, if only for the reasons implied in an answer to Ludwig Wittgenstein's question: "Why can a dog simulate pain? Is he too honest?" Wittgenstein, *Philosophical Investigations*, trans. G. E. M. Anscombe, ed. Anscombe and Rush Rhees (Malden, Mass.: Blackwell, 1997), 90.

21. This is the source of Marx's closeness to Rousseau and why capitalism is a denial of humanness, even if there is nothing more human than to want to maintain capitalism.

22. See the discussion in McWilliams, *The Idea of Fraternity in America*, chap. 3.

23. Emerson's term is in "The Divinity School Address," in *Essays and Lectures*, ed. Joel E. Porte (New York: Library of America, 1983), 79. For a discussion, see "Nietzsche's Political Aesthetics," in *Nietzsche's New Seas*, ed. Michael Gillespie and Tracy B. Strong (Chicago: University of Chicago Press, 1991).

24. *DA* II, iii, 1 Pléiade, 678–80.

25. Foucault does not cite this passage from *DA* in *Surveiller et Punir* (Paris: Gallimard, 1975); he does however cite Tocqueville and Beaumont's reports on prisons, 239-42. See Gustave Auguste de Beaumont de la Bonninière and Alexis, comte de Tocqueville. *Système pénitentiaire aux États-Unis et de son application en France; suivi d'un appendice sur les colonies pénales, et de notes statistiques, Augm. du Rapport de M. de Tocqueville sur le projet de réforme des prisons, et du texte de la loi adoptée par la Chambre des députés* (Paris: C. Gossselin, 1845), 446.

26. Democracy in Rousseau designates on the other hand only the form of administration where the government (as opposed to the sovereign) is made up of all the people. Rousseau does not apply the notion of democracy to sovereignty. There is nothing in *The Social Contract* that makes impossible a government of the one, or of the few. But this government (*l'administration*) must, for there to be political right, correspond to a sovereignty of the common or general. As the sovereign is unitary and made up of that which is common (in the sense described above) it will be able to deal only with matters that are general or common. See the detailed discussion in Strong, *Jean-Jacques Rousseau*, chap. 3.

27. Recall here Tocqueville's story of two Englishmen from different classes who run into each other "*aux antipodes*" and spend their time together avoiding an encounter, *DA* II, iii, 2 Pléiade, 680–81.

28. *DA* I, ii, 9 Pléiade, 321.

29. In America, humans are "born equal rather than become so." *DA* II, ii, 3 Pléiade, 615. I cannot refrain from noting that it is a sign of the limitations of Louis Hartz's reading of America (*The Liberal Tradition in America*) that when using this passage as his epigraph, in the first two editions, "equal" is given as "free" (with an erratum slip added to the second edition).

30. *DA* II, iii, 1 Pléiade, 680. Pierre Manent also cites this passage during an interesting discussion of the status of the other in democracies. See *Tocqueville and the Nature of Democracy*, 48 ff.

31. Lawler, *Restless Mind*, 41.

32. *DA* II, 1, 17 Pléiade, 587.

33. There are obvious links here to Marx's argument that humanity is realized with the *Gattungswesen*.

34. *DA* II, i, 17 Pléiade, 583. See the discussion of democratic poetry in Strong, "Politics and Transparency," in *Liberal Modernism and Democratic Individuality, Essays on the Work and Thought of George Kateb*, ed. Austin Sarat and Dana Villa (Princeton, N.J.: Princeton University Press, 1996), hereafter cited as as "Politics and Transparency."

35. Ibid., 584.

36. Ibid., 585.

37. Ibid., 586.

38. Ibid., 585.

39. I am not sure that Tocqueville would have gone this far, but the thought extends in this manner. It is exemplified best in the work of George Kateb. See his "Walt Whitman and the Culture of Democracy," in *The Self and the Political Order*, ed. Tracy B. Strong (Malden, Mass.: Blackwell, 1992) (reprinted with changes in Kateb, *The Inner Ocean* [Ithaca, N.Y.: Cornell University Press, 1994], and Strong, "Politics and Transparency."

40. *DA* II, i, 3 Pléiade, 526.

41. *DA* II, i, 17 Pléiade, 587.

42. Ralph Waldo Emerson, "Sovereignty of Ethics," in *Lectures and Biographical Sketches, The Complete Works*, ed. Edward Waldo Emerson (Boston: Houghton Mifflin, 1903), 10:199. Thanks to George Kateb for tracking down this citation. On Emerson, see Stanley Cavell, *In Pursuit of the Ordinary* (Cambridge, Mass.: Harvard University Press, 1988). Emerson dined with the Tocquevilles in Paris on 31 May 1848. He had been introduced by Richard Milnes, Lord Houghton, and recommended to them by John Stuart Mill. See Emerson, *The Journals and Miscellaneous Notebooks* (Cambridge, Mass.: Belknap Press, 1973), 10:532, and *Letters* (New York: Columbia University Press, 1939), 4:78 (letter to Lidian, 25 May 1848). I have found no account of the interaction between Tocqueville and Emerson, although Tocqueville thought well enough of him to propose him for election as a foreign member to the *Académie des Science Morales* in 1855; he was not elected. See letter from Tocqueville to Adolphe de Circourt, 25 January 1855, in *Oeuvres* (Paris: Gallimard, 1983), 18:240.

43. Strong, "Politics and Transparency," 584.

44. Though I cannot go into it here, there is a close genealogical relation of this text to Nietzsche's *Use and Misuse of History for Life*.

45. For a discussion of this in American literature, see Strong, "Politics and Transparency."

46. Tocqueville, *Voyages en Amérique*, Pléiade I, 30–31.

47. *DA* II, ii, 13 Pléiade, 650.

48. See the discussion in Strong, *Jean Jacques Rousseau*, chap. 1.

49. *DOI*, ii; *OC*, iii, 192–93.

50. *DOI*, ii; *OC*, iii, 191.

51. *DA* II, iv, 7 Pléiade, 846.

52. "Despotism, which is, in its nature, fearful sees in the isolation of humans the clearest sign of its continuance." *DA* II, ii, 4 Pléiade, 616.

53. *Correspondance anglaise*, in *Oeuvres*, 48.

54. For example, *DA* II, ii, 4 Pléiade, 620.

55. *DA* II, ii, 4 Pléiade, 616.

56. For an elaboration of this, see Strong, "Contract, Governance, and Contingency," in a book edited by Henrik Bang (forthcoming).

57. The next several paragraphs draw upon my "Politics and Transparency."

58. I might note that for me the most disappointing part of *The Idea of Fraternity in America* is the section on Emerson. Albeit with the advantage of twenty-five years of hindsight, let me offer the following pages as what might have been said.

59. That this does not mean withdrawal is clear from Emerson's own involvement in abolitionist politics of his time. On the other hand, he chose not to live at Brook Farm, not wanting, he said, "to remove from my present prison to a prison a little larger."

60. I must insist that community is not the same as commonalty.

61. Emerson, *Essays and Lectures*, 599 (my italics), hereafter cited as EL. See also the discussion in George Kateb, *Emerson and Thoreau* (Thousand Oaks, Calif.: SAGE, 1996).

62. Martin Heidegger, *Poetry, Language, Thought* (New York: Harper & Row, 1973), 165.

63. Aside from *The House of the Seven Gables*, "The Celestial Railroad," and other well-known texts, see Hawthorne, "Fragments from the Journal of a Solitary Man," in *Tales and Sketches* (New York: Library of America) 487–500.

64. *EL*, 277–79.

65. *EL*, 259.

66. *EL*, 57; one sees some echoes of this in the recent work of Benjamin R. Barber, *An Aristocracy of Everyone* (New York: Ballantine, 1992).

67. G. W. F. Hegel, *The Phenomenology of Spirit*, trans. A. V. Miller (New York: Oxford University Press, 1979), 397.

68. *EL*, 79.

69. *EL*, 476.

70. *EL*, 483.

71. I recognize this as bald assertion: for an argument, see Strong, *Jean-Jacques Rousseau*, chaps. 3 and 4.

72. *DA* II, ii, 4 Pléiade, 617.

73. *DA* II, ii, 4 Pléiade, 616–20.

74. See, however, the analysis of Madison in McWilliams, "Leo Strauss and America," *Review of Politics* (Spring 1998): 231–46.

75. Michael Walzer, *Obligations* (Cambridge, Mass.: Harvard University Press, 1970) 113; see J. Peter Euben, "Walzer's Obligations," *Philosophy and Public Affairs* I, no. 4 (summer 1972), 438–59, especially 445.

76. Robert Frost, "In the Clearing," in *In the Clearing* (New York: Holt, Rinehart and Winston, 1962), 16.

77. *DA* I, introduction to Pléiade 7.

78. And yet his attitude towards Machiavelli (at least *The Prince* and *History of Florence*) is negative. See his letter to Royer-Collard, 25 August 1836, in *SL*, 109–11.

79. *DA* I, introduction to Pléiade 17–18.

80. *Discours à l'Académie des sciences morales et politiques*, Pléiade II, 1216.

81. Tocqueville to Beaumont, 9 September 1850, *SL*, 186: "[I]t is not reason but passion that rules the world, or at least, reason only makes its way when she finds some passion that is willing to accompany her."

82. Letter to Kergorlay, *OC*, xiii, 2, 128–29. Cited from Pléiade II, 1654.

83. And indeed his contemporaries reacted. See Robert Darnton, "Readers' Response to Rousseau," in *The Great Cat Massacre and Other Episodes in French Cultural History* (London: Penguin, 1991), especially 235–38. See discussion in Strong, *Jean-Jacques Rousseau*, 8–12

84. For a full(er) elaboration of these claims see Strong, *Jean-Jacques Rousseau*, chaps. 1 and 2.

85. L. E. Shiner, *The Secret Mirror: Literary Form and History in Tocqueville's Recollections.* (Ithaca, N.Y.: Cornell University Press, 1988), 16. Rousseau writes rather that in modern times there are no longer any secrets (draft of a letter to Beaumont, *OC*, iv, 1020).

86. *DA* I, introduction to Pléiade 7; compare to Burke at the end of *Thoughts on French Affairs*.

87. See the table of polarities in Shiner, *The Secret Mirror*, 90.

88. *S*, 134. It is probable that Emerson was at this dinner. See note 42.

89. *S*, 120–21. Emerson, on the other hand, had gone to hear Blanqui give a speech. See *The Journals*, ed. William Gillman (Cambridge, Mass.: Harvard University Press), 10:323.

90. *S*, 140.

6

"Damn Your Eyes!" Thoreau on (Male) Friendship in America

Norman Jacobson

> In the busy streets, domains of trade,
> Man is a surly porter, or a vain hectoring bully,
> Who can claim no nearer kindredship with me
> Than brotherhood by law.
> —Henry David Thoreau, "In the Busy Streets,
> Domains of Trade"

In an age when all that is solid melts into airwaves, what are the prospects for intimacy, especially friendship? This is not so recent an issue as we might imagine. Alexis de Tocqueville was struck by one aspect of the problem: if all that had for the longest time been regarded as private becomes public, can there exist a genuine public order at all? That is, under such conditions is political community possible? Thoreau came at the problem from the opposite side: can intimacy flourish when the values proper to a public order, particularly one shaped by the idea of a social contract, become the test of all relationships, not excluding friendship? He thought not, and in his testy way made a case against such a touchstone, a case that seems appropriate for taking some measure of the present situation. Not least, because he was bold enough to hold himself up for scrutiny as an example of one crushed by such circumstances.

In his chronicle, "A Week on the Concord & Merrimac Rivers," Thoreau has a passage some thirty pages in length devoted to the topic of friendship.[1] It is probably the most perceptive exploration of friendship conducted by an American. Thoreau has much to tell us about what kind of people we are, about what we have made of ourselves owing to our vaunted practicality and competitiveness, about ourselves as parties to a contract and as ideologists of individualism. The term individualism itself is quite modern, an invention of Tocqueville during his extended visit to America. By individualism, Tocqueville did not mean seeking to know and to become oneself, an aspiration that stretches back beyond the Greeks. What he referred to was a new ideology that had come into the world with democratic equality: namely, a turning inward, sometimes eventuating in an edgy, even menacing defense of our rights, of our persons, our concerns, and our property. Individualism can be easily bent to serve egoism.

"Don't tread on me" was, and remains to this day, a noble response to tyranny. But in a mass democracy, where the tyrant is likely to be us, its strident advocacy eventuates in the sovereign individual. The individual becomes a city unto himself, as well as a critic of the other cities of the plain, high places, and shore. We tip our lances in passing greeting to one another and develop foreign policies thought suitable to relate to other sovereign individuals such as ourselves. The results, as well we know, are not entirely satisfactory. What is won is individuality of a certain kind; what is lost is equally apparent. Since we live by treaty with one another, community is no simple achievement. We might ache for communion with others, but our reality is often a lonely, undifferentiated, drifting purposelessness, which we dignify with the name of freedom.

We will not be possessed, we must possess ourselves, utterly, like a commodity, an object. Hands off, this is my property: my self is my property, still another commodity. I have rights over my own body, as if my body and I are distinct entities. My self owns my body; but who owns my self? Be it resolved: that the body of each and every man, woman, and child is his or her own property, in which he or she has a sovereign right. One is led to inquire: how much a pound? Generally, only two alternatives present themselves: either I possess myself or am possessed by the other.

Each of us becomes a version of Raymond Chandler's Philip Marlowe trudging down his own mean streets. In the American democracy, "[t]he woof of time," Tocqueville wrote, is "every instant broken and the track of the generations effaced. Those who went before are soon forgotten; of those who will come after, no one has an idea." So it is no wonder, having no past and willing no particular future, except that of moving on, moving on, to God knows where, every American, in Tocqueville's words, "shuts himself up tightly within himself, and insists upon judging the world from there." I quote Tocqueville, because he is writing about Thoreau's America.

Talk of shutting oneself up tightly within oneself and judging the world from there brings us more directly to Thoreau. An acquaintance once said of him, "I love Harry, but I cannot like him; and as for taking his arm, I should as soon think of taking the arm of an elm tree." And for good reason, for as a child he had already earned the nickname "The Judge" by regular visitors to the household. Yet this same Harry, this great wooden being, will write on friendship, and how he will write!

No "thought is more familiar" to the aspirations of men than friendship, Thoreau begins. "All men are dreaming of it, and its drama, which is always a tragedy, is enacted daily." Think of it: we dream friendship and live tragedy. Just what the tragedy is all about, we shall soon see. Friendship is:

> the secret of the universe. You may tread the town, you may wander the country, and none shall ever speak of it, yet thought is everywhere busy about it. . . . We are dreaming that our Friends are our Friends, and that we are our Friends' Friends. Our actual Friends are but distant relations of those to whom we are pledged. We never exchange more than three words with a Friend in our lives on that level to which our thoughts and feelings almost habitually rise. One goes forth prepared to say "Sweet Friends!" and the salutation is "Damn your eyes!" But never mind; faint heart never won true Friend. O my Friend, may it come to pass, *once*, that when you are my Friend, I may be yours.[2]

So Thoreau begins, a cross between a lyric poet and a lovesick schoolboy. So Thoreau begins, like the rest of us American middle-class utilitarian daydreaming romantics. Who has not whispered to the trees, to the sky, the stars, or to the sea, "O my Friend, may it come to pass, once, that when you are my Friend, I may be yours?" "Nobody understands me"— poor Henry Thoreau, poor Henry American: he hides behind his Puritanical bachelorhood, and doesn't have a friend. Poor Henry Adams, poor Henry American: he hides behind the cathedral of his intellect, and doesn't have a friend. Poor Henry James, poor Henry American: he hides behind the prickly hedge of his style; where is his friend? Pity all the American Henrys—and Herman, too, and Nathaniel, and sad, austere, Tommy Eliot. Pity poor Ez Pound, and Scotty Fitz, and Ernie, who became a papa without ever having found a friend. Poor friendless American; poor whiteskinned striver who doesn't have a friend, while himself capable of boundless friendship, of superb friendship, of divine friendship even. Poor Henry American—poor Charlie Brown.

Yet, let us not be too hasty, let's see what friendship means to Thoreau, what this dream and this torment; why the yearning, for him and for so many others, must end in tragedy. The tragedy, according to Thoreau, lies in this: "How often we find ourselves turning our backs on our actual Friends, that we may go and meet their ideal cousins." "Good for you, Hank," says Sam Clemens. Still, Thoreau's very sense of friendship is an ideal sense, itself conceived in individualism. "Would that I were worthy," he sighs, "to be any man's Friend." Would, we hear him say in the next breath, that any man were worthy to be mine. In fact, the trouble is that actual friendships are simply not ideal enough for Thoreau. "What is commonly honored with the name of Friendship is no very profound or powerful instinct. Men do not, after all, love their Friends greatly." So there we are. Friendship demands a great devotion, but the capacity to love greatly is a gift, perhaps not that prodigally diffused among any population maybe not everyone is capable of it.

Thoreau, however, demands nothing less than that friends, in his words, be "transfigured and translated by love in each other's presence." That they be "purified, refined, and elevated." That true friendship make a man "honest," a "hero," even a "Saint." Alas, "there are," he laments, "only two or three couples in history." No doubt. So much for the ideal.

Yet, Thoreau's profundity on the matter rests not so much with the bare statement of the ideal, however elevated, as with his uncanny perceptiveness of reality: the ability to fathom his own soul, the better to read ours; the power to see through false relations, and the artistry to present this falseness to us with surpassing fidelity. What arrests us is not his whining as a citizen, but the piercing quality of his words as a cool observer.

Listen to Thoreau's critique of actual friendship in America, however romantic or inaccessible the ideal:

> If one abates a little the price of his wood, or gives a neighbor his vote at a town meeting, or a barrel of apples, or lends him his wagon frequently, it is esteemed a rare instance of Friendship. . . . To say that a man is your friend, means commonly no more than this, that he is not your enemy. Most contemplate only what would be the accidental and trifling advantages of Friendship, as that the friend can assist in time of need, by his substance, or his influence, or his counsel . . . [But] such services are particular and menial. . . . Even the utmost good-will and harmony and practical kindness are not sufficient for Friendship, for Friends do not live in harmony merely, as some say, but in melody. We do not wish for Friends to feed and clothe our bodies—neighbors are kind enough for that—but to do the like office to our spirits.[3]

Note that Thoreau here is attacking the typical American utilitarian impulse, while he himself is expounding "Friendship-for-Friendship's Sake" not as a utility, not as instrumental to anything at all. Friendship, he says, has no other goal than this: to confront "the sincere with the sincere," to bring together "man with man." And such simply does not exist, except as an ideal, in America. "What is commonly called Friendship," he remarks, "is only a little more honor among rogues."

However much I am tempted to pin Thoreau's attitude to friendship in the epigram, "Friendship is too precious a sentiment to be wasted on friends," I am compelled to listen further to the sad tale of the crippling effect of utilitarian considerations upon friendship in America, or, perhaps, in all societies in a democratic age. Typically, much of the critique proceeds by way of comparison to friendship that is at the same time both "natural" and "noble," that is, which identifies the primitive and the ideal: Fenimore Cooper's Natty Bumppo and Chingachgook, Herman Melville's Ishmael and Queequog, and Mark Twain's Huck and Jim. Thoreau's own characters, invented in his literary imagination, are called Henry the Fur Trader and the Indian Wawatam.[4]

This friendship, no doubt projected outward upon a "safe" target, that is, one thought to be in certain ideal ways superior and in other more practical ways inferior to the protagonist of the story, was so pure and so beautiful, the love of Henry the Fur Trader and Wawatam, that by contrast what the white, civilized American calls friendship is a farce, a melancholy joke. We tend, Thoreau writes, to "count our Friends on our fingers," but "they are not numerable." We wish their applause, he says, but a true friend owes his friend nothing. We tend to evaluate our friends by their "performance," he tells us, by value received. But a true friend, if he judges at all, does so on the basis of his friend's "aspirations." Utility is the test of neighbors and fellow citizens, and that is as it should be. But never of friends. And American society means nothing so much as the elevation of utility to a standard by which all must be measured, even friendship. Thoreau adds a "word of entreaty and advice to the large and respectable nation of Acquaintances, beyond the mountains;—Greetings. My most serene and irresponsible neighbors, let us see that we have the whole advantage of each other; we will be useful, at least, if not admirable, to one another."

The tragedy is, that by seeking to be useful at all, Americans at the same time guarantee that they be used by none. Given this practice, intimate friendship is an impossibility.

Thoreau concludes on what seems an utterly unexpected and ominous note: "Ah my dear Strangers and Enemies, I would not forget *you*. I can well afford to welcome *you*. Let me subscribe myself Yours ever and truly—your much obliged servant. We have nothing to fear from our foes; God keeps a standing army for that service; but we have no ally against our Friends, those ruthless Vandals."

There we have it, at last. It was bound to come out that way. Thoreau knows. His Yankee soul whispers to him of the perils of intimacy, of dropping the guard, above all, of dependence. The American tames the vandal, he domesticates the barbarian within as well as without, all by the trick of elevating usefulness to first place among the tests of human beings and their relations to one another. The dread of being vandalized, torn open, ruthlessly misused—that is, according to Thoreau, the true American dread of friendship, including his own dread.[5]

But the free, independent American will not run the risk of vandalization by intimates, nor will he be chewed and swallowed, however delicate and devoted the diner. Even a bit of nibbling around the edges terrifies us. We are prickly; we don't go down easily. Our hides are tough. But how we also crave communion with others, on our own terms. No wonder we take pride in the impenetrability of our individual surfaces. We own our selves, like so much merchandise; and we alone have exclusive right to ourselves as property. No wonder also we grieve: we mourn the death of the ideal friend who will put an end to the awful isolation of our being. Do we mourn also a part of ourselves stillborn? Is it the death of the garden, the Walden Pond that we have lost, while the dream, to our sorrow, persists? The garden pond to which we invite our friend to dwell with us in perfect concord and serenity—the dream, at least, seems still to have us in its grasp.

Thoreau is one of a nation of brothers, but then, why not a nation also of friends? Why not? "One goes forth prepared to say 'Sweet Friend!' And the salutation is 'Damn your eyes!'" That is, one goes forth as a hero of the spirit to say "Sweet Friend" but one finds no companion spirit there to respond, only one's own brother. Thoreau calls it "brotherhood by law": no friendship there, only contractual obligation, at best.

So we have the garden, Walden, the secret place of our individuality, the spot deep in the recesses of our soul, impenetrable to others except by invitation. We invite, we entreat, we say "Sweet Friends!" But we will not open ourselves to communion, cannot do so, to our brothers and equals, our colleagues, and our rivals. Poor Henry American indeed.

Perhaps such friendships as Thoreau and we dream about are not laid in heaven after all, but in traditional communities. Perhaps Thoreau's warrior of the soul, that fierce and implacable individual, that disdainful and heroic fellow who put in an appearance in the essay "On Civil Disobedience," is a natural aristocrat trying to steer a true course all but awash in the equalitarian sea of uniformity and lack of distinction.

Uniqueness, stoicism, lofty ideas, privacy, differentiation and distinction, and heroism: a sprawling political democracy is by no means a spawning ground favorable to such human qualities. Join the crowd, we say, and how's tricks, we say, and how's the missus and the kiddies? Thoreau replies, "A good morning to you Sir, and damn your eyes!" Damn your prying, judging, hungry eyes, damn your insatiable democratic eyes.[6] And so our eyes are compelled to turn back upon ourselves—American intellectuals and literary gents are wont to call this "the moral sense." And so we socialized, practical-minded citizens turn our gaze inward, but only briefly. Then, aghast at the bleak and forbidding landscape there, we go back to being our customary superficial selves.

Only Thoreau is resolved to plague us to the very end, without mercy. He insists on pointing a finger at our other self, the one we are so eager to flee, and shouting, "Look, take a look at that, will you! That's *you* also!" But that sort of teaching, that sort of prophecy, is an enemy to the social affections, where those affections are grounded in utility. It is as if we have, all of us, conspired with one another to place "No Trespassing" signs along the boundaries of tens of millions of Waldens, emerging from our individual fastnesses only for the purposes of a more commodious existence. If nothing else, Thoreau reminds us that barter is no substitute for a more fulfilling, if riskier, commerce.

NOTES

1. Henry David Thoreau, "A Week on the Concord & Merrimac Rivers," in *The Writings of Henry David Thoreau* (Boston: Houghten Mifflin, 1906). All subsequent quotations from Thoreau are from this source (hereafter cited as "The Week").

2. Thoreau, "The Week."

3. Ibid.

4. Add to the list the Henry Morgan of Mark Twain's *A Connecticut Yankee at King Arthur's Court* and Ernest Hemingway's character of the same name in *To Have and Have Not*, appropriately called Hank in our casual age. Does anyone have a clue as to why all the Henrys?

5. The same idea is given a different, more optimistic, if sacrificial, twist by Eric Hoffer: "People who eat you up and pick your bones are not monsters. Actually it is your task to see to it that as you are swallowed, bite by bite, you ennoble the eater so that he becomes as much a part of you as you of him. Perhaps all mutual devotion is mutual devouring." Read by Hoffer from his notebook to the author in 1962.

6. Francis Parkman's response to the rude curiosity of the buffalo hunters and trappers he encountered along the Oregon Trail asking: Who are you? What do you do? Where you from? Where you going? Parkman, *The Oregon Train* (New York: Putnam, 1895).

7

Jane Addams and Democratic Citizenship

Bob Pepperman Taylor

These are not, however, the days of miracles, and I suppose it will be granted
that I am not to expect a direct revelation.

—Abraham Lincoln[1]

There is a noticeable air of self-criticism in Jane Addams's first book of
essays, *Democracy and Social Ethics*, when she reprimands philanthropists
for patronizing the poor. A part of Addams's project in this early work is
to help others learn, as she has herself, that the most important needs of
the poor include dignity and civic equality. The "charity visitor"[2] learns
to appreciate this equality, but perhaps only after difficult beginnings.
While she may have originally been motivated by a philanthropic impulse,
if the charity worker is open to the people she works with and lives
among, she learns over time to think of them as individuals with whom
to share a civic life, rather than as cases to be managed. In another early
paper, "The Objective Value of a Social Settlement," Addams explains that
she hopes her work at Hull House will be identified more with the "duties of good citizenship" than with the philanthropic movement,[3] and that
all residents of Hull House were "pledged to devote themselves to the
duties of good citizenship."[4] When Addams described herself as an "incorrigible democrat,"[5] it is clear that this commitment to democracy
grew out of her experiences as a reformer and political activist.[6] Her life
at Hull House taught her the beauty of building a democratic community,
and the ugliness of demeaning the poor through a condescending philanthropy.

Consider this passage from *Democracy and Social Ethics*, where Addams
elaborates on the character of the charity visitor's civic education:

130

She reaches the old-time virtue of humility by a social process, not in the old way, as the man who sits by the side of the road and puts dust upon his head, calling himself a contrite sinner, but she gets the dust upon her head because she has stumbled and fallen in the road through her efforts to push forward the mass, to march with her fellows. She has socialized her virtues not only through a social aim but by a social process.[7]

The social process Addams alludes to here is the process whereby middle-class reformers like the charity visitor, like herself, fall into the dust as a result of class arrogance. Such humbling lessons, however, are the beginning of political wisdom. Now the reformer is in a position to recognize the degree to which all social classes "are bound together in ethical development."[8] Such recognition is built upon a learned respect for the potential of all members of the political community. "The writer has long ceased to apologize for the views and opinions of working people, being quite sure that on the whole they are quite as wise and quite as foolish as the views and opinions of other people."[9] Having learned such lessons herself, Addams can write, most powerfully in *Twenty Years at Hull-House*, of her neighbors with such unsentimentality, such moral power, and such dignity. She can write not as a charity visitor but as a citizen.[10]

Jean Bethke Elshtain suggests that Addams's writings teach us about the importance of particularity in democratic political thinking, about how to avoid the kind of dogmatism and abstraction that infect much contemporary political life. "Her immersion in the particular, her ability to articulate wider social meaning through powerful depictions of individual suffering or joy, hope or despair, sets her apart from all who write abstractly about experience."[11] It is true that Addams was never tempted by the terrifying ideological commitments found across the modern political spectrum that led Albert Camus to despairingly observe that "what counts now is whether or not one has helped a doctrine to triumph, not whether or not one respects a mother and spares her suffering."[12] For Elshtain, Addams teaches us "how to do social theory from the inside out."[13] Such teaching grows out of the way Addams learned of civic equality from her life at Hull House. She conveyed these lessons through the power of her simple, direct, and sometimes beautiful description of these experiences.[14]

The essay "Charitable Effort" referred to above, however, shows that Addams offers more lessons for the democratic theorist than those identified by Elshtain. The final passage elaborates on the theme of humility and citizenship, and speaks in general terms that can apply to all members of a democratic community:

The Hebrew prophet made three requirements from those who would join the great forward-moving procession led by Jehovah. "To love mercy" and

at the same time "to do justly" is the difficult task; to fulfil the first requirement alone is to fall into the error of indiscriminate giving with all its disastrous results; to fulfil the second solely is to obtain the stern policy of
withholding, and it results in such a dreary lack of sympathy and understanding that the establishment of justice is impossible. It may be that the
combination of the two can never be attained save as we fulfil still the third
requirement—"to walk humbly with God," which may mean to walk for
many dreary miles beside the lowliest of His creatures, not even in that peace
of mind which the company of the humble is popularly supposed to afford,
but rather with the pangs and throes to which the poor human understanding is subjected whenever it attempts to comprehend the meaning of life.[15]

In this passage alone, I think, Addams earns our attention as a political thinker and democratic citizen. Accepting the prophet Micah's distinctions, Addams not only suggests that justice, mercy, and humility before
God are required of us, she also discerns the extraordinary difficulty of
meeting these requirements. Justice is an obvious political good, but it is
a stern and harsh and blunt instrument that not uncommonly fails to make
necessary but subtle moral distinctions among cases and individuals.
Mercy is the corrective to this harsh virtue, yet mercy alone can undermine the demands of justice by failing to give individuals their proper due
(or, more negatively, failing to restrain them in appropriate ways). Addams
suggests the degree to which these two moral precepts are only imperfectly balanced in the practice of political life. There is no theoretical "resolution" to be discovered, no formula allowing us to simply or routinely
balance these competing virtues.

The enactment of these qualities is so difficult, so ambiguous, that we
are only likely to apply both to the degree that we "walk humbly with
God." The implication is not that "walking with God" will somehow supply us with the resolution to the problems raised by these conflicting demands of justice and mercy, but rather that our humility before God is a
constant and necessary reminder of the resolutions we seek, the tenuous-
ness of our grasp on the moral demands of political life and public policy.
We are required to seek justice and mercy, so it is not a moral option to
simply withdraw from political judgment. But such judgment must always be approached with the strongest sense of the imperfection of our
own evaluations and assessments. Citizenship requires a humble recognition of this problem, just as it requires that we recognize the essentially
uncertain and ambiguous moral nature of public judgment. This is particularly true in a democracy, where all citizens' views are given political
standing; each of us must continually struggle to respect the views of others even when they conflict with our interests, or even more troublingly,
with our judgments. Only a certain kind of democratic humility will al-

low us to listen to other citizens when their voices seem discordant with our own.

Addams came to her understanding of democratic citizenship through the experience of living at Hull House, and this understanding informed her local, national, and international political activism throughout her life.[16] Addams's political life provides us with numerous examples of her own attempt to live up to Micah's injunction, and I will mention just two here by way of illustration. First, consider her campaigns to oust Alderman John Powers of Chicago's Nineteenth Ward. When Addams moved to Hull House, located in Powers's ward, she found herself at odds with the alderman and his political organization. The initial conflict focused on sanitation and garbage collection. Addams fought for, and was granted by the mayor, the ward contract to collect the garbage, only to have this arrangement subsequently eliminated by an ordinance sponsored by Powers.[17] Addams's battle over garbage turned into general opposition to Powers, and she led three unsuccessful electoral campaigns against him.

It is not surprising that Addams's experiences with Powers left her appalled by the corruption of his administration—Addams began her career, after all, as a fairly conventional Progressive reformer. What is surprising is the result that these experiences had on her thinking about politicians like Powers. In *Democracy and Social Ethics*, Addams's outrage has turned into a much more nuanced discussion of political reform. She continues to disapprove of Powers's motives, the narrowness of the private advantage that drives his political calculations, and she speculates about the evolution of a "higher morality" to guide a future democratic politics.[18] On the other hand, she fully recognizes the "kindness" of the political boss, the way in which he delivers services and goods to constituents at critical moments in their lives, and she insightfully suggests that at least the people of her ward share with the political boss a democratic relationship to which many reformers don't even aspire. Reformers, in fact, often "fix their attention so exclusively on methods [of administration] that they fail to consider the final aims of city government. This accounts for the growing tendency to put more and more responsibility upon executive officers and appointed commissions at the expense of curtailing the powers of the direct representatives of the voters."[19] The reforms they promote are dangerously detached "from the rest of life," and the reformers "speak and write of the purification of politics as of a thing set apart from daily life."[20] In contrast, the ward boss is a genuine representative of his constituents:

> Men living near to the masses of voters, and knowing them intimately . . . minister directly to life and to social needs. They realize that the people

as a whole are clamoring for social results, and they hold their power because they respond to that demand. They are corrupt and often do their work badly; but they at least avoid the mistake of a certain type of business men who are frightened by democracy, and have lost their faith in the people.[21]

In this chapter, "Political Reform," there is no mistaking Addams's continued disapproval of the ward boss and urban political machine generally. However, it is also clear that she has gained a respect for this form of politics and has learned to appreciate the integrity that can grow out of it. In *Newer Ideals of Peace*, published five years after *Democracy and Social Ethics*, she scolds anti-machine reformers in even stronger terms: "In portraying the evil he is fighting, he does not recognize, or at least does not make clear, all the human kindness upon which it has grown. In his speeches he inevitably offends a popular audience, who know that the evil of corruption exists in all degrees and forms of human weakness, but who also know that these evils are by no means always hideous, and sometimes even are lovable."[22]

What is striking about these reflections on urban political reform is the degree to which Addams's own evaluations are complex and open to the lessons of experience. Rather than allowing her opposition to Powers to harden into a self-righteous tirade against the corruption of the machine and ignorance of the voters, she recognized the moral stakes were more ambiguous. She continued to campaign for political reform, but refused to demonize her opponents or to shield her own camp from scrutiny. These qualities influenced the very conception of political reform she developed in the course of these events. Addams maintained her integrity while respecting and learning from the opposition. This style of democratic citizenship allows disagreement among friends and citizens, and yet, paradoxically, it may promote civic unity more than the self-righteousness of many reform activists.

Turning to Addams's opposition to World War I, the first fact to note about her pacifism is how morally perilous she believed it was. Pacifists in wartime, Addams writes, are confronted by profound dangers and suffering. First, they are tempted by seemingly opposed vices: "Strangely enough he [the pacifist] finds it possible to travel from the mire of self-pity straight to the barren hills of self-righteousness and to hate himself equally in both places."[23] Second, the social isolation generated by pacifist convictions creates additional wounds that compromise the possibility of living a complete and healthy moral life, a life that requires a kind of civic friendship or at least inclusion: "I concluded that to the very end pacifists will occasionally realize that they have been permanently crippled in their natural and friendly relations to their fellow citizens."[24]

The agony of the war, for Addams, was in part the agony of being shut out of the shared life of her political community. She "longed desperately for reconciliation" with her "friends and fellow citizens."[25]

Political isolation is obviously difficult on many levels, but Addams emphasized the degree to which it constituted a moral handicap in her life. Rather than engaging in debate and deliberation with her fellow citizens, she felt compelled to stick with her own evaluations of the political world.

> We [pacifists] slowly became aware that our affirmation was regarded as pure dogma. We were thrust into the position of the doctrinaire. . . . It therefore came about that ability to hold out against mass suggestion, to honestly differ from the convictions and enthusiasms of one's best friends did in moments of crisis come to depend upon the categorical belief that a man's primary allegiance is to his vision of the truth and that he is under obligation to affirm it.[26]

Addams does not deny that "a man's primary allegiance is to his vision of the truth." But she does write about this as though it is a perilous position to be forced into, a choice forced upon individuals in extreme moments when democratic community and debate are no longer fully available. Even then, Addams refused to retreat completely into her own moral universe; John Farrell notes that, "[u]nlike many pacifists, she strove to understand those who supported war."[27] Moral individualism was forced upon pacifists not by the fact of their minority opinions, but because of the inability of the state and the political community generally to view dissent during wartime as anything but disloyalty. Many commentators have noticed that despite the strength of her convictions, Addams suffered grave doubts about her pacifism during the war.[28] James Weber Linn portrays the pain of separation Addams felt during this period: "She had spent her life in seeking identification of her own spirit with the spirit of democracy. . . . Her profoundest conviction had been of the worth and sanctity of the opinions of others. And now suddenly she found fellowship with the majority refused, and her interpretation mocked."[29] Sandra Herman, however, captures the full power of Addams's problem when she observes that "[f]or Jane Addams, loyalty to one's own vision was an overly individualistic doctrinaire belief."[30] Addams distrusted moral commitments generated in political isolation as much as she suffered the social torments of that isolation.

When Addams found herself in a political position where she dissented, standing outside the acceptable parameters of political debate, she had the strength of character to do so. She viewed this act, however, as morally dangerous, almost debilitating. It is remarkable to note the degree to which Addams attempted to maintain her connection with the political community during this time, despite its harsh rejection of her. Regardless of her continued objection to the war, her deep (and astute) skepticism about the democratic goals of the war, and her work with the Women's International League for Peace and Freedom to do what she could to bring about the war's end, she nonetheless allowed Hull House to be used as an Army draft registration station.[31] In addition, she accepted Herbert Hoover's request that she serve the Department of Food Administration by speaking around the country on behalf of food conservation during the war (this while she was under surveillance by the Justice Department).[32] Addams maintained the integrity of her vision, while finding as much common ground with her opponents as she could. She served the political community to the degree that she could, even while being vilified by that community.[33] In this case, as well as in her disputes with Alderman Powers, Addams combined an exemplary strength of conviction with respect for her opponents. Yet she managed to combine this intensity of conviction with a noticeable humility about her own judgments. This humility allowed her to seek and promote political unity even while engaging in often fierce political debate.[34] Addams's life provides illustrations that approximate her understanding of the moral demands of democratic citizenship.[35]

While serving as chair of the school management committee of the Chicago school board in the early years of the twentieth century, Addams deeply angered the head of the Chicago Teachers Federation, Margaret Haley. The teachers had been embroiled in bitter struggles over salary and promotion policy, and when Addams gained a position of leadership on the board, Haley had hoped that she would be a strong advocate for the teachers. Instead, Addams consistently supported compromise positions, and this moderation made Haley think that Addams was weak and perhaps opportunistic and unprincipled. "I told her [Addams] I did not believe in any compromise that compromised a principle," Haley reported. "Miss Adams [sic] if she is anything to Chicago is an ethical and moral leader and not a compromiser."[36] She later said to a friend, "We had made the mistake in Chicago of considering Miss Addams as a moral leader and treating her as such and expecting her to do in very difficult positions what a William Lloyd Garrison would do."[37] This assessment of Addams's weakness as a civic leader is seemingly shared by a later biographer who argues that during World War I, "[s]he had not the strength to stand with Norman Thomas and tell her countrymen they were wrong."[38] The idea here, as in Haley's comments, is that Addams was not as brave or clear-sighted or committed as we might expect and desire from such a figure. The implication is that, despite her virtues, Addams at times failed to maintain the courage of her convictions.

In contrast to this view of Addams's character and actions, a more admiring biographer, John C. Farrell, suggests that when Addams suffered the ostracism and isolation of those who opposed the war, she took comfort in the strength of her private vision. "In this crisis she came to reaffirm categorically that man's primary alliance must be to his own individual vision of the truth."[39] Where one biographer sees weakness, another finds an individual strength of commitment.

These alternative evaluations of Addams reflect a broader debate in the secondary interpretations of her life and ideas. On the one hand, Addams is most commonly portrayed as "Saint Jane," a heroine, one of the greatest women in American history.[40] These portraits emphasize Addams's eccentric strength of character, the supposed altruism and selflessness of her life, and her courage in the face of political and social opposition. On the other hand, this admiring literature has generated an inevitable revisionism that aims to puncture the balloon of Addams's saintliness: here she is portrayed as dithering and confused, as ambitious, even cowardly.[41]

Both assessments are flawed. Praise of Addams frequently underemphasizes the moral ambivalence of her political positions, portraying her as having a kind of immovable character, while failing to capture the complexity of the facts surrounding her political style and development. We have seen, for example, that Farrell is right to suggest that in the end the war forced Addams to cultivate her private moral sensibilities. He is wrong, however, to imply that for Addams this represents the pinnacle of moral life—we have seen that the truth is quite to the contrary. Critics, on the other hand, frequently fail to measure Addams by her own standards, mistaking their own for hers. We can admit that it is true that Addams failed to live up to the example of William Lloyd Garrison, but we must deny the conclusion drawn. Addams explicitly avoided cultivating a style similar to the abolitionists,[42] but her pacifism during the war proves that this did not prevent her from taking unpopular positions and sticking to them in the face of intense public hostility.[43]

Not only are both of these assessments flawed, they are flawed in a similar way. What critics like Haley and champions like Farrell share is a view of citizenship in which morality is a privately (and perhaps mysteriously) attained quality that is brought, in its entirety, to political life. Political integrity, in this view, is evaluated by the degree to which an individual citizen maintains this vision in the face of debate and even opposition; Farrell's disagreement with Haley concerns only his assessment of the degree to which Addams lived up to this standard. Addams, on the other hand, thought of the life of the democratic citizen quite differently. Her own view of her dissent during the war is that it was a personal tragedy rather than a triumph—a necessary tragedy, perhaps, but a tragedy nonetheless. The isolation she suffered was a kind of wound, not only to her social but to her moral needs. The moral life of the citizen is most accurately understood and experienced as a process, she believed, in which citizens pursue and discover and live their moral life together as best they can. Rather than generating the type of certainty and self-righteousness desired by Haley and seemingly discovered by Farrell, we have seen that Addams in reality embodied and promoted a kind of democratic humility, which is one of the most difficult yet essential qualities of citizens.[44]

The view of citizenship adopted by both these admirers and critics assumes that the character of good citizens is in some sense completely self-contained, and therefore calm, confident, unconflicted. Clark Cochran has described good civic character as a kind of "wholeness," which "refers to the ability of character to be true to itself in all situations. The left hand does know what the right is doing. The person does not work against himself, is not torn apart from within, but is at peace with himself."[45] It is precisely this kind of character that Haley hopes to find and Farrell thought he did find, but neither is compatible with the kind of humility Addams promoted and strove to represent. In contrast to her interpreters, democratic equality demands for Addams the strong sense that one could be wrong, that when we are set against our fellows we might be making a terrible mistake, that when we are forced to separate ourselves from the course taken by the majority, this is a painful and potentially crippling act, isolating us and making our own deliberations about public affairs too private or narcissistic to be trustworthy. What democracy needs from its citizens is not only courage and vision but uncertainty as well. One must do what is right, but it is wrong to be smug or overly self-confident in thinking we know for sure what the right actually is. In fact, it wouldn't be wrong to suggest that even when doing what one must, good civic character will be haunted by doubt, especially when it finds itself up against the considered judgment of other citizens. For Addams, good citizens in times of civic conflict are necessarily conflicted, uncertain, and in turmoil, and it couldn't possibly be otherwise. Since the civic community is a part of our moral life, our alienation from that community is an alienation from a part of ourselves. If we really approach other citizens as civic equals, as equally implicated in a common life, we cannot help but be torn when our judgment differs widely or strongly from theirs. When we "walk humbly with God," we recognize the limitations of our own judgment, as well as the degree to which we share these limitations with all other citizens.

A second characteristic of the more conventional modern view of citizenship is that it assumes, even promotes, a kind of individual pride. How can I feel so morally confident, so sure that I am right even if that means that my brothers and sisters are wrong? Because, quite simply, there is nothing to chasten and humble my view of myself. It is not true that contemporary liberal morality necessarily produces some form of moral relativism;[46] it does often enough, but this is by no means necessary. What *is* necessary is that even when absolute moral principles or rights or methods are appealed to, the final moral judge is none other than myself, and who is better than I, whom I know to be driven by all the right motives, and to be wiser than all others?[47] A belief in God is no guarantee that such self-confident moralism won't emerge. Still there is certainly no powerful reason for this moralism not to surface without a recognition of some authority greater than myself.[48]

Richard Rorty has recently argued that the great seers of the Progressive period, John Dewey and Walt Whitman, are to be praised for promoting a humanism that attacks all appeals to the sacred or to divine authority, a humanism committed to Whitman's proposition that "[i]t is not consistent with the reality of the soul to admit that there is anything in the universe more divine than men and women."[49] For Rorty, the genius of the Progressive period is captured by Whitman's belief that we can and must replace the worship of God with the worship of ourselves: "We are the greatest poem because we put ourselves in the place of God: our essence is our existence, and our existence is in the future. Other nations thought of themselves as hymns to the glory of God. We redefine God as our future selves."[50] Only such a view, for Rorty, is compatible with the dignity of free men and women. Rorty believes that Ralph Waldo Emerson was right to suggest that in a democracy, "the only sin is limitation,"[51] that the only view compatible with a commitment to democratic progress is one that elevates each individual to a level of ultimate moral value. To think of men and woman as in any way subordinate to God is to constrain and make a mockery of their freedom. Democracy must replace the love of God with the love of humanity. There must be no limitation placed on the free, potentially infinite development of human individuality.

To the degree that Rorty's description captures the spirit of the Progressive age, it is clear that Addams is more of a dissenter from the orthodoxy of the period than is often recognized.[52] The position promoted by Rorty, from Addams's view is a dangerous idolatry. One of the gravest dangers in a democracy is the temptation to arrogance. The freedom promoted by democracy threatens to teach individuals and the democratic community as a whole that their wills, desires, and interests have no legitimate constraints, that there is no higher moral standard than what they choose, and that therefore what they choose must be right and good because they choose it. Addams's fear is not only of the materialism of consumer society and the debasing of moral standards by economic interests in a capitalist economy—although these are real enough problems.[53] Self-righteousness is perhaps an even more dangerous possibility if citizens interpret their democratic freedom as the kind of liberation Rorty describes. If we are replacing God, after all, our wants and judgments must themselves be God-like. Addams once observed that "Self-righteousness has perhaps been responsible for more cruelty from the strong to the weak, from the good to the erring than any other human trait."[54] Democracy can be particularly vulnerable to this vice of arrogance. Addams's conception of democratic citizenship theoretically and practically stands as a rebuke to the conception Rorty locates and praises in Addams's generation.[55]

This is not to deny that Addams shared, to some extent, significant qualities and inclinations with many of her reform-minded colleagues from the Progressive era. To see this, consider the confidence she occasionally expressed in the benefits of modern, bureaucratic, scientific, political management. In one passage, for example, she considers the constituent services provided by urban machine politicians. Political reformers, she concludes, are impotent as long as they fail to understand that the local alderman represents, in contemporary urban form, a real "manifestation of human friendliness" and "village kindness" when he keeps track of deaths and provides his constituents with Christmas turkeys.[56] She then continues the thought with one of the most remarkable comments from her writings:

> A mother who eats her Christmas turkey in a reverent spirit of thankfulness to the alderman who gave it to her, might be gradually brought to a genuine sense of appreciation and gratitude to the city which supplies her little children with a Kindergarten, or, to the Board of Health which properly placarded a case of scarlet-fever next door and spared her sleepless nights and wearing anxiety, as well as the money paid with such difficulty to the doctor and the druggist.[57]

In this passage, Addams not only seems remarkably confident about the ability of bureaucratic institutions to effectively serve their clients; in addition, she seems to be promoting an idea of civic friendship that equates the affection one can feel for a local politician with that which one might feel for an impersonal bureau. Elsewhere, she writes of her friend Julia Lathrop as having a remarkable quality for loving institutions as most of us can only love friends: "She possessed the devotion of friendship itself for organization and for even units of government which most people are able to extend only to individuals."[58] She almost seems at times to believe that the modern state will not only serve our interests, but will be our friend as well.

Such a respect for reform political institutions seems to reflect the Progressive commitment to the efficiency of modern scientific management;

increasingly centralized political institutions are the answer to the unique problems raised by modern industrialism and urban society.[59] For example, in *A New Conscience and An Ancient Evil*, Addams recommends turning to public health officials to combat prostitution,[60] and in *The Second Twenty Years at Hull-House* she pleads for increasing federal intervention in child welfare policy:

> There was evidently confusion in the minds of many of our fellow countrymen between self-government and local government. Americans have thought for a long time . . . that unless government is localized they do not exercise self-government at all. Such a conception, if persisted in, must narrow our notion of government and circumscribe our national life. We forget that politics are largely a matter of adjusted human relations through any unit of government which best serves the purpose.[61]

Only the federal government is in a position to address many of our modern problems, but this need not worry us about the democratic control and character of government. In these observations, Addams appears to be expressing a view of the large and professionalized government advocated by many of her contemporaries. Here she shares with John Dewey, for example, an insensitivity to the problem of designing democratic institutions to control increasingly centralized and impersonal public policy. How are we to assure that these centralized and impersonal institutions generate the kind of commitment and community found in more local institutions? Like Dewey, she does not suggest that such institutions will be easy to build or maintain, but like him she also seems to believe that there is no principled or theoretical reason to worry about the project itself.[62] The point is not that Addams wasn't right to observe that many contemporary political problems must be addressed at the national level, and that the complexity of many of these problems requires the growth of bureaucratic expertise. Rather, it is that she did not always appear to be troubled by the problem of how to make such institutions expressive of and accountable to democracy.

Yet, despite these Progressive moments in Addams's writings, there are alternative themes that continually emerge in contrast. When she writes in *Newer Ideals of Peace*, for example, that "[i]t is necessary from the very beginning to substitute the scientific method of research for the a priori method of the school men if we would deal with real people and obtain a sense of participation with our fellows,"[63] what she has in mind by "scientific method" has little to do with technical expertise, as it would for a Herbert Croly or a Walter Lippmann. Rather, it is her way of signaling the simple rejection of dogma in public debate, "science" being her expression for open-mindedness, the alternative to dogmatic closed-mindedness.

In fact, when one looks at Addams's discussions of public service, it is clear that her image of the virtuous public servant has much less to do with technical or scientific expertise, or the promotion of "reason,"[64] than it does with the deep commitment to pursuing the public good that she expects from these officials. When she praised the Chicago board of health, it was on the grounds of the characters and commitments of the officials and their placement in a public rather than private or partially interested institution. "All of these officials had accepted without question and as implicit in public office, the obligation to carry on the dangerous and difficult undertakings for which private philanthropy is unfitted, as if the commonality of compassion represented by the State was more comprehending than that of any individual group."[65] These individuals are to be admired less for their expertise than for their commitment to public service.

The view of the political community emerging in many of Addams's writings stands in significant tension with more conventional Progressive values.[66] She contends, for example, that what is needed overall in city government is "a more diffused local autonomy."[67] More powerfully, she criticized reformers for patronizing the "poor and ignorant foreigners of the city," as, for example, when they called for middle-class citizens to vote selflessly on behalf of this less advantaged constituency:

> It would be difficult to suggest anything which would result in a more serious confusion than to have each man, without personal knowledge and experiences, consider the interests of the newly arrived immigrant. . . . In truth the attitude of the advising reformer was in reality so contemptuous that he had never considered the immigrants really partakers and molders of the political life of his country.[68]

Here the image of the political community is of citizens contributing to public life on an equal footing, rather than of clients and professional administrators and condescending philanthropists. While there is certainly Progressive rhetoric to be found scattered throughout Addams's writings, these moments frequently, and importantly, give way to a stronger, less commonly noted and exemplary, democratic sensibility.[69] As Allen F. Davis suggests, Addams "was less interested in a search for order than in a quest for peace and justice, less interested in a cult of efficiency, than in a search for community."[70]

Addams's lesson about democratic citizenship is a hard one. We long to understand, theoretically and philosophically, the answer to questions about how to balance justice and mercy in our political choices. But basically, these questions are less about theory than they are about the character and sensibilities of the citizens addressing them.[71] In contrast to more conventional views, Addams suggests that the demands of citizenship are fundamentally ambiguous and wrought with tensions. These tensions will inevitably lead to a kind of moral messiness even in the best of democratic regimes. Theory cannot resolve this messiness; learning the humility of "walking with God" is our best hope as democratic citizens.

So Addams's teaching is intellectually frustrating as well as hard to live. Michael Walzer once wrote: "Politics at its best is the art of overcoming pride and every sort of individual caprice while still associating honorable men."[72] Here we are back to the problem of how it is possible in practice to seek justice and love mercy, all the while walking humbly with God. Seeking justice and loving mercy assume our freedom and the legitimacy of our judgment. They require a self-confidence in our abilities and the rightness of their exercise. What could be more fundamental to "honorable men?" But pride is the almost inevitable offspring of such self-confidence and freedom. How are we to maintain a humility that tempers but does not damage or cripple our ability to exercise our rightful freedom? In *Democracy and Social Ethics*, Addams suggests that humbly walking with God demands a fraternal openness and concern for our fellows, a deep commitment to our fundamental civic equality and interdependence, and a charity even toward those whose political views we are quite certain are wrong.

NOTES

1. Abraham Lincoln, "Reply to Chicago Emancipation Memorial, Washington, D.C.," 13 September 1862, in *Lincoln: Speeches and Writings, 1859–1865* (New York: Library of America, 1989), 361.

2. This is Addams's phrase. See Jane Addams, "Charitable Effort," in *Democracy and Social Ethics* (New York: Macmillan, 1902), 13–70 (hereafter cited as *Democracy and Social Ethics*).

3. Addams, *The Social Thought of Jane Addams* (Indianapolis, Ind.: Bobbs-Merrill, 1965), 61.

4. Addams, *Twenty Years At Hull-House* (New York: Macmillan, 1938), 126–27.

5. Addams, *The Second Twenty Years At Hull-House* (New York: Macmillan, 1930), 29.

6. John C. Farrell writes, "Perhaps this is as good a summary as is possible of Jane Addams' first decade at Hull House: learn to trust democracy." Farrell, *Beloved Lady* (Baltimore, Md.: Johns Hopkins University Press, 1967), 78 (hereafter cited as *Beloved Lady*).

7. Addams, *Democracy and Social Ethics*, 69.

8. Ibid., 263.

9. Ibid., 122.

10. In what are still among the loveliest words written about Addams, Walter Lippmann's eulogy upon her death included these observations: "She had compassion without condescension. She had pity without retreat into vulgarity. She had infinite sympathy for common things without forgetfulness of those that are uncommon. That, I think, is why those who have known her say that she was not only good, but great. For this blend of sympathy with distinction, of common humanity with a noble style is recognizable by those who have eyes to see it as the occasional but authentic issue of the mystic promise of the American democracy." Quoted from Allen F. Davis, *American Heroine* (New York: Oxford University Press, 1973), 291.

11. Jean Bethke Elshtain, "A Return To Hull House: Reflections on Jane Addams," *Cross Currents* 38 (Fall 1988): 262 (hereafter cited as "Return To Hull House").

12. Quoted in Jean Bethke Elshtain, *Augustine and the Limits of Politics* (South Bend, Ind.: University of Notre Dame Press, 1995), 70.

13. Elshtain, "Return To Hull House," 266.

14. Addams's hostility toward ideological thinking is gently expressed when she comments about the socialists that frequented Hull House, "I should have been glad to have had the comradeship of that gallant company had they not firmly insisted that fellowship depends upon identity of creed." Quoted from *Twenty Years At Hull-House*, 187. This quality was not admired by all of Addams's associates. Rosika Schwimmer, the Hungarian peace activist Addams worked with extensively, distrusted Addams and called her "slippery Jane" and "claimed it was impossible to pin her down to a particular ideological position." See Davis, *American Heroine*, 219.

15. Addams, *Democracy and Social Ethics*, 69–70.

16. Addams's career was divided between her work at Hull House, perhaps the most famous and successful of all the settlement houses in the United States, and her peace activism with the Women's International League for Peace and Freedom, for which she received the Nobel Peace Prize in 1931. In addition, she and her colleagues at Hull House have been credited with having played an integral role in the development of American sociology through their influence on scholars at the University of Chicago and their collection of demographic data from Chicago. See Mary Jo Deegan, *Jane Addams and the Men of the Chicago School, 1892–1918* (New Brunswick, N.J.: Transaction Books, 1988).

17. See James Weber Linn, *Jane Addams* (New York: D. Appleton-Century, 1935), 168–77.

18. Addams, *Democracy and Social Ethics*, 275.

19. Ibid., 223.

20. Ibid.

21. Ibid., 224–25.

22. Addams, *Newer Ideals of Peace* (Chautauqua, N.Y.: Chautauqua Press, 1907), 57.

23. Addams, *Peace and Bread in Time of War* (New York: Macmillan, 1922), 139 (hereafter cited as *Peace and Bread*).

24. Ibid.,197.

25. Ibid., 143.

26. Ibid., 150–51.

27. Farrell, *Beloved Lady*, 215.

28. For example, see Merle Curti, "Jane Addams on Human Nature," *Journal of the History of Ideas* 22 (1961): 247; Sondra R. Herman, *Eleven Against War* (Stanford, Calif.: Hoover Institution Press, 1969), 116; Daniel Levine, *Jane Addams and the Liberal Tradition* (Madison: State Historical Society of Wisconsin, 1971): 222; Linn, *Jane Addams*, 183.

29. Linn, *Jane Addams*, 333.

30. Herman, *Eleven Against War*, 116.

31. Farrell, *Beloved Lady*, 176.

32. Davis, *American Heroine*, 247.

33. For the anger directed at Addams during and after the war, see Davis, *American Heroine*, chaps. 13 and 14.

34. Addams's response to the war provides an interesting contrast to Randolph Bourne's. Addams fundamentally agreed with Bourne's analysis of the war, and she reprinted copies of his essay, "War and the Intellectuals," for distribution to the Women's Peace Party. But she never allowed her despair about the war to completely demoralize her and undermine her fundamental faith in democracy, as it did for Bourne. See Charles Forcey, *The Crossroads of Liberalism* (New York: Oxford University Press, 1961), 281, and Richard J. Ellis, *The Dark Side of the Left* (Lawrence: University Press of Kansas, 1998), 99–100.

35. Sometimes these demands to balance justice with mercy and humility led Addams to take positions that made her uncomfortable. For example, Addams vigorously supported seating African-American delegates at the Progressive Party convention of 1912, but accepted their exclusion upon losing this battle to Theodore Roosevelt. Mary Jo Deegan points out that Addams felt anguish over this compromise: "Perhaps because of this painful choice of 'democratic' values over her own, Addams was aided in her later decision to opt for the latter when she was tested on the pacifism issue." Deegan, *Jane Addams and the Men of the Chicago School*, 302.

36. Davis, *American Heroine*, 133.

37. Ibid., 134.

38. Levine, *Jane Addams and the Liberal Tradition*, 223.

39. Farrell, *Beloved Lady*, 19.

40. Allen F. Davis notes that "Probably no other woman in any period of American history has been venerated and worshipped the way Jane Addams was in the period just before World War I." Davis, *American Heroine*, 200. See 198–200 for illustrations of her popularity.

41. The biographies by Addams's nephew James Weber Linn, *Jane Addams*, and John C. Farrell, *Beloved Lady*, are the most uncritically admiring. Rivka Shpak Lissak, *Pluralism and Progressives* (Chicago: University of Chicago Press, 1989), and essays by Jill Conway, "Jane Addams: An American Heroine," *Daedalus* 93 (Spring 1965): 761–80, and "Women Reformers and American Culture, 1870–1930," *Journal of Social History* 5 (Winter 1971–72):164–77, provide three of the most critical, even angry, assessments of Addams. For a moderately debunking but also generally respectful biography, see Davis, *American Heroine*.

42. Addams approved of not taking the "attitude towards" President Woodrow Wilson during the war "by which the Abolitionists so constantly embarrassed President Lincoln during the Civil War." Addams, *Peace and Bread*, 44.

43. See note 33.

44. One of the difficulties of thinking about the virtues of democratic citizenship is the degree to which these virtues are sometimes incompatible with one another. Just as Addams teaches us the need for a kind of democratic humility, so there are times when especially the excluded must cultivate a strong sense of pride in order to stake their rightful claim to democratic recognition. Think, for example, of the inspiring character of Frederick Douglass in this regard.

45. Clark E. Cochran, *Character, Community, and Politics* (Tuscaloosa, Ala.: University of Alabama Press, 1982), 21.

46. For the assertion that it does, see, for example, Allan Bloom, *The Closing of the American Mind* (New York: Simon & Schuster, 1987).

47. "For such is the nature of men, that howsoever they may acknowledge many others to be more witty, or more eloquent, or more learned; Yet they will hardly believe there be many so wise as themselves: For they see their own wit at hand, and other mens at a distance. But this proveth rather that men are in that point equall, than unequall." Thomas Hobbes, *Leviathan*, (1651; reprint, New York: Penguin, 1968), 184.

48. "Only religion possesses the majesty, the power, and the sacred language to teach all of us, the religious and the secular, the genuine appreciation for each other on which a successful civility must rest." Stephen L. Carter, *Civility* (New York: Basic Books, 1998), 18.

49. Richard Rorty, *Achieving Our Country* (Cambridge, Mass.: Harvard University Press, 1998), 22.

50. Ibid., 22

51. Ibid., 34.

52. Addams is most often thought of as a kind of illustration of mainstream liberal progressivism, such as when Leon Fink writes, "If John Dewey best expressed the precepts for democratic commitments among intellectuals, Jane Addams likely offered their most thorough-going example." Leon Fink, *Progressive Intellectuals and the Dilemmas of Democratic Commitment* (Cambridge, Mass.: Harvard University Press, 1997), 20.

53. Note, for example, her outrage at the commercialization of entertainment and art, in Jane Addams, *The Spirit of Youth and the City Streets* (New York: Macmillan, 1912), 98.

54. *Second Twenty Years at Hull-House*, 301.

55. Just as Vaclav Havel stands as a rebuke to our own generation when he writes, "We are still under the sway of the destructive and thoroughly vain belief that man is the pinnacle of creation, and not just a part of it, and that therefore everything is permitted to him." Vaclav Havel, *The Art of the Impossible* (New York: Knopf, 1997), 19.

56. Addams, *Democracy and Social Ethics*, 240.

57. Ibid., 266.

58. Addams, *My Friend, Julia Lathrop* (New York: Arno Press, 1974), 169.

59. It is a commonplace of the literature on the Progressive era that this was the period in which middle-class reformers championed expertise and social science as the tools for controlling and managing the new urban industrial America. For example, Steven Diner writes, "Historians have shown that the new professionals of the Progressive Era formed a middle class that substantially created the modern bureaucratic culture of contemporary America." Diner gives a striking example of this demand for expert management: "The leader of the playground movement in Pittsburgh explained in a speech in 1896 that immigrant and working-class children did not know how to play." The implication, of course, was that recreational experts would teach them. Steven J. Diner, *A Very Different Age* (New York: Hill and Wang, 1998), 199, 74.

60. Addams, *A New Conscience and an Ancient Evil* (New York: Macmillan, 1912), 183.

61. Addams, *Second Twenty Years at Hull-House*, 23. See, too, *A New Conscience*, 124; *Newer Ideals of Peace*, 168. Finally, consider this passage from *Second Twenty Years at Hull-House* (16): "It was hard to prove to the community that efficiency is also tenderness; that untrained service results in cruelty, and that the last things to depend upon are the vagaries of a self-seeking politician."

62. See John Dewey, *The Public and Its Problems* (Athens, Ohio: Swallow Press, 1954).

63. Addams, *Newer Ideals of Peace*, 28.

64. Kevin Mattson argues that the theory of citizenship to emerge during the Progressive period replaced virility and property ownership with the values of "enlightenment" or "rationality" as the foundation upon which citizenship was to be built. Kevin Mattson, *Creating a Democratic Public* (University Park: Pennsylvania State University Press, 1998), 80.

65. Addams, *Twenty Years at Hull-House*, 311.

66. Rogers M. Smith writes of what he calls "centrist progressivism" and its commitment not only to nationalism and administrative efficiency, but to nativism as well. See Smith, *Civic Ideals: Conflicting Visions of Citizenship in U.S. History* (New Haven, Conn.: Yale University Press, 1997), 413.

67. Addams, *Newer Ideals of Peace*, 35.

68. Ibid., 48–9.

69. The reason for the lack of recognition of these elements probably has more to do with neglect of Addams as a thinker in her own right than anything else. As pointed out in note 52 above, Addams is usually thought of more as an actor who embodied certain Progressive principles than an independent thinker. As a result, her writings haven't always been given the intellectual scrutiny they deserve by students of the period. As Jean Bethke Elshtain has recently written, Addams is "[o]ne of the great dreamers of American democracy, someone we seem to have forgotten or remember but dimly." Elshtain, "Jane Addams: A Pilgrim's Progress," *Journal of Religion* 78 (July 1998): 339.

70. Davis, *American Heroine*, 102.

71. "Moral consistency is not to be found in the principles of a theory, but in the practice of good judgment. As Aristotle argues, the benchmark of morality is not what the principles say, but what the *phronimos*, the man of practical

wisdom, does. Judgment is more a question of character, of ethics, than of theory." Niko Kolodny, "The Ethics of Cryptonormativism: A Defense of Foucault's Evasions," *Philosophy and Social Criticism* 22 (September 1996): 70.

72. Michael Walzer, *Obligations* (Cambridge, Mass.: Harvard University Press, 1970), 201.

Citizens
(Aristocratic and Democratic)

8

The Natural History of Citizenship

Dennis Hale

America invites all men to become citizens; but it implies the dogma that there is such a thing as citizenship.
—G. K. Chesterton, *What I Saw in America* (1922)

CITIZENSHIP AS A PROBLEMATIC

Whatever America might once have implied about the existence of citizenship, contemporary political science is filled with earnest doubts and rancorous debate: about what citizenship was, is, and can be under modern conditions, in America or in the world. To borrow the language of contemporary social theory, citizenship has become a problematic, which explains the outpouring of books and articles on a theme that a generation ago was almost completely neglected.[1]

It is not my aim here to review the citizenship literature, but it will be helpful to summarize the propositions this body of work has advanced; for while the work is the product of many minds, there is a remarkable consistency of result.

1. The first proposition is that real citizenship is so unlikely in modern nation-states that it is no longer possible to take the idea seriously. The impossibility thesis rests firmly on several facts about modern states that have troubled political thinkers at least since Jean-Jacques Rousseau. First and foremost is the problem of scale: modern states are so large that the individual citizen has shrunk to arithmetical insignificance. To make matters worse, increased scale has brought in its wake complex systems of management and control that further

151

exclude most citizens from any significant participation in public life. And in this inhospitable environment, the attractions of civic life must compete with the responsibilities of family and work. Most of the time, citizenship loses out.[2]

2. The second proposition asserts that our ideas about citizenship come from societies so different from our own, whose political institutions were so antithetical to modern liberal values, that the concept of citizenship must be reconstructed from the ground up before it can be taken seriously. Athens (the source of so many ideas about political things) practiced slavery and imperialism, refused to allow women to be citizens, and enforced rigid distinctions between native and foreign-born. Sparta and Rome were even worse. Any appeal to the ancient ideal of citizenship, therefore, must be deeply suspect, or at best irrelevant.[3]

3. It follows that modern citizenship must be fundamentally different from ancient citizenship—otherwise it would be impossible to attain, or be unworthy of attainment. When we see things from the proper perspective, in fact, we see that ancient citizenship is merely one type of citizenship, among many others—and among these others may be a type more suitable to our present circumstances and values.[4]

4. When it comes to defining the characteristics of this more suitable, modern citizenship, commentators are not of one mind. But the ideal involves the following components:

   —Equality. All distinctions that imply inequality, hierarchy, or difference are incompatible with the equality that contemporary scholars see as the heart and soul of citizenship. It follows from this proposition that American citizenship, like ancient citizenship, falls far short of the ideal, or (alternatively) that citizenship as it has actually been practiced in America for most of our history should be considered simply one of many types (or visions) of citizenship—and a morally suspect type, at that. Awareness of this failing will smooth the path toward a better citizenship in the future.[5]

   —Rights. Citizenship implies equal rights, even when citizens are (regrettably, though perhaps remedially) unequal in other respects— for example, in wealth or social standing. There is an important school of thought that sees citizenship as primarily a claim to rights, or as a form of legal protection against oppression by officials. "Citizenship," the Supreme Court has said, "is the right to have rights," and a diverse array of scholars has insisted on the close connection between citizenship and an expanding number of rights, including not just the classic rights, such as speech and assembly, but also new forms of property and privilege, such as government benefits.[6]

—Democracy. But real citizenship (the citizenship whose possibility is denied by proposition 1) implies something more than the equal protection of the laws, or the possession of various rights, however numerous. It implies very clearly that all of those who share the status of citizen will participate in ruling. Citizenship without political participation seems to most modern commentators—and citizens—to be a contradiction in terms. Most would agree, for example, that all those residents of the United States who were denied the vote in the nineteenth century, whatever their legal status might have been, were in fact only second-class citizens, even when they enjoyed rights: to own property, to be tried by a jury, to freely choose an occupation or residence.[7] Being a citizen (according to this view of the matter) implies not just legal protection but also the broadest possible participation in the task of ruling. Like the ancient citizenship from which it differs in so many other respects (and which so many modern commentators reject as a model), modern citizenship is held to involve "ruling and being ruled"—however paradoxical it might seem to apply Aristotle's formula to a modern state.

—Inclusion. Citizenship is ennobled by inclusion. Modern scholarship generally argues that an exclusive conception of citizenship quickly degenerates into nationalism or xenophobia. As enlightenment spreads, the circle of citizenship will expand with it. It follows, therefore (although this would seem to aggravate the impossibility thesis) that a wider political jurisdiction is to be preferred, wherever possible, to a narrower one: Europe is better than France, the United States is preferable to Georgia, cosmopolitan is better than parochial.[8]

Equality, rights, participatory democracy, inclusion: if these are the elements of the modern understanding of citizenship, it follows that the obstacles to the realization of such a vision are hierarchy and inequality, a focus on obligations rather than rights, representative as opposed to direct democracy, and an exclusive rather than inclusive definition of citizenship.

These obstacles are, of course (the principle of representation excluded), the principal elements in the older conception of citizenship that we are now urged to reject. And we might willingly do so if the institution of citizenship were something that could be redesigned from scratch, like a car or a couch.

But if, like so many political institutions, citizenship has its own nature and dynamic, then perhaps it cannot be redesigned from scratch, in which case we might learn much by attempting to reconstruct what I am calling here, somewhat grandly, "the natural history of citizenship."[9] Looked at from this comparative and historical perspective, the institution of citizenship displays a remarkably stubborn consistency, and what appear to be contemporary problems and puzzles have an ancient and honorable ancestry.

ANCIENT CITIZENSHIP

The idea that we might learn about modern citizenship by studying ancient citizenship will seem a dubious proposition to many scholars. They will insist that each time and place generates its own civic institutions, so that it is wrong to speak of citizenship as such. Premodern polities were so radically different from modern nations that any comparison is likely to mislead. Ancient cities were small, homogeneous, and intensely religious; they embraced slavery and war; they excluded women from public life; and they demanded total devotion to public life, rejecting the most elemental guarantees of privacy and personal liberty.[10]

The modern liberal state, by contrast, exists to preserve private liberty and prosperity. The claims made by the polity on the citizen are superficially modest: the citizen has simply to mind his own business, take care of his family, and obey the law. The virtues such a polity requires are those generated by commerce, although most of the founders of modern liberalism assumed a moderate Christianity in the background to help the citizen behave himself. It is not the liberal state's function to cultivate excellent souls, or to supply the citizenry with opportunities to seek honor, eminence, or noble actions; indeed, such vanity is dangerous when mixed with political ambition. The Good Life might be found in the household or in the marketplace, but not in the assembly.

All of this is true. But there are continuities as well as discontinuities between ancient and modern politics. For example, it is instructive to note in the accounts of ancient cities the many ways in which ancient and modern politics are similar, a discovery all the more surprising because the similarities are found amidst so many differences. Despite the differences in scale, in social arrangements, in economic and household life, we can easily recognize in Athens and Rome phenomena and character types from our immediate surroundings. Among the former: class conflict, greed, ambition, patriotism, loyalty, and betrayal. Among the latter: the arrogant nobleman, the stolid bourgeois, the resentful proletarian. We can also recognize certain familiar tendencies at work beneath the surface. Then, as now, the rich and the poor faced each other across a gulf defined by different aims, interests, and experiences. The power of one class could not increase except at the expense of another. The natural divisions in the community could easily be exploited by clever politicians aiming to expand their own power or the power of their faction. Even some of the techniques (defamation of character, politically motivated lawsuits, benefits exchanged for votes) have changed little in 2,500 years.[11] And as always, there was the permanent conflict between public and private good, pulling citizens and statesmen first in one direction, then another.[12]

This elemental distinction between private and public has many permutations—between what is "mine" and what is "ours;" between what is good for me and my own, and what is good for the city; between what is just and what is convenient. While the ancient city strove to subordinate the private to the public, the tension between them never disappeared, because it is a consequence of the creation of political communities. The city for the first time inducts the individual into a relationship that transcends kinship, and with it the laws of the household and of the body, and therefore creates the possibility of tension between "mine" and "ours."[13] The proper understanding of citizenship is therefore fundamental to any coherent account of politics; and there is no better place to begin this effort than with Aristotle's *Politics*.

THE ARISTOCRATIC ORIGINS OF CITIZENSHIP

In Aristotle's account, citizenship is the social invention that makes the city possible. Because it was a different kind of association from the family, the city required a different basis for membership. Citizenship was a child of necessity. In this case, the need was to govern men who were (in Aristotle's words) "equal and free" and whose obedience could therefore not be compelled.[14]

The city created a different kind of membership, but also a different kind of hierarchy, based on virtue of a new sort: "the virtue that belongs to a citizen," or what Aristotle defines as "understanding the governing of free men" from the point of view both of the ruler and of the ruled.[15] The route to citizenship might lie through military service or noble birth; but the honor attached to participation in public life is not the same thing as military valor or ancestral pride. As Paul Rahe has noted, the citizen's distinctive virtue is the ability to reason correctly about the public good, and to use the gift of speech to urge salutary measures on his fellow citizens.[16] In the ancient city we can see, for the first time, the emergence of political virtue as a distinctive form of honor.

This virtue is not an ideal, but a necessity; without it, the city could not exist. All who possess such virtue should be invited into the ranks of citizens; those who do not should be excluded. The best constitution is one in which this principle is followed scrupulously, but Aristotle concedes that there are many forms of constitution other than the best, many compromises even in good constitutions, and many constitutions that are simply mistaken.[17]

In Aristotle's account, nobody made the citizens equal and free. They simply were so when the city came into being. Citizenship in its earliest form was an invitation to such men—the heads of well-to-do families and free farmers with enough means to be self-supporting—to think of themselves in a different way, as partners in a wider association rather than as the heads of rival and potentially warring families or clans. Because they were free, no wider association would be possible without their participation, and because of their autonomy, the political association was not necessary for their survival. They were already surviving well enough without it. Though some cities might appear to have been formed for the purposes of protection or prosperity, these aims ("mere life") could be, and have been, achieved in much smaller and less comprehensive associations. The city must have come into existence, Aristotle concludes, for some reason beyond "mere life"—that is, "for the sake of noble actions." And it is in this sense that the political association is the most comprehensive association, making possible the fullest expression of man's nature.[18]

Citizenship, therefore, was not a democratic idea originally, but an aristocratic one. In ancient cities, citizenship was a status at first open only to those whose participation was essential to the creation or functioning of the association. It was as exclusive as membership in a high-class men's club, perhaps more so, because unlike club membership, citizenship in its original form could not be purchased, but was open only to those who were free and equal by birth—that is, who were not dependent upon others for their survival.[19]

Everyone else was excluded: foreigners (whose participation was not essential to the local association) and dependents of freemen (slaves, household members, and hangers-on) who were, by virtue of their dependence, under the care and authority of someone else. These principles excluded the vast majority of the adult residents of a typical ancient city, even under a democratic constitution, on the grounds that they were not free, and therefore not equal to those who were free. The democratic assembly that condemned Socrates was open to the participation of roughly twenty-five to thirty percent of the city's residents. The vast majority of Athenians were not eligible for what we would consider full Athenian citizenship, even under its most democratic constitution. Under other political circumstances, citizenship was narrower still.[20]

When we first encounter citizenship, it wears the mask of privilege, highly prized and jealously guarded; every extension of civic honors in ancient cities was taken reluctantly, and usually under duress—for example, foreigners (and sometimes slaves) who served a Greek city in wartime were occasionally granted citizenship as a reward for their services. But this was a rare event.[21]

We find also citizenship closely tied to family and faith—the modes of membership and association that it transcended but did not destroy. Ancient cities were collections of extended clans and large households, each with its own family deities. One entered the city by first passing through the doorway of the family, embracing the city's cults only after embracing those of the clan—but without abandoning the family devotions either. The wider association was constructed on a foundation of narrower, but older associations, anchoring the city in the familiar, but making possible a conflict between old and new, between the world of the household and the world of the city.[22]

Citizenship was at first an invitation to share in governing. A citizen was (in Aristotle's well-known formula) one of those "entitled to participate in office, deliberative or judicial."[23] Other residents of the city enjoyed what we (but not they) would call rights—at times, even slaves had certain rights as did foreigners (for example, the right to own property, including other slaves), and even, to a limited degree, so did women. But only citizens could share in honors, that is, only citizens could rule.[24]

It follows that the citizenry would have seemed, to citizens and noncitizens alike, a rather special group, jealous of its prerogatives and inclined at times to be rather fussy about its special role in the city—and a frequent irritant to those left out. "Is it lawful for you to scourge a man who is a Roman, and uncondemned?" This was the response of the apostle Paul to the soldiers who arrested him—meaning, I am a Roman citizen, and therefore I have certain rights, and a certain dignity, and both must be respected by the authorities whatever they might think of my ideas. In Paul's exchange with the centurions, the chief captain says: "With a great sum obtained I this freedom" (that is, Roman citizenship, which was purchasable in those latter, decadent days of the empire). Paul's response is as eloquent as it is haughty: "But I was born free" (Acts 22: 28–29).

Citizens shared this special status by virtue of their independence, which was determined by birth into one of the independent families. Birthright citizenship implied two important principles: (1) ruling belongs to those who are capable of ruling themselves, whose families have enough resources to escape the authority of others,[25] and (2) keeping the association together requires that it not be stretched too far beyond the natural boundaries of the family and clan. Foreigners—regardless of their wealth, noble birth, or special virtue—could not be encompassed within the narrow circle of fellow citizens, a form of exclusiveness that proved difficult to maintain in the long run, as we shall see below.

The implication, clearly, is that citizens are better than noncitizens. They are superior both to foreigners and to native-born noncitizens. Citizenship was exclusive and parochial and existed quite comfortably with the aristocratic ranking of society, under which the few ruled and were ruled in turn, while the many were simply ruled.

THE PLEBEIANIZATION OF CITIZENSHIP

In the beginning, civic rights belonged only to those who could effectively claim them. Sometimes this meant a struggle to subdue or to limit arbitrary rule by a prince; at other times it meant that those who served the city were given special rewards, such as public recognition of their importance (honors). Or, the city's most important men might withhold their support (in arms or taxes) in exchange for concessions; in extreme cases they could depose the ruler.[26]

But over time, as political conditions became more settled, what was important to the few became important to others as well (although not immediately to the many). Inevitably, men from lower social ranks sought the status of citizen, and increasingly they were successful in doing so. But why did men from lower ranks want to be citizens in the first place, and why did rulers find it appropriate, or expedient, to open what once had been closed?

The demand to be included in the ranks of citizens was almost certainly not, initially, a demand to share in ruling per se. The plebeianization of citizenship was driven primarily by two other concerns: (1) the plebeians' need to defend their interests against abuse by patricians, and (2) the desire of the plebeians for dignity.

Ancient cities were elaborately hierarchical. The many who did not rule nevertheless enjoyed certain rights (as we would say), or privileges, as noted earlier: to contract, to engage in business, to own property other than land. The right to share in offices, however, must have conferred a decisive advantage on those who were willing to take advantage of their position, and before long the most prosperous plebeians were demanding entrance to the assembly and even to the magistracy, along with the right to own land and to marry into the patrician class.[27]

The second concern is harder to document. But it is easy to imagine the process by which successful plebeians became restive and then resentful at being denied this final recognition of their merit: the dignity afforded by entrance into the *sanctum sanctorum* of citizenship. However merit is defined, those who are convinced that they have it will demand the appropriate honors. An aristocracy that insists on withholding such recognition exposes itself to danger on two fronts: first, it is dangerous to insult residents who have become powerful in fact, if not in theory; and second, refusal undermines the aristocracy's moral authority through the tacit acknowledgment that merit is unattainable by those born outside the charmed circle and is therefore simply an accident of birth rather than a true accomplishment.

Thus, the extension of citizenship has an almost inexorable quality to it. Aristotle recognized the reason: those who have the means to destroy the regime must be persuaded to support it, and the simplest way to accomplish this is to give them a share in ruling, even when their participation is a source of disturbance to the old constitution. For this reason, Rome invited the plebes into the army to help defeat the Gauls and extended full citizenship in return for their service—an invitation that led eventually to heightened class conflict and civil unrest.[28]

THE WIDENING CIRCLE

In the same way that citizenship was extended downward to include the plebes, it was also extended outward to encompass a wider territory as the once-exclusive privilege of citizenship was made available to foreigners. This process paralleled the transformation of the city into an empire and was especially important in Rome.

As Rome grew and prospered, due in part to the effectiveness of its civic institutions, the original city acquired clients at greater and greater distances from the capital. The free residents of these far-off places eventually sought equality with their Roman rulers. The very success of civic institutions, in other words, encouraged their geographic dispersal, and the circle of citizenship widened finally to encompass all of Italy and then much of the empire as well.[29] This process was already far advanced when Paul had his encounter with the centurions, an incident that richly portrays the clash between aristocratic and imperial citizenship. Paul, an upper-class Jew, a citizen and (formerly) a servant of Rome, was arrested by a captain of guards who had purchased his own citizenship. In fact, both were subjects of a far-flung empire stretching from Britain to Persia, whose subjects spoke a thousand tongues, rather than citizens of a small, homogeneous city.

But stretching citizenship beyond the city's walls and beyond the aristocracy were possibilities inherent in the institution from the beginning. So, therefore, were the conflicts that accompanied this process of expansion: between rich and poor, ruler and client, city and empire. By the time Aristotle wrote the *Politics*, in fact, these conflicts had already acquired a lurid history in Athens. That Aristotle's categories of analysis are so immediately familiar to us—the arrogant rich, the sober bourgeois, the resentful poor—suggests that perhaps, despite the passage of time, the central problem presented by modern citizenship is not very modern after all.

In the light of this history, what appear to be the elements of this problem?

First, the logic of citizenship is expansion. Beginning with a core of aristocratic citizens, the institution will grow to accommodate the demands of newcomers and plebes for place, and the state's need for additional resources. Citizenship expands because it confers advantage and honor to those who acquire it, at the same time holding the association together and making it succeed.

Second, and despite this logic, the essence of citizenship—ruling—is the natural province of a minority, for two reasons: (1) the deliberation required by decision-making can accommodate only a fraction of potential deliberators at any moment,[30] and (2) the excellence required by ruling is not equally distributed but belongs only to the few, a category that includes a smaller or greater number depending upon a variety of circumstances, such as the state of civic education.

Third, the plebeianization of citizenship is associated with an important shift in emphasis from ruling to the defense of rights and interests. Those who stand outside the ruling circle see that their rights and interests are threatened by the greater power of those on the inside. Their initial motive for seeking entry into the ruling circle is thus not to rule but to defend themselves against those who do. That they might ultimately acquire an interest in ruling—in statesmanship, in fact—is a possibility that depends on civic education for its fulfillment. But if the circle of citizens widens rapidly enough or far enough, it will be difficult to devise forms of civic education that can keep up with the demand or that can embrace the entire mass of newly minted citizens.

In the meantime, however, both the plebeianization of citizenship and the growth of the association from city to empire, cause the numbers of citizens to increase, contributing to the problem identified earlier: if there are many citizens, no citizen's share of the time devoted to deliberation can be at all large. As the process continues, the share shrinks to insignificance, and citizenship loses its connection to ruling. And in any case, newer citizens, less drawn to ruling and less prepared for the disciplines of self-government, are likely to see citizenship as useful only for the protection of private rights and interests.

Like so many other good things, then, it would appear that citizenship has a natural tendency to self-destruct.

MODERN CITIZENSHIP

The aspects of modern citizenship that trouble us are not new; they were present at the creation, and are difficulties to be lived with rather than eliminated. But living with them requires that we understand them clearly. Restated in terms more directly relevant to our contemporary debates, the problem of citizenship has the following natural components:

1. Most of a country's citizens are not citizens in the fullest sense; real citizenship is the possession of a minority. This was true in Athens, and it is true in America and in other modern democratic states, although not for the same reasons. Athens excluded the majority of its inhabitants on the grounds that they were not fit to exercise public judgment or because they were foreigners. The modern liberal state excludes no significant category of adult residents from citizenship; even the foreign-born face relatively modest hurdles. But the scale of modern states accomplishes what the law does not: it excludes most people from active participation in governing, even when it is scrupulous about protecting their rights. The end result is similar: in Athens and America alike, the community is governed by a small fraction of its adult population.[31]

   This is not a matter that offers us any choice. Citizenship as ruling requires deliberation, and deliberation cannot be conducted over great distances, or in the midst of a crowd, or by millions of people at once. It requires face-to-face encounters among people who take seriously the business at hand.

2. Unlike an ancient city, however, a modern state does not have to be governed by the same minority continually; the politically active class can be freshened by rotation. Something like this happens in many organizations or in small towns as the most active members pass their burdens to others. What matters is the presence in society of a large class of citizens-in-waiting—individuals who can rise to the occasion of service and judgment, even if such opportunities must be infrequent. This is what we expect when we impanel a jury, whose members may not have performed any public service, but from whom we expect extraordinary judgment and discretion.

   Furthermore, all citizens, even those who do little more than vote, are continually called upon to make judgments on difficult public questions. However small each citizen's share of collective judgment might be, we cannot ignore the cumulative weight of such individual contributions. The quality of the whole will depend, inevitably, on the quality of the parts.

3. Citizens are not equal, however, in their capacity to make the public judgments that citizenship requires and they cannot be made equal by administrative fiat or social engineering. Judgment is a political art, after all. This does not mean that public policy should not aim at nurturing the capacity for public judgment in as many

citizens as possible—this is what civic education is for. Nor does it
mean that we must seek out only those citizens who belong to the
most favored classes. Good citizens, while hard to find, can be found
in every class and among all walks of life. But it does mean that we
should place a high value on all those methods of selecting potential judges and deliberators that enable us to make relevant discriminations among citizens.[32]

4. It is important to nurture such capacities for reasons of state because
it is dangerous to a democratic regime if an increasing percentage
of the populace is incapable of rendering prudent judgments. Real
citizens have a counterintuitive incentive in modern states as in ancient ones: however much it might diminish each citizen's share of
sovereignty, it is nevertheless a sound policy to encourage a wider
distribution of the skills necessary to ruling. But to do so requires that
we face squarely the problem of civic education in the modern state,
and to begin a very brief consideration of this puzzle, I invite the
reader to join in a thought experiment.

CITIZENSHIP AND CONTEXT

Where are we likely to encounter a cross-section of our fellow citizens?
At the ballpark? The freeway at rush-hour? The registry of motor vehicles?

Imagine yourself in one of these places. Now look around, and think
about the people you see, not just as a crowd of strangers, but as fellow
citizens: colleagues in the republic and shareholders in the enterprise of
ruling. If you are honest, this experiment may leave you feeling a little
queasy.

Now vary the circumstances. Instead of the ballpark or the freeway,
imagine your neighborhood polling place on election day. In my own
neighborhood, election day brings a fairly typical turnout for an American election—roughly half the electorate for presidential elections, maybe
a third for a state or local election. Many of my neighbors grew up in the
neighborhood, and they greet each other as old friends, exchanging ban-
ter with election workers holding signs and passing out leaflets. It is a
pleasant atmosphere and inspires far fewer misgivings than a day on the
freeway or a trip to the motor vehicle registry. Still, there is at least this
one misgiving: where have all the other voters gone?

Change the picture again. Imagine now that you are a member of a jury,
one of twelve given the task of judging innocence or guilt. You and your
fellow jurors will come from varied circumstances and walks of life; in
fact, you will probably never again spend so much time with such a de-
mographically heterogeneous group. Several jurors have not been edu-

cated beyond high school and only one or two have professional degrees. Most are financially comfortable, but no one is wealthy. Their ages range from the early twenties to the middle sixties, they are a mixture of racial and ethnic backgrounds, and their number includes both men and women.

Nothing about these people suggests that they have been selected from among the nation's most virtuous or outstanding citizens, and you are not at all sure of their ability—or your own, if you are still being honest—to judge fairly an especially complex case. But as you begin your delibera-tions you notice something that pleases you: the members of the jury are taking their responsibilities very seriously. The judge has told you of your importance to the administration of justice and may also have noted the important role that juries have played in the evolution of free institutions of government. You were impressed by the gravity of the circumstances and the weight of your responsibility, and as far as you can tell, your fel-low jurors were impressed as well. By the time you have completed your deliberations, it is your considered opinion that you, and they, have risen to the occasion and rendered a sensible verdict.[33]

In this experiment we have constructed concentric circles. The largest circle embraces a mass; the smallest circle embraces a committee. But it is a condition of this experiment that any of the people in the larger circle might also be found in the smallest—although not, of course, all at once. In constructing these circles, we are not separating the wheat from the chaff, or the cream from the milk. Nor are we, to borrow James Madison's language, "refining" public opinion by "passing [it] through the medium" of a body of citizens chosen for their wisdom. We might well encounter a fellow juror on the freeway or at the ballpark, where we might entertain gloomy thoughts about his or her conduct and character. Or our fellow juror might be one of our neighbors who failed to vote. What changes in this experiment is not the sample, but the context.

The first context, in which we meet our fellow citizens in anonymous public spaces, is social rather than political. It is a truism that social con-texts in the United States have become looser, less well governed by rules about such things as noise, public behavior, modes of dress and address, and so forth. The result is that public spaces may seem to many people threatening rather than inviting, driving citizens farther into their private shells and away from public involvement.

The second context is political: voting is a public act, widely held to be either a privilege or an obligation of American citizens (notice the ambi-guity). A declining percentage of Americans bothers to vote, even in presi-dential elections presenting very clear choices. Voting is a weak behav-ior: it fails to stir the deepest passions, and a great many people, at least in recent decades, do not take it very seriously. Many theories have been offered to explain why this is so, but they are not our interest at the moment. For now we can leave it at this: voting is the minimum action associated with American citizenship. Below this minimum, citizenship loses all connection to ruling and becomes only an assertion of rights.

The third context, which is judicial, differs in interesting ways from the second. Compared to voting, service on a jury is time consuming, emotionally and intellectually draining, and obligatory. Unlike the refusal to vote, refusal to serve on a jury is a felony. Like the military draft, jury service reminds us that we can be called upon to make sacrifices for the public good and to meet a difficult challenge as a matter of duty—a realization that sometimes comes as a (salutary?) shock.

In our tradition, the word *voting* is almost subliminally linked with the idea of *right*, as in the right to vote. Not so with the word *jury*. We hear often of the right to be tried by a jury but we hear much less often of the right to be a juror. Jury service is associated with obligation (jury *duty*) along with paying taxes and registering for the draft, one more task that many citizens would (and do) gladly avoid.

Voting is a form of mass political behavior—and a weak behavior, as noted above. Furthermore, the context within which voting takes place has in recent times become increasingly unstructured as parties and campaigns have changed, especially at the presidential level. Modern campaigns are more often than not contests between individuals rather than between mass political organizations, and they take place increasingly in an electronic void of sound bites and infomercials. Jury service is carried out in an intimate context that is extremely structured and that changes very slowly. We also have the testimony of former jurors that the process leaves a permanent mark—especially if the trial is long or complicated. Voting takes very little out of us, and some people cannot remember a week after an election for whom they voted, or even *if* they voted. Jury service can take a great deal out of us, and is often an unforgettable experience.

Voting is voluntary. It involves participation in politics; we may participate or not, as we wish. Jury service is compulsory. Voting is private and anonymous. On a jury, by contrast, citizens are forced to reveal their opinions, preferences, and judgments in public, and usually cannot practice other than what they preach. Voters may seek their private advantage in the voting booth: in fact, contemporary election theory expects that voters will be motivated by private calculation. The so-called median voter model describes a rational actor seeking to advance his private interests—maximizing his benefits while minimizing his burdens.[34] Jurors, by contrast, are expected to set aside private interests, and to reveal any possible biases, or conflicts of interest, before being sworn. Any attempt by a juror to do what voters are supposed to do—use the process to advance a private agenda—would be considered in contempt of court.

Jury service differs from voting in yet another way: even though both voters and jurors are expected to deliberate, only jurors work in a context that is actually conducive to deliberation. Deliberation requires certain preconditions—access to information, time in which to consider it, openness to opposing views, a forum in which debate is both encouraged and regulated, and a commitment to subordinate private interest to the public good.

There is a pattern to these contexts—from the fluid, unstructured context of social encounters, to the more ordered but still relatively fluid world of elections, to the extreme formality of the jury's chambers. As the context becomes more structured and more deliberate, the quality of citizenship is strengthened. The more citizens are asked to do, the more likely they are to rise to the occasion, provided that the occasion is presented in the appropriate context. Citizenship survives—the survival of the jury is one piece of evidence for this. But American life is increasingly inhospitable to the contexts within which citizenship can flourish.

Consider the qualities we have identified with citizenship: structure, compulsion, publicity, deliberation, and formality. Americans profess a dislike for all of these things. We like to be open, to be free to choose, to be private, to do things spontaneously and quickly rather than deliberately, and to be informal. If citizenship is to be strengthened, we will first have to learn to appreciate things that we do not, as a people, like very much. One of these qualities will give us particular trouble: compulsion. Americans do not like to be told what to do. But there is an irreducible element of compulsion involved in the experience of citizenship, and part of the task of civic education is to remind ourselves of what expectations we can impose on ourselves and, in so doing, on one another.[35]

However, unlike the theme of citizenship itself, the theme of civic education has not enjoyed a contemporary revival and it is easy to see why. It is much easier to devise a strategy that increases rights than one that increases the citizenry's ability to exercise those rights responsibly or to carry out the obligations associated with citizenship. The very phrase "civic education" conjures the musty aroma of 1950s grade-school civics lessons or Progressive-era training sessions for immigrants. Both forms of civic education sought to teach facts and values simultaneously: to inform school children and immigrants about how American government worked and to inculcate in them the appropriate reverence for the process and its results.[36]

But the natural history of citizenship suggests very strongly that the most important aim of civic education is neither information nor reverence; it is character formation. The political association is possible only because some of its members, at least, are willing to care for it and to subordinate their private advantage to the public good. The larger the proportion of such members, the stronger the association will be, whether the association is a city, a nation, or a private organization. This is a truism, as old as politics. Nearly as old is the ancient method of achieving this end, by keeping the city as small as possible, gathering in one embrace family, religion, fellowship, and market.

The difficulty is to achieve the character formation required by citizenship in the very different circumstances presented by the modern state.[37] We cannot do so with methods imported from ancient cities, but we might nevertheless learn something about civic education from a focus on the natural history of citizenship; and I will end this essay with a few observations drawn from my own reading of this history.

1. As Aristotle noted, the exercise of citizenship-as-ruling involves a particular kind of knowledge (which should not be confused with information of the how-a-bill-becomes-a-law variety). Aristotle defines this knowledge as "understanding the governing of free men from the point of view of both the ruler and the ruled." The educated citizen has acquired, in other words, the knowledge, through experience, of what it means to be responsible for the association and its members.

   It is immediately apparent that a large part of this knowledge can be acquired in contexts that are not strictly political, or in organizations that are not vested with formal public authority: citizens can learn how to care for the most comprehensive association by caring for lesser associations, such as churches, unions, political parties, fraternal organizations—even university departments.[38] The knowledge of how to rule is transportable from one context to another, in part because it is not a purely technical knowledge. It follows that part of the strategy of civic education in the modern state should be to multiply the opportunities for people to exercise responsibility, both in explicitly political contexts (town meetings, school committees, party organizations, etc.) and in private organizations as well. It follows also that modern citizenship, like ancient citizenship, builds on the lesser but more familiar associations of family, religion, work, and neighborhood. That these lesser associations will sometimes conflict with the wider association is part of the nature of citizenship, a tension to be lived with rather than overcome.

2. If learning to care for the association is one element in the character formation required of citizenship, learning to take care of oneself is another, and is probably prior in sequence. This is a difficult matter.

A certain portion of the community is, by obvious necessity, dependent upon others for its care, and we are all, by turns, members of this portion at the beginning and at the end of our lives. In between, there are misfortunes that place us in temporary need of public assistance. But the modern state encourages other, less natural forms of dependence. Alexis de Tocqueville worried about the "soft despotism" that would follow on this dependence, and the modern mania for finding victims everywhere suggests that he was right to worry. Victims require protection and then restitution, and both require larger and more powerful and more bureaucratic governments. An important part of the strategy of civic education, then, is to encourage as much as possible the development of habits of independence and responsibility, especially among children and adolescents, but also among adults.

3. In civic education it is important to find the right balance between what G. K. Chesterton called "the romance of citizenship"[39] and what Tocqueville called "self-interest, rightly understood."[40] Like the idea of community, the idea of citizenship often provokes a syrupy sentimentalism that obscures an important fact about civic engagement: namely, that it is hard work. Citizenship has its pleasures, no doubt, and there are times when politics can be fun; but Socrates was mostly right, after all, to suggest that ruling involves "solving other people's problems for them," and that such a task would have little appeal to anyone with better things to do. This is not what we want to tell children. But we do need to acknowledge, and carefully teach, that caring for the association is an activity that comes at a price, even when the price is worth paying. Still, no one who has served in an official capacity, or even as an officer of a private organization, will deny that caring for the association is often frustrating, tedious, and even heart-breaking labor.[41] And while such work may seem very far from the "noble actions" that Aristotle saw as the aim of the city, there is more than a little democratic nobility in doing well those tasks that simply must be done. This seems a realistic and even uplifting standard against which to measure the experience of citizenship in modern times.

NOTES

1. There has been a dramatic increase in the scholarly attention paid to citizenship over the past twenty-five years—a marked contrast to the 1950s and 1960s. For example, there is no entry for *citizenship* in the 1968 edition of the *International Encyclopedia of the Social Sciences*, but the Boston College library has more than five hundred titles on citizenship published since 1975.

2. John Schaar, *Legitimacy in the Modern State* (New Brunswick, N.J.: Transaction Books, 1981), 15–53; Robert Putnam, "Bowling Alone: America's Declining Social Capital," *The Journal of Democracy* (January 1995), 65–78, and "Tuning In, Tuning Out: The Strange Disappearance of Social Capital in America," *Political Science* 28 (Winter 1995), 664–83. For a richer body of empirical data on civic engagement, see Sidney Verba, Kay L. Schlozman, and Henry E. Brady, *Voice and Equality: Civic Voluntarism in American Politics* (Cambridge, Mass.: Harvard University Press, 1995).

3. Judith N. Shklar, *American Citizenship: The Quest for Inclusion* (Cambridge, Mass.: Harvard University Press, 1991).

4. Rogers M. Smith, *Civic Ideals: Conflicting Visions of Citizenship in U.S. History* (New Haven, Conn.: Yale University Press, 1997).

5. Ibid., 470–506. See also Jane Mansbridge, *Beyond Adversary Democracy* (Chicago: University of Chicago Press, 1983).

6. *Trop v. Dulles*, 356 US 86 (1958); Mary Ann Glendon, *Rights Talk: The Impoverishment of Political Discourse* (New York: Free Press, 1993), 31–32.

7. James Kettner, *The Development of American Citizenship: 1608–1870* (Chapel Hill: University of North Carolina Press, 1978), 287–333.

8. Shklar, *American Citizenship*. See also Kenneth L. Karst, *Belonging to America: Equal Citizenship and the Constitution* (New Haven, Conn.: Yale University Press, 1989), especially chap. 3.

9. The phrase is inspired by Bertrand de Jouvenel, *On Power: The Natural History of its Growth* (Indianapolis, Ind.: Liberty Fund, 1997).

10. Paul Rahe, *Republics Ancient and Modern: Classical Republicanism and the American Revolution* (Chapel Hill: University of North Carolina Press, 1992), bk. 1, chap. 1.

11. See, for example, Kathleen Freeman, *The Murder of Herodes and Other Trials from the Athenian Law Courts* (Indianapolis, Ind.: Hackett, 1963), 54–86, 173–81, and 229–34.

12. The discussion of ancient citizenship in this paper is based on the following sources: Aristotle, *Politics* (New York: Penguin, 1981); F. E. Adcock, *Roman Political Ideas and Practice* (Ann Arbor: University of Michigan Press, 1964); G. Glotz, *The Greek City and its Institutions* (New York: Routledge & Kegan Paul, 1969); A. H. M. Jones, *Athenian Democracy* (Baltimore, Md.: Johns Hopkins University Press, 1986) and *Sparta* (Oxford: Blackwell, 1967); Michael Crawford, *The Roman Republic* (Cambridge, Mass.: Harvard University Press, 1982); A. N. Sherwin-White, *The Roman Citizenship* (Oxford: Clarendon Press, 1973); Victor Ehrenberg, *The Greek State* (Oxford: Blackwell, 1960); Peter Riesenberg, *Citizenship in the Western Tradition: Plato to Rousseau* (Chapel Hill: University of North Carolina Press, 1992); Paul Rahe, *Republics*; Alfred E. Zimmern, *The Greek Commonwealth* (Oxford: Clarendon Press, 1911); C. Nicolet, *The World of the Citizen in Republican Rome* (Berkeley and Los Angeles: University of California Press, 1980); and John Thorley, *Athenian Democracy* (New York: Routledge, 1996).

13. On this point see Wilson Carey McWilliams, *The Idea of Fraternity in America* (Berkeley and Los Angeles: University of California Press, 1973), 9–63.

14. Aristotle *Politics*, bk. 1, ch. 1, 2, and 7.

15. Aristotle *Politics*, bk. 3, ch. 4.

16. Rahe, *Republics*, 23–54.

17. Aristotle *Politics*, bk. 3, ch. 5.

18. Aristotle *Politics*, bk. 1, ch. 1 and 2; bk. 3, ch. 6 and 9.

19. Reisenberg, *Citizenship*, 35–36.

20. Jones, *Athenian Democracy*, 10–11. See also Glotz, *The Greek City*, 126–27; and Ehrenberg, *The Greek State*, 97. Riesenberg says of Rome, in its republican period, that "less than a tenth of the population governed the rest" (57).

21. Jones, *Athenian Democracy*, 19; Nicolet, *The World of the Citizen*.

22. Jones, *Athenian Democracy*, 10–11.

23. Aristotle *Politics*, bk. 3, ch. 1.

24. Jones, *Athenian Democracy*, 10–11; Riesenberg, *Citizenship*, 27–30, 35–37.

25. Aristotle *Politics*, bk. 3, ch. 5. "Ruling oneself" had a meaning beyond economic self-sufficiency and the possession of leisure. It was the mark of the gentleman that he could discipline his own passions; one first glimpses the rule of the "statesman" in the phenomenon of self-rule (bk. 1, ch. 3).

26. Crawford, *The Roman Republic*, chap. 3; Riesenberg, *Citizenship*, 3–4.

27. Riesenberg, *Citizenship*, 27–30. Conflict between office-holding patricians and free farmers excluded from official honors led to the reforms of Solon, in which the right to hold office was first extended downward. In Plato's *The Republic*, when Thracymachus observes that "each ruling group sets down laws for its own advantage," the implication is that the behavior referred to is normal (bk. 1, 338e).

28. Reisenberg, *Citizenship*, 57.

29. The circle was not widened easily. The demand by the Latins and Campanians (in 338 B.C.) to be included with Rome as "one people and one state" was first received by Rome as an act of rebellion, and proposals to grant citizenship to non-Romans were a frequent source of conflict within Rome. See Nicolet, *The World of the Citizen*, chap. 1. When proposing to grant citizenship to foreigners in A.D. 40, the emperor Claudius (as recorded by Tacitus) observed that it was the exclusiveness of Athens and Sparta, "their policy of holding the conquered aloof as alien-born," that led to their downfall (Nicolet, 25).

30. This is true even in a small assembly or meeting. See Bertrand de Jouvenel, "The Chairman's Problem," in *The Nature of Politics: Selected Essays of Bertrand de Jouvenel*, ed. Dennis Hale and Marc Landy (New Brunswick, N.J.: Transaction Books, 1988), 108–18.

31. Under its most democratic constitution, only 25 to 30 percent of Athenian residents were eligible for Athenian citizenship, which entitled them to sit in the Assembly, and to serve as jurors, magistrates, and other officers. Sidney Verba and Norman Nie have concluded that only about 11 percent of the American population can be classed as fully active citizens who participate in the full range of political activity available to American citizens, from voting to serving as officers in a political organization. Twice as many Americans, 22 percent, engage in no political activity at all. Sidney Verba and Norman H. Nie, *Participation in America* (New York: Harper & Row, 1972), 21.

32. For example, judges once chose jury foremen based on a quick "read" of a juror's profession, experience, and demeanor—an admittedly unscientific procedure subject to all kinds of *invidious* as opposed to *relevant* discriminations.

But this method at least acknowledged that a jury foreman should be first among equals, rather than a name picked from a hat.

33. Harry Kalven Jr. and Hans Zeisel, *The American Jury* (Boston: Little, Brown, 1966). Obviously, not all juries function as idyllically as the caricature.

34. Mancur Olsen, *The Logic of Collective Action* (Cambridge, Mass.: Harvard University Press, 1965).

35. An encouraging sign is the movement in many states to discourage evasion of jury duty and to shorten the list of exemptions. For a description of one class of reforms, see David E. Kasunic, "One Day/One Trial: A Major Improvement in the Jury System," *Judicature* 67 (August 1983): 79–86.

36. Civic educators have usually assumed that students, having learned how American institutions operate, would naturally be reverential toward them, an assumption which may not be justified. For an interesting discussion of the conflict between political knowledge and the demands of citizenship, see Harvey Mansfield Jr., "The Teaching of Citizenship," *Political Science PS* 17 (Spring 1984): 211–15.

37. This task resembles the larger problem of defining and achieving the political good more generally, as discussed by Bertrand de Jouvenel in *Sovereignty: An Inquiry into the Political Good* (Indianapolis, Ind.: Liberty Fund, 1997).

38. There is much evidence on this point in Verba, Schlozman, and Brady, *Voice and Equality*. We can also learn much about citizenship, I believe, by thinking about the complex meanings attached by academics to the phrase "good departmental citizen."

39. The phrase appears in G. K. Chesterton, *What I Saw in America* (New York: Dodd, Mead & Co., 1922), 16.

40. Alexis de Tocqueville, *Democracy in America*, ed. Phillips Bradley (1835; reprint, New York: Knopf, 1945) 2:121–24.

41. For a discussion of how citizens learn to appreciate this problem, see the chapter entitled "How Order Came to the Mining Camps" in Josiah Royce, *California, from the Conquest in 1846 to the Second Vigilance Committee in San Francisco: A Study of American Character* (Boston: Houghton Mifflin, 1886).

9

Political Parties, the Constitution, and Popular Sovereignty

Sidney M. Milkis

I am honored to be included in a Festschrift for Wilson Carey McWilliams. In his teaching and writing, Carey McWilliams has encouraged us to reflect on friendship and politics, on "fraternity in America." With passion and reason, he has championed the importance of political fraternity in sustaining self-rule in the United States. He has also revealed how fragile political friendship is in the American republic. Like a modern-day Anti-Federalist, McWilliams denies that the Constitution provides adequately for an active and competent citizenry. Indeed, the promise of the Constitution to rest ultimate authority in the people has depended on the endurance of Anti-Federalist principles and practices, in a localized politics that "personalizes public life, conveys dignity, and encourages participation." The waning of this sort of politics, he warns, is at the core of our decrepit civic culture—the cause of our present political discontents.[1]

This essay is written in celebration of McWilliams's defense of our fragile civic culture. It pays special attention to political parties, which he has long defended as critical agents of popular rule. Political parties were formed in the early part of the nineteenth century as a means of engaging the attention of ordinary citizens, and with localistic foundations that were critical for the maintenance of an engaged citizenry. The American tradition of local self-government, which preceded and was only partly modified by the "more perfect Union" formed in 1787, played a critical part in relating the private order to the public life of the United States. As Alexis de Tocqueville observed in the 1830s, this tradition went well beyond the legal division between the national and state governments and left considerable discretion to counties and townships. The vitality of townships and counties depended on the well-founded idea in the United

States that "each man [was] the best judge of his own interest and best able to satisfy his private needs." The practice of leaving townships and counties in charge of their "special interests," in turn, cultivated civic attachments, by giving each individual "the same feeling for his country as one has for one's family." Happily, Tocqueville concluded, "a sort of selfishness makes [the individual] care for the state."[2]

Like Tocqueville, the Anti-Federalists and their Jeffersonian descendants viewed the states and localities as the schools of American democracy. But they were more concerned than Tocqueville seemed to be that the original Constitution provided inadequate support for provincial institutions. As the Pennsylvania Minority[3] warned, its very preamble, beginning with the words, "We the People of the United States," betokened a "compact between individuals entering into a state of society, and not that of a confederation of states." The other features of the Constitution—granting the essential powers of national security and commerce to the national government—supported this stated end, leaving the states and localities, the *Federal Farmer* lamented, "a mere shadow of power."[4] Thomas Jefferson and his political allies would echo this refrain, viewing Alexander Hamilton's domestic and foreign policy initiatives as confirmation of the Anti-Federalist warnings against "a consolidation of the States into one government."[5]

As McWilliams has told us, "Anti-Federalist concerns" found a "reflection in American political parties."[6] Born of the Jeffersonian and Jacksonian democracy, political parties were conceived as localized political associations that could provide a vital link between rights and community in the United States; they would do so by balancing state and local communities, championed by the Anti-Federalists and the national government, which the Federalists sought to strengthen with the Constitution of 1787. Traditional political parties satisfied Jefferson's desire for a "graduation of authority," in which national unity would grow out of local wards.[7] As Jefferson wrote in a letter to Samuel Kercheval: "In government, as well as in every other business of life, it is by division and subdivision of duties alone, that all matters, great and small, can be managed to perfection. And the whole is cemented by giving to every citizen, personally, a part in the administration of public affairs."[8] Although cautious in his support of partisanship, Jefferson founded the Republican Party as a necessary means to the end of civic obligation, as an institutional device that welded the personal and the public.[9] "Aristocracy," Tocqueville observed, "links everybody from peasant to king in one long chain. Democracy breaks the chain and frees each link."[10] "In the United States, political parties would attempt to reforge the chain," McWilliams has written, "giving its metal a new democratic casting."[11]

LOCALIZED PARTIES AND CONSTITUTIONAL REFORM

The origins and organizing principles of American political parties yielded a highly mobilized and highly competitive, locally oriented democracy that subordinated the powers of the national government to the prerogatives of the states and localities. As V. O. Key argued in 1964: "Federalism in our formal governmental machinery includes a national element independent of the states, but in our party organization the independent and national element is missing. Party structure is more nearly *confederative* than *federal* in nature."[12]

The confederative form of parties seemed to defy the "more perfect Union" created by the Constitution of 1787. Indeed, even though the early development of party organizations organized national electoral followings for presidential candidates, these political associations were shaped by decentralizing institutions such as the nominating convention and patronage system. That the traditional party was rooted in the local community was no accident, nor was it merely a pragmatic adjustment to political events. Political parties were founded as part of a program to modify the original Constitution so that it would conform in practice to many of the principles of Anti-Federalism. These political associations served the purposes of those who shared the Anti-Federalist commitment to local self-government but joined Jefferson in accepting the Constitution as a work in progress, hoping to shape it by amendment, interpretation, and practice.[13]

Ironically, one of the leaders of this revisionist project was James Madison, who had played a critical part in writing and ratifying the Constitution. Donald Brand describes "Madison's philosophical and political about-face from the time he co-authored *The Federalist* to the time he wrote pieces more Anti-Federalist in spirit" as "one of the most perplexing episodes in the American Founding period."[14] Madison's statements about property and majority rule at the time of the Constitution gave no hint that he saw the need for strong political associations to cultivate an active and competent citizenry. To the contrary, he celebrated the Constitution for the way it separated the cup of power from the lips of the people. In the normal course of events, the majority would be indifferent, if not avowedly hostile to the rights of property, and all too likely to carry out "wicked projects" that sought to distribute property equally and thus deny individuals the fruits of their own labor. Writing as Publius, Madison argued in *The Federalist* 10 that the control of the majority lies in "extending the sphere" in which critical political relationships and associations form, so that a majority would necessarily be composed of diverse and narrow factions that would be unlikely to agree about much or for long.[15]

As Madison wrote in a letter to Thomas Jefferson in October 1787—an extraordinary postmortem on the Constitutional Convention—"Divide et impera, the reprobated axiom of tyranny, is under certain qualifications, the only policy, by which a republic can be administered on just principles."[16] Or, as Madison put it somewhat more delicately in *Federalist* 51, "In the extended republic of the United States, and among the great variety of interests, parties, and sects which it embraces, a coalition of a majority of the whole could seldom take place on any other principles than those of justice and the general good."[17]

Within this scheme of government, the states and localities were to play an important role, but they were to be transformed from the principal sites of political authority into mere interests, which added to the variety and diversity of factionalism. The state legislatures would effectively defend "local interests," Alexander Hamilton observed, and could be relied on "to erect barriers against the encroachments of the national authorities."[18] As Madison put in *Federalist* 51:

> In a single republic, all the power surrendered by the people is submitted to the administration of a single government; and the usurpations are guarded against by a division of government into distinct and separate departments. In the *compound republic* of America, the power surrendered by the people is first divided between two distinct governments, and then the portion allotted to each subdivided among distinct and separate divisions. Hence a *double security arises to the rights of the people.* The different governments will control each other, at the same time that each will be controlled by itself (author's italics).[19]

Given their collaboration on *The Federalist Papers,* and given Madison's brilliant efforts to create a new national regime capable of remedying the "mortal diseases of popular government," Hamilton had good reason to believe that Madison would support his efforts as secretary of the treasury in the Washington administration to seize the governing initiative. Yet, by the winter of 1791–1792, Madison was becoming the philosophical and congressional leader of an opposition group that would soon harden into the Jeffersonian Republican party, a group Hamilton and his political allies dismissed derisively as representing a recrudescence of Anti-Federalism.

Hamilton's program required a liberal—"elastic"—interpretation of the national government's authority, and some discretion for the judiciary in drawing the boundary between the state and national power: this discretion anticipated a significant extension of executive power. The power of the more decentralizing institutions—Congress and state governments— was necessarily subordinated in this enterprise. More than the policies themselves, Hamilton's interpretation of the Constitution persuaded Madison that he had underestimated the warnings of the Anti-Federalists that the original constitutional design portended a unitary system that would destroy the delicate balance of federalism. In the aftermath of Washington's Neutrality Proclamation of 1793, issued without consulting Congress, Madison wrote to Jefferson in June 1793 expressing a far less sanguine view of the Constitution than in the *The Federalist Papers*. "I must own my surprise that such a prerogative should have been exercised," he stated. "Perhaps I may have not attended to some parts of the Constitution with sufficient care, or may have misapprehended its meaning."[20]

Written during the critical period of partisan maneuvers in 1791 and 1792, Madison's essays in the *National Gazette* reveal his revised thoughts on the original Constitution—his fear that it provided inadequately for executive accountability—had caused him to reformulate the arguments of *Federalist* 10.[21] Whereas Madison originally feared that the security of liberty would be violated by a majority faction bent on a misconceived notion of economic justice, requiring institutional arrangements to divide and filter the voice of the people, his concern about Hamilton's program focused on the need to arouse a "common sentiment" among the states against government consolidation, a task that informed the creation of the Republican Party.[22]

As such, Madison, the chief architect of the "Constitution-against-parties," played a leading role in founding the first majority party.[23] The Republican Party was dedicated to strengthening the decentralizing, and therefore supposedly more popular, institutions of the Constitution—the Legislature and the states—against the encroachments of national administrative power. In *The Federalist Papers*, Madison defended the Constitution's strengthening of the national government as necessary to "break and control the violence of faction."[24] His revised understanding of government and society championed political centralization, that is, a consolidation of public opinion under the banner of the Republican Party, as a way of defending state and local interests against governmental centralization. Combining political centralization and governmental decentralization, Madison argued, was the "proper object" to unite former Anti-Federalists—"those who are most jealously attached to the separate authority reserved to the states"—and the more ardent republicans of the Federalists—"those who may be more inclined to contemplate the people of America in light of one nation":

> Let the former continue to watch against every encroachment, which might lead to a gradual consolidation of the states into one government. Let the latter employ their utmost zeal, by eradicating local prejudices and mistaken rivalships, to consolidate the affairs of the states into one harmonious

interest; and let it be the patriotic study of all, to maintain the various authorities established by our complicated system, each with its respective constitutional sphere; and to erect over the whole, one paramount Empire of reason, benevolence, and brotherly affection.[25]

Republicanism of the 1790s faced its greatest danger and found its greatest opportunity in resistance to the Alien and Sedition Acts, passed and administered by the Federalists to stifle criticisms in the Jeffersonian press. In his report on the 1799 Virginia Resolutions, Madison appealed "to the intermediate existence of the state governments between the people and [the national government], to the vigilance with which they would decry the first symptoms of usurpation, and to the promptitude with which they would sound the alarm to the public."[26] As if to underscore the defects of the arguments of *The Federalist Papers*, Madison defended the right of the Virginia assembly to declare the Alien and Sedition Acts unconstitutional, but only as a matter of "opinion"—to "excite reflection" among the people in the various states and to encourage their cooperation in resisting the offensive statutes. Just as the judiciary's rulings "enforced the general will," Madison hoped the resistance of the states to the Federalist government might "lead to a change in the legislative expression of the general will—possibly to a change in the opinion of the judiciary."[27] The reference to a Rousseauan general will was not frivolous; rather, it reflected Madison's revised understanding of the Constitution, in which government must rest not merely on effective institutional arrangements, but also on national opinion, cultivated by civic associations in the states and localities.[28]

Madison's report figured prominently in the election of 1800, the "Revolution of 1800," as Jefferson called it. An advocate of strengthening the national government at the time of the founding, Madison was now committed to a doctrine, later set forth in Jefferson's first inaugural address, that celebrated "the state governments in all their rights as the most competent administrations for our domestic concerns and the surest bulwarks against anti-republican tendencies."[29] Madison's alliance with Jefferson helped revitalize a tradition dedicated to local self-government, thus ensuring that federalism—the interplay between one nation and many local communities—would be a central feature in the dynamic of American constitutional government.

JACKSONIAN DEMOCRACY AND THE CREATION OF A PARTY SYSTEM

"Out of the original clash" between the Federalists and the Republicans, James Piereson has written, "there developed in America the tension between party politics, on the one hand, and governmental centralization and bureaucracy, on the other."[30] Similarly, the emergence of open party conflict altered the Constitution, which was now joined to a doctrine of local self-government. But Jefferson and Madison were dedicated to transforming government, not necessarily to establishing a permanent, formal two-party system. Once the Federalists and their program of executive aggrandizement were defeated, they hoped, the Republican Party could safely wither away, restoring the nonpartisan character of the Constitution. The country, Jefferson assured an anxious political ally, would see a "rapid return of general harmony," and her countrymen would "[move] in phalanx in the paths of regular liberty, order, and sacrosanct adherence to the constitution."[31] Unlike the Federalists, the Republicans were not merely a party, a faction that degraded the general harmony. As Jefferson declared in 1811, "the republicans [were] the *nation*."[32]

By the 1820s, Jefferson's claim that the Republicans embodied a new national consensus seemed justified. Indeed, the Federalists had grown so weak by 1816 that they had stopped fielding national tickets; in 1820, the Republican president, James Monroe, was reelected without opposition. The complete triumph of the Republicans over their Federalist rivals, ushering in the so-called "Era of Good Feelings," appeared to restore the nonpartisan character of the Constitution, albeit on terms favored by the Republicans. The Republican Party did not wither away, historian James Roger Sharp has written, but it "became bloated and shapeless."[33] With the demise of the Federalists, the motivation for Republicans to unite behind a single national ticket was greatly reduced; moreover, the centralized party organization of the Republicans coexisted uneasily with their commitment to local self-government. Consequently, the national party structure they formed, dominated by the congressional caucus, broke down by 1824, when four major candidates ran for the presidency, each representing not only his own ambitions for office, but also the aspirations of a sectional constituency. The presidential choice of the Republican caucus, William Crawford of Georgia, finished third in electoral votes behind Andrew Jackson of Tennessee and John Quincy Adams of Massachusetts, both of whom had been nominated by their state legislatures. The powerful Speaker of the House, Henry Clay, came in fourth. Party politics had been displaced by narrow factionalism.

The task of transforming party politics into a formal institution after the 1824 election fell to militant Republicans, such as Martin Van Buren of New York and Thomas Ritchie of Virginia. The outcome of this election, in which Adams was selected by the House of Representatives even though Jackson had more popular and electoral votes, persuaded Jacksonian reformers that the Constitution's vulnerability to centralized administration had not been corrected by Jeffersonian democracy. The controversy stirred by the election was further aroused by its aftermath: Adams's selection of Henry Clay, who had orchestrated his victory in the House, as secretary of state; and the president's first State of the Union Address, proposing an active role for the federal government in the economy and society. With the weakening of the national party structure, Van Buren lamented, a system of personal and local factions displaced the "common sentiment" that had upheld republican principles, thus favoring champions of "consolidation."[34]

Adams's ascendance to the White House was abetted by James Monroe's earlier policy of conciliation—the president's effort to complete the triumph of the Republicans over the Federalists by persuading moderate Federalists to join his administration. Adams was one of the more prominent of these converts. His position as secretary of state in the Monroe administration advanced the cause of so-called National Republicans who sought to challenge orthodox republican commitments. Van Buren considered Monroe's policy of national unification a disaster; by abandoning militant partisanship for impartiality, the president made a revival of Federalism possible. The spectacle of a fragmented and apathetic electorate allowing the House to select the neo-Federalist Adams as president revealed the need to establish political parties as permanent institutions.

The Jacksonian ambition to revitalize partisanship gave rise to the Democratic Party. Styling themselves as orthodox Jeffersonians, Democratic Party leaders, as Van Buren put it, sought "to draw anew and . . . re-establish the old party lines."[35] Whereas the Federalists, dedicated to strengthening national power and proscribing popular rule, did not need a popular party to advance their program, the Republicans and their heirs, the Jacksonian Democrats, stood in need of "an extraneous force to secure harmony in its ranks." The Federalist ambition to create an administrative republic did not require an elaborate party apparatus rooted in the states and localities; rather the Federalists sought to center government responsibility in the executive, which would cultivate and maintain the support of commercial interests through the disbursement of bounties, licenses, and tariffs. The executive would wed commercial interests to state power—and develop, in turn, a stable commercial republic. In contrast, the task of the Jacksonian Democrats was to organize public opinion in support of government decentralization. Dedicated to the tradition of local self-government and to the provincial liberties that supported it, the Republicans were successful, Van Buren counseled, as long as they were "wise enough to employ the caucus system . . . and to use in good faith the influence it is capable of imparting to the popular cause."[36]

As the leader of the Republican caucus, Van Buren (the junior senator from New York) supported Crawford in 1824. But the collapse of the congressional caucus required that Van Buren turn to Jackson, hoping to link the Tennessean's personal popularity with a new party organization. In truth, Van Buren considered Jackson's great personal popularity to be both a threat and an opportunity. As he put it to Ritchie, the great task was to "substitute party principle for personal preference."[37] The success of this partisan strategy ensured that Jackson's appeal to the people was not entirely direct; instead, his election campaigns and policy fights would be waged through the new Democratic Party, which called for a return to the principles set forth in Jefferson's first inaugural address.

The Jeffersonians had merely tolerated the Republican Party as a temporary agent to advance the doctrine of local self-government; by the mid-1820s, Jacksonian reformers began to defend parties as indispensable allies of local democracy. "Although this is a mere party consideration, it is not on that account less likely to be effectual," Van Buren wrote in calling for Jackson's candidacy to be linked with the emergence of a new party; "considerations of this character not infrequently operate as effectively as those which bear upon the most important questions of constitutional doctrine."[38] By the 1830s, Jacksonians were defending political parties, indeed, a party system, as constitutional doctrine.

Just as Jeffersonian democracy gave rise to a party that established a formidable wall between the national government and the states, so Jacksonian democracy fortified this barrier. Similarly, the alliance between the Constitution and local self-government was strengthened. The Jacksonians' ambition to make partisanship part of the "living Constitution" was embodied by the Democratic Party, which organized voters on the basis of principles that were militantly decentralizing, as was the very process of party politics they established.

Jacksonian democracy thus had established the "confederate" form of political organization that became the distinguishing feature of representative government in the United States. The Jeffersonian emphasis on political centralization comported with national parties, which rested on the nomination of presidential tickets by the congressional caucus. As this national structure weakened, state party organizations emerged as key actors in national, as well as in state and local politics. The Jacksonian political reforms institutionalized this political devolution. With the collapse of "King Caucus" after 1824, presidential tickets soon were nominated by national conventions, which were dominated by state party organizations. Implicit in the idea of the national convention was that the delegates' authority sprang directly from the rank and file, that they came, as Jackson put it, "fresh from the people."[39]

The Jacksonian political philosophy, rooted in the understanding that "consolidation" was a chronic problem, encouraged a much bolder assault on national institutions and programs than the Jeffersonians had undertaken. After his election in 1828, Jackson withdrew the federal government from the realm of internal improvements. Military power, especially the army, was kept to a minimum. Jackson's fiscal policy was to hold down expenditures. Most significantly, the Bank of the United States, which Jeffersonians had learned to live with, was dismantled and its deposits were reinvested in selected state banks. As such, the strengthening of the presidency during Jackson's stay in the White House, as Marvin Meyers has written, "mobilized the powers of government for what was essentially a dismantling operation."[40] As Jackson pointed out in his veto of legislation that would have renewed the national bank's charter, Democrats believed that the "true strength" of the Union consisted "in leaving individuals and States as much as possible to themselves—in making itself felt, not in its power, but in its beneficence; not in its control, but in its protection; not in binding the States more closely to the center, but leaving each to move unobstructed in its proper orbit."[41]

So dominant had this doctrine of local self-government become by the end of Jackson's presidency, that even the Whig (former National Republican) opposition, led by Adams and Clay, dedicated to expanding the economic and social responsibilities of the national government, imitated the Jacksonian brand of national politics. By 1840, the Whigs subscribed to the Jacksonian style of democracy, shaped by the convention system and widely disbursed patronage appointments that held the national councils of power accountable to the states and localities. In part, the Whigs' acceptance of Jacksonian politics was strategic, an acceptance of popular campaigns and practices so as to avoid the fate of the Federalists. "The cry of aristocracy takes with certain folks," John C. Spencer wrote to Thurlow Weed in 1831, "and there is no way to meet it but to clamor louder than our adversaries."[42]

Equally significant, the Whigs, no less than the Democrats, had an appreciation of the importance of local self-government in the tradition of popular rule in the United States. The Massachusetts Whig statesman Edward Everett gave voice to this understanding in his review of Tocqueville's *Democracy in America*, in which he reserved special praise for Tocqueville's recognition of New England town meetings as the "primary schools" of liberty. "On the whole," Everett wrote in hearty agreement, "no element of American liberty is more essential than the unobtrusive, humble, domestic, municipal organization. Everything is done by the neighbors; by the people, whose interest and comfort are to be promoted. It is the curse of *centralization*, that it puts power into the hands of those who know not Joseph."[43]

The Democratic and Whig parties were national organizations, but they celebrated a national idea that complemented a deep and abiding respect for localized politics and governance. Indeed, the Jacksonian theory of governance was not one of states' rights per se, but of local community. To be sure, Democrats believed that local rights were best guaranteed in national politics by states' rights. As Tocqueville recognized, however, the power of state governments was challenged by reformist aspirations that sought to devolve power to counties and townships.[44] New York Governor Horatio Seymour proclaimed this doctrine of local self-government in a widely distributed Fourth of July oration in 1856, delivered in Springfield, Massachusetts. "The democratic theory takes away control from central points and distributes it to the various localities that are most interested in its wise and honest exercise," he observed. "It keeps at every man's home the greatest share of political power that concerns him individually. It yields it to the remoter legislative bodies in diminishing proportions as they recede from the direct influence and action of the people." Such a system of local self-government, Seymour instructed, was not based on a naive view of "the people's wisdom and patriotism"; rather, it was dedicated to the proposition that republican government rested on right opinion, which was nurtured by "the great theory of local self-government" and the parties that made it effective:

> This system [of local self-government] not only secures good government for each locality; but it also brings home to each individual a sense of his rights and responsibilities; it elevates his character as a man; he is taught self-reliance; he learns that the performance of his duty as a citizen, is the best corrective for the evils of society, and is not led to place a vague, unfounded dependence upon legislative wisdom and inspirations. The principle of local and distributed jurisdiction, not only makes good Government, but also makes good manhood.[45]

Seymour's defense of local self-government was not empty rhetoric. The decentralizing spirit of Jacksonian democracy influenced reform not only at the national level, but also in the states. By the 1840s, constitutional reform had spread to most of the states, including most of those in the South, and devolved considerable power from the state capitals to the counties and townships. In New York, for example, the constitutional convention of 1846 created small electoral districts to give better representation to local patches of opinion; made most state and local positions, hitherto appointed by either the governor or legislature, elective offices; and decentralized patronage. Before these changes, Democratic reformer Jabez Hammond wrote, the "central power [of the state] reached every county, and was felt by every town in the state. The convention of 1846 [has] wholly annihilated this terrible power."[46]

Such action did not go unchallenged. Many Democratic leaders, including Van Buren, were somewhat taken aback by the radical devolution loosed by Jacksonian democracy. At the New York constitutional convention of 1821, in fact, Van Buren had opposed the direct election of justices of the peace, powerful officials whose patronage he thought essential to the New York Democratic Party's dominance. When taunted by his political enemy, De Witt Clinton, for not trusting the people, Van Buren replied that direct popular election would give the opposition, minority faction in New York control over as many as half of the state's justices of the peace. More penetratingly, Van Buren believed that the Democratic Party had the special function of protecting the principle "first formally avowed by Jean-Jacques Rousseau that the right to exercise sovereignty belongs inalienably to the people."[47] Subjecting all offices to direct election favored wealthy figures of reputation, such as Clinton, Van Buren argued; majority rule and the rights of the average citizen required the support of a disciplined state party organization that could exercise firm control over public opinion and government action. The humble members of society—the farmers, the mechanics, the laborers—required a disciplined party organization to achieve unity and to make their will effective in the councils of government. Thus, as John Casais has written, "While it possessed a legislative majority the [New York Democratic Party] would rule, protecting the common man from his own enemies, and, in a Rousseauan way, from his own folly."[48]

The Anglo-American devotion to provincial liberties, as Tocqueville observed, would not easily abide such a centralized instrument of the "general will." Indeed, Van Buren's party suffered the consequences for challenging the sovereignty of local opinion in the New York state elections of 1824, which returned Clinton and his allies to power. Two years later, an amendment was added to the 1821 constitution giving "the people in their several towns, at their annual elections," the power to choose justices of the peace.[49] Thereafter, Van Buren's ideal of a rigorously disciplined, united party as a guide to public opinion had to be modified, acquiescing to popular aspirations for the direct election of local officials. The Regency, as the New York Democratic party was known, led the fight at the 1846 state convention for reforms that would subject all judicial offices to popular election. At the same time, this recognition of local self-government enabled the Democratic Party to endure as an important intermediary between government and society and thus to remain an essential agent of popular rule.

The Whig press charged that Jacksonian reforms went too far, investing "a revolutionary, fickle and radical spirit in politics" that undermined the republican character of the state constitution. "Our judges are to be chosen directly by the people!" lamented the *American Whig Review* in the wake of New York's 1846 constitutional convention. "And that serene and elevated region, which the winds and waves of political excitement have, till this time, respected, is to be thrown open to their utmost violence."[50]

Tocqueville shared the Whig concerns about the popular, decentralizing thrust of the Democratic Party. Although he admired the Americans' "taste for local freedom," considering it a critical corrective to their excessive attention to private concerns, Tocqueville feared that Jacksonian democracy might make it impossible for the national government to attend to those few, critical matters "important enough to attract its attention." He praised American democracy for achieving government centralization, which involved the government in such matters as foreign policy and national commerce, even as it avoided administrative centralization, involving the national government in "secondary concerns," better left to states and localities. Although the Jeffersonian Republicans sought to organize voters in support of government decentralization, they accepted institutions such as the national bank as a necessary evil, thus stopping well short of a full-scale dismantlement operation. And yet, militant Jacksonian reformers now threatened to destroy the delicate balance between government centralization and administrative decentralization. Jackson, himself, according to Tocqueville, was a popular, but not a strong leader— "the majority's slave"—who threatened to deprive the federal government of that limited government centralization without which a nation could not "live, much less prosper." In attacking the Bank of the United States, Jackson merely flattered the "provincial jealousies" and "*decentralizing passions*" that had brought him to power.[51]

But Jacksonian Democrats defended the political reforms of the 1830s and 1840s as necessary to prevent the consolidation that they considered a threat to constitutional government in the United States. Jackson was no slave of the majority, they claimed. Indeed, there was no popular demand to terminate the bank; Jackson, through the medium of the party organization and press, convinced the people that this relic of Hamiltonian nationalism was not only bad public policy but also unconstitutional. Moreover, as his stand against John C. Calhoun in the nullification crisis of 1832 revealed, Jackson's commitment to devolution was hitched to the rising spirit of democratic nationalism. As John O'Sullivan argued in his review of *Democracy in America* that appeared in the Jacksonian press, the president did not "shrink from responsibility; on the contrary, . . . by the freedom and firmness with which he used his legislative veto, and asserted his right to act upon the Constitution, as he understood it, [he] developed the energies of government in a point where they had been previously dormant, and thus left it more efficient than he found it."[52] What Tocqueville did not appreciate, as Jackson's Senate ally Thomas Hart Benton, alleged in his memoirs, was that the president's attack on the bank was rooted in Jeffersonian principles, that it meant "going back to the constitution and the foundation of party on principle."[53] The renewal of party conflict did not weaken federal authority, but linked it vitally with the public.

The Jacksonians did not see themselves as dishonoring the free enterprise system. Rather, they denied that free enterprise, properly understood, was linked to centralized government. Jacksonian Democrats hoped to unleash the commercial spirit from government-created monopolies, such as the national bank. Only then would commercialism conform to the Jacksonian understanding of "natural rights," whose clarion call of "equal rights to all and special privileges to none" promised political and economic independence to the producing "bone and sinew" of the country.[54] This independence required local self-government, a deep and abiding effort, as Governor Seymour put it, "to distribute each particular power to those who have the greatest interest in its wise and faithful exercise."[55]

The localized parties of Jacksonian democracy gave political effect to this decentralized polity, linking it to public causes and national developments. With the transition from the age of Hamilton and Jefferson to Jackson, Tocqueville observed, "great" parties, based on the leading principles of government, ceased to exist. They were replaced by "small" parties that eschewed principles for material and provincial interests. "This had been a great gain in happiness but not in morality," he concluded.[56] But, as George Pierson observed, Tocqueville may have failed to appreciate how these diminutive parties could engage Americans in public deliberation and judgment, the very practices that nurture a civic culture.[57] To be sure, the Jacksonian concept of "the people" was limited; it did not apply to African Americans, women, or American Indians. Nor did the localized party system, animated by patronage practices and entertaining partisan displays such as torchlight parades, cultivate political debate that reached the highest note on the scale. But the limitations of this popular revolution should not blind us to the fact, as Robert Wiebe argues, that "something profoundly important occurred in nineteenth century America that acquired the name democracy."[58] Once established, it penetrated deeply into American society, dominating the political perceptions and voting habits of the people. Thereafter, calls for justice, indeed demands for rights, would have to come to terms with the "tenacity of this highly mobilized, highly competitive, and locally oriented democracy."[59]

CONCLUSION: PARTY POLITICS AND THE STRUGGLE FOR NATIONAL COMMUNITY

The confederate form of party organization legitimized during the Jacksonian era endured well into the twentieth century. Even the rise of the Republican Party in the 1850s as a result of the slavery controversy and the decline of the Whigs did not alter the essential characteristics of the party system in the United States; and these characteristics—decentralized organization and hostility to centralization of power—ultimately short-circuited the efforts of radical Republicans to complete their program of Reconstruction after the Civil War.

In truth, like their Whig forbears, Republicans were diffident in their opposition to the Democratic doctrine of local self-government. Senator Stephen A. Douglas, the author of the 1854 Kansas-Nebraska Act, justified northern Democrats' defense of "popular sovereignty" in the territories on the basis of this theory of government, proclaiming in his 1858 debates with Abraham Lincoln, that government in the United States was "formed on the principle of diversity in the local institutions and laws, and not on that of uniformity." "Each locality," Douglas continued, "having different interests, a different climate and different surroundings, required different local laws, local policy and local institutions, adapted to the wants of the locality."[60] To Republicans, this marked the triumph of petty particularism over the principles of the Declaration of Independence, rightly understood. Still, Abraham Lincoln pledged not to interfere with slavery where it was already established, a promise he reiterated in his first inaugural address, in which he disavowed "any purpose, directly or indirectly, to interfere with the institution of slavery in the states where it exists."[61]

Given their tepid opposition to local self-government, Republicans saw little purpose in dismantling the localized party system; rather, to the dismay of Progressive reformers such as Herbert Croly, they more or less took "over the system of partisan organization and discipline originated by the Jacksonian Democrats." As Croly would put it in *Progressive Democracy*, this party system "bestowed upon the divided Federal government a certain unity of control, while at the same time it prevented increased efficiency of the Federal system from being obnoxious to local interests."[62]

Considering the creation of a national program, let alone a social democratic party in the United States, impractical, Progressives looked to revive the national character of the original Constitution as an agent of reform. Progressive democracy glimpsed a national community, in which new political institutions such as the direct primary, initiative, and referendum would forge a direct link between public opinion and government representatives. Progressives hoped, as Herbert Croly put it, "to give democratic meaning and purpose to the Hamiltonian tradition and method." Progressive democracy rested on the possibility of creating a "modern," independent executive that might become, as Theodore Roosevelt put it, "the steward of the public welfare."[63]

Progressive democracy came into its own with Franklin D. Roosevelt's New Deal. Yet the expansion of the central government's power that followed from the New Deal realignment did not result in the formation of a national state that Progressive reformers such as Croly had anticipated, one that established national regulations and welfare programs that were expressions of a shared understanding of principles. Rather, the reconstituted executive was hitched to a plebiscitary politics that exposed the fragile sense of citizenship in American political life.[64] In the final analysis, the limits of Progressivism—the danger of resurrecting Hamiltonian nationalism—point to the limits of the original Constitution, the "Madisonian system" that Madison, himself, came to view as defective.

This constitutional defect required political parties, which might arouse a common sentiment against "consolidation." Progressive reformers understood that the development of a more purposeful national government meant loosening the hold of traditional parties on the loyalties and voting habits of citizens. But they failed to appreciate the purpose these parties served as effective channels for democratic participation.[65] Political parties, which embodied the principle of local self-government, were critical agents in counteracting the tendency of citizens to shut themselves up in a limited circle of domestic concerns out of reach of broader public causes. By enticing Americans into neighborhood organizations and patronage practices that were beyond their tiny private orbits, traditional party organizations helped to show individuals the connection between their private interests and public concerns. Similarly, highly decentralized party structures ensured that national campaigns and controversies focused on the partisan activities of townships, wards, and cities, thus cultivating a delicate balance between local and national community.[66] Drawn into political associations by the promise of social, economic, and political advantage, Americans might also learn the art of cooperation and form attachments to government institutions. As Tocqueville put it in a nice turn of phrase, "Public spirit in the Union is . . . only a summing up of provincial patriotism."[67]

Progressive reformers' faith in national democracy, in the whole people, betrayed them, McWilliams has taught us, "for they ignored or slighted the implication that we all begin in a world of particulars, from which the human spirit ascends, on any account only slowly and with difficulty." Still, he cautions, "while the Progressives may have overestimated the reach of the spirit, unlike so many of our contemporaries, they never forgot that its yearning perennially strains against the possibilities."[68]

In truth, we must not allow the present discontents of the American people to blind us to the shortcomings of the nineteenth century polity—certainly, there was no "golden age" of parties. Progressive reformers had good reasons for viewing political parties and the provincial liberties they upheld as an obstacle to economic, racial, and political justice. The resurrection of Hamilton nationalism they favored, which required the weakening of political parties, yielded a stronger executive that became the principal agent for undertaking domestic and international responsibilities that must be assumed by all decent commercial republics. The nobility of the modern presidency comes from, to use Woodrow Wilson's phrase, its "extraordinary isolation," which provides great opportunity for presidents to leave their mark on the nation, even as it subjects them to a volatile mass democracy that makes popular and enduring achievement unlikely.[69]

Even as he has condemned Progressivism for weakening the foundations of our civic culture, McWilliams has celebrated its greatest accomplishments. In honoring him, we should recognize that politics does not allow us to have all the good things. In the end, our inquiries necessarily leave us with a dilemma—with the recognition that any regime, no matter how just, must rely on countervailing principles and institutions to correct its most dangerous tendencies.

It is appropriate, then, to end this essay by acknowledging the complexity and richness of contemporary political life. In the final analysis, the rise and decline of localized democracy in the United States demands that we come to terms with a legacy that yields a more active and better equipped national state—the national resolve to tackle problems such as forced radical segregation at home and Communism abroad—but one without adequate means of common deliberation and public judgment.

NOTES

1. Wilson Carey McWilliams, "The Meaning of the Election," in *The Election of 1996*, ed. Gerald Pomper (Chatham, N.J.: Chatham House, 1997), 255–61.

2. Alexis de Tocqueville, *Democracy in America*, ed. J. P. Mayer (1835; reprint, New York: Doubleday, 1969), 68, 82, 95.

3. As the title indicates, this essay reflects the opinions of those delegates to the Pennsylvania ratifying convention who opposed the adoption of the Constitution. The essay expresses not only the minority delegates' reasons for opposing the Constitution, but also their resentment over the tactics that the Federalists employed in gaining the approval of the convention.

4. "The Address and Reasons of Dissent of the Minority of the Convention of the State of Pennsylvania to their Constituents," in *The Antifederalists*, ed. Cecilia M. Kenyon (Indianapolis, Ind.: Bobbs-Merrill, 1966), 45–46; Richard Henry Lee, "Letters from the Federal Farmer," in *The Antifederalists*, II, 213.

5. James Madison, "Consolidation," in *The Writings of James Madison*, ed. Gaillard Hunt (New York: Putnam, 1906), 6:67.

6. McWilliams, "The Anti–Federalists, Representation, and Party," *Northwestern University Law Review* 84, no. 1 (Fall 1989): 12–38.

7. McWilliams, "Tocqueville and Responsible Parties: Individualism, Partisanship, and Citizenship in America," in *Challenges to Party Government*, ed. John Kenneth White and Jerome Mileur (Carbondale, Ill.: Southern Illinois University Press, 1992), 195.

8. Thomas Jefferson to Samuel Kercheval, 12 July 1816, in *The Portable Thomas Jefferson*, ed. Merrill Peterson (New York: Viking, 1975), 557.

9. Frequently, historical literature will refer to the Jeffersonian party as the "Democratic-Republicans." The use of this term may help us distinguish the Jeffersonian Republican party from the Republicans that formed in the 1850s in response to the slavery controversy. But the name most frequently, almost exclusively, used by Jefferson and his supporters is Republican, not Democratic-Republican. More to the point, the link between the Jeffersonian Republicans and the Republican Party of the 1850s is deliberate. The founders of the latter meant to indicate that they—and not the Jacksonian Democrats—were the loyal followers of the Jeffersonian tradition.

10. Tocqueville, *Democracy in America*, 508.

11. McWilliams, "Parties as Civic Associations," in *Party Renewal in America: Theory and Practice*, ed. Gerald Pomper (New York: Praeger, 1980), 59.

12. V. O. Key Jr., *Politics, Parties, and Pressure Groups* (New York: Crowell, 1964), 334 (italics added).

13. McWilliams, "Democracy and the Citizen: Community, Dignity, and the Crisis of Contemporary Politics in America," in *How Democratic Is the Constitution?* ed. Robert Goldwin and William A. Schambra (Washington, D.C.: American Enterprise Institute, 1981), 91.

14. Donald R. Brand, "Reformers of the 1960s and 1970s: Modern Anti–Federalists?" in *Remaking American Politics*, ed. Richard A. Harris and Sidney M. Milkis (New York: Westview, 1989), 50 n. 50.

15. Alexander Hamilton, James Madison, and John Jay, *The Federalist Papers* (New York: New American Library, 1961), no. 10, 83 (hereafter cited as *Federalist*).

16. Madison to Jefferson, 24 October 1787, in *Writings of James Madison*, 5:31.

17. *Federalist* 5, 325.

18. *Federalist* 85, 526.

19. *Federalist* 51, 323.

20. Madison to Jefferson, 13 June 1793, *Writings of James Madison*, 6:131.

21. The Jeffersonian scholar Lance Banning challenges the proposition that Madison's thought changed dramatically from the time he coauthored *The Federalist Papers* to the time he wrote the *National Gazette* essays. Madison was never as committed to nationalism as was Hamilton, Banning argues. He became a

leader of the Republican opposition to support his long-standing view of the Constitution as "that middle ground . . . between state sovereignty and an excessive concentration of authority in distant, unresponsive hands." See Banning, *The Sacred Fire of Liberty: James Madison and the Founding of the Federal Republic* (Ithaca, N.Y.: Cornell University Press, 1995), especially chaps. 1, 10, and 11. Without denying that Madison favored a federal republic, it seems clear that he became doubtful that the original Constitution sustained such a vital mean between national and state sovereignty. Moreover, Madison came to believe that minority rather than majority factionalism posed the greatest threat to liberty, and that this threat called for the creation of a political party to assert the will of the people. This concern to awaken a vigorous and active public represented a significant revision, if not a direct contradiction, of Madison's position in the *The Federalist Papers.* As Stanley Elkins and Eric McKitrick write of Madison's revised understanding of factions: "Parties are still a necessary evil. But in Madison's mind the emphasis is now mainly on the 'necessary.' " See Elkins and McKitrick, *The Age of Federalism* (New York: Oxford University Press, 1993), 267.

22. This discussion draws on two essays that have called attention to Madison's party papers, and to the importance of the debate about party government. See James Piereson, "Party Government," in *The Political Science Reviewer* 12 (Fall 1982): 2–52, and Harry Jaffa, "A Phoenix From the Ashes: The Death of James Madison's Constitution (Killed by James Madison) and the Birth of Party Government" (paper presented at the annual meeting of the American Political Science Association, Washington, D.C., 1977).

23. The term "Constitution-against-Parties" was coined by Richard Hofstadter. See Hofstadter, *The Idea of a Party System: The Rise of Legitimate Opposition in the United States, 1780–1840* (Berkeley and Los Angeles: University of California Press, 1969), especially chap. 2.

24. *Federalist* 10, 77.

25. "Consolidation," *National Gazette* 6 (5 December 1791): 68–9, reprinted from *The Writings of James Madison.*

26. "Report on the Resolutions," House of Delegates, Virginia, Session 1799–1800, *Writings of James Madison*, 6:405.

27. Ibid., 402–3.

28. See, for example, Madison's essay "Universal Peace," which invokes Rousseau in arguing that the "will of the government . . . must be made subordinate to, or rather the same with, the will of the community." Quoted from *National Gazette* (2 February 1792) in *The Writings of James Madison*, 6:89.

29. Thomas Jefferson, "First Inaugural Address," 4 March 1801, in *The Portable Thomas Jefferson*, 293.

30. Piereson, "Party Government," 51.

31. Jefferson to James Sullivan, 9 February 1797, *The Writings of Thomas Jefferson*, 7:118.

32. Jefferson to William Duane, 28 March 1811, *The Writings of Thomas Jefferson*, 9:313 (Jefferson's italics).

33. James Roger Sharp, *American Politics in the Early Republic: The New Nation in Crisis* (New Haven, Conn.: Yale University Press, 1993), 284.

34. Martin Van Buren, *Inquiry Into The Origin and Course of Political Parties in the United States* (New York: Hudson and Houghton, 1867), 4–6. In the face of these developments, Jefferson endorsed Van Buren's plan to reintroduce party competition. Responding to Van Buren's concern that Adams and his political allies were but disguised Federalists, Jefferson wrote in a letter dated 29 June 1824: "Tories are tories still, by whatever name they may be called." *The Writings of Thomas Jefferson*, ed. Paul Leicester Ford (New York; Putnam, 1899), 10:316. For an excellent discussion of Van Buren and the critical part he played in renewing party competition, see James Ceaser, *Presidential Selection: Theory and Development* (Princeton, N.J.: Princeton University Press, 1979), chap. 3.

35. Van Buren to Thomas Ritchie, 13 July 1827, *Martin Van Buren Papers*, Library of Congress, Washington, D.C.

36. Van Buren, *Inquiry Into The Origin and Course of Political Parties in the United States*, 4–6. The congressional caucus had become the leading institution of national party organization by the election of 1800. A caucus of each party's members of Congress was held to choose its nominees for president and vice president; the caucus's decision was then coordinated with party organizations in the various states so that electors were selected as instructed agents, pledged to support their party's ticket.

37. Van Buren to Ritchie, 13 July 1827, *Martin Van Buren Papers*.

38. Van Buren to Ritchie, 13 July 1824, *Martin Van Buren Papers*.

39. Andrew Jackson to James Gwin, 23 February 1835, in *Niles Register* vol. 7, no. 12 (4 April 1835): 80.

40. Marvin Meyers, *The Jacksonian Persuasion: Politics and Belief* (Stanford, Calif., Stanford University, 1957), 28.

41. Andrew Jackson, "Veto Message," 10 July 1832, in *Messages and Papers of the Presidents*, ed. James D. Richardson (New York: Bureau of National Literature, 1897), 3:1153.

42. John C. Spencer to Thurlow Weed, "Jacksonian Democracy and the Rise of the Nominating Convention," cited in James Alton Chase, *Essays on Jacksonian America*, ed. Frank Otto Gatell (New York: Holt, Rinehart and Winston, 1970), 88.

43. Tocqueville, *Democracy in America*, 63; Edward Everett, "On the *Democracy in America*, Alexis de Tocqueville," *North American Review* 43 (July 1836), 197–99 (Everett's italics).

44. Tocqueville noted that the townships and municipal life were strongest in New England, but everywhere, even in the South, he detected the gravitational pull of local self–government: "County and township are not constituted everywhere in the same way, but one can say that the organization of township and county in the United States everywhere depends on the same idea, viz. that each man is the best judge of his own interest and the best able to satisfy his private needs. So township and county are responsible for their special interests. The state rules but does not administer. One finds exceptions to that principle, but no contradictory principle." Tocqueville, *Democracy in America*, 82.

45. Horatio Seymour, "The Democratic Theory of Government," speech delivered 4 July 1856, in *Seymour and Blair: Their Lives and Services*, ed. David G. Croly (New York: Richardson, 1868), 49, 52.

46. Jabez D. Hammond, *Life and Times of Silas Wright* (Syracuse, N.Y.: Hall and

Dickson, 1848), 670. For an overview of constitutional reform in the states during the Jacksonian era, see George P. Parkinson Jr., "Antebellum State Constitution-Making: Retention, Circumvention, Revision," (Ph.D. diss., University of Wisconsin, 1972).

47. Van Buren, *Inquiry Into the Origin and Course of Political Parties*, 11; *Reports of the Proceedings of the New York Constitutional Convention, 1821* (New York: De Capo Press, 1970), 341, 353–54. For an excellent discussion of Van Buren's struggle to balance party organization and direct election of local officials, see J. A. Casais, "The New York State Constitutional Convention of 1821 and Its Aftermath," (Ph.D. diss., Columbia University, 1970), especially chap. 9.

48. Casais, "The New York State Constitutional Convention of 1821 and Its Aftermath," 295.

49. "Amendments to the Constitution of 1821, Ratified September, 1826," in *The Federal and State Constitutions*, ed. Francis Newton Thorpe (Washington, D.C.: U.S. Government Printing Office, 1909), 5:2651.

50. "Responsibility of the Ballot Box; With An Illustration," *The American Whig Review*, (November 1846): 440.

51. Tocqueville, *Democracy in America*, 262–76; 392–93 (Toqueville's italics).

52. John O'Sullivan, "European Views of Democracy—Number II. (M. De Tocqueville)," *United States Magazine and Democratic Review* 2, no. 8 (July 1838): 355.

53. Thomas Hart Benton, *Thirty Years View; or, A History of the Working of the American Government for Thirty Years, From 1820 to 1850* (New York: Appleton, 1854), 224.

54. Jackson, "Farewell Address," 12.

55. Seymour, "The Democratic Theory of Government," 51.

56. Tocqueville, *Democracy in America*, 175.

57. George Wilson Pierson, *Tocqueville and Beaumont in America* (New York: Oxford University Press, 1938), 765.

58. Robert W. Wiebe, *Self-Rule: A Cultural History of American Democracy* (Chicago: University of Chicago Press, 1995), 6.

59. Stephen Skowronek, *Building A New American State: The Expansion of National Administrative Capacities, 1877–1920* (Cambridge: Cambridge University Press, 1982), 40.

60. *The Lincoln-Douglas Debates of 1858*, ed. Robert W. Johannsen (New York: Oxford University Press, 1965), 126–127. On the Democratic ideology and its support of local self-government, see Bruce Collins, "The Ideology of the Ante-Bellum Northern Democrats," *American Studies* 2, no. 1 (1977): 102–21.

61. *Messages and Papers of the Presidents*, ed. James D. Richardson, 20 vols. (New York: Bureau of National Literature, 1897): 7:3206.

62. Herbert Croly, *Progressive Democracy* (New York: Macmillan, 1914), 99, 347.

63. This phrase comes from Roosevelt's 1909 "New Nationalism" address, given in Osawatomie, Kansas. See *The Works of Theodore Roosevelt* (New York: Scribner's, 1926), 17:349.

64. I make this argument in *The President and the Parties: The Transformation of the American Party System Since the New Deal* (New York: Oxford University Press, 1993).

65. Jane Addams was highly critical of machine politics in Chicago. At the same time, she warned her fellow reformers that the ward bosses ruled in spite of their vices because they practiced "simple kindness" in the community day in and day out. "[I]f we discover that men of low ideals and corrupt practice are forming popular political standards simply because such men stand by and for and with the people, then nothing remains but to obtain a like sense of identification before we can modify ethical standards." Addams, "Why the Ward Boss Rules," *The Outlook* (2 April 1898), reprinted in William L. Riordan, *Plunkitt of Tammany Hall*, ed. Terrence J. McDonald (Boston: Bedford Books, 1994), 122.

66. See Michael McGerr, *The Decline of Popular Politics: The American North, 1865–1928* (New York: Oxford University Press, 1986), especially chap. 2. McGerr argues that the promise of entertainment, no less than petty favors, drew Americans to local party organizations. Presidential campaigns, in particular, were occasions for "spectacular partisan displays" in communities that made elections highly emotional episodes. Still, McGerr insists, spectacular displays were not simply a matter of entertainment nor emotional identification with a party: "[Nineteenth] century campaigns tied parades and fireworks to long expositions of issues on the stump and in the press. In a sense, the excitement of partisan display could lure men into dealing with complex issues such as slavery. Popular politics fused thought and emotion in a single style accessible to all—a rich unity of reason and passion that would be alien to Americans in the twentieth century" (41).

67. Tocqueville, *Democracy in American*, 162.

68. McWilliams, "Standing At Armageddon: Morality and Religion in Progressive Thought," in *Progressivism and the New Democracy*, ed. Jerome Mileur and Sidney M. Milkis (Amherst: University of Massachusetts Press, 1999).

69. Woodrow Wilson describes the "extraordinary isolation" of the president in "Constitutional Government in the United States," in *The Papers of Woodrow Wilson*, ed. Arthur S. Link (Princeton, N.J.: Princeton University Press, 1974), 18:114–115.

10

Lincoln and the Politics of Refounding

Joseph Romance

> While they were there, Cain attacked his brother Abel and murdered him. Then the LORD said to Cain, "Where is your brother Abel?" Cain answered, "I do not know. Am I my brother's keeper?" The LORD said, "What have you done? Hark! your brother's blood that has been shed is crying out to me from the ground."
>
> —Gen. 4:8-10[1]

> If the last generations of your country appeared without much luster in your eyes, you might have passed them by and derived your claims from a more early race of ancestors. Under a pious predilection for those ancestors, your imaginations would have realized in them a standard of virtue and wisdom beyond the vulgar practice of the hour.
>
> —Edmund Burke, *Reflections on the Revolution in France*

THE DILEMMA OF FOUNDINGS

The problem of the founding of a political institution continually weighs on all subsequent political activity, for the founding moment sets political institutions in motion and these institutions focus and direct later political actors in their grand and minor endeavors. All foundings, whatever their virtues, are definite problems in the making. No founding is so powerful as to erase all previous attachments and old memories, and these—together with differing views of recent events—are a constant source of conflict over the meaning of the founding itself. It is highly likely that no founder, or collection of founders, is wise enough to solve all the problems that present themselves at the founding moment; and thus there is a need for continual reinterpretation.[2] The founders force later political leaders to walk a tightrope: how can they transform flawed institutions without weakening the very bonds that hold a society together?[3]

Yet, the power of the founding is certainly based, in part, on the restraints it demands of later politicians. This restriction on freedom is both necessary and problematic. The very success of the founding is partially measured by its capacity to summon a great deal of awe from later generations. The founding moment creates the institutions and political rituals of a nation and inaugurates a collective memory that connects later people to that founding moment, seeking to restrict the hearts and minds as well as the habits of later generations. This sense of historical obligation, although imprecise and difficult to measure, is nonetheless very real.

I would like to explore the thought of one reformer who handled this challenge of respecting the founding, while reforming it, with great political acumen: Abraham Lincoln. He presided over profound and painful changes in America. Yet, he did so by preserving the essential constitutional framework of the American Founders and, in the act of amending it, he placed it on firmer ground. His genius was to successfully redefine the founding, thus the meaning of American citizenship, without breaking asunder the edifice that James Madison and Alexander Hamilton had wrought. Lincoln, though, engaged in an active preservation of the founding by carefully reinterpreting the Constitution and its debt to the Declaration of Independence. By bringing the Declaration back into our understanding of the founding, Lincoln was able to recall an older civic teaching, one that reminded citizens of their communal responsibilities to the Union and to each other. To engage in such an active preservation is to achieve something quite subtle and less appreciated in the history of politics.[4] While some might see Lincoln's actions as fundamentally revolutionary precisely because of the sacrifice and changes that the Civil War demanded, it is more compelling to see Lincoln as the preserver of the regime.[5] This opinion rests on the unmistakable fact that, despite all the changes that occurred during the 1860s (and they were breathtaking), the survival of the regime was paramount in Lincoln's mind and, in the end, this survival is Lincoln's most fundamental legacy.

This essay will address four issues. First, I will discuss actions of the framers of the Constitution. In particular, we need to consider carefully the Founders' awareness of their role and, especially, their binding of subsequent generations to the structures proposed by the Constitution. In this regard, I will look carefully at a section of *The Federalist Papers* in which Madison deals explicitly with the founding moment. Second, I will argue that Lincoln—a man devoted to the Union, yet very ambitious—was self-consciously aware of the constrained relationship between his generation and the founding. Third, we need to directly address slavery, the problem that was left unsolved by the founding and had to be addressed by Lincoln. Finally, I argue and conclude that Lincoln's main task was not merely to satisfy his own ambition or to solve the slavery question. Rather, the particular issue of slavery must be understood as part of a larger dilemma: what is the relationship between two American founding doctrines, the democratic principle of self-rule of citizens and the universal principles that must be accepted, regardless of elections and majorities? The existence of the Union itself meant a bond of citizenship that presumed respect among citizens and between the generations. The respect required that all citizens support the higher principle of the Union. It is thus not surprising that in Lincoln's last public address he urged flexibility in working out the details of Reconstruction; yet, when considering fundamental ideas like equality, he maintained that, "[i]mportant principles may, and must, be inflexible."[6] For Lincoln, important principles came from his reinterpretation of the American founding and the egalitarian aspects found in the Declaration of Independence. Harry Jaffa draws attention to Lincoln's thoughts concerning the founding and I rely upon his perceptive reading of Lincoln's writings.[7] However, I believe that Jaffa slights the ambiguous qualities of the Declaration that allowed Lincoln to interpret the founding in a more Christian and less individualistic light.

Lincoln was a democratic theorist of the first order, one who was acutely aware of the limitations of democracy. The problem for any democracy, as Plato reminds us, is that it might be quite incapable of collective moral judgment.[8] Lincoln deserves our praise because he tried to navigate the distance between principle and expediency that continually haunts the democratic experiment. Lincoln's teachings are all the more necessary as America enters a new century: a time of continued cultural diversification and the apparent, nearly universal, ascendancy of democratic practice. The vitality of democracy, however, must be predicated not only on a triumph of practice, but also the ascendancy of principle.

MADISON'S FOUNDING MOMENT

Nations, like men, are teachable only in their youth; with age they become incorrigible. Once customs are established and prejudices rooted, reform is a dangerous and fruitless enterprise; a people cannot bear to see its evils touched, even if only to be eradicated.

—Jean-Jacques Rousseau, *The Social Contract*

Apart from their inherent importance, the American Founders deserve discussion because of the tremendous respect accorded them by Lincoln himself. The framers of the Constitution were powerfully aware of the difficulty of the founding moment.[9] Whatever the public's willingness to innovate, though, there was no agreement regarding the exact nature of desirable change. The war for independence meant that many differences among political leaders were suppressed in the hopes of achieving the more immediate goal of defeating the British.[10] Yet obviously, once that rather pressing goal was achieved, differences of opinion resurfaced and forced renewed debates about the meaning of liberty, federalism, republicanism, and the public good.[11]

What is quite apparent is that the authors of the U.S. Constitution were strongly interested in creating a new commercial republic and one in which a citizen's desire for political involvement had to be channeled through a distant national government. Along the way, citizens would be encouraged to think more about matters of personal liberty and less about matters of collective freedom.[12] Thus, Madison and company established a large nation with a strong national government, uniformly representative, and limited by a complex system of checks and balances. In creating this kind of government, what was lost—the communal life and the robust sense of political participation that the Anti-Federalists defended— was balanced by the inherent stability and potential power of this new system and its enhancement of individual liberty.[13]

Furthermore, the Constitution was, through its system of checks and balances, bound to limit political actors. This sense of limitation was necessary regardless of the virtues of individual citizens. Madison's argument in *Federalist* 55—"Had every Athenian citizen been a Socrates, every Athenian assembly would still have been a mob"—is a classic, even shocking, statement on this point. On the whole, the pursuit of liberty, understood as private and personal, took precedence over all other political matters. And this pursuit of liberty must be understood as springing from the natural well of universal human ambition.

Madison and Hamilton were aware that their project was sharply, even bitterly, contested and recognized for the radical departure it was. Thus, we should not be surprised by Madison's fear upon hearing a proposal for a second convention that, "the very attempt at a second Convention strikes at the confidence in the first; and the existence of a second by opposing the influence to influence, would in a manner destroy an effectual confidence in either, and give a loose to human opinions."[14] The Founders wanted to attach citizens to the national government in a new and subtle way. Just as important, however, was their desire to create an enduring regime. To do this, Hamilton and Madison relied not simply on functioning institutions, but on the working of time to create an ever increasing sense of veneration that made the foundation of national government stronger as the years passed. They envisioned a future in which virtually everyone involved in American politics would be constrained by the political system created by the Constitution. Yet, one could ask: what constrained the Founders themselves? The desire for fame that so animated the Founders was something to be controlled, because what wins fame is not always clearly distinguished from what deserves infamy.[15]

This need is readily apparent when we read Madison's writings in the *The Federalist Papers*. In numbers 37, 38, and 39, Madison focuses on the importance of the founding and its meaning for America. In *Federalist 37*, Madison opens with a plea for moderation in the debates over the Constitution and an analysis of the goals most important for government: security, energy, and stability. But the imperatives of government raise the question of whether the demands for security will overwhelm the imperative to maintain liberty. Before Madison answers this query, though, he proceeds through a rather odd digression—in the fashion of David Hume—about the difficulty of knowing anything at all. In fact, nature itself offers us only confusion and obscurity. Moving to politics, Madison reminds his audience of the foibles of history and how difficult it is to frame any good set of laws. Men are frail and prone to sharp disagreements that make the entire process of republican government suspect. Given the myriad of problems facing the writing of any laws and the inherent instability of language, Madison urges his audience to marvel at the ability of the Constitutional Convention to surmount these difficulties. This claim that the convention overcame so many difficulties eases a troubled mind about the compromises that must be accepted by ratification. But Madison's argument rests on the proposition that there are few, if any, natural standards by which to judge the Constitution or any similar founding effort to carry theory into practice.

In *Federalist 38*, Madison continues his argument that the founding is an extraordinary event. The past he recounts is a sobering one, full of violence, in which foundings were the achievements of singular men, themselves acting with special, prudent secrecy. Madison insists that, historically, "the task of framing it [a new government] has not been committed to an assembly of men; but has been performed by some individual citizen of pre-eminent wisdom and approved integrity."[16] Foundings were inherently undemocratic and even un-republican. America represents a breakthrough in political thinking because deliberations about the founding were both public and collective.

Having accomplished his goal of making us respect the difficulty inherent in the act of founding, Madison is only now ready to define republicanism—and it is a sobering definition. In *Federalist 39*, Madison presents the "sufficient" grounds of republicanism. He retains relatively little of the ancient ideal, limiting republicanism to the idea of holding office for set times and for appointments either "directly or indirectly, by the people."

He tells us that this limited definition is the best that can be hoped for in our world with human nature being what it is.

Madison's remarks in these papers serve to remind his audience how difficult a founding is; America's situation, while extraordinary, was not a permanent departure from human experience, but an isolated moment that had to be seized.[17] Given human nature, which Hamilton reminds us is characteristically "ambitious, vindictive and rapacious," we cannot rely on the virtue of citizens.[18] Instead, we must place our faith in institutional structures that will channel humanity's natural ambitions. This faith, however, demands that people not question too seriously the institutions of government. Individual ambition must be directed elsewhere in its search for fulfillment. The Founders, creating institutions that would frame all subsequent politics, reserve to themselves the ultimate glory. As Joshua Miller perceptively argues:

> They [the Federalists] agreed, explicitly, that the people could create, alter, or abolish their governments whenever they chose to do so; [but] the Federalists stipulated that, for acts of "the people" to be valid, they had to act all at once and together. . . . The Federalists ascribed all power to a mythical entity that could never meet, never deliberate, never take action. The body politic became a ghost.[19]

By creating such a ghostly body politic, the Founders created two problems for men like Lincoln. First, the founding was seriously flawed because of the compromises that slavery forced upon the Founders; second, some men have the same great ambitions that the Founders had and would chafe at the restraint of the laws. What to do with such great ambition and how to solve old problems became Lincoln's political aim. In acting the way he did, Lincoln solved both the immediate problem facing the nation and the more perennial political problem that he, himself, embodied.

LINCOLN'S AMBITIONS

> It is to deny, what the history of the world tells us is true, to suppose that men of ambition and talents will not continue to spring up amongst us. And, when they do, they will as naturally seek the gratification of their ruling passion, as others have done before them. The question then, is, can that gratification be found in supporting and maintaining an edifice that has been erected by others?
>
> —Abraham Lincoln, "Address to the Young Men's Lyceum of Springfield, Illinois, January 27, 1838"

It is a well established belief among students of American history that Lincoln was an extremely ambitious man.[20] Born to an undistinguished and relatively poor family, Lincoln, according to his most recent biographer, consciously rejected his father's "unambitious, unsuccessful way of life."[21] Lincoln desired not only political, but financial and social success. He worked hard from very early in his life to reach the kind of status he thought he deserved.[22] As such, he is hardly a unique figure in political life. Yet Lincoln's ambition, reaching beyond private life and orthodox politics, led him to wrestle with the Founders themselves.[23]

This great sense of self-importance is apparent in one of Lincoln's earliest speeches, commonly called the "Address to the Young Men's Lyceum of Springfield, Illinois." It was originally entitled "The Perpetuation of Our Political Institutions." Throughout this text Lincoln is in agreement with the conventional political attitudes of the day and, in particular, he assents to much of the Founders' argument.[24] Lincoln argues that the Founders have already given us an adequate system of laws and the only issue is to simply maintain that orderly government:

> We find ourselves under the government of a system of political institutions, conducing more essentially to the ends of civil and religious liberty, than any of which the history of former times tells. . . . We toiled not in the acquirement or establishment of them—they are a legacy bequeathed us, by a once hardy, brave patriotic, but now lamented and departed race of ancestors. Theirs was the task (and nobly they performed it) to possess themselves, and through themselves, us, of this goodly land; and to uprear upon its hills and its valleys, a political edifice of liberty and equal right; 'tis ours only, to transmit these, the former, unprofaned by the foot of an invader; the latter, undecayed by the lapse of time, and untorn by usurpation—to the latest generation that fate shall permit the world to know.[25]

Lincoln next proceeds, however, to discuss how this legacy is eroding. Disorder, arising from a disregard for the law, threatens the nation. Not surprisingly, much of the problem can be traced to the existence of slavery. Furthermore, the problems that slavery generates are not confined solely to one side of the issue. First, slavery encourages its opponents to see the laws of the land as unjust and, thus, not worthy of respect. This strikes at the reverence necessary for any regime. The carefully calibrated machine the Founders created is breaking down, and, in times of crisis, "men of sufficient talent and ambition will not be wanting to seize the opportunity, strike the blow, and overturn that fair fabric, which for the last half century, has been the fondest hope, of the lovers of freedom."[26]

Ambition motivated the Founders in the first place, but later generations also seek their fortune in the province of fame; however, they find a field already "harvested, and the crop is already appropriated." Such a reality is bound to frustrate those of the highest ambition. Such men would not be satisfied to simply add their names to the ongoing "monuments of fame." Such a man, an American Caesar or Napoleon, "thirsts and burns for distinction; and, if possible, it will have it, whether at the expense of emancipating slaves, or enslaving freemen."[27] The reader should notice that Lincoln has, in effect, equated the motivation of both sides of the slave controversy. The same basic desire for distinction animates all. Although this ambition is constant, its ability to express itself waits for the right moment. Slavery, with all its attendant controversy, merely provides the excuse for such unbridled ambition.

This stark image sets the stage for Lincoln's solution. Earlier in the text, we note that he had prescribed a reverence for the laws. Now we learn, though, that such reverence must come from a proper relation to the founding and, interestingly enough, the revolution. The fading of political memory of that time was at the root of popular detachment from the laws. Americans must find a new pillar of strength to overcome the failing memories and can only turn to an iron rationality:

> Passion has helped us; but can do so not more. It will in the future be our enemy. Reason, cold, calculating, unimpassioned reason, must furnish all the materials for our future support and defense. Let those materials be moulded into general intelligence, sound morality and, in particular, a reverence for the constitution and laws.[28]

The attempt to balance emotion with reasoned reverence is reminiscent of Alexis de Tocqueville's notion of the reasoned patriotism of self-interest rightly understood.[29]

Slavery was the preeminent failure of the Founders and the crucial test of any political life of that era. Yet, by an appeal to reason, could Lincoln convince America to give up slavery? The appeal to reason may not work, not simply because of the passionate appreciation of the new nation, but because of the play of self-interest in owning slaves and dominating others. Lincoln had to find a new equilibrium between an emotional commitment to the Union and a reasoned understanding of all sides in this debate. Lincoln's greatness consisted in a careful appreciation of what reasoned reverence meant. To solve the problems of Union, reason and the emotion of reverence were both essential.

SLAVERY AND AMERICAN POLITICS

What, to the American slave, is your Fourth of July?

—Frederick Douglass

As far back as the 1780s, Thomas Jefferson had shuddered, "Indeed I tremble for my country when I reflect that God is just: that his justice cannot sleep for ever."[30] Jefferson certainly seemed to hope that the dilemma created by slavery would eventually solve itself naturally. It was expected by some and hoped for by many that slavery would wither away as conditions changed in the South and attitudes and manners evolved throughout the nation. Time would be the healer.

To some, this called for the removal of this issue from politics altogether. As J. David Greenstone has argued, the second generation of political leaders—the Jacksonians—was seriously intent on eliminating the slavery debate entirely from the world of political discourse.[31] American political leaders embarked on a political journey punctuated by a series of wrenching detours: the Missouri Compromise, the Compromise of 1850, the Kansas-Nebraska Act.

Each compromise was marked by severe strain on the political system, and each antidote's calming effects evaporated more quickly than the previous cure. The issue would not go away. The legacy bequeathed by the Founders to their "caretaker" successors had contained two ideals: natural right and democratic practice. The universal principles of equality and freedom did not sit well with the institution of slavery.[32] Just as powerful was the demand that localities could and should decide such matters for themselves, leaving the question of slavery in the hands of the majority. Furthermore, the practice of slavery was bound to cause problems in the attitudes of all citizens—slave and freeman alike. Earlier in his political career Lincoln had learned that slavery had a corrupting influence on the slave owner because it was "highly seductive to the thoughtless and giddy headed young men."[33] And, because of expansion, slavery remained a constant problem as citizens moved west. The basis of America's growth—the westward expansion—constantly recalled to the nation its most urgent dilemma.

Something had to give, and the resulting controversy led to four possible policies. First, there were increasing numbers of people in the South who defended slavery as an absolute good. This was a relatively new trend in southern thinking about slavery. For much of the early nineteenth century, southerners took Jefferson's earlier view that slavery was an evil institution that had to be accepted and there was hope for its eventual demise. By the 1850s, this was no longer the southern view.

The second option was the eradication of slavery, a position associated with the abolitionists, that was revolutionary in its own way, since it presumed that the principles at stake were more important than the institutions laid down by the Constitution. Increasingly, the abolitionists' rhetoric was a harsh attack on the founding and its achievements. We can see why Lincoln singled out the abolitionists as the first threat to order in America in his "Address to the Young Men's Lyceum." In William Lloyd Garrison's censorious remark, "The compact which exists between the North and the South is a covenant with death and an agreement with hell."[34] It is not surprising, then, that Lincoln never joined the abolitionists and was always wary of the movement's extremism.[35]

The third position was the most clearly democratic and was closely associated with Judge Stephen A. Douglas—popular sovereignty. Douglas was maintaining the purest of democratic principles. An issue as diverse as slavery cannot be settled at the national level, he argued, and must be channeled away from the federal level so as not to disrupt the country as a whole. To have no position on the question of slavery was certainly democratic in a way; however, it highlighted the potential failure of democracy to even consider moral questions.[36]

Lincoln took a fourth position. Slavery must be pointed toward extinction, and the shared nature of the Union meant that it must end on terms equitable to all. The apparent difficulty of this position did not deter Lincoln from pressing this course. Lincoln's famous address accepting his nomination as Republican candidate for senator included his observation that

> the institution of slavery ought to be placed in the very attitude where the framers of this Government placed it, and left it. . . . In my opinion it will not cease till a crisis shall have been reached and passed. A house divided against itself cannot stand.[37]

Given the failure of the Founders' expectation that slavery would eventually end, the framers' intention required, not abolition, but constant pressure by political measures to keep slavery contained where it would die a definite, if not instant, death.

> They [the Founders] did not mean to assert the obvious untruth, that all were then actually enjoying that equality, nor yet, that they were about to confer it immediately upon them. In fact they had no power to confer such a boon. They meant simply to declare the right, so that the enforcement of it might follow as fast as circumstances should permit.[38]

Of course, this reading is contingent on Lincoln's interpretation of the founding. Yet Lincoln's goal was to convince the people that his reading of the founding was the correct one.[39]

Part of Lincoln's goal was to reintroduce the notion of what it meant to be an American citizen, by thinking again about the founding. Lincoln's intent stands in contrast to much of what passed as arguments for and against slavery, appealing to the self-interest of those involved. The slave owners obviously had a great self-interest in the system, and often identified all objections to the system as one of different interests; many opponents of slavery were men who defended free labor, and Lincoln was certainly aligned with that movement. There was a danger, however, that this sort of contention reduced the moral argument to one of political will and power, making the conflict about two different economic systems. Such political thinking often resulted in disturbing resolutions to this most perplexing issue. There was a movement afoot to simply let the South go from the Union. This might purify the North but it would make false the promise of the founding, which aimed to create out of great diversity one Union dedicated to certain principles. Another solution might be the conquest of the South by the North. In a sense, of course, that is what actually happened, but Lincoln's view was subtler. It was Lincoln's task to rediscover the moral principles of the founding and teach them to all Americans—North and South. In so doing, Lincoln would pay homage to the Founders while challenging the founding itself.

Lincoln wanted to return the argument to the moral plane, yet he did not want to surrender the argument to rigid and perfectionist abolitionists.[40] He had to travel between the Scylla and Charybdis of expedient interest and moral principle. Lincoln would ultimately prefer the moral argument that slavery must end. Yet, this moral principle had to be balanced with a defense of the political universe created by the Founders: the Union itself. The preservation of the Union had a moral force that equaled the demands of ending slavery. Moreover, as we shall see, the Union's moral claim was not limited to the terms of the Constitution, for it included the Constitution's animating principles, contained in that other great American document, the Declaration of Independence. Lincoln, thus, subtly expands our notion of the founding by paying a great tribute to the founding moment when he said, "I am exceedingly anxious that this Union, this Constitution, and the liberty of the people shall be perpetuated in accordance with the original idea for which that struggle was made."[41] This is the active force of preservation that Lincoln brought forth. If his methods were not always pure, his final goal remained a fixed star to guide his immediate movements.

LINCOLN'S SOLUTION

Let us re-adopt the Declaration of Independence, and with it, the practices, and policy, which harmonize with it. Let north and south—let all Americans—let all lovers of liberty everywhere—join in the great good work. If we do this, we shall not only save the Union; but we shall have saved it, as to make, and to keep it, forever worthy of the saving.

—Abraham Lincoln, "speech on Kansas-Nebraska Act," 16 October 1854

His reverence for the Declaration of Independence made Lincoln both revolutionary and respectful of the past. One is reminded of Rousseau's observation about the Lawgiver and the people in the *Social Contract*.[42] Rousseau remarks that people are not always ready for the laws to be enacted; yet, this certainly implies that there is a people that nevertheless exists, waiting to eventually receive those laws.

> For nations, as for men, there is a time of maturity which they must reach before they are made subject to law; but the maturity of a people is not always easily recognized; and something done too soon will prove abortive.[43]

Rousseau's abstract theory is made concrete in Lincoln's life and actions. America had not fully learned what its founding meant, so Lincoln proceeded to explicate the founding and the Constitution. The Constitution, however, only mentions the creation of institutions, since the Founders consciously omitted the Declaration's principles from the Constitution's text. This did not surprise Lincoln because he knew that the Declaration and its statement that "all men are created equal," was "for future use."[44] Lincoln's task was to bring the principles of the Declaration to the forefront of debate. What were those principles?

Jaffa is right to point out Lincoln's emphasis on the Declaration as offering us the "transcendent goal" of equality.[45] Jaffa argues, though, that we should understand the Declaration on Lockean grounds. These grounds stress the right of self-preservation, which belongs to us in a prepolitical state of nature. Self-preservation would seem to offer some support to slave owners, since a strict Lockean doctrine imposes no imperative duty to others. Furthermore, fear of the slave, and a general concern about safety, may allow the continuation of slavery. According to Jaffa, Lincoln attempts to shift our understanding of the Declaration toward an appreciation of civil society, and equality becomes an affirmative goal of government. As Jaffa writes:

> Lincoln's interpretation of "all men are created equal" transforms that proposition from a pre-political, negative, minimal, and merely revolutionary norm, a norm which prescribes what civil society ought not to be, into a transcendental affirmation of what it ought to be.[46]

This interpretation is essentially true; however, I think it fails to highlight the non-Lockean and especially Christian aspect of American culture, which the Declaration was designed to include by its careful ambiguities. (As Jefferson later suggested, the Declaration was designed to appeal to the "harmonizing sentiments of the day.")[47]

The text of the Declaration is open to interpretation because it is ambiguous. This ambiguity allows Lincoln to offer an interpretation more in keeping with the nation's Christian heritage and less aligned with a strict Lockean reading. Lincoln's readings of the text treat creation as the design of the whole, rather than merely as an original state. Thus, the phrase "created equal" comes to define a fundamental quality and not a negative absence of claims. Lincoln's appeal for equality and the ending of slavery resonates with the biblical teaching, "You, my friends, were called to be free; only do not turn your freedom into license for your lower nature, but be servants to one another in love."[48] This older idea is echoed in Lincoln's observation that those who criticize the Declaration "insist that there is no right principle of action but self-interest."[49] Lincoln, then, can be said to articulate the Declaration's second, and decidedly more religious and less selfish, voice against a Lockean reading of American politics.

Lincoln's transformation is especially important because the Constitutional Convention consciously omitted, or suppressed, the Declaration's doctrine; the Constitution made no mention of natural rights as the Declaration had. As Edmund Randolph told the assembly, the Constitution does not deal with natural rights, but with those rights "modified by society."[50] Conventions such as slavery violate natural rights and it would be imprudent to call attention to this fact. The framers combine a disinclination to openly acknowledge slavery (referring to "other persons") with an equal disinclination to emphasize its violation of natural rights. By bringing the Declaration back into our discussions, Lincoln rearticulates the critique of slavery (and possibly even points toward a critique of other conventions such as property, something used to justify slavery). Lincoln, in his first debate with Douglas, reminded his audience that equality was "guaranteed by the Laws of God, and it is asserted in the Declaration of Independence."[51]

Thus, for Lincoln, America was based on the Declaration's ideal of self-government of free men, a principle that can be realistic only to the extent that equality is maintained for all. Lincoln certainly believed that the Declaration announced to the world that we were a nation—one people—and a nation of free and equal citizens. Furthermore, this one people and their Declaration were a beacon of principle for the entire world because, as Lincoln observed, "I had thought the Declaration contemplated the progressive improvement of the condition of all men everywhere."[52] As J. David Greenstone has argued, Lincoln believed that the Declaration "proclaimed his nation's 'covenantal' status as a special people with 'an ancient faith,' a status that imposed solemn responsibilities on them."[53]

Lincoln argued in 1858 that this "covenantal bond" was elastic enough to include new people, and points us to a greater appreciation of the whole that makes up America:

> We have besides these men—descended by blood from our ancestors— among us perhaps half our people who are not descendant at all of these men, they are men who have come from Europe—German, Irish, French, and Scandinavian. . . . If they look back through this history to trace their connection with those days by blood, they find they have none, they cannot carry themselves back into that glorious epoch and make themselves feel that they are a part of us, but when they look through that Old Declaration of Independence they find those old men say that "We hold these truths to be self-evident, that all men are created equal," and then they feel that the moral sentiment taught in that day evidences their relation to those men, that it is the father of all moral principle in them, and that they have a right to claim it as though they were blood of the blood, and flesh of the flesh of the men who wrote the Declaration, and so they are.[54]

The end of slavery can only come about when the people recognize abolition's necessity; when they are ripe for this teaching, as Rousseau would tell us. Lincoln aimed to preserve the people, united by the institutions of the Constitution, and teach them the true meaning of the people as embodied in the Declaration. In so doing, Lincoln amended the Constitution by the ideals of the Declaration.[55] At one point in his debates with Douglas, he refers to Douglas as amending the Declaration; thus Lincoln virtually conflates the two documents with a decided emphasis on the moral superiority of the Declaration.[56] They became, in actuality, part of the same whole, which was the founding. To understand one required understanding the other. The founding forged a "we" that would, over time, realize its collective identity and its collective responsibility. Thus, Lincoln served both to change and preserve the founding moment. And, in forging this "we," he called upon not only America's religious past. He evoked, in his war speeches, a new civic religion that reminded North and South of their shared responsibilities as citizens. We must now turn to Lincoln's final accomplishments, achieved during the Civil War, to educate a divided country.

HEALING THE WOUNDS

All the American revolutionaries knew that democracy was a problem in need of constant solution, in constant need of moderation, in constant need of institutions and measures to mitigate its defects and guard against its dangers.

—Martin Diamond, *The Revolution of Sober Expectations*

Despite all his hopes, war came. There is something significant in the fact that Lincoln honestly did not expect war. He seemed to think that the bonds of Union would win out, and when they failed, he set about forcibly reforming these bonds. Many commentators point to Lincoln's famous observation that "I claim not to have controlled events, but confess plainly that events have controlled me."[57] While this is certainly a true confession in part, we should not exaggerate it to the detriment of Lincoln's accomplishments. Lincoln certainly did not achieve reform in the way he wanted to and he did not achieve all that he wanted. Nonetheless, the goals he set out to achieve largely came to pass, and, more importantly, he provided a way in which the American people could understand what was transpiring. Lincoln provided meaning to a confused audience. As Garry Wills reminds us: "[T]he Civil War is, to most Americans, what Lincoln wanted it to mean. Words had to complete the work of guns."[58] Lincoln confirmed his role as a statesman, and all statesmen are in part educators whose fundamental tools are words.

Lincoln wanted above all else to hold the nation together and to make it a land of free men. Both goals were inextricably linked. As Lincoln reminded the nation as he campaigned for the presidency, one side in the debate was right and one side wrong. Moral principles must, at some level, reach certainty and universality.

> If slavery is right, all words, acts, laws, and the constitutions against it, are themselves wrong, and should be silenced, and swept away. If it is right, we cannot justly object to its nationality—its universality; if it is wrong, they cannot justly insist upon its extension—its enlargement. . . . LET US HAVE FAITH THAT RIGHT MAKES MIGHT, AND IN THAT FAITH, LET US, TO THE END, DARE DO OUR DUTY AS WE UNDERSTAND IT.[59]

It was just as important to recognize the imperative of Union, and this imperative made Lincoln realize the communality of all men. If Lincoln could see some communality with the slaves, we should also recall that he could see his bond with the slave owners too. To believe in the centrality of Union must mean just that—that northerners were united with southerners. As Wills points out, the "Second Inaugural Address" refers to "American slavery" and discusses the war God gave to both the North and South.[60] Early in his career, Lincoln had told an audience that if they had been born in the South, they almost certainly would have been like slaveholders. The lesson Lincoln learned from this was to recognize the fraternal bonds, in this case guilty bonds, that united all Americans—North and South. Hence, Lincoln was most forgiving, even as he sternly insisted on the transformation of American politics. He understood the need to compromise with his fellow citizens because he knew them as his brothers; yet, like a good brother, he insisted on the best from those around him. If he insisted on sacrifice, it was only to fortify the bonds that should unite all those who are members of a common endeavor.

> We are not enemies, but friends. We must not be enemies. Though passion may have strained, it must not break our bonds of affection. The mystic chords of memory, stretching from every battlefield, and patriot grave, to every living heart and hearthstone, all over this broad land, will yet swell the chorus of the Union, when again touched, as surely they will be, by the better angels of our nature.[61]

From the first moment of his administration, Lincoln understood that the connections uniting America must be maintained and those connections ran from North to South and from the present to the past.

This lesson concerning the connections among citizens is of profound significance for a democracy. The dangerous tendency of democracies is the belief that the majority makes right and that the majority is simply an aggregate of personal, contemporary preferences and interests. In the effort to educate democracy, there is a certain kinship between Lincoln and Socrates. Lincoln understood the need to criticize and demand more of his fellow citizens than they might be willing to immediately give while never breaking the civic bond, just as Socrates was led to observe that his philosophizing was tied to his commitment to the community he knew best.

> I shall do this [engage in philosophic questioning] to everyone I meet, young and old, foreigner or fellow-citizen; but especially to you my fellow citizens, inasmuch as you are closer to me in kinship.[62]

Socrates, as a private citizen, exhorted individual citizens to think; Lincoln, as an active politician, urged the entire nation to forgive and remember.

> With malice toward none; with charity for all; with firmness in the right, as God gives us to see the right, let us strive on to finish the work we are in; to bind up the nation's wounds; to care for him who shall have borne the battle, and for his widow, and his orphan—to do all which may achieve and cherish a just, and a lasting peace, among ourselves, and with all nations.[63]

To some commentators, this language strikes an all-too-religious note and Lincoln is held responsible for mythologizing a new civic religion for America. This charge is quite accurate in many ways. Lincoln's rhetoric grew more religious in tone as the war dragged on. If he did call upon the cadences of the Bible, it was certainly to recall the most profound Judeo-Christian messages—righteousness and forgiveness. Lincoln's rhetoric was not built upon a hollow worship of the false god of patriotism; rather, his message was couched in religious terms because it resonated with a religious people, and the themes of justice are central to the language they spoke and understood.

Lincoln's new civic religion was more moral than the civic religion developed by the Founders, and, in important ways, more inclusive, expansive and, thus, more democratic.[64] This civic religion taught Americans to forgive the past transgressions of war and slavery and offered everyone a chance to be included in the promises held out by the Declaration and the founding it inaugurated. The understanding of the founding was democratized, emphatically denying any notion of exclusion in American politics and, thus, enabling all citizens—regardless of race or ethnicity and eventually gender—to fully participate in American politics. This is Lincoln's moral and inclusive project. Lincoln's efforts also included an expansive and democratic aspect. By expanding our understanding of the founding to include the Declaration, and thus amending the Constitution, he opened up the possibility of criticizing the institutions created by the Founders. Of course, citizens had to be committed to the Union, but the meaning of that Union and citizenship remained open to interpretation that the revolution and founding, together, bequeathed to later generations. Lincoln articulated the voice of possibilities that the framers had seemingly silenced. Such democratized ideas were built upon a firm and unwavering moral commitment that self-interest was not the foundation of American politics.[65]

Lincoln served the founding by refounding the United States; and in the act of preserving the nation, he reformed it. Although the cost may have been great, Lincoln was, in a certain sense, the Burkean figure of his generation—following Edmund Burke's maxim that, "a state without the means of some change is without the means of its conservation."[66] Lincoln finally achieved both the moral goal of ending slavery and his personal goal of great political success. And it is not surprising that we hold Lincoln—and, Lincoln virtually alone—as equal to, if not surpassing, the greatness of the founding generation.

NOTES

1. *The New English Bible* (New York: Cambridge University Press, 1972).

2. See J. David Greenstone, *The Lincoln Persuasion* (Princeton, N.J.: Princeton University, 1993), 241. In particular, see Greenstone's thoughtful discussion of "rule-ambiguity."

3. Commentary on foundings and America can be found in Hannah Arendt, *On Revolution* (New York: Penguin Books, 1963); Forrest McDonald, *Novus Ordo Seclorum* (Lawrence: The University Press of Kansas, 1985); Hanna Pitkin, *Fortune*

Is A Woman (Berkeley and Los Angeles: University of California Press, 1984); Sheldon Wolin, "Contract and Birthright," in *The Presence of the Past* (Baltimore, Md.: Johns Hopkins University Press, 1989); and Jean Yarbrough, "Republicanism Reconsidered: Some Thoughts on the Foundation and Preservation of the American Republic," *Review of Politics* 41 (Winter 1979), 61–95.

4. We might recall Niccolò Machiavelli's intriguing praise of Numa, rather than Romulus, as the central figure in effectively founding Rome.

5. Garry Wills, *Lincoln at Gettysburg* (New York: Simon & Schuster, 1992), and James McPherson, *Abraham Lincoln and the Second American Revolution* (New York: Oxford University Press, 1990), see Lincoln as a revolutionary figure.

6. Abraham Lincoln, "Speech on Reconstruction, Washington, D.C.," in *Abraham Lincoln: Speeches and Writings 1859–1865*, ed. Don E. Fehrenbacher (New York: Library of America, 1989), 2: 701.

7. Harry Jaffa, *Crisis of the House Divided* (Chicago: University of Chicago Press, 1982), 322. Jaffa makes clear that Lincoln exaggerates Jefferson's "nonrevolutionary" aspects.

8. Plato, *The Republic of Plato*, trans. Allan Bloom (New York: Basic Books, 1968), 557a–561a.

9. See Alexander Hamilton, James Madison, and John Jay, *The Federalist Papers* 16, ed. Clinton Rossiter, (New York: Penguin, 1961) (hereafter cited as *Federalist*).

10. *The Debate on the Constitution* (New York: Library of America, 1993), 21.

11. See Ralph Ketcham, *Framed for Posterity* (Lawrence: University Press of Kansas, 1993).

12. See Wilson Carey McWilliams, "Democracy and the Citizen: Community, Dignity and the Crisis of Contemporary Politics in America," in *How Democratic Is the Constitution?* ed. Robert Goldwin and William Schambra (Washington, D.C.: AEI, 1980), 86–7.

13. The case for the Constitution is most famously made by Madison in *Federalist* 10, 51, and 55. See also *Federalist* 63, in which Madison argues that representation in America is based on "the total exclusion of the people in their collective capacity" from ruling. This is echoed by "An Old Whig I," a critic of the new Constitution, who wrote, "THAT COMMON PEOPLE HAVE NO BUSINESS TO TROUBLE THEMSELVES ABOUT GOVERNMENT," in *The Debate on the Constitution*, 125, (emphasis in original).

14. James Madison to Governor Edmund Randolph," *The Debate on the Constitution*, 746.

15. Many of these themes are dealt with by Douglass Adair, "Fame and the Founding Fathers," in *Fame and the Founding Fathers*, ed. Trevor Colburn (New York: Norton, 1974).

16. *Federalist* 38.

17. See Jay's observation in *Federalist* 64 that "there are frequently occasions when days, nay even hours are precious," and "there are moments to be seized as they pass."

18. *Federalist* 6.

19. Joshua Miller, *The Rise and Fall of Democracy in Early America* (University Park: Pennsylvania State University Press, 1991), 112–13. See also *Federalist* 49.

20. This was the considered judgment of Lincoln's contemporaries and occupies a central role in more recent accounts. See Richard Hofstadter, *The American Political Tradition* (New York: Random House, 1948), 92–134; Edmund Wilson, *Patriotic Gore* (New York: Oxford University Press, 1962), 99–130; and most recently, J. David Greenstone, *The Lincoln Persuasion*. Lincoln's law partner William Herdon once observed, "His ambition was a little engine that knew no rest."

21. David Herbert Donald, *Lincoln* (New York: Simon & Schuster, 1995), 152.

22. See Edmund Wilson, "Abraham Lincoln: The Union as Religious Mysticism, "in *Eight Essays* (New York: Doubleday, 1954).

23. I have learned a great deal on this subject from Greenstone, *The Lincoln Persuasion*.

24. Harry Jaffa has an extensive and insightful commentary on the speech in *Crisis of the House Divided*, chapter 9. See also Donald, *Lincoln*, 80–3.

25. Abraham Lincoln, "Address to the Young Men's Lyceum of Springfield, Illinois," in *Abraham Lincoln, Writings and Speeches, 1832–1858* (New York: Library of America, 1989), 1:28.

26. Ibid., 32.

27. Ibid., 34.

28. Ibid., 36. See also Lincoln's later speech, "Address to the Washington Temperance Society of Springfield, Illinois," in *Abraham Lincoln: Speeches and Writings, 1832–1858*, 81–90.

29. I am indebted to Rogers Smith for this observation (personal communication to the author).

30. Thomas Jefferson, "Notes on the State of Virginia," in *The Portable Thomas Jefferson*, ed. Merrill D. Peterson (New York: Penguin, 1988), 215.

31. Greenstone, *The Lincoln Persuasion*, see especially sec. 2.

32. We should of course recall Lincoln's staunch and continual defense of free labor. See Hofstadter, *The American Political Tradition*, 104.

33. Donald, *Lincoln*, 166. This reveals Lincoln's ability to see things from the other side. On this point see Lincoln's "Fragment on Slavery" in *Abraham Lincoln: Speeches and Writings, 1832–1858*, 303. In that fragment, Lincoln recognizes that the principle of slavery can be easily extended once it is first accepted.

34. Quoted in Edmund Wilson, *Patriotic Gore*, 91.

35. Lincoln hesitated in joining the Republican Party, in part, because he feared that it was too dominated by abolitionists.

36. For a clear summary and analysis of Douglas's position, see Jaffa, *Crisis of the House Divided*, chaps. 3–8.

37. Lincoln, "Speech at Springfield, Illinois," in *Abraham Lincoln: Speeches and Writings, 1832–1858*, 470.

38. Lincoln, "Speech on Dred Scott Decision," in *Abraham Lincoln: Speeches and Writings, 1832–1858*, 398. See Wills, *Lincoln at Gettysburg*, 87, for a discussion of this passage.

39. The argument that slavery would have definitely ended is, of course, open to debate. Lincoln certainly thought that if it was contained it would eventually decline.

40. Hofstadter argues the exact opposite point—that Lincoln was trying to move "the slavery question out of the realm of moral and legal dispute." See *The American Tradition*, 113.

41. Lincoln, "Address to the New Jersey Senate at Trenton, New Jersey," in *Abraham Lincoln Speeches and Writings, 1859–1865*, 209. See on this point, Wills, *Lincoln at Gettysburg*, chap. 2.

42. Jean-Jacques Rousseau, *The Social Contract*, bk. 2, ch. 7–10 (1762; reprint, New York: Penguin, 1968). For an excellent analysis of Rousseau's idea of the "people" and the "Lawgiver" in *The Social Contract*, see Hilail Gildin, *Rousseau's Social Contract* (Chicago: University of Chicago Press, 1983), 67–91.

43. Rousseau, *The Social Contract*, bk. 2, ch. 8.

44. Lincoln, *Abraham Lincoln: Speeches and Writings, 1832–1858*, 399.

45. Jaffa, *Crisis of the House Divided*, 318.

46. Ibid., 321.

47. Jefferson, "Letter to Henry Lee, May 8, 1925," in *Jefferson: Writings*, ed. Merrill D. Peterson (New York: Library of America, 1984), 1501.

48. Gal. 5:13–14. See also Rom. 8:20–22, I Cor. 12:26, and Gal. 3:28 with its emphasis on the law and wholeness of the universe. In Romans, Paul writes: "For the created universe waits with eagerness for God's sons to be revealed. It was made the victim of frustration, not by its own choice, but because of him who made it so; yet always there was hope, because the universe itself is to be freed from the shackles of mortality and enter upon the liberty and splendor of the children of God. Up to the present, we know, the whole created universe groans in all its parts as if in the pangs of childbirth."

49. Lincoln, *Abraham Lincoln: Speeches and Writings, 1832–1858*, 315.

50. See Charles Warren, *The Making of the Constitution* (Cambridge, Mass.: Harvard University Press, 1937), 392–393.

51. Lincoln, *Abraham Lincoln: Speeches and Writings, 1832–1858*, 504–5.

52. Ibid., 400.

53. Greenstone, *The Lincoln Persuasion* 282.

54. Lincoln, *Abraham Lincoln: Speeches and Writings, 1832–1858*, 456.

55. This is very clear in his "Speech at Chicago, July 10, 1858." Lincoln tells his audience to return to the principles of the Constitution as intended by the Founders, which he believed meant holding to the notion of equality articulated by the Declaration. See *Abraham Lincoln: Speeches and Writings, 1832–1858*, 458.

56. Ibid., 477.

57. Lincoln, "Letter to A. G. Hodges, April 4, 1864," in *Abraham Lincoln: Speeches and Writings 1859–1865*, 586.

58. Wills, *Lincoln at Gettysburg*, 38.

59. Lincoln, *Abraham Lincoln: Speeches and Writings, 1859–1865*, 129–30 (Lincoln's emphasis).

60. Wills, *Lincoln at Gettysburg*, 186.

61. Lincoln, "First Inaugural Address," *Abraham Lincoln: Speeches and Writings, 1859–1865*, 224.

62. Plato, *The Apology of Socrates*, ed. Hugh Tredennick (New York: Penguin, 1987), 61.

63. Lincoln, "Second Inaugural Address," in *Abraham Lincoln: Speeches and Writings, 1859–1865* 687.

64. For a discussion of the religious imagery in Lincoln's thought, particularly the Gettysburg Address, see Wills, *Lincoln at Gettysburg*, 87–89.

65. Of course, Lincoln could only articulate an ideal that still significantly eludes us.

66. Edmund Burke, *Reflections on the Revolution in France* (Indianapolis, Ind.: Hackett, 1987), 19.

11

The Ordinary Hero and American Democracy

Gerald M. Pomper

Let us now sing the praises of famous men,
the heroes of our nation's history. . . .
Some there are who have a left a name behind them
to be commemorated in story.
There are others who are unremembered . . .
and it as though they had never existed. . . .
—Ecclesiasticus, 44: 1–9

If a man has any greatness in him, it comes to light, not in one flamboyant
hour, but in the ledger of his daily work.
—Beryl Markham, *West With the Night*

Heroes teem in Western literature and political life, providing lessons for contemporary American democracy. Two initial examples may help our learning.

In ancient times, Achilles, angered by the loss of his mistress, refuses to fight the Trojans. Relenting only when his dearest friend is slain, the demigod vengefully defeats the enemy leader Hector in single combat. As Achilles too prepares to die, he brings the Greeks to the eve of their historic victory, and is eternally remembered as the hero of the Trojan War.

Three millennia later, a bomb ignites, turning a New York subway car into an inferno. The lives of dozens of people are spared when an off-duty policeman, with the uninspiring name of Denfield Otto, grabs a fire extinguisher and douses the spreading flames. Bewildered by reporters and the president of the United States, who praise his quick response, Otto

214

tersely declines admiration. "I don't consider myself a hero," he says, "I only did my job."[1] Who is the real hero?

Our immediate response is to choose Achilles, the exceptional individual who voluntarily acts in an extraordinary manner. Indeed, it is this type of person for whom the Greeks invented the very word *hero*. As Achilles did for his army, we look to heroes to protect us and preserve our society. Our storybooks picture heroes as dramatic figures, as traditional biographies focus on the unique personal characteristics of their subjects. In contemporary politics as well, we search for the charismatic leader who will easily solve the complex problems of modern life.

This view, however, has serious—and worrisome—implications. There are very few people or demigods like Achilles. Relying on such heroes makes human welfare contingent on the exceptional, often arbitrary, and uncertain help of these unique individuals. The successful resolution of political crisis comes to depend on the chance that extraordinary people will be found, somehow, to meet such crises, or on luck, the ability of people to achieve an ennobling transformation in critical times.

These implications are particularly serious in a democracy. The faith of democracy is that the populace has enough collective wisdom and character to choose able leaders and to work out its collective problems. But this faith hardly fits a populace that depends on heroes such as Achilles. Rather, reliance on heroes easily leads to disdain for the citizenry of democracy, pointedly expressed by the French playwright Jean Anouilh:

> Listen, my friend, there are two races of beings. The masses teeming and happy—common clay, if you like—eating, breeding, working, counting their pennies; people who just live; ordinary people; people you can't imagine dead. And then there are the others—the noble ones, the heroes. The ones you can quite well imagine lying shot, pale and tragic; one minute triumphant with a guard of honor, and the next being marched away between two gendarmes.[2]

A similar distinction is made by playwright Bertolt Brecht, but from a different perspective. One of Brecht's dramatic characters regretfully reflects Anouilh's desire for noble exemplars: "Unhappy the land that has no heroes." But another character, Galileo, responds with a more generalized trust in humanity: "Unhappy the land that is in need of heroes."[3]

Democracy cannot wait for demigods; it requires "ordinary heroes," superficially undistinguished people who can do what is necessary in extraordinary moments. These people become heroes not by luck or a miraculous metamorphosis. They become heroes by fulfilling their responsibilities as they have always done, but in a situation in which their qualities are particularly needed. Heroism is potentially widespread, but usually unseen, until induced by external events.

James Madison recognized the limits of heroism when he argued in *The Federalist Papers* that government must be designed for use by ordinary people: "It is vain to say that enlightened statesmen will be able to adjust these clashing interests, and render them all subservient to the public good. Enlightened statesmen will not always be at the helm."[4]

As Madison taught us, a successful democracy cannot depend on great men and great women. Instead, to Madison, self-government requires appropriate institutional arrangements that will curb the evils of factions, promote the selection of wiser officials, and transform the conflict of personal ambitions into the common good, so that "the private interest of every individual may be a sentinel over the public rights."[5]

Madison prioritizes institutions over individuals. But the traditional hero is unconfined by institutions. Indeed, he may be dangerous because he scorns such constraints, as the Greeks themselves recognized in the practice of ostracism, exiling persons who had become overly prominent. Achilles subverts the institutionalized discipline of the Achaean armies, valuing his personal gratification over the success of his comrades. When he returns to battle, he does so only to settle an individual blood grudge, not as a leader of his forces. Even as he glorifies his name, Homer warns of this hero's rage,

> murderous, doomed, that cost the Achaeans countless losses,
> hurling down to the House of death so many sturdy souls,
> great fighters' souls, but made their bodies carrion,
> feasts for the dogs and birds.[6]

Contrast Denfield Otto, the New York policeman, who respects institutions and accepts their prescriptions. He is the type of person with whom democracy is comfortable. The heroes of democracy are ordinary people who occasionally do heroic deeds, as they meet the ideal prescriptions of their institutional responsibilities. Though greatly diverse in social class and background, ordinary heroes usually explain their performance in the same way. "I was just doing my job," they say, like Denfield Otto, emphasizing their social and institutional responsibilities rather than their personal qualities.

Their job—sometimes a self-designated mission as much as a paid position—brings them into a situation where they act heroically, but not self-consciously, out of custom, habit, and the regular practice of their vocation. This fundamental sense of duty is also exemplified by accountants who uncover corruption and by teachers who inspire deprived pupils to read. Through the same quiet heroism, slaves were brought to freedom over the Underground Railroad. Outside of America, children were rescued in the Nazi Holocaust by nurses and social workers who felt they had no choice but to follow the life-saving rules of their professions.

Heroism does not proceed only from duty, however, which can be used to excuse inaction or even to condone evil. Such perversion of duty is exemplified by subordinates who acquiesce in their superiors' brutality or corruption, and then seek exoneration for "just doing my job." There must be more than obedience to superiors; there must also be a commitment to the higher values of their institutionalized work, such as honesty, legality, protection, and well-being.

Two ordinary heroes, Peter Rodino and Frances Kelsey, exemplify the concept in recent American political history. At a particular time and place, they did what they did at other times, putting the values of their institutions into exemplary practice. In a crisis, they did their accustomed work on a larger stage, to the benefit of American society. To appreciate their contributions, the concept of democracy's "ordinary hero" must be distinguished from many accepted, but diverse, usages.

CONCEPTIONS OF THE HERO

Heroism is rife in America, to judge by popular sources. *Newsweek*, for example, has honored "everyday heroes," as it termed a "diverse bunch—doctors, social workers, a single mother, a basketball great, and energetic high-school students [who] each recognized a need, and found an innovative way to meet it."[7] Showing a different ideological slant, *Mother Jones* gives annual "Heroes" awards to "grassroots activists," commended for "the dailiness of heroism that makes history happen," such as a Marine resisting the Persian Gulf War and a farm labor organizer.[8]

From still another perspective, the Heinz Family Foundation, proclaiming that "Heroes Walk Among Us," provides $25,000 annual awards for such persons as the U.S. surgeon general and the chairman of the Chiron Corporation in recognition of their "significant and long-term contributions to the betterment of humanity." Amnesty International bestows the accolade more broadly. It offers the title of "Quiet Hero" to those "individuals who in the sanctity and privacy of their own homes will help us save prisoners who are in danger" by displaying a decal, endorsing a protest to the prime minister of China, and contributing as little as $15.[9]

Heroes apparently might be anyone we like a lot. But heroism, to be meaningful, must be defined by more than popularity or good citizenship. We need to draw some conceptual distinctions and to examine their implications for democratic thought.

Heroism involves three elements: the person, his or her deeds, and the impact of the action. All of these are relevant, but they are combined in different ways in different interpretations. As explicated below, my portrayal of the ordinary democratic hero places little emphasis on personal characteristics, instead stressing customary, institutionally-prescribed deeds that, in a situation of crisis, have exceptional effects.[10]

For analytic purposes, we can conceive of polar differences on each of the three characteristics: persons, deeds, and impact. Persons may be classified as rare or ordinary, their deeds as extraordinary or customary, and the impact of these deeds as exceptional or commonplace. These polar opposites, when combined in alternative ways, produce eight ideal types, presented in the table below. The table also provides suggestive illustrations of individuals and social roles drawn from literature, history, and daily life, although particular examples may not always fit precisely.

A Typology of Heroes

Person	Deeds	Impact	Example
Rare	Extraordinary	Exceptional	Achilles
Rare	Extraordinary	Commonplace	Sisyphus
Rare	Customary	Exceptional	Washington
Rare	Customary	Commonplace	Billy Budd
Ordinary	Extraordinary	Exceptional	Medal of Honor winner
Ordinary	Extraordinary	Commonplace	Dorothea
Ordinary	Customary	Exceptional	Democratic hero
Ordinary	Customary	Commonplace	Classroom teacher

The most frequent conception of the hero is the romantic literary portrait, the rare individual who does extraordinary deeds having exceptional impact—such as the archetype, Achilles. But rare individuals can also act in other ways, and have different impact, as suggested in the next three ideal types. There can be individuals of rare qualities who do extraordinary deeds that have no exceptional impact. The appropriate example might be Sisyphus, a renowned mythic individual who valiantly and endlessly, but vainly, rolls a rock almost to the mountain summit, only to see it fall, in commonplace fashion, to the valley below.

To further illustrate the categorization, we can think of rare individuals who become known as heroes through their customary activities, rather than through glorious deeds. George Washington was an extraordinary individual who won acclaim for his personal magnetism from his contemporaries even before his historical apotheosis. His impact on American and world history is obviously great. Yet Washington's deeds were not extraordinary in themselves. A reluctant general and president, he was notable for his dutiful and careful work, not for striking originality. He is properly remembered not for any individual deeds of valor, but for using his power "gently and self-effacingly."[11]

Billy Budd, the hero of Herman Melville's novel, completes this group. Billy is a rare individual, a Christ-like seaman of striking physical and personal presence. But Billy does nothing outside of the ordinary work of a deckhand, until he is falsely accused of mutiny, convicted of an accidental murder, and hanged without protest. His death distresses his mates and captain, but has no further impact.

We are particularly interested here in persons characterized, sometimes deprecatingly, as "ordinary." Sometimes they do extraordinary deeds, which have great impact. Illustrative is the solider who, briefly and atypically, embodies the virtues of military duty in an unusual burst of courage. Such heroes earn the recognition of the Medal of Honor for "bravery beyond the call of duty."

There are other ordinary people who perform extraordinary deeds even if the impact of these actions is commonplace or unrecognized, such as the nurses and doctors who do their daily rounds in emergency rooms. In her conclusion to *Middlemarch*, George Eliot provides a moving example. Summarizing the lifetime benevolence of Dorothea, the novel's heroine, Eliot draws a great moral lesson, that "the growing good of the world is partly dependent on unhistoric acts; and that things are not so ill with you and me as they might have been, is half owing to the number who lived faithfully a hidden life, and rest in unvisited tombs."[12]

The most complete contrast to the literary conception among heroic types would be an ordinary individual who does customary deeds with only commonplace impact, such as a classroom teacher. As one champion of such "anonymous heroism" puts it: "[T]he bravest things we do in our lives are usually known only to ourselves. No one throws ticker tape on the man who chose to be faithful to his wife, on the lawyer who didn't take the drug money, or the daughter who held her tongue again and again."[13]

The final group comprises democratic heroes, people ordinary in their personal characteristics and their deeds, who yet have a considerable impact on the world, particularly in politics. To honor democracy, we must do more than speak "in praise of famous men." We need to recognize, with Sidney Hook, that a hero may be "any individual who does his work well and makes a unique contribution to the public good. . . . Daily toil on any level has its own occasions of struggle, victory, and quiet death."[14] But democratic heroes are more than praiseworthy citizens. They are distinctive because of the extraordinary impact of their institutional performances.

The nature of democratic heroism may be illuminated by discussing one recurring attribute of heroes: courage. The military veterans of the Normandy invasion of 1944 fit well into our category of democratic heroes:

> They look no different from the other guys who hang out at the Grange Hall or the ones who bowl in the Friday league. But talk to them, the heroes of Omaha and Utah Beach and the others, and they have a thousand tales to tell.
>
> That is just the point. Most led ordinary lives before their supreme test on D-Day, and ordinary lives afterward as well. Most do not see themselves as heroes, and they talk hesitatingly, if at all, about the scenes of carnage that met them on that gray morning in 1944.
>
> Yet, as Donald Boyce, 69 years old, from Carmichael, Calif., said here in Normandy over the weekend, they got the job done. . . . "Somehow or other," he said, "a bunch of people who were only civilians—they told us what to do, they trained us—and we went out and battled a professional army and made Europe free."[15]

Military heroism is the most common illustration of courage. Most often, physical courage is emphasized—the infantryman charging toward the enemy, the firefighter running into a burning building to rescue a trapped child. But this kind of courage is exceptional by its very nature and applies to only some kinds of heroes.

Democratic heroes, both men and women, also show courage. It is not always the dramatic courage of medal winners in war, but the steady performance of the tasks customary in their institutions, whatever the difficulties. This "courage of constancy"[16] is evident in self-descriptions by these ordinary heroes. Recurrently, they refer to their "job," their customary, vocational activities. It is shown by the collective, if individually unspectacular, achievement of the Normandy invasion, where "none had to be larger than life to deserve our salute."[17] It is marked by a firefighter in San Francisco, reporting her colleagues' remembrance of the rescue of four children from a burning building:

> "I found William first. . . ." He shook his head slowly.
>
> "It was the other guys," he said. "I just followed them."
>
> "Then I found Jamie Frank. I just helped," he murmured. "The others are the real heroes."
>
> "It was pretty satisfying," the officer said. "But you should get the story from the rest of the crew. I didn't do much." And so on.[18]

Heroism need not be restricted to extraordinary individuals and need not wait upon horrific conditions. We can also find democratic heroism among ordinary people doing their customary work with an extraordinary impact. Two Americans—a legislator and a civil servant—exemplify the contributions of democratic heroism.

PETER RODINO

We have recently marked the twenty-fifth anniversary of a decisive moment in American politics, the resignation of President Richard Nixon under threat of impeachment and removal from office. Congressman Peter Rodino of New Jersey precipitated the resignation when the House Judiciary Committee, under his leadership, thrice indicted Nixon for acting "contrary to his trust as President and subversive of constitutional government, to the great prejudice of the cause of law and justice and to the manifest injury of the people of the United States."[19]

The passage of time makes it useful to recount the constitutional crisis of 1972–74. The story began with a break-in at the Democratic National Committee's offices in the Watergate building complex in Washington during the presidential election campaign of 1972. The incident drew only limited attention before Nixon's triumphant reelection, but skilled investigative reporting led to a televised inquiry by a special Senate committee, the revelation of a series of executive branch offenses, paralleled by extensive White House efforts to thwart the spreading investigations and to repress evidence. Late in 1973, resolutions to impeach Nixon were referred to the House Judiciary Committee. At the end of July 1974, the committee concluded that Nixon's conduct "warrants impeachment and trial, and removal from office." Ten days later, Nixon left the White House in disgrace.

Nixon's impeachable conduct involved far more than individual vices. The incumbent president came close to subverting the basic democratic processes of the United States. He and his collaborators spied on their opponents, burglarized offices, employed the IRS, the FBI, the CIA, the Justice Department and other federal agencies to violate his opponents' constitutional rights, put government appointments and policy up for sale, and engaged in an extensive cover-up of these and other actions.[20] His peaceful removal from the presidency sustained American constitutional democracy.

Peter Rodino was the hero of this critical episode. In recalling his prominence, we illustrate the concept of democratic heroism. The committee chairman was not a "great man," neither before nor after the Nixon investigation. Rather, he was an ordinary man, who had "greatness thrust upon him." In a personal interview,[21] he agreed that, without the impeachment crisis, he would be remembered only by "the people who are especially interested, the scholars who write and record." Rodino had achieved the respect of his congressional colleagues, but he had won little public attention. He was, in legislative slang, "a workhorse not a show horse." Yet, in a decisive moment, he met the challenge.

Rodino was not typecast to be a hero. Relatively short, with a distinct urban accent, almost too carefully groomed, he could not be mistaken for Jimmy Stewart of *Mr. Smith Goes to Washington.* Coming out of a decaying urban political machine in Newark, New Jersey, he embodied the declining New Deal Democratic coalition. First elected in 1948 as an advocate of Harry Truman's Fair Deal, he consistently supported liberal programs, including repeal of the Taft-Hartley labor law, coauthored by his Republican predecessor in Congress.

Proud of his ethnic heritage, he referred to his base constituency as "Italian-Americans," and devoted himself to casework on behalf of newer Italian immigrants. As blacks moved into the once-solidly Italian North Ward of Newark in his congressional district, he became active in support of civil rights legislation, and added more nonwhites to his staff.

Until the Watergate scandal, even after a quarter of a century in Congress, Rodino had made little impact on the general public. Former colleagues of his had been elected mayor of Newark, and U.S. senators, or had been nominees for governor of New Jersey, but Rodino stayed in the House, serving a patient apprenticeship, contributing to the watershed 1960s legislation on civil rights, and managing the landmark immigration revision of 1965. No law bore his name, and he became chair of the Judiciary Committee almost by accident.

What accounts for the ability of a journeyman legislator to master a severe constitutional crisis? In other nations, deposing the head of the government commonly brings troops into the streets and unending political bitterness. Nixon's resignation, by contrast, brought almost universal relief to the nation, and Nixon ultimately would receive a respectable state funeral. Rodino's deft management of the impeachment inquiry must be given a considerable share of the credit for these results. But how can we explain Rodino's personal accomplishment?

The quick answer would be that the congressman "rose to the occasion," that he became on this occasion something of an overachiever, akin to a Medal of Honor winner, destined to revert to his obscure character once the crisis was past. That explanation would be only a put-down of Rodino, neglecting his institutional role. Even more important, it would imply the normal incapacity of democracy and its dependence on good luck and the rare savior.

Using the concept of the democratic hero, however, we look for heroism among ordinary people doing their customary work with exceptional impact. Rodino exemplified this type. The congressman was effective not because he was acting differently from his usual manner. His accomplishment was based on precisely those same qualities he had shown throughout his legislative career. As he himself put it:

> I believe that the very characteristic traits that made it possible for me to be effective in other roles—to be fair, to be decent, without fanfare, without showmanship—were the same in the role that I played as well during the impeachment crisis. That is the role that I've been playing all along. I was just the same Peter Rodino that I've been all the time from the very first day that I came to the Congress, from the very first speech that I made on the floor of the House.

Rodino was a politician in an institution of politicians; his virtues are the accustomed virtues of his breed. These virtues, however, are generally condemned by the public and the mass media. Congress, the most openly political of the branches of government, is also the least esteemed. While Americans abstractly favor democracy, they seem really to want a "stealth democracy," unmarred by the compromises, maneuvers, and ambiguities of a free politics. "They dislike compromise and bargaining, they dislike committees and bureaucracy . . . and they dislike debate and publicly hashing things out."[22]

Rodino was not an extraordinary individual, but one who succeeded by using typical tricks of the political trade. By building a record, he won a place on the congressional agenda. By proceeding cautiously, he gained more attention and support. By pursuing consensus across party lines, he gained broader backing. By compromising on some issues, he won agreement on the central questions. By his evident patriotism, he gained national acceptance of Nixon's condemnation.

Careful research is one of the traits valued in Congress. The first step in the impeachment process, under Rodino's direction, was the production of a large reference book on the arcane subject. The research led less to intellectual enlightenment than to a changed political climate. "There was now a book on impeachment. It wasn't an undefinable topic any more. . . . Nobody read a line of the book, but everybody held it and looked at the last page to see that it was 718 pages long."[23]

Another trait of Rodino's, valued in Congress, is caution. Although initially inclined toward impeachment, he made no public judgments—in contrast to other liberal Democrats. He insisted on formal House authorization of the impeachment inquiry to give it greater legitimacy. To preserve his impartial stance, he even disguised his reading materials on impeachment when traveling, using false cover pages. For the same reason, he vetoed the appointment of a staff member who had signed a pro-impeachment telegram.

Majority Leader Tip O'Neill valued this quality, using it to convince other House members that Rodino's committee should direct the impeachment inquiry. Yet even O'Neill grew impatient, pressing Rodino to begin the investigation quickly. "They wanted me to push," the New Jersey congressman remembers. "I told O'Neill in no uncertain words, that I was going to do it my way. I don't mind being called cautious, because I believe that when one is responsible for making decisions that are going to affect the future of the country, one doesn't treat those issues by making snap judgments. Maybe we ought to have a little more of that."

American politicians are seekers of consensus. In seeking consensus, Rodino deliberately courted House Republicans. He appointed John Doar, a Republican, as special counsel for the impeachment investigation and separated Doar's assistants from the normal partisan staff. The ranking Republican member was included in all aspects of the inquiry and given an early opportunity to hear the White House tapes. Junior Republicans were encouraged to take independent positions and led in framing the actual articles. In the end, the bipartisan approach worked, as seven of the committee's seventeen Republicans voted for Nixon's removal from office.

Compromise, the politician's particular art, was vital in winning this consensus. Originally, five counts were lodged against Nixon. Rodino agreed to dispense with the most political of these charges, which condemned Nixon for the secret bombing of Cambodia. Over Rodino's limited objections, the committee also passed over the president's questionable tax returns. By focusing on three central questions of constitutional illegality, Rodino assembled a strong majority.

Like most congressmen, Rodino is also an old-fashioned patriot. His House office was decorated with an American flag and other nationalistic symbols. The walls of his inner office featured autographed portraits of all recent presidents but Nixon. A decade after accomplishing the only removal of a president from office in American history, Rodino still conveyed a guileless patriotism as he remembered his reaction to the impeachment vote. Normally, one would expect the victor in a political battle to feel exaltation in his triumph. But Rodino's response was quite different:

> I went inside to a little cubby-office that I had and there was John Doar, and I looked at him, and there was nothing I could say, and I know we all looked solemn. Then I asked them to excuse me and went into the other room. I picked up the telephone and called my wife, and I said to her, "Well, I guess you know. And I pray to God we did the right thing." And then I broke down and cried.[24]

Rodino happened to be in a particular position at a particular time when he could affect the course of American history. He continued as chair of the committee until his retirement, celebrated for his action but limited in ambition. Despite his new fame, he withdrew his name from consideration as a vice presidential nominee in 1976 because "I wanted to stay on and do the job I was doing."

The successful outcome of the impeachment investigation is a personal tribute, yet it is also significant as a tribute to the characteristics and ability that are widespread in a nation. As the congressman acknowledged, "We've had many people who had humble beginnings and may not have been extraordinary until the time came that something happened and they were there."

Successful popular government cannot await great men and great women. It requires democratic heroes, apparently unremarkable people who can do what is necessary at extraordinary moments. In the impeachment crisis, Peter Rodino did what he would do at other times but on a larger stage. This workhorse politician embodied the democratic heroism of a man "just doing his job."

FRANCES KELSEY

Frances Kelsey is our second example. In 1962, working as a staff scientist for the Food and Drug Administration, she prevented the introduction of the drug thalidomide into the United States. Sold abroad as a mild sedative widely used to treat insomnia, it had become the third largest-selling drug in Germany and was available in 45 countries, often without a prescription. This drug, when taken by pregnant women, was soon found to cause serious harm to their fetuses, leading eventually to the birth of children without arms and legs, a condition called phocomelia.[25]

By her action, Dr. Kelsey prevented the birth of hundreds of handicapped children and spared their parents immense pain. In acknowledgment of her work, Dr. Kelsey received a presidential citation and worldwide recognition, and her discovery led to major legislation giving the FDA authority to monitor the effectiveness, as well as the safety, of new drugs. Surely she is a hero.

Frances Kelsey is a sharp personal contrast to Peter Rodino. The individual characteristics are quite different, but the theme is consistent: a woman and a scientist-bureaucrat, rather than a man and a lawyer-politician; a reserved Canadian from the midwestern plains, rather than a gregarious Italian-American from Newark's dense streets; an office without plaques and degrees that reflects standard government issue, still laden with packing boxes after two and a half years' occupancy, rather than the photographs and flags that symbolize power in a congressional office. But both are democratic heroes.

Kelsey resists efforts to depict her work as heroic and avoids probes into her personal feelings or motivation. Earlier in her career, she had been involved in another notable inquiry, when her graduate adviser found that the base of a sulfa elixir prescribed for pediatric patients was essentially antifreeze, diethylene glycol, and consequently responsible for serious injuries and deaths, particularly of children. A psychologist might infer that this investigation made her a crusader for children's health and that her zeal was further stimulated by her later becoming the mother of two. Yet, even when working on embryo metabolism of new drugs, she said her motivation was "just scientific interest." Kelsey finds her most significant research to be work on the pituitary gland and on antimalarial drugs.

Throughout her career, Kelsey emphasized the quotidian canons of scientific investigation. After graduating from medical school, she worked for the *Journal* of the American Medical Association as an editorial associate, reviewing drug studies submitted for publication, and was struck by "the poor quality of the studies that came in." Later, at FDA, this experience aroused her skepticism, when "I found that those [inadequate authors] were the ones doing the studies on drug applications,"[26] and that "many of the studies in support of safety of the new drugs were done by investigators whose work had not been accepted for publication in the *Journal*."[27]

In appearance and in her work, Kelsey is best seen as a scientist working for a bureaucracy and trying to further the purposes of that bureaucracy—safe drugs. For the FDA, thalidomide's review was but an example, ultimately exceptional in its consequences, of typical practices. At the time, FDA was a small agency, housed in "grim" prefabricated buildings on the Mall in Washington, D.C., with drug reviews conducted by only seven full-time physicians who had only sixty days for an initial decision. Bureaucratic routine caused Kelsey to be named chief investigator of thalidomide. She had just joined the agency, moving to Washington when her husband was appointed to a position at the National Institutes of Health. "Since I was new, it was decided that I should be given a simple preparation to start on and that's how the thalidomide application was assigned to me."[28]

The drug went through three stages of review. Initially, it was presented as a drug for insomnia, its widest usage, although it also seemed to relieve morning sickness in pregnancy. It is notable that Kelsey and her associates first delayed approval of thalidomide for purely technical reasons, as demonstrated in this list of detailed, undramatic objections:

> [T]he animal data were not reported in full detail. . . . [T]he chronic toxicity data were incomplete . . . deficiencies relating to details of the manufacturing process. . . . The asymmetrical carbon atom in the molecule was noted

... insufficient cases had been studied ... the claims of safety were not adequately supported.

After these technical issues were raised, the drug company submitted a new application, only to meet new objections. Kelsey had begun to worry about a possible connection between thalidomide and a nervous system problem, peripheral neuritis, a condition of painful tingling and numbness in the arms and legs. These doubts came from a note in a British journal, but Kelsey found that warning almost by accident as she was looking up references on another drug. The manufacturer, W. S. Merrell, still wanted to go ahead and sell thalidomide while adding a warning label.

Kelsey remained obdurate. She began to wonder about the long-term effects of the drug, which had never been tested, particularly on fetuses. Her skepticism was increased by the absence of any data on the use of thalidomide during the first two trimesters of pregnancy. Before the FDA could act to ban the drug, reports came from Germany and Australia of congenital defects in babies born to mothers using thalidomide. Merrell withdrew its application—but not before at least seventeen deformed American children had been conceived. In the rest of the world, unrestrained by the FDA, 12,000 new lives were ruined.[29]

Throughout the thalidomide review, Kelsey's concern was professional precision, not a sentimental protection of children. She disdained the Merrell application because it was "sloppy" and lacked complete data on the tests employed and on the samples, controls, and investigators, and it even included mistranslations of the original German research articles. Procedures were easily abused: "We got the impression from a new drug application that maybe [only] forty or fifty doctors had the privilege of trying it out. . . . They came back with a [dangerously large] list of over a thousand doctors all over the states. . . . They didn't bother keeping records."

Perhaps these qualms were only lucky guesses. As she put it, "[T]here was something that I just didn't like about the drug. Maybe that's woman's intuition or something foolish, but I don't think so." Rather than inexplicable intuition, her caution stemmed from informed judgment: "I was not prepared to see the type of applications that were submitted, because I lived in sort of an academic dream world, I guess. . . . [Their research] was so superficial and so anecdotal."

Kelsey and her associates' repeated objections brought complaints from the manufacturer. "They called my boss that I was dragging my feet. . . . nit-picking and asking for unnecessary stuff. There were some raised eyebrows." In the circumstances, the politically prudent action would have been to accept the manufacturer's assurances and promises of careful marketing. But Kelsey held to a singular goal, the withdrawal of the drug, and she achieved her aim.

Even later, when she was famous, Kelsey published only two short medical journal articles about thalidomide. She and the agency refrained from making political capital of the incident, which was only revealed months later when a Senate committee chaired by Estes Kefauver broke the story as part of an effort to amend the drug safety laws. Once the thalidomide story became news, the law was swiftly amended to give FDA its expanded jurisdiction over new drugs. Kelsey, although politically inactive, makes the shrewd political judgment: "[I]f you want the law to change, you have to have something that affects children. Because that did it overnight."

Recently, Kelsey's action has incurred criticism and ridicule in a way that illuminates, although unintentionally, the character of her heroism. Dr. Steven Harris, an opponent of FDA regulatory practice, correctly points out that the FDA already had authority over the safety of drugs even before the thalidomide case and that the 1962 amendments added power over efficacy, not safety (although they also made it easier for the FDA to assess safety). "It was only by the sheerest chance that the red-tape" delayed thalidomide until the connection was made to birth defects, he alleges. Rather than a hero, he denigrates Kelsey as only "a delay-causing bureaucrat . . . allowing Europeans to serve as first-class 'guinea pigs' for Americans, in a case where (quite literally) guinea pigs themselves would not have done an adequate job."[30] He regrets the new powers gained by the FDA, arguing that the agency has harmfully delayed many desirable drugs and has limited patient choice.[31]

Harris's policy position has some validity, and complaints about FDA delays have recently led Congress to require speedier drug trials. In criticizing Kelsey for her caution, however, he ironically praises her "ordinary" virtues. We expect a good bureaucrat—and a good scientist—to be careful, to apply objective rules, to act on the basis of the relevant evidence. "Red tape" is simply an abusive term for established procedures.

As a scientist, Kelsey waited for reliable data, which could have been provided by proper and feasible clinical tests. Her caution was particularly appropriate at the time, given the absence of any system for international exchange of information about new drugs. For example, German scientists had some suspicions about birth defects, but they checked with U.S. hospitals and found no unusual cases and therefore dropped their investigation, not knowing that thalidomide was not approved for use in the U.S. Contrary to Harris's rhetorical attack, Kelsey did not experiment on humans, European, or American. The terrible effects on European humans, however, did justify her bureaucratic protection of American patients.

There was another consequence to this story, unintended but large. An American woman, a pregnant Arizona broadcaster named Sherry Finkbein, borrowed the drug from her husband who had used it for insomnia on an overseas trip. When Ms. Finkbein learned of the likely deformities of her fetus, she flew to England to have an abortion, which was then illegal in the United States. Her difficulties spurred the movement to legalize abortion, probably the most divisive political issue of the last three decades.

What made Frances Kelsey a hero? She was a typical scientist and bureaucrat, not a person of rare talent. Her actions were the customary work of her job, not glorious exceptions to her daily routine. Her colleague in the thalidomide investigation, Lee Geismar, provided the refrain of these individuals: "It was just my job. I just went to work and did my job. I never set out to do anything extraordinary."[32]

The heroic aspect of Frances Kelsey is the exceptional impact of her ordinary deeds. The story has an element of luck, but good luck is the remains of good design, as Thomas Edison commented. By devotion to the high standards of the scientific enterprise, by commitment to the objective procedures of effective bureaucracy, by doing her ordinary job well at an exceptional time, Frances Kelsey became a democratic hero.

THE POLITICAL USES OF DEMOCRATIC HEROISM

Rodino and Kelsey are personally attractive heroes, but politics is more than a story of individuals. Such heroes can promote democracy in three ways.

First, the particular decency of persons such as Rodino and Kelsey testifies to the more general goodness of humanity, or at least to the potential of goodness. Democracy at bottom rests on such optimistic faith, or else we must accept the grim, selfish world described by Thomas Hobbes. Good actions by some role models can also inspire further good actions in others, adding new evidence of the worthiness of democracy's trust in "common" people.

These examples are still more telling when the role models are "ordinary." It is always inspiring when we witness exceptional acts of goodness, but these acts can also occasion regret, precisely because of their rarity. A chilling example is provided by the most fearsome experience in western history, the Nazi Holocaust. Those "Righteous Gentiles" who rescued Jews certainly deserve our praise. But, if these good people were "only" exceptional people, their laudatory behaviors could also create despair because they suggest that most people accepted, at least passively, the brutality of their time. To see rescuers as exceptional "is in fact to make such people seem essentially different from you and me, and thus not really, not challengingly, relevant to our daily lives."[33]

On the other hand, we can draw happier conclusions when goodness is not confined to uniquely estimable individuals. Even in the evil of the Holocaust, we can draw a deeper inspiration from the French village of Le Chambon, where the entire community cooperated to hide and save Jews. This enclave of morality provides a lesson in "the banality of goodness," and evidence that "the instinct for love ran deep in unexpected places, and was present not only among leaders or highly gifted people."[34] We come to a more optimistic, and more democratic, conclusion when we see rescuers as the true, if bolder, representation of fundamental human sentiments.

Heroism provides a second contribution. The political actions of these individuals remind citizens of their collective experience, of the existence of a community beyond themselves. The self-government of democracy requires more than the promotion of self-regarding actions; heroes bring this larger vision into view. The actions of heroes may encourage others to foster their own communal participation, to increase their actual exercise of democratic responsibilities. They heed Alexis de Tocqueville's admonition: "[T]he rulers of our time sought only to use men in order to make things great; I wish that they would try a little more to make great men."[35]

To Ralph Waldo Emerson, a hero can make others into heroes. "With the great, our thoughts and manners easily become great. We are all wise in capacity, though so few in energy. There needs but one wise man in a company, and all are wise, so rapid is the contagion. . . . Thus we feed on genius, and refresh ourselves from too much conversation with our mates, and exult in the depth of nature in that direction in which he leads us."[36]

Heroes become leaders when they inspire similar actions by others, by followers. A democratic hero, to be effective, cannot act alone. "The leader most needs followers. When those are lacking, the best ideas, the strongest will, the most wonderful smile have no effect. . . . It is not the noblest call that gets answered, but the *answerable* call. . . . The leader is one who mobilizes others toward a goal shared by leader and followers"[37]

Martin Luther King, Jr.'s leadership of the modern civil rights movement exemplified this contribution of heroism. While King was the public voice of the movement, he was effective not so much because of his eloquence but because of his example. By going to jail, reluctantly yet nonviolently, he inspired others to collective sentiment.[38] Blacks became more conscious of their common needs, and whites became more conscious of the common humanity they shared with blacks. Fostering involvement and community, King advanced America's founding ideal: equality.

In a third contribution, heroes may take actions that improve and defend the democratic process itself and increase more general understanding and appreciation of that process. "The 'potential hero' in a democracy sees what others do not. His will to action is stronger. His knowledge of what must be done to realize what he sees is surer. . . . His loyalty to the democratic ideal compels him to make this insight the common faith of the majority."[39]

Democratic heroes act successfully within democratic institutions. Their proudest boast might well be: "The system worked."[40] Peter Rodino worked within the legislative system to maintain constitutional liberty. Frances Kelsey worked within the bureaucratic system to advance children's health. They are not extraordinary characters, but they did foster American democracy in their customary work. They personify the character of American democracy anticipated by Tocqueville:

> If there are few instances of exalted heroism or of virtues of the highest, brightest, and purest temper, men's habits are regular. . . . [G]enius becomes more rare, information more diffused. The human mind is impelled by the small efforts of all mankind combined together, not by the strenuous activity of a few men.[41]

Their experiences also remind us of Benjamin Franklin's answer to a woman who asked, at the end of the Constitutional Convention, what kind of government the Founding Fathers had designed. Rather than relying on the unique virtues of a king, Franklin said, the framers had placed their hopes in the people, creating "A republic, if you can keep it."[42] Each of us may need to be a hero to keep our nation.

NOTES

I am grateful for the stimulating research of Marlene Pomper, and the helpful critiques of Miles, Marc, and David Pomper, Rayna Pomper, Erika Siegel, Milton Finegold, Ruth Mandel, Maureen Moakley, and Marc Weiner.

1. Felicia Lee, "One Man's Impromptu Act of Bravery," *New York Times*, 22 December 1994, sec. B, p. 7.
2. Jean Anouilh, *Point of Departure*, act 2.
3. Bertolt Brecht, *Life of Galileo*, scene 13.
4. Alexander Hamilton, James Madison, and John Jay, *The Federalist Papers* (New York: Modern Library, 1941), no. 10, 57 (hereafter cited as *Federalist*).
5. *Federalist* 51, 337.
6. Homer, *The Iliad*, trans. Robert Fagles (New York: Penguin, 1990), bk. 1, p. 77, lines 2–5.

7. "Everyday Heroes," *Newsweek* 125 (29 May 1995): 26–39. A few years earlier, the magazine offered "A 51-Gun Salute to Everyday Heroes," in vol. 110 (6 July 1987): 62–79.

8. "Heroes, Heroines," *Mother Jones*, January–February 1992, 43–50.

9. School children's heroes include a Little League coach, Superman, and Mr. T, who bested George Washington and Abraham Lincoln in a poll of eighth graders. See Tonya Huber Emeigh, "Native American Heroines: The Biography in the Curriculum," *The Educational Forum*, 52 (Spring 1988): 256.

10. In this interpretation, the vital causal factor (in social science terms, the critical independent variable) is the crisis event, rather than the individual. Crisis then stimulates an appropriate institutional response to the situation from involved individuals.

11. See James T. Flexner, *Washington: The Indispensable Man* (Boston: Little, Brown, 1973), xvi.

12. George Eliot, *Middlemarch* (1871–72; reprint, New York: Bantam, 1985), 766.

13. Peggy Noonan, *What I Saw at the Revolution* (New York: Random House, 1990), 253.

14. Sidney Hook, *The Hero in History: A Study in Limitation and Possibility* (Boston: Beacon, 1943), 239.

15. R. W. Apple, "Looking Back," *New York Times*, 7 June 1994, sec. A, p.1.

16. The phrase is from novelist Cormac McCarthy, *All the Pretty Horses* (New York: Vintage, 1992), 235.

17. William McDonald, writing about the film *Saving Private Ryan* in *New York Times*, 26 July 1998, sec. 2, p. 16.

18. Caroline Paul, *Fighting Fire* (New York: St. Martin's Press, 1998), 217.

19. House, Committee on the Judiciary, *Impeachment of Richard M. Nixon, President of the United States*, 93d Cong., 2d sess., 1974, 3–4.

20. New evidence on Nixon's crimes has recently become available with release of extensive White House tape recordings. See Stanley Kutler, *Abuse of Power* (New York: Free Press, 1997).

21. All unattributed quotations are from a personal interview by the author of Congressman Rodino in his Washington office, 15 April 1983.

22. John Hibbing and Elizabeth Theiss-Morse, *Congress as Public Enemy* (Cambridge: Cambridge University Press, 1995), 18–19.

23. Jimmy Breslin, *How the Good Guys Finally Won* (New York: Viking, 1975), 71–72

24. To add to the emotional strain, Bob Woodward and Carl Bernstein report, this incident occurred soon after Rodino had been informed that a kamikaze pilot was said to be heading for the committee offices. See Woodward and Bernstein, *The Final Days* (New York: Avon, 1976), 31.

25. Frances O. Kelsey, "Denial of Approval for Thalidomide in the U.S.," in *Medicine and Health Since World War II: Four Federal Achievements* (Bethesda, Md.: National Library of Medicine, 9 December 1993).

26. All unattributed quotations are from a personal interview by the author of Dr. Kelsey at FDA headquarters, Rockville, Md., 3 February 1998.

27. Kelsey, "Denial of Approval for Thalidomide in the U.S.," 7.

28. Ibid., 8.

29. Sheryl Gay Stolberg, "Their Devil's Advocates," *New York Times Magazine*, 26 January 1998, 20. Perhaps ironically, thalidomide recently has been approved by the FDA, under very strict controls, for use in treating leprosy and ulcers caused by AIDS. Dr. Kelsey raised no objections to the new use, and the earlier victims supported its reintroduction.

30. Harris, Steven, M.D., "The Right Lesson to Learn from Thalidomide," <http://www.aces.uiuc.edu:8001/Liberty/Tales/Thalidomide.html > (1992) (accessed 7 October 1997).

31. It is remarkable to me that I learned of this critique only because Kelsey herself gave it to me, despite its criticism of her greatest life achievement. This action itself manifests her commitment to scientific objectivity.

32. Lisa Fine, "Caretaker of the Curatives," *Washington Post*, 23 January 1997, M01.

33. Pierre Sauvage, "Ten Questions," in Carol Rittner and Sondra Myers, eds., *The Courage to Care: Rescuers of Jews During the Holocaust*, (New York: New York University Press, 1986), 139.

34. Robert McAffee Brown, "They Could Do No Better," in Rittner and Myers, *The Courage to Care*.

35. Alexis de Tocqueville, *Democracy in America*, ed. Phillips Bradley (1835; reprint, New York: Vintage, 1954), 2:347.

36. Ralph Waldo Emerson, *Representative Men* (1850), in *Essays & Lectures* (New York: Literary Classics of the United States, 1983), 626–27.

37. Garry Wills, *Certain Trumpets* (New York: Simon & Schuster, 1994), 13, 17.

38. See John Lewis, *Walking With the Wind* (New York: Simon & Schuster, 1998), chap. 7, and Wills, *Certain Trumpets* , 218–19

39. See Sheldon S. Wolin, *Politics and Vision* (Boston: Little, Brown, 1960), chap. 1; Hook, *The Hero in History*, 232–33.

40. These were President Gerald Ford's first public comments after he succeeded Richard Nixon.

41. Tocqueville, *Democracy in America*, 2:350.

42. Farrand, Max, ed. *The Records of the Federal Convention of 1787* (New Haven, Conn.: Yale University Press, 1923), 3:85.

12

Wilson Carey McWilliams and Communitarianism

Mac McCorkle and David E. Price

Equally at home taking the measure of Aristotle or John Winthrop or Newt Gingrich, Wilson Carey McWilliams stands out as one of the most impressive and diverse practitioners in the field of political thought. For over twenty years, he has been producing postelection analyses for the American presidential year volumes edited by his Rutgers colleague, Gerald Pomper, and shorter election analyses for such publications as *Commonweal*.[1] McWilliams's collection *Beyond the Politics of Disappointment?* contains his presidential-year essays through 1996 and additional essays about the 1994 and 1998 midterm congressional elections.[2] For over thirty years, he has engaged in serious political theory. Indeed, his 1973 tome *The Idea of Fraternity in America* presaged much of what has now become a central debate in political theory—the question of "communitarianism" as an alternative to liberalism (and conservatism) on the Western ideological spectrum.[3] In fugitive scholarly essays after *Fraternity*, he has quietly continued to develop his position in the so-called "liberal-communitarian debate."[4]

The mix of contemporary election analyses and political theory has given an unparalleled, multilayered dimension to McWilliams's work. Purists in both election analysis and political theory could find him guilty of taking distracting detours when he mixes realms in his writings. However, in our view, his writings have developed a middle-ground perspective that enriches both realms.

It is probably futile to hope that his election analyses can become influential models ultimately leading to the elevation of standard campaign punditry. Yet hope springs eternal. It is far more reasonable to expect that returning his work to the forefront of intellectual discussion will significantly enrich the liberal-communitarian debate. That is the main purpose of our essay.

Numerous thinkers of varying perspectives have danced with the basic communitarian theme that Enlightenment liberalism's emphasis on individual rights and its lack of emphasis on social obligation are politically inadequate.[5] And we do not suggest that McWilliams has defined the real or perfect communitarian position. Indeed we are in closer agreement with the politics of the more moderate and hopeful line of communitarian thought being pioneered by *The Responsive Community* editor Amitai Etzioni and coeditor William Galston.[6]

We also recognize that McWilliams hardly fits the profile of a dispassionate historian. He is instead a very engaged political theorist—and something of an old-fashioned moralist as well. Thus he is willing to make strongly polemical judgments and to make major intellectual leaps across historical contexts.[7]

Nevertheless, in traveling from the highbrow of political theory to the lowbrow of contemporary election horseraces, McWilliams has confronted, framed, and fleshed out essential questions for the maturation of contemporary communitarian thought. His work grapples with theoretical issues in the context of American history that more moderate thinkers like Etzioni and Galston, as well as the influential, left-leaning communitarian thinker Michael Sandel, have so far papered over or simply ignored.[8] Ultimately, however, McWilliams's own work can benefit by confronting policy advances in the work of Etzioni, Galston, and Sandel.

McWILLIAMS'S ELECTION ANALYSES:
THE POLITICS OF DISAPPOINTMENT

"The essays are impressionistic, but far more than journalism or mere speculation," political scientist Susan Herbst has aptly written in reviewing McWilliams's *Politics of Disappointment*. "They are all thoughtful reflections on how elections, as political moments, highlight the decline in a coherent American political culture."[9] His election essays display very little in common with journalistic treatments that glorify the making of presidents or congressional majorities. He does not fall for the journalistic fallacy of equating electoral victories with mastery of the modern American political situation.

Like the Progressive era intellectuals portrayed in Daniel Aaron's classic work *Men of Good Hope: A Story of American Progressivism*, the often-disappointed McWilliams is still a "man of good hope." On some occasions in his analyses, he even indulges in the hope that the election of a new (Democratic) president will lead to a new era of "civic equality." Yet, the view that pervades McWilliams's analyses is that the American political earth has parted over the last three decades and left a yawning chasm between the populace and the federal government. Even as the economy sustained its long boom after the 1996 elections, the percentage of the public expressing "trust in the government in Washington to do what is right" remained below one-third. This vote of no confidence represented the reverse image of the mid-1960s when a two-thirds supermajority expressed trust in the federal government.[10]

Agreeing with conventional punditry, McWilliams sees Ross Perot and his emergence as a serious presidential candidate in 1992 as personifying the gulf between citizen and government. However, rather than accepting the conventional placing of Perot in the "tradition of prairie populism," McWilliams emphasizes that "the legacy of Perot's candidacy. . . pointed to our distance from Populism's promise and to the endangered status of democratic citizenship." In contrast to "the federation of localities and associations" which emerged as the People's Party in 1892, Perot's movement one hundred years later "was constructed from the top down." Perot merely proved that in today's media-driven politics "with grand salesmanship and enough money it is possible to become a major force without passing through the primaries or parties."[11]

Yet McWilliams refuses to engage in a Menckenesque condemnation of the American people.[12] Indeed, McWilliams takes the opposite tack. He goes so far as to compliment Ronald Reagan's political savvy in appearing to embrace the religious right wing's "sense of grievance" and "feeling of disadvantage in relation to secular culture." In his 1996 election analysis, McWilliams even declares: "Virtually all of us are feeling at least somewhat baffled and considerably overwhelmed. *Our experience is an ever-closer match to the paranoid position.*" McWilliams here is invoking and defying Richard Hofstadter's influential view in *The Paranoid Style in American Politics and Other Essays* that only a remnant of maladjusted, right-wing fanatics are significantly troubled by modern America's progress.[13]

So, gazing over the horizon beyond Bill Clinton, McWilliams can still see the possibility of a right-wing redefinition of the American political universe. In response to President Bill Clinton's 1996 slogan about building a bridge to the future, McWilliams sardonically declared, "The bridge America really needs, in the nearest possible future, is one linking citizens with their government."[14]

But he refuses to settle for the typical journalistic finger-pointing at Clinton and the rest of today's political class. He instead targets the constitutional framers and their handiwork for the lack of connection between citizen and government:

A big part of the problem is inherent in the nature of the regime. In the framing of our institutions, distance between government and people was designed; the unique quality of American constitutionalism, wrote James Madison, lies in the "total exclusion of the people in their collective capacity" from any share in rule. And at the time, Antifederalists warned that the Constitution's politics . . . were weighted to the advantage of elites.[15]

McWilliams ends his 1996 analysis by calling for a "new Progressive movement" that would act in an opposite fashion from its elitist predecessor in the early twentieth century. Rather than relying on disinterested academic and administrative expertise, he hopes for a new movement attempting to "revitalize politics" through a return to "party organizations that are local, closer to citizens, and better able to provide them with a public voice."[16]

Protecting the democratic legacy of Populism from such current pseudo-outsiders as Perot, empathizing with the religious rank-and-file, identifying the Constitution as a major source of our contemporary political problems, and calling for a revival of political parties—these views are hardly the stuff of standard campaign commentary. They furthermore go beyond being intellectual bons mots thrown out to spice up his analysis. As the next section shows, they instead stem from a distinctive, religiously-grounded communitarianism that McWilliams forges in *Fraternity* and subsequent writings. As we go on to demonstrate, his significant engagement with Anti-Federalist criticism of the Constitution, with Populism, and political parties is virtually absent not only in standard campaign commentary but also in the writings of such other communitarian thinkers as Sandel, Etzioni, and Galston.

McWILLIAMS'S RELIGIOUS COMMUNITARIANISM

McWilliams's unique style and patterns of thought provide *Fraternity* with the aura of an eclectic virtuoso performance—perhaps best titled "Wilson Carey McWilliams Does American Thought"—rather than a work that rams home one underlying thesis. In an admiring fashion, Robert Booth Fowler describes *Fraternity* as "a cornucopia of (not necessarily brief) essays on all sorts of thinkers, ideas, and eras in American history. It sprawls; it wanders; it enlightens; it argues."[17]

Yet, underneath all of *Fraternity*'s dazzling eccentricities, McWilliams maps out a discernible communitarian viewpoint on American history, a perspective he continues to develop throughout his later writings. It is neither some vague allegiance to a faddish, existentialist notion of community nor a romantic *Gemeinschaft* dream—both of which he specifically dismissed in *Fraternity*.[18] His American communitarianism is instead unapologetically religious, predominantly Protestant and Puritan in origin.

In *Fraternity*, McWilliams locates the intellectual origins of American communitarianism in John Winthrop's 1630 lay sermon "A Model of Christian Charity" to his fellow migrating Puritans. Aboard the Arabella flagship, Winthrop declared:

> We must entertain each other in brotherly affection; we must be willing to abridge ourselves of our superfluities for the supply of others' necessities; we must uphold a familiar commerce together in all meekness, gentleness, patience, and liberality. We must delight in each other, mourn together, labor and suffer together; always having before our eyes our commission and community in the work, our community as members of the same body.[19]

In his encyclopedic commentary on American political theory, James Young identifies this emphasis on "a current of fraternal politics rooted in Puritanism" as distinguishing McWilliams's viewpoint from most other communitarian thinkers. It certainly contrasts with a strict Hartzian view that America was born, and has always remained, an Enlightenment liberal country. In *Fraternity*, McWilliams bluntly declared: "Puritanism . . . was here first."[20]

This original Puritan communitarian strain, however, quickly became a dissenting, rather than a dominant, political tradition. "Louis Hartz's seminal *The Liberal Tradition in America*," McWilliams acknowledges in *Fraternity*, "has demonstrated beyond the need for formal argument the degree to which conscious and formal thought about politics has shaped itself in terms of the categories of Enlightenment liberalism." He further concedes:

> The United States government was . . . founded on liberal doctrines, and deviation from them has had a suspect, alien quality. . . . And so much of the American experience seems to confirm the great liberal theses. The creation of American institutions was almost the visible demonstration of the struggle against nature, the social contract, the superiority of individual decision, science and contrivance over custom and natural law.[21]

Thus, while the religious influence of the Puritan errand dominated the settling of the new world, the secular influence of the Enlightenment dominated the founding of the new nation.

McWilliams sees this historical bifurcation as making American culture "deeply dualistic." In effect, although granting much political ground to the Hartzian view, McWilliams refuses to see Enlightenment liberalism as the hegemonic common sense of the American people. "The domination of its [American] formal thought by the Enlightenment does not exclude an informal tradition in symbols, rituals, and arts and letters based on very different notions of man and politics." Subsequent migrations from Europe and Africa to the New World reinforced this mainly religious traditionalism. "The United States drew its first great wave of immigrants from what was the last migration of the religious age and subsequent immigrants to America were largely traditional peoples who embodied or readily imbibed the religious heritage."[22]

McWilliams sees the cultural embeddedness of this religious impulse as providing American communitarianism with substantial populist potential. In *Fraternity*, McWilliams briefly characterizes Anti-Federalism as the first populistic force in the new nation:

> Most [Anti-Federalists] agreed that a larger union was needed, but they were insistent that it be tied intimately to the people, which required that it be built on the basis of locality. They were aware that a large state not only limits the number who can participate but makes it easier for the well-to-do and the educated to organize, and more difficult for the poor.[23]

In his writings after *Fraternity*, McWilliams more elaborately features the Anti-Federalists as presenting a populist alternative that shared the emphasis of Puritanism on a "coherent moral community." McWilliams even portrays Anti-Federalism's dissent as paving the way—to a large degree, unintentionally—for the emergence of locally-based political parties. He depicts parties as providing the "closest possible approximation of Anti-Federalist ideas of political friendship and strong representation" by being "rooted in local communities and in political fellowship."[24]

McWilliams sees Thomas Jefferson as belatedly giving formal articulation to this Anti-Federalist view. From his Monticello retirement in 1816, increasingly discontented with the limitations of the political system, Jefferson wrote that America desperately needed a new localist, "ward-republic" system "where every man is a sharer in the direction . . . and feels that he is a participator in the government." McWilliams sees Jefferson as providing a theoretical rationale for what he had been attempting to accomplish as the first presidential standard-bearer of the first American party (Democratic-Republican) in the 1790s. Jefferson's belated declaration completes the circle to the Puritan legacy because he explicitly based his ward-republic idea on the New England town meeting.[25]

This dissenting communitarian tradition struggled to survive in the twentieth century. Religious traditions initially remained strong "among [urban] immigrants and in rural areas, where Enlightenment standards touched lightly." It was thus no accident that "the great protests against the dehumanization of industrialism came first from the farms" and then (in a somewhat more uncertain fashion) from ethnic laborers in the cities. McWilliams especially portrays the Populists of the 1890s as "devoted to religious values" and drawing their "ideal from the Testaments." From an institutional perspective, he sees the locally based political parties of the nineteenth century as the main embodiment of this populist potential in American political life. But parties in the twentieth century were under attack from the Progressive reform mentality that placed a priority on centralized and bureaucratized expertise.[26]

Despite seeing this legacy of Puritan communitarianism as an alternative to Hartz's "liberal tradition," McWilliams acknowledges the political divide in America is something more than a conflict between classes or warring ethnic groups. The conflict between secular liberal and religious communitarian options often represents the split intellectual personality of the archetypal American. Most Americans want to avoid having this "fundamental discord between biblical religion and secular rationalism" to erupt within themselves. As McWilliams puts it, they have held on to "some attachment to both traditions and preferred a downy equivocation to the discipline of the dialectic."[27]

McWilliams treats this usual religious compromise as a victory for secular individualism. Compromised civil religion has displayed a "complacent cosmic optimism [that] identified what passed with the Divine will, assuring men that America was as perfect as conditions permitted, and might become better through 'progress' combined with faith." This American corruption of Puritanism's "inner-worldly asceticism" led to the connection of respectable "Protestantism with the capitalist spirit" in American life.[28] The course of the Puritan inheritance was a story of depletion and decline. McWilliams even sees the reformist Social Gospel of Walter Rauschenbusch as somewhat infected by civil religion. The main saving graces in *Fraternity* are the religious communitarian elements in the African-American political tradition, which Reverend Martin Luther King Jr. voiced in the civil rights movement, and the critique of American capitalist optimism found in such nineteenth-century dissenters as Nathaniel Hawthorne, Herman Melville, and Mark Twain, and twentieth-century African-American writers as Ralph Ellison and James Baldwin.[29]

Like such other historical critics of liberal progress as Christopher Lasch and E. P. Thompson, McWilliams wants more to highlight communitarian aspects of premodern traditionalism as critical foils to the liberal present than to launch a full-scale apologia for premodern society.[30] He thus tries to get some critical distance from parts of the Puritan legacy. Yet his criticisms usually focus on the decline in religious faith as the source of problems. For example, he states in *Fraternity*: "The religious tradition has not been uniformly beneficial. *Deprived of their basis in faith, manipulated and twisted*, religious ideas of fraternity have encouraged violent millennialism, revivalist frenzy, and political quietism." Similarly, he characterizes Puritan-like witch hunts as the desperate convulsions of a fading religious communitarianism floating unanchored from its theological moorings. They stem, according to him, from a people's unspoken "awareness that 'community' among them is a delusion" and that "the necromancer is inside the self."[31]

Moreover, such actions as Puritan leader Winthrop's driving out of dissidents Anne Hutchinson and Roger Williams hardly seem to faze him. McWilliams even criticizes both dissidents for teaching "a doctrine whose implications led directly to individualism" through opposing "the positive moral obligations and the negative force of guilt which Winthrop hoped to inculcate as supports for man and fraternity in New England."[32]

He also strives to disassociate any of his critical observations about the Puritan-populist legacy from the more fundamental attacks on its reactionary side in Richard Hofstadter's *Age of Reform*. McWilliams's embrace of religious, participatory, decentralized, and localist elements in the American reform tradition from the Puritans to Black Power is almost an exact reverse mirror image of Hofstadter's embrace of more professionalized, centralized, and nationalist elements. While acknowledging progressive (if not communitarian) aspects to the Protestant-populist tradition, Hofstadter's basic message is that America needs to get beyond it. Despite acknowledging its erratic nature, McWilliams's message is that the communitarianism of this tradition represents America's main hope for recovery.[33]

COMPARING THE COMMUNITARIANISM OF SANDEL AND ETZIONI-GALSTON

In large outline, Sandel's recent work *Democracy's Discontent: America in Search of a Public Philosophy* resembles the portrait of American intellectual history in McWilliams's *Fraternity*. Both books depict a dominant Enlightenment liberalism privileging the isolated self and individual rights versus an alternative, dissenting tradition defending community and social obligation. Both also see their alternative tradition as being on the political left wing (although incorporating some right-wing discontent) and as experiencing decline over the course of American history.

Etzioni, however, rejects what he calls this "old communitarian" vision. In his *Essential Communitarian Reader* Etzioni pointedly criticizes Sandel's writings as its latest manifestation. He sees himself as directing the development of a "new communitarianism" that represents "a third way of thinking" occupying the political center. Galston characterizes it as "liberalism properly conceived" or "communitarian liberalism."[34]

Etzioni's distinction between his and Sandel's general position on the political spectrum appears more or less accurate. Yet, in terms of historical and theoretical viewpoints, the example of McWilliams defies and confounds Etzioni's distinction between old and new communitarianism. For in opposition to McWilliams, Sandel and Etzioni-Galston end up on the same side over such key dividing-line issues as the treatment of Madisonian constitutionalism, the populist tradition, and political parties. These essential differences all trace to the religious roots of McWilliams's communitarianism versus their more secular orientations.

It is true that openness to religion in the public square is a chief element of contrast that Sandel claims for his communitarian outlook against liberalism. In his 1994 review of John Rawls's *Political Liberalism*, Sandel criticizes Rawls's "ideal of public reason" for holding that citizens have to avoid delving into their "moral and religious" beliefs when addressing "fundamental political and constitutional questions." Rawls's position in favor of the naked public square, according to Sandel, presents "an unduly severe restriction that would impoverish political discourse and rule out important dimensions of public deliberation."[35]

Moreover, in *Democracy's Discontent*, Sandel demonstrates special intellectual solicitude for "persons encumbered by religious convictions." He criticizes liberal as well as conservative Supreme Court justices for failing to accord "greater respect to the [religious] claims" of the Amish, Orthodox Jews, Seventh-Day Adventists, and Native Americans. He also concludes that a central weakness in late twentieth-century jurisprudence is its "fail[ure] to take religion seriously."[36]

Yet it seems no accident that Sandel's protected religious groups are small and on the periphery of American political life. In Sandel's rendition of communitarian thinking (and of American public philosophy generally), examples of formative religious thinking are few and far between. Although writing from Massachusetts Bay, the Harvard professor chooses to bypass Winthrop and his "Model of Christian Charity," all successor Puritan divines, as well as the rest of Puritan thought and culture. *Democracy's Discontent*, moreover, has no Great Awakenings, one passing mention of evangelical abolitionism, no Social Gospel, no Reinhold Niebuhr, and only one reference to Martin Luther King Jr. as a preacher.[37]

In essence, Sandel chooses to look past Jerusalem and to find the historical source of American communitarianism in Athens. He posits the original hegemony in the American political culture of the "civic republican tradition"—the transatlantic communitarian persuasion traced by J. G. A. Pocock (among others), to the eighteenth-century English commonwealthmen, and through the sixteenth-century Italian republics, and all the way to Aristotle and his *Politics*. And within this tradition, Sandel strives to encompass what he sees as James Madison's effort in the Constitution "to save American republicanism from the deadly effects of private pursuit of happiness."[38]

The contrasting example of McWilliams's religious communitarianism puts special pressure on Sandel's secular account. McWilliams essentially shares—and his later writings specifically incorporate—Sandel's philosophical argument in his 1982 work *Liberalism and the Limits of Justice*[39] for the communitarian origins of the person. Rejecting John Rawls's liberal understanding of persons coming into the world as morally "unencumbered" free agents, Sandel there elaborates the view that "where the self is unencumbered . . . no person is left for self-reflection to reflect upon." Yet McWilliams argues that the Puritan tradition ignored by Sandel is the prime exponent of this communitarian account of personhood in American history. As McWilliams writes in a 1985 essay:

> In their [the Puritans'] teaching . . . [h]uman beings are part of the order of creation, and can be understood only in relation to the whole in which they participate. This principle pervades nature, and it evidently holds true in political life. . . . [I]ndividual liberty . . . is possible only within political society; the existence of the whole is the condition of the freedom of the part, and it can be said following Aristotle, that the *polis* is prior to the individual in the order of nature.

To make his communitarian point, McWilliams of course relies on Winthrop's "Model of Christian Charity." Yet, as he also points out, such eighteenth-century Puritan preachers as Gilbert Tennent attacked the desire to be "a sort of independent being" and condemned the temptation of people "against the Law of Nature, to seek a single and independent state in order to secure their Ease and Safety."[40]

McWilliams's communitarian challenge extends beyond the Puritans. He applies Sandel's critique of "unencumbered" Rawlsian liberalism to the Madisonian framers of the Constitution portrayed by Sandel as belonging to his civic republican communitarian tradition. The framers, he argues in a 1986 essay:

> held that human beings are by nature free beings who are morally independent and primarily self-centered. In this doctrine, nature is defined by origins, and hence by the body; the decisive evidence of human freedom is the fact that we come into the world in separate bodies, and so remain. By nature, individuals are *unencumbered*, without duties to others or claims on them [italics added].

McWilliams thus claims that "Rawls follows Locke and the Framers" in espousing this liberal, individualistic view of the self.[41]

Although the connections that McWilliams draws between Aristotle and the Puritans and between the framers and Rawls may be strained, he nevertheless makes clear that no self-respecting thinker of a communitarian bent can ignore the legacy of Winthrop and the contrast with the Madisonian framers.[42]

The communitarianism of Etzioni and Galston hardly wears the same kind of secular blinders that narrow Sandel's view of American history. The title of Etzioni's 1996 work, *The New Golden Rule*, establishes that the Judeo-Christian ethos is hardly foreign to his political vocabulary. Galston similarly declares in *Liberal Purposes* that one of his chief concerns is "the characteristic liberal incapacity to understand religion." While expressing concern about some of the religious outsider groups that capture Sandel's attention, Galston goes much further in recognizing that most Americans have been, and remain, "vastly more religious . . . in both ritual and belief" than citizens in other Western democracies.[43]

Yet the ultimate conclusion in the Etzioni-Galston communitarian outlook remains much the same as Sandel's view: American religious traditions from Puritanism and beyond play no formative political role. In striking contrast to McWilliams, Etzioni goes out of his way to distance his view from the Puritan errand into the wilderness. In his 1993 work *The Spirit of Community*, Etzioni calls for "a moral reawakening without Puritanism" because its legacy is too much of "a rigid social order maintained through fear and conformity and denying dissent." Etzioni even entitles *Spirit*'s manifesto-like introduction "A New Moral, Social, Public Order— Without Puritanism or Oppression." His first communitarian declaration in the introduction was: "We hold a moral revival in these United States is possible without Puritanism."[44]

At the end of *Liberal Purposes,* Galston provides a formal theoretical statement of position that further illuminates his difference with McWilliams's religious communitarianism. Various "thinkers along the political spectrum," writes Galston, "have contended that liberalism is dependent on . . . the accumulated moral capital of revealed religion." However, he claims that this view is "mistaken" because his communitarian liberalism "contains *within itself* the resources it needs to declare and to defend a conception of the good and virtuous life that is in no way truncated or contemptible." Galston acknowledges that his communitarian liberalism has gained and needs supplementary "support" from the religious tradition in the American context. He is acutely aware that religion continues to provide many Americans with "both the *reasons* for believing . . . [political] principles to be correct and the *incentives* for honoring them in practice." Yet he emphatically concludes that the religious contribution involves no "*essential content and depth.*"[45]

In a later essay, Galston makes even more evident that American religion makes no intellectual contribution to his communitarian outlook. There he criticizes the "Enlightenment project" of Kantian, or non-communitarian, liberalism for its single-minded pursuit of the goal of individual autonomy. He unfavorably juxtaposes this misguided Enlightenment project with what he endorses as the "Reformation project." To McWilliams and many others, the essence of something called the Reformation project would focus on belief in (as Martin Luther put it) "the priesthood of all believers" with its positive participatory and egalitarian as well as its negative exclusivist and separatist implications. Galston's analysis of the Reformation project, however, focuses only on the negative side of the Protestant legacy and the challenge of "managing" all the conflicting diversity in religious beliefs.[46]

In *Liberal Purposes*, the heroes of Galston's Reformation project are George Washington, James Madison, and the other framers because they endorsed "American religion in the most general of terms" but cabined its divisive tendencies in the Constitution. In particular, he holds up Washington as evidencing the wise outlook of the framers. The first president in his "Farewell Address" declared: "Of all the dispositions and habits which lead to political prosperity, religion and morality are indispensable supports. . . . The mere politician, equally with the pious man, ought to respect and cherish them." But according to Galston, "Washington's view is not that religion provides premises essential to the validity of liberal arguments. It is rather that only a relatively small number of citizens can be expected to understand and embrace liberal principles on the basis of purely philosophic considerations."[47]

Along with a number of conservative intellectuals, McWilliams expresses disdain for this instrumental approach to religion. He agrees with Galston that the framers saw religion as a "mythology" that "*supports* but does not *define* the moral order." Yet he condemns rather than embraces this legacy. "The Framers were concerned to make religion harmless, rendering it solely subject to political society without even the hope of rule." He is especially outraged by the instrumental attitude expressed in Benjamin Franklin's statement that "Publick Religion" should concentrate as much on making "good Citizens" as on making "good Presbyterians." He endorses Melville's view that Franklin was a "Machiavelli in tents"—which, according to McWilliams, means that he was "a combination of ancient and modern duplicity and self-seeking."[48]

One can legitimately wonder if the framers get the short end of the intellectual stick from McWilliams's and Galston's inadvertently mutual agenda to separate their founding legacy from the American religious tradition. They both strain to ignore the view held by Reinhold Niebuhr and others that the Reverend John Witherspoon's teaching at Princeton had a formative influence on Madison and that the concept of original sin lurks between the lines of *Federalist* 10 and 51.[49] McWilliams is probably the bigger culprit here in his effort to paint the framers into an unholy Hobbesian-Lockean posture that sees "human beings . . . at war with nature, seeking the mastery that will force nature to yield to . . . a political regime . . . consequently dedicated to the pursuit of power."[50]

The larger problem, nevertheless, lies with Galston's caricatured treatment of American religion. While recognizing its status as a major "sociological fact," he strains to deny its intellectual influence. *Liberal Purposes* contains no exemplars of left-leaning religious thinking. Galston acts as if neither the Puritans nor any other religionists had any "mind" that helped to form or define American community-oriented liberalism. But the tradition of reform Christianity, not the constitutional tradition of the framers, led the way on such reform efforts as the abolition of slavery. Ignoring all its progressive moments, Galston treats the "socio-religious Protestant nexus" as reflecting the unthinking "traditional morality" of American society that needs to be accommodated and managed to avoid a lapse into right-wing reaction. In other words, according to Galston's one-dimensional view, the American Protestant tradition amounts to little more than a monolithically conservative civil religion.[51]

Perhaps the most telling way to challenge Galston's position is to point out that taking it seriously would mean that McWilliams's religious communitarianism could provide no "essential content and depth" to contemporary American political theory.[52] Surely Galston does not take his secularist position that seriously.

We hope to have established that McWilliams's religious perspective provides a fuller historical picture of American communitarianism. Our next section tries to show why the secular communitarian frameworks of Galston, Etzioni, and Sandel need to confront the political and theoretical insight that McWilliams's religious communitarianism supplies.

COVENANT THEORY AS THE MISSING LINK IN THE COMMUNITARIANISM OF SANDEL AND GALSTON

From the view of high political theory, McWilliams, Sandel, and Galston all meet at Aristotle's ancient ideal of the citizen in the polis.[53] One of their common goals is to modernize and democratize the Aristotelian view so that it values mass political participation throughout society. This is a tall order even for this trio of gifted thinkers. McWilliams's distinctive effort to achieve a contemporary synthesis of Aristotle and the Puritans may well represent the most ambitious and elusive project among the three.

Yet the major problems encountered by Sandel and Galston stem from their respective failures to find a coherent way onto the democratic path that McWilliams locates through his embrace of the covenant idea in Puritanism.

In *Democracy's Discontent*, Sandel is unequivocal in staking out neo-Aristotelian ground. "It is only as participants in political association," he writes in conscious and favorable paraphrase of Aristotle, "that we can realize our nature and fulfill our highest ends." He explains that "participating in politics . . . means deliberating with fellow citizens about the common good and helping to shape the destiny of the political community."[54]

But Sandel's participatory neo-Aristotelian sentiments run directly into the reality of what the essential original figure in his American republican tradition—James Madison—thought about popular participation during the founding era. He acknowledges that the Madisonian constitutional system—featuring an extended republic and a governmental scheme of checks and balances—was designed to "save republican government by making it less dependent on the virtue of the people." According to Sandel, "the point of republican government" for Madison "was not to give the people what they want but to do the right thing. This meant placing government in the hands . . . of the virtuous" few who could govern without "consulting the people directly." In other words, as Thomas Pangle comments, "Sandel cannot help but acknowledge the aristocratic dimension in American civic republicans' arguments. But Sandel never really comes to terms with these arguments."[55]

Galston more clearly recognizes the serious tension in this neo-Aristotelian embrace of the framers. Galston and Etzioni firmly treat the Madisonian constitutional system as a historical "given"—or what Etzioni calls a "core element"—in their moderate communitarianism. Furthermore, unlike Sandel, Galston acknowledges that this political conception moves some distance from the pure Aristotelian civic republican conception because it treats formal political participation among the citizenry as merely optional. Galston nevertheless asserts that his pro-Madisonian position "does not thwart democratic participation."[56]

It would be unfair to dismiss the late twentieth-century thought of Sandel or Etzioni-Galston as too elitist and anti-communitarian simply because it begins with the late eighteenth-century framers. McWilliams's support of the seventeenth-century Puritans—with their clearly exclusivist hierarchy based on religious belief—would be subject to the same kind of ahistorical attack. The telltale problem with both Sandel's and Etzioni-Galston's communitarian viewpoints is the murkiness with which they trace the legacy of the framers in the subsequent course of American history. They fail to explain how their Federalist tradition becomes more democratic-participatory or progressively communitarian. Their mutual silence on the Populist insurgency of the 1890s only reinforces the question.[57]

The main institutional thread emanating from Sandel's and Galston's Federalism seems to lead ineluctably away from popular politics and toward the Supreme Court. In moving through American history, they both lavish attention on intellectual disputes about Supreme Court cases and the arguments of constitutional theorists. While sometimes arguing for a judicially activist stance, both Sandel and Galston distance themselves from typical liberal commentators in eclectically arguing for judicial passivism on some issues and deference to community standards (on such issues as pornography). Yet these differences with standard liberal jurists are still matters of degree, rather than kind—the theoretical equivalent of the quarrels, for example, between the aging Justice Felix Frankfurter and the rest of the Warren Court. In embracing judicial guardianship to the significant extent that they do, both Sandel and Galston seem to espouse more a contemporary version of Plato than of Aristotle. [58]

In contrast, especially after *Fraternity*, McWilliams reinforces the democratic nature of his communitarianism by heading in an explicitly extra-constitutional direction to embrace the legacy of American political parties.[59] He champions the ideal of the political party as the best "means of narrowing the affective distance between citizens and representatives" established in the Madisonian constitutional design. At its best, the party system, according to McWilliams, has served as "a second system of representation based on locality, memory, and conviction."[60]

As McWilliams recognizes throughout his writings, the reality of American political parties has been messier than his portrayal of the ideal. Yet he can rely on such authoritative figures as Walter Dean Burnham to make the populist case for party politics. Their shared conclusion is that throughout American history party politics has provided the lower economic orders with their "best hope of organizing 'countervailing collective power' against those who are 'individually'—or organizationally—powerful." At the same time, unlike interest groups concerned merely about the defense of private wants, parties in McWilliams's view are capable of reconciling and transforming them into shared public values.[61]

Parties certainly deserve better than the virtually silent treatment that they receive from Sandel and Galston. On the opening page of *Democracy's Discontent*, Sandel renders the uncontroversial current judgment that "the political parties are unable to make sense of our condition." But he then proceeds to act as if parties played no noteworthy role in American history and fails to consider any need for their revitalization. Galston's *Liberal Purposes* even fails to contain an index reference for parties. In elsewhere discussing the role of political parties, Galston limits them to functioning as (unintended) extensions in the Madisonian constitutional design of checks and balances on mass political participation. He even reverts to the individualist language of public-choice ideology, pronouncing that "party competition may be understood on the analogy of free market competition" where citizens are largely relegated to the role of passive consumers.[62]

Sandel's and Galston's failure to take political parties more seriously is not just another example of an intellectual dodge that raises questions about the democratization of their respective Federalist outlooks. It possesses central theoretical significance, because McWilliams proposes the party idea as the political symbol of a synthesis between the extreme poles of individualism and what he critically characterizes as folk "communalism."[63]

An undeniable element in McWilliams's thought is his opposition to the way that the modern individualist age of capitalism, science, and technology melts almost everything solidly traditional into air. Yet his ultimate Aristotelian understanding is that "the idea of the *polis*" rises above the communalism of "blood-right" and "is applicable to men of different clans." Although antithetical to political individualism, McWilliams's American-style parties at the same time can constitute "great rivals of political communalism" because they "accept and presume the continued existence of the political society and a common government, recognizing the larger political whole and hence, to some degree, their own partiality."[64]

McWilliams sees this party idea as stemming from the covenant fraternity idea that the Puritans brought to the New World. Although grounded in the Hebrew scriptures and with parallels in other cultures, covenant theology became, in Perry Miller's phrase, "the marrow of American Puritan divinity." The New World situation, as McWilliams sees it, ruled out the possibility of relying on any Old World sense of organic community:

> America could not begin by relying on the source of immemorality, the deep-seated emotions and common customs that were the unthought foundation of solidarity in older nations. Political commitments had to be understood as the results of decision, covenant, or contract.[65]

In other words, while certainly encumbered in a traditionalist historical context, the act of becoming a Puritan communitarian in the New World was still a choice. That is the ultimate political importance of what the Puritans preached in their covenant theory. "Puritan theorists," acknowledges McWilliams, "argued that men only 'discovered' the existence of bonds already in existence and written in the character of those who made the covenants." Yet, the key political point was that the Puritans saw "the formal act of deliberation and agreement" as "pledg[ing] men in the flesh to obligations that had existed only as abstractions. Duties which might have bound the individual to any set of like-minded men bound him to the particular set of like-minded men with whom he had engaged in the art of covenanting." Although the original Puritan covenant was limited to believers, it made a decisive egalitarian step away from ancient theory by basing membership on one's choice of belief rather than one's immutable social status.[66]

Sandel sometimes appears to be in search of such middle ground between individualism and folk communalism. In a 1987 symposium, he even describes the distinguishing goal of his communitarianism as an "intermediate self-understanding that lies between the purely parochial, radically unreflective, situated self and the radically unencumbered self."[67] But trapped in his secular theoretical framework, Sandel sees elements of voluntarism and choice as inextricably connected to liberalism's impoverished social contract theory between isolated selves. Thus, at one point in *Limits of Justice,* he sweepingly dismisses "voluntary association" as mere Rawlsian pseudo-communitarianism.[68]

This dismissal sweeps political parties off Sandel's map. As McWilliams emphasizes, while possessing some of the non-voluntarist cultural embeddedness that Sandel seems to admire, American parties have involved "the art of associating together" and at bottom constitute voluntary "civic associations." Because he verges on dismissing the possibility of people *choosing to be communitarian,* Sandel's outlook virtually limits him to working with only the ascriptive, Old World elements of nationalism and ethnicity. This puts him in the doubly unfortunate situation of relying on organic elements that can ignite in a reactionary fashion but always quickly burn out in the New World. [69]

Galston's theory has the same need to provide a more convincing voluntarist explanation of how individuals come together to unite as a people in the New World context. An uncharitable reading denies that his theory has any foundation in genuine democratic consent. Instead, as conservative Peter Lawler has acidly written, wise Aristotelian elites "must deceive . . . in order to rule." Galston indeed sees the dominance of liberal individualist contract theory as part of the problem, rather than part of the solution. In *Liberal Purposes,* Galston nevertheless affirms that sufficient grounds for genuine democratic agreement "on the virtues needed to sustain such societies" exist. By the terms of his own argument, only such a religiously-inspired notion as the covenant ideal could give to the great mass of people the "reasons for behaving [in] . . . and the incentives for honoring" a commitment to democracy. At the same time, however, he is boxed in by his stubborn position that no such religiously inspired ideal provides any "essential content and depth" to the framers' achievement.[70]

Clearly, Sandel's, Etzioni's, and Galston's historical as well as theoretical outlooks could benefit from sustained engagement with McWilliams's religious communitarianism. This hardly means that Sandel, Etzioni, Galston, or any other communitarian must wholeheartedly embrace McWilliams's account of the Puritan tradition. Other scholars have found the Puritan tradition ultimately to be more modern, capitalistic, and more compatible with the constitutional mainstream of subsequent American political thought.[71] Still others reject McWilliams's linking of Puritan covenant theology with American political parties and search for more clearly spiritual or dissenting tributaries.[72]

An eye-opening engagement with the Puritan tradition may even repel some erstwhile communitarian thinkers. It could lead them to reconsider the comparative merits of a thoroughly secularized, deontological liberalism or move on to a more radical secular alternative. Or, it may simply drive some to swear off the search for any substantial grounding in the origins of American history and political theory. But as McWilliams's work proves, any communitarian outlook that claims to be present at the creation cannot get away with skipping past the Puritan tradition.[73]

ON McWILLIAMS'S COMPARATIVE POLICY DEFICIT

In moving away from the realms of history and theory to policy, the comparative advantage switches to Etzioni and Galston as well as to Sandel, while the critical spotlight turns on McWilliams. He has described his *Fraternity* as "attempting to set a stage for policy suggestions . . . rather than to make them." But in the view of some observers, the writing of mere political prefaces seems to describe the entire corpus of McWilliams's work. Critics charge him with offering "only utopianism." Even those sympathetic to his work raise questions about the shape of "the political institutions that would embody his . . . soulcraft" and "the political difficulties that would accompany those institutions."[74]

This charge regarding the lack of praxis in McWilliams's work is actually overblown. After *Fraternity*, he repeatedly articulates a policy strategy consistent with his theoretical outlook. This strategy is a pro-party variant of comprehensive campaign finance reform. Beyond dramatically restricting or abolishing the influence of private money, McWilliams envisions the channeling of public funding to the parties with the effect of revitalizing "party organizations that are local, closer to citizens, and better able to provide them with a public voice." However, as McWilliams himself would acknowledge, campaign finance reform is, at best, a necessary and procedural but not a sufficient and substantive source for renewing the communitarian base of American politics.[75]

Moreover, even in terms of incremental reform, McWilliams's reliance on campaign finance reform pales in comparison to Etzioni and Galston's portfolio of "third way" policies. In such works as *Capital Corruption: The New Attack on American Democracy*, Etzioni has strongly advocated campaign finance reform. But Etzioni and Galston have also been major activists in the "New Democratic" movement's championing of new policy ideas with communitarian overtones. These include community policing, college scholarships in exchange for national service, significant expansion of the Earned Income Tax Credit subsidy for the working poor, securitized mortgage arrangements to make homeownership more affordable, "second-chance" homes for unwed teenage mothers, and "restorative justice" for juvenile offenders.[76]

Etzioni and Galston have awkwardly backed these policies out of the parking lot of political theory, and these third-way policies are hardly invulnerable to criticism. Yet McWilliams has failed to take seriously the third-way policy thrust, portraying it only as a "mongrel" political tactic of President Clinton and his allies to preempt Republican popularity by "poaching on the territory of the other party."[77]

This dismissal is particularly odd since Galston's and Etzioni's policy work addresses moral and religious concerns raised in McWilliams's work. Over a decade ago, for example, McWilliams was deploring that "[m]odern America is all too frequently a place of shattered families." But Galston and Etzioni are the ones now directly challenging liberal notions of lifestyle neutrality and are making the communitarian policy case for the usual superiority of the two-parent family. McWilliams even earlier hinted about the need to relax the strict separation of church and state because "any concern for the civic equality of the poor is bound to consider help from the church in performing that civic role." However, despite his restricted instrumental conception of religion's political role, Galston is the one now actively promoting the communitarian case for allowing faith-based organizations a more active role in antipoverty programs.[78]

Moreover, in his political activity, Galston could be viewed as following the communitarian ideal in McWilliams's writings rather than his own intellectual writings. For more than a decade, he has been channeling his communitarian insights into an effort to revitalize the oldest American political party. As an adviser to Walter Mondale's 1984 presidential campaign, he shelved his intellectual reserve and advocated populist identification with "a tradition which pitted the individual and the small community against the large and impersonal forces of big business and big government." And, during the first half of the Clinton years, he served as a chief policy adviser and intellectual defender of a presidential agenda that at least fitfully attempted, as McWilliams acknowledges, to sound "chords of memory" by framing its policies under the umbrella label of the "New Covenant."[79]

In comparison, McWilliams evidences not a failure of nerve but an overlay of intellectual inhibitions against such mainstream activity on the national front. On the one hand, his wish for thoroughgoing renewal leaves him uninspired by moderate incremental measures. On the other hand, the antistatism of his Anti-Federalist leanings leads to wariness about any action mandated from the national governmental level even if it is ostensibly designed to further communitarian purposes. In *Fraternity*, McWilliams fatalistically declares:

> In the modern state, civic fraternity is impossible and the best, or rather the safest, approximation of justice is procedural rather than substantive, limited to external conduct, and leaves the development of man's justly fearful spirit to others than the state.

McWilliams later reaffirms his belief that although "human beings are meant to live in the polis . . . we cannot realize that goal in our great industrial states."[80]

These inhibiting beliefs not only over-determine McWilliams's reluctance to embrace Etzioni-Galston's third-way, incremental measures but also put him on the horns of an intellectual dilemma. Like the view of New Left historian William Appleman Williams, his antistatism threatens to cut off any affiliation with the nationalist sweep of virtually all progressive reform in the twentieth century.[81]

McWilliams attempts to resolve the dilemma by belatedly ratifying extinguished examples of communitarian governmental experimentation at the national level. In *Fraternity*, McWilliams looks back and praises New Deal experiments—such as the Subsistence Homestead and Farm Security programs—which were "aimed at creating fraternity among the disadvantaged . . . and across the racial line." In the 1980s, he applauds the Community Action Program (CAP) of the Johnson administration's too-brief War against Poverty in the 1960s for "enlisting public policy in the cause of . . . community."[82] These fleeting backward looks, however, fail to provide any direction from McWilliams on how to engage future policy challenges.

The striking failure in McWilliams's work is that he has never endeavored to map out the decentralizing direction implied in his writings and flesh out a vision for what might be called communitarian federalism. Yet, at the end of *Democracy's Discontent*, Sandel squarely puts the concept on the communitarian agenda.

While embracing the framers, and even showing a relatively generous attitude to the centralizing elements in mid-twentieth-century Progressivism in their historical context, Sandel believes the evolution of the national welfare state now to be exhausted.[83] He therefore looks to "the unrealized possibilities implicit in American federalism" for a "political vision that offers an alternative to the sovereign state and the univocal identities such states require. It suggests that self-government works best when sovereignty is dispersed and citizenship formed across multiple sites of civic engagement." In thus advocating what he calls the structural differentiation of federalism against Rousseau's "undifferentiated" general will, Sandel necessarily rids himself of any debilitating intellectual taboos against endorsing regimes involving political choice and voluntarism.[84]

To illuminate this vision of a communitarian federalism, Sandel even turns to Jefferson's description of the local-based ward system used by McWilliams as his theoretical ideal for political party associations. In his 1816 statement, Jefferson stated:

> The elementary republics of the wards, the country republics, the state republics and the republic of the Union, would form a gradation of authorities . . . [w]here every man is a sharer in the direction of his ward-republic, or some of the higher ones, and feels that he is a participator in the government of affairs, not merely at election day in the year but every day.[85]

McWilliams has consistently acknowledged that Jefferson was here envisioning a governmental, not a party, structure, and he knows that his application of this statement to parties is a creative stretch. Jefferson remained hostile in theoretical perspective to the idea of strong party competition and, in McWilliams's words, was close to being a "single-party" theorist.[86] Given Jefferson's practical role as the first party-builder and fellow-traveling sympathizer with Anti-Federalist complaints, McWilliams has some intellectual grounds in making this transference. Yet, in using this Jeffersonian statement as a governmental ideal, Sandel is returning to Jefferson's original intent.

Without explicitly saying so, Sandel appears to promote Hannah Arendt's view of Jefferson's ward-republic idea as the reincarnation of the Greek polis. Yet, in her recent work, *American Virtues: Thomas Jefferson on the Character of a Free People*, Jean Yarbrough forcefully rejects this understanding. She portrays Jefferson as searching for the same ideological synthesis in governmental structure that McWilliams found in the American-style party ideal. According to Yarbrough:

> [T]he wards are best understood as a kind of modern hybrid, in which political participation is no longer the highest human activity, but neither is it simply instrumental. The wards play a positive role in forming and preserv-

ing the character of a free people by drawing them out of their merely private concerns and into the larger common world in which they are immediately involved.[87]

The Jeffersonian ward-republic ideal is also a fitting governmental structure for McWilliams in light of its connection with the Puritan covenant ideal. As Sandel recognized, Jefferson specifically identified "the townships of New England" as the model for his ward-republics. Yet, such scholars as Daniel Elazar and Donald Lutz have further traced the New England "mode of town formation" to the "civil covenant" structure originally inspired by Puritan theology. "The New England town," in Elazar's words, "was the highest embodiment of the Winthropian covenanted community."[88]

The rationalist in Jefferson undoubtedly would hesitate to connect the religious covenant to his ward-republic ideal. Yet, he would feel the same way about his historical legacy as the founding architect of the American party system. Both are examples justifying, in McWilliams's words, Jefferson's "ironic" place as the enduring symbol for the "diverse voices" of American reform opposition.[89]

And although envisioning decentralization, his 1816 statement is at odds with the conventional Jeffersonian position that the best government governs least. As historian Christopher Tomlins has written, "The polity Jefferson sought, although decentralized, was by no means a decentered one." Jefferson rather envisioned replicating the structure of the New England governmental network that had presented (what he called) a solid "phalanx" of opposition across the region to his embargo policy against England. In explaining this ideal of a layered governmental network to John Tyler, he even foresaw the structure as capable of operating in a nationalist fashion:

General orders are given out from a centre to the foreman of every hundred [ward], as to the sergeants of an army, and *the whole nation* is thrown into energetic action, in the same direction in one instant and as one man, and becomes absolutely irresistible. Could I once see this I should consider it as the dawn of the salvation of the republic.[90]

AN INCREMENTAL MODEL FOR COMMUNITARIAN FEDERALISM: NORTH CAROLINA'S SMART START

Although Sandel provides only a sketchy picture of communitarian federalism, he suggestively points to the example of Robert Kennedy—a political figure who represents, according to one of Etzioni's and Galston's allies in the third-way movement, "the prototypical New Democrat." Kennedy's innovative policy work—such as the Bedford-Stuyvesant model for Community Development Corporations—mainly involved federal governmental cooperation with the private sector. Yet Kennedy also recognized the need for governmental decentralization without abolition of federal authority or directionless block grants to state or local governments. As he moved into his tragically foreshortened 1968 presidential candidacy, Kennedy wrote about the goal of updating Jefferson's ward-republic "vision of a participating democracy" while still pursuing "our great cooperative efforts" for national purposes.[91]

An apt model now existing at the state laboratory level is the Smart Start initiative begun by North Carolina's consciously third-way "New Democratic" Governor Jim Hunt. State government serves as the catalytic agent in Hunt's Smart Start, offering funding to counties for a designated menu of developmental assistance for preschool children. These include family literacy programs, immunization and other preventive health screenings, loan assistance to day-care operators, support for caregiver training, and the matching of federal support to help at-risk preschoolers.[92]

In the Smart Start model, the centralized government possesses no veto power over the policy options selected at the local level. A distinctive procedural element requires counties to demonstrate a local consensus in favor of their choice. Local boards of major institutional participants (including representatives from social service agencies, day-care operators, educators, local elected officials, civic and business leaders) and parents must come to agreement on the policy choices and manage the use of the state funding.[93]

This is not direct democracy or a perfect structure for public deliberation. But it does bring down the political debate over policy options to the local level. In particular, it turns local leaders' failure to agree into a political liability for all of them.

Smart Start has become a signature issue for Governor Hunt and North Carolina Democrats.[94] Frustrated Republicans in control of the state house first tried to attack Smart Start as just another bureaucratic program. Unable to make this charge stick, GOP opponents then actually turned to criticizing Smart Start for failing to possess the uniformity found in a bureaucratically driven program. Its lack of centralized control certainly exposes Smart Start to the possibility of questionable local spending and management of resources. Alexis de Tocqueville worried that a modern society would "find it hard to tolerate attempts at freedom in a local community" due to "numerous blunders and is apt to despair of success before the experiment is completed."[95] But as Smart Start moves statewide into every county, it has gained overwhelming popular support that Republican criticisms show no signs of denting.[96]

As a last-ditch compromise formulation during an era of divided government, the federal government has already resorted to this kind of centralized menu with decentralized choice in the case of such initiatives as health coverage for uninsured children. The national goal is to cover children whose family income is above the current Medicaid level but still too low to allow purchase of private-market insurance. The federal menu (inserted in the 1997 budget bill) allows the states to use federal funding for expansion of Medicaid coverage, subsidization of private insurance, or some combination of both. Its passage in Washington and quick implementation by the states provide a stunning contrast to the deadlock that killed the Clinton administration's blueprint for national health care reform.[97] In an irony that McWilliams would appreciate, this hybrid Smart Start model may have succeeded precisely because it reverses Herbert Croly's dictum and uses Jeffersonian decentralizing means to achieve national ends.[98]

CONCLUSION

If the true test of accomplishment is whether or not a theorist can develop an unassailable political position, even McWilliams would get a failing grade. But in our view, nobody would deserve a higher mark. While McWilliams has not been able to remove all the roadblocks facing American communitarian thought, other thinkers cannot get very far down the road by ignoring or avoiding engagement with his work. Yet the communitarian movement also needs McWilliams to engage the third-way policy proposals of Etzioni and Galston and the concept of communitarian federalism addressed by Sandel. In the coming years, we look forward to such constructive family deliberations among McWilliams and other thinkers.

NOTES

1. Wilson Carey McWilliams, "The Meaning of the Election," in *The Election of 1976–1996: Reports and Interpretations*, ed. Gerald M. Pomper (New York: McKay, 1977; Chatham, N.J.: Chatham House, 1981, 1985, 1989, 1993, 1997).

2. McWilliams, *The Politics of Disappointment: American Elections, 1976–1994* (Chatham, N.J.: Chatham House, 1995) and *Beyond the Politics of Disappointment? American Elections, 1980–1998* (Chatham, N.J.: Chatham House, 2000).

3. McWilliams, *The Idea of Fraternity in America* (Berkeley and Los Angeles: University of California Press, 1973) (hereafter cited as *Fraternity in America*).

4. For background and key selections, see Charles Taylor, "Cross-Purposes:

The Liberal Communitarian Debate," and other essays in *Liberalism and the Moral Life*, ed. Nancy L. Rosenblum, (Cambridge, Mass.: Harvard University Press, 1989); *Communitarianism and Individualism*, ed. Shlomo Avineri and Avner de-Shalit (Oxford, U.K.: Oxford University Press, 1992); and *Liberals and Communitarians*, eds. Stephan Mulhall and Adam Swift (Oxford, U.K.: Blackwell, 1992).

5. Robert Booth Fowler, *The Dance of Community: The Contemporary Debate in American Political Thought* (Lawrence: University of Kansas Press, 1991); see also Fowler's *Enduring Liberalism: American Political Thought Since the 1960s* (Lawrence, Kans.: University of Kansas Press, 1999).

6. Amitai Etzioni began publishing *The Responsive Community* in 1990. On William Galston's central role and the general history of the publication, see Etzioni's introduction to *The Essential Communitarian Reader* (Lanham, Md.: Rowman & Littlefield, 1998). See also Etzioni, "A Moderate Communitarian Proposal," in *Political Theory* 24, no. 2 (May 1996): 155–71.

7. For a provocative argument from a historian against the conventional hostility of historians to this approach, see David R. Harlan, *The Degradation of American History* (Chicago: University of Chicago Press, 1997).

8. For evidence of Michael Sandel's influence as a communitarian thinker, see *Debating Democracy's Discontent: Essays on American Politics, Law, and Public Philosophy*, ed. Anita L Allen and Milton C. Regan Jr. (New York: Oxford University Press, 1998).

9. Professor Susan Herbst goes on to explain, "De Tocqueville and his concerns loom as a phantom over the book." Susan Herbst, review of *Democracy's Feast: Elections in America*, ed. Herbert Weisberg, and McWilliams, *The Politics of Disappointment*, in *Party Politics* 3, no. 4 (October 1997): 565–66. This statement could apply to the entire corpus of McWilliams's writings. He begins sixteen of the twenty chapters in *Fraternity in America* with epigrams from Tocqueville. However, we have shied away from the formidable task of treading on the highly contested ground of Tocqueville's thought and attempting to assess McWilliams's use of him. See Stephen Schneck, "New Readings of Tocqueville's America: Lessons for Democracy" and the comments of McWilliams and Delba Winthrop, *Polity* 25, no. 2 (Winter 1992): 283–314. See also Peter Berkowitz, "The Art of Association," *New Republic* 44, (June 24, 1996); review of Joshua Mitchell, *The Fragility of Freedom: Tocqueville on Religion, Democracy, and the American Future*).

10. Fowler, *Dance of Community*, 78 (characterizing McWilliams as "self-consciously a member of the party of hope"); Daniel Aaron, *Men of Good Hope: A Story of American Progressivism* (New York: Oxford University Press, 1958). See McWilliams, *Politics of Disappointment*, 20 (Carter 1976), 168, and 172 (Clinton 1992). On government and public opinion, see David Broder, "Trust in Government Edges Up," *Washington Post*, 10 March, 1998, A15; "Confidence in the National Government Has Not Rebounded in the Nineties," *Public Perspective* (February-March 1998): 30–39; Gary Orren, "Fall From Grace: The Public's Loss of Faith in Government," in *Why People Don't Trust Government*, ed. Joseph Nye et al. (Cambridge, Mass.: Harvard University Press, 1997), 72–107. In *1996 Elections*, 250, McWilliams cites similar poll data.

11. McWilliams, *Politics of Disappointment*, 159–61.

12. For McWilliams's critical attitude toward H. L. Mencken, see *Fraternity in America*, 510, and 514–15; McWilliams, "American Pluralism: The Old Order Passeth," in *The Americans: 1976*, ed. Irving Kristol and Paul Weaver (Lexington, Mass.: Lexington Books, 1976), 310.

13. McWilliams, *Disappointment*, 90; "The Meaning of the Election, " in *Election of 1996*, ed. Gerald Pomper, 248 (author's italics). Cited hereafter as Pomper, *Election of 1996*. Richard Hofstadter, *The Paranoid Style in American Politics and Other Essays* (New York: Knopf, 1965). For a recent and finely nuanced appreciation of Hofstadter's work, see Michael Kazin, "Hofstadter Lives: Political Culture and Temperament in the Work of an American Historian," *Reviews in American History* 27, no. 2 (June 1999): 334–48.

14. McWilliams, in Pomper, *Election of 1996*, 254-55.

15. Ibid., 260.

16. Ibid.

17. Fowler, *Dance of Community*, 77.

18. McWilliams, *Fraternity in America*, 6 (existentialism), 99 (*Gemeinschaft*).

19. Ibid., 141, quoted from *The American Puritans*, ed. Perry Miller (New York: Doubleday, 1956).

20. James P. Young, *Reconsidering American Liberalism: The Troubled Odyssey of the Liberal Idea* (Boulder, Colo.: Westview, 1996): 294; Louis Hartz, *The Liberal Tradition in America* (New York: Harcourt Brace, 1955); McWilliams, *Fraternity in America*, 113.

21. McWilliams, *Fraternity in America*, 96–97.

22. Ibid., 98–99.

23. Ibid., 203.

24. McWilliams, "Ambiguities and Ironies: Conservatism and Liberalism in the American Political Tradition," in *Moral Values in Liberalism and Conservatism*, ed. W. Larson Taitte (Austin: University of Texas Press, 1995), 193; "The Anti-Federalists, Representation, and Party," *Northwestern University Law Review* 84, no. 1 (1989): 36. For a provocative argument that pushes the Anti-Federalists farther in the direction of intentionally founding the party system, see Michael Allen Gillespie, "Political Parties and the American Family," in *American Political Parties and Constitutional Politics*, ed. Peter W. Schramm and Bradford P. Wilson (Lanham, Md.: Rowman & Littlefield, 1993), 17–43.

25. McWilliams, "Parties as Civic Associations, " in *Party Renewal in America*, ed. Gerald M. Pomper (New York: Praeger, 1980), 56; quoting Jefferson to Samuel Kercheval, 12 July 1816, in *The Life and Selected Writings of Thomas Jefferson*, ed. Adrienne Koch and William Peden (New York: Modern Library, 1944), 56. For McWilliams's discussion in *Fraternity in America* of Jefferson's ward concept, see 219–20. For more on Jefferson and parties and on McWilliams's use of Jefferson's local-ward concept, see 254–55 in this book.

26. McWilliams, *Fraternity in America*, 105–6, 397, and 399 (immigrants, farmers, laborers, and Populists). On religion and Populism, see Rhys H. Williams and Susan M. Alexander, "Religious Rhetoric in American Populism: Civil Religion as Movement Ideology," *Journal of the Scientific Study of Religion* 33, no. 1 (March

1994): 1–15 (surveying numerous sources). On parties, see McWilliams, *Fraternity in America*, 484, and 498–502; "Civic Associations," 51–68; "Liberty, Equality, and the Problem of Community," in *Liberty and Equality under the Constitution*, ed. John Agresto (Washington: American Historical Association, 1983): 128; "Politics," *American Quarterly* 35, nos. 1–2 (1983): 19–38; "Tocqueville and Responsible Parties: Individualism, Partisanship, and Citizenship in America," in *Challenges to Party Government*, ed. John K. White and Jerome M. Mileur (Carbondale: Southern Illinois University Press, 1992): 190–211; "Two Tier Politics and the Problem of Public Policy," in *The New Politics of Public Policy*, ed. Marc K. Landy and Martin Levin (Baltimore, Md.: Johns Hopkins Press, 1995): 275; McWilliams, *Election of 1996*, 260.

27. McWilliams, *Fraternity in America*, 105 (fundamental discord); "The Bible in the American Tradition," in *Religion and Politics*, ed. M. J. Aronoff (New Brunswick, N.J.: Transaction Books, 1984), 28 (downy equivocation); "Leo Strauss and the Dignity of American Political Thought," *Review of Politics* 60, no. 2 (Spring 1998): 240; "Religion and the American Founding," in *Princeton Seminary Bulletin* 8, no. 3 (1987): 46–56; "American Pluralism," 317; McWilliams and Hale, "The Constitutional Convention and the Founding Principles," in *Principles of Constitutional Order: The Ratification Debates*, ed. Robert L. Utley Jr. and Patricia B. Gray (Lanham, Md.: University Press of America, 1989), 16.

28. McWilliams, *Fraternity in America*, 105. Thus McWilliams strives to separate the Puritan intellectual legacy from the connection that Max Weber drew between "the Protestant ethic" and "the spirit of capitalism." See Weber, *The Protestant Ethic and the Spirit of Capitalism*, trans. Talcott Parsons (1904; reprint, New York: Scribner, 1958). For McWilliams's citation of Leo Strauss in support of his non-Weberian view of the Puritans, see "Leo Strauss," 241, citing Strauss in *Natural Right and History* (Chicago: Chicago University Press, 1952), 60–62.

29. McWilliams, *Fraternity in America*, 482 (Rauschenbusch), 599 (the civil rights movement and "the continuing political power of the biblical tradition"); see also "Bible," 33–34. McWilliams also sees strong biblical influences in Hawthorne, Melville, Ellison, and Baldwin. *Fraternity in America*, 301–27 (Hawthorne), 328–71 (Melville), 570–617 (Ellison and Baldwin); "Bible," 14, 27–28, and 34–36. He does not make the same strong biblical claim about Twain. But McWilliams suggests that a Calvinist realism lay at the base of Twain's political thought and led to his rejection of the individualism found in "pietistic Protestantism . . . [and] the creed of the Enlightenment as well." McWilliams, *Fraternity in America*, 431.

30. See, Christopher Lasch, *The One and Only True Heaven: Progress and Its Critics* (New York: Norton, 1991); E. P. Thompson, *The Making of the English Working Class* (New York: Vintage, 1963).

31. McWilliams, *Fraternity in America*, 40, 49 (authors' italics). Could it be that Amy Gutmann was referring to McWilliams when she described a communitarian as someone who "wants to live in Salem, but not believe in witches"? Gutmann, "Communitarian Critics of Liberalism," *Philosophy and Public Affairs* 14, no. 3 (Summer 1985): 319.

32. McWilliams, *Fraternity in America*, 144.

33. For McWilliams on Richard Hofstadter, see *Fraternity in America* 396, 399, and 400 n. 39. See also McWilliams, "American Pluralism," 305 ("Not xenophobic in any strict sense, populists did not admire social pluralism or cultural diversity"). Although using Hofstadter as a foil to help highlight McWilliams's contrasting view, we are not suggesting that McWilliams's work focuses on debate with Hofstadter. Yet, it is interesting to note that Hofstadter singled out his father, Carey McWilliams, *A Mask for Privilege: Anti-Semitism in America* (Boston: Little, Brown, 1948), as "characteristic of the indulgence which Populism has received" in painting the origins of anti-Semitism "simply as an upper-class phenomenon" and ignoring the reality that "the Greenback-Populist tradition activated most of what we have of modern, popular anti-Semitism in the United States." Richard Hofstader, *Age of Reform: From Bryan to FDR* (New York: Vintage, 1955), 80–81 n. 3. For positive comments from Hofstadter on Populism as part of the liberal reform tradition, see *Age of Reform*, 18. See also Kazin, "Hofstader Lives," 339. Kazin is author of *The Populist Persuasion: An American History* (New York: Basic, 1995), rev. ed. (Ithaca, N.Y.: Cornell University Press, 1998).

34. Etzioni, introduction to *Communitarian Reader*, x-xi. For Galston's characterization of his position as "liberalism properly conceived," see "Defending Liberalism," *American Political Science Review* 76, no. 3 (September 1982): 621–29. Throughout the 1980s, Galston pursued this rhetorical strategy of "defending liberalism properly conceived" from the dominant form of liberalism displayed in such thinkers as John Rawls and, less emphatically, from such "communitarians" as Sandel. This approach culminated in Galston's major work, *Liberal Purposes: Goods, Virtue, and Diversity in the Liberal State* (Cambridge: Cambridge University Press, 1991). For criticism of Galston's "liberal" strategy in *Liberal Purposes*, see Peter Augustine Lawler, "Is William Galston Really a Liberal?" in *Community and Tradition: Conservative Perspectives on the American Experience*, ed. George W. Carey and Bruce Frohenn (Lanham, Md: Rowman & Littlefield, 1998). But by 1990, Galston was also embarking with Etzioni on editing *Responsive Community* and drafting the inaugural 1990 "Communitarian Manifesto." On his "liberal communitarianism," see Galston, "A Public Philosophy for the 21st Century," *Responsive Community* 8, no. 3 (Summer 1998): 21. See also Galston, "Social Mores Are Not Enough," *Responsive Community* 7, no. 4 (Fall 1997): 16–20 (simply referring to himself as "a 'communitarian'").

35. Sandel, review of Rawls, *Political Liberalism*, *Harvard Law Review* 107 (May 1994): 1776.

36. Sandel, *Democracy's Discontent*, 61, 67, and 68–71.

37. Ibid., 23 (mentioning religious influence on abolitionism), 349 (noting the role played by "black churches in the civil rights movement"), and 61and 64 (favorably noting the argument of Puritan dissenter Roger Williams for separation of church and state). See also Jean Bethke Elshtain's review of Sandel's *Democracy's Discontent*, "Mario Cuomo Isn't Your Daddy," *New Oxford Review* 63 (December 1996): 25 ("Sandel pays too little attention to the religious sources of American democracy"); Elshtain and Roger Beem, "Can This Republic Be Saved?"

in *Debating Democracy's Discontent*, 196–97; James T. Kloppenberg, *The Virtues of Liberalism* (New York: Oxford University Press, 1998), 162 ("Sandel's republicanism is deaf to the pervasive religiosity of American political discourse").

38. J. G. A. Pocock, *The Machiavellian Moment: Florentine Political Thought and the Atlantic Republican Tradition* (Princeton, N.J.: Princeton University Press, 1975). While claiming an Aristotelian heritage for his American republican tradition, Sandel decides "to leave aside the question" of its transmission through Machiavelli and the court-country debates of eighteenth-century England. *Democracy's Discontent*, 371–72 n. 33.

39. Sandel, *Liberalism and the Limits of Justice* (Cambridge: Cambridge University Press, 1982), 180.

40. McWilliams, "American Founding," 48, and "The Arts and the American Political Tradition," in *Art, Ideology, and Politics*, ed. Judith H. Balfe and Margaret Wyszomirski (New York: Praeger, 1985), 17.

41. McWilliams, "The Discipline of Freedom," in *To Secure the Blessings of Liberty: First Principles of the Constitution*, ed. Sarah Baumgartner Thurow (Lanham, Md.: University Press of America, 1988): 32–33, 51 n. 69, and 52 n. 72 (specifically relying on Sandel in his critique of Rawls and contemporary liberalism).

42. In a commentary on McWilliams's "Discipline of Freedom" essay, Jeffrey Tulis puckishly and insightfully notes his distinctive attempt to forge a Christian Aristotelian synthesis. See Tulis, "Constituting Liberty," in Thurow, *Blessings of Liberty* 64 (noting McWilliams's appeal to a "forgotten Aristotelian world" while still providing a "Presbyterian slant on that perspective"). In contrast to McWilliams, many scholars draw major dividing lines between the Aristotelian tradition and the Puritans. For a sample of the range in this scholarship, see Miller, *The New England Mind: The Seventeenth Century* (Cambridge, Mass.: Harvard University Press, 1939), 92–97, 117–20, 157, and 194–95; and Stephen Innes, *Creating the Commonwealth: The Economic Culture of Puritan New England* (New York: Norton, 1995), 57–58, 99, and 109–11, 164–66. Indeed, "Christian Aristotelianism" is usually seen as far more characteristic of the intellectual status quo that the Puritans and the general Reformed tradition split apart. See Michael P. Zuckert, *Natural Rights and the New Republicanism* (Princeton, N.J.: Princeton University Press, 1994). For more on McWilliams's view of the Puritans versus that of other scholarship, see pages 250–51 in this book.

43. Etzioni, *The New Golden Rule: Community and Morality in a Democratic Society* (New York: Basic Books, 1996); Galston, *Liberal Purposes*, 13.

44. Etzioni, *New Golden Rule*, 255; *The Spirit of Community: The Reinvention of American Society* (New York: Simon & Schuster, 1993), 1, 41.

45. Galston, *Liberal Purposes*, 295–304, and "Defending Liberalism," 629 (Galston's italics). Without citing any specific works, Galston identifies Irving Kristol and Jurgen Habermas as examples of thinkers from opposite sides of the political spectrum who espouse the "religious capital" view. But perhaps the most influential American source is Daniel Bell, *The Cultural Contradiction of Capitalism* (New York: Basic Books, 1976).

46. Galston, "Two Concepts of Liberalism," *Ethics* 105, no. 3 (April 1995): 525,

526; see also "Value Pluralism and Political Liberalism," *Report from the Institute for Philosophy and Public Policy* 16, no. 2 (Spring 1996): 2, 3. For a concise summary regarding the egalitarian implications of the Reformation generally and such ideas as the "priesthood of all believers," see Thomas A. Spragens Jr., *Civic Liberalism: Reflections on Our Democratic Ideals* (Lanham, Md: Rowman & Littlefield, 1999): 150–52.

47. Galston, *Liberal Purposes*, 265–67.

48. McWilliams, "Bible," 22, 24, 29; "Science and Freedom: America as a Technological Republic," in *Technology in the Western Political Tradition*, ed. Arthur M Melzer et al. (Ithaca: Cornell University Press, 1993), 102. For conservative rejection of this instrumental approach to religion, see Peter Augustine Lawler, "William Galston," in *Community and Tradition*, 147, 159; Philip E. Johnson, "The Swedish Syndrome," review of *The Culture of Disbelief: How American Law and Politics Trivialize Religious Devotion* by Stephen L. Carter, *First Things* 38 (December 1993): 48–49.

49. For a more religious interpretation of Madison's thought, see Reinhold Niebuhr, *The Irony of American History* (New York: Scribner, 1952). For historical background on the Madison-Witherspoon connection, see John Murrin, "Religion and Politics in America from the First Settlements to the Civil War," in *Religion and American Politics: From the Colonial Period to the 1980s*, ed. Mark A. Noll (New York: Oxford University Press, 1990), 41–42. See also Jeffrey Hayes Morrison, "John Witherspoon and the Public Interest of Religion," *Journal of Church and State* 41, no. 3 (Summer 1999): 567 n. 65. In terms of our own perspective on religion and politics, we would characterize it as far more "Niebuhrian" that McWilliams's viewpoint. For McWilliams's early and critical view of Niebuhr, see "New Orthodoxy for Old Liberalism," *American Political Science Review* 56, no. 4 (December 1962): 874–85.

50. McWilliams, "Bible," 22.

51. Galston, *Liberal Purposes*, 266. For evidence that the idea of a monolithic religious conservatism is not accurate in today's political context, see Gustav Niebuhr, "Among a Religious Electorate, Overlooked Corners," *New York Times*, 8 May 1999, sec. A, p. 13.

52. For more on McWilliams's "Presbyterian slant," see Tulis, "Constituting Liberty," 64.

53. McWilliams indeed sees Galston as sharing "Straussian fellow-traveler" status with himself. "Leo Strauss," 231. As with Tocqueville, rather than entering into the argument about what Aristotle "really thought" about political participation and the citizen of the polis, we are simply noting the agreement in the understanding of McWilliams, Sandel, and Galston. For a recent survey and criticism of scholarship on this subject, see Tim Duvall and Paul Dotson, "Political Participation and *Eudaimonia* in Aristotle's Politics," *History of Political Thought* 19, no. 1 (Spring 1998): 21–34. See also Bernard Yack, *The Problems of a Political Animal: Community, Justice, and Conflict in Aristotelian Political Thought* (Berkeley and Los Angeles: University of California Press, 1993).

54. Sandel, *Democracy's Discontent*, 6, 7.

55. Ibid., 129, 131; Thomas Pangle, "The Retrieval of Civic Virtue: A Critical Appreciation of Sandel's *Democracy's Discontent*," in Allen and Regan, *Debating Democracy's Discontent*, 25.

56. Galston, *Liberal Purposes*, 43, 225, 295; Etzioni, *New Golden Rule*, 200.

57. See McWilliams, "Democracy and Power in America," review of *The Democratic Wish*, by James A. Morone, *Review of Politics* (1992): (describing Federalism's problem with the democratic tradition in America). For Galston's critical comments about populism generally, see *Liberal Purposes*, 11 ("commitment to equality can all too easily turn into the populist resentment of distinctions"), 248 (expressing concerns about "popular rancor against the claim of liberal democratic excellence"). In contrast, Sandel emphasizes the community-oriented "producer" element in civic republicanism, which many scholars also find in the 1890s Populist movement. See Thomas Goebel, "The Political Economy of American Populism from Jackson to the New Deal," *Studies in American Political Development* 11, no. 1 (Spring 1997): 109–48. Sandel places the late nineteenth-century Knights of Labor in this tradition, and other scholars frequently picture the Knights as strong allies of the Populist movement. Sandel, *Democracy's Discontent*, 185–200, and Goebel, "American Populism," 132. Yet, along with his silence on Populism and its elements of political radicalism, Sandel goes out of his way to emphasize the Knights' early conservative middle-class allies, such as *Nation* editor E. L. Godkin, while ignoring their coal-mining, working-class bases as well as their use of strikes. *Democracy's Discontent*, 185–90, 198. On the Knights, see William Forbath, *Law and the Shaping of the American Labor Movement* (Cambridge, Mass.: Harvard University Press, 1989).

58. Sandel, *Democracy's Discontent*, 86–89 (passive stance favoring legislative restrictions on pornography commerce); 103–8 (activist stance in support of striking down sodomy laws against homosexuals). On Sandel's "judicial imperialism," see Spragens, *Civic Liberalism*, 136. For evidence of Galston's tendency toward judicial activism, see *Liberal Purposes*, 49, 52; "Community, Democracy, Philosophy: The Political Thought of Michael Walzer," *Political Theory* 17, no. 1 (February 1989): 126–29 (criticizing Michael Walzer's "anti-platonic" democratic position against judicial review). For a pro-Frankfurter view of the Warren Court, see Alexander Bickel, *The Supreme Court and the Idea of Progress* (New York: Harper & Row, 1970).

59. In his early years, before fully embracing parties as the saving grace of mainstream American politics, McWilliams was attacked for his "anti-constitutionalist" tendencies. See Herman Belz, "New Left Reverberations in the Academy: The Anti-Pluralist Critique of Constitutionalism," *Review of Politics* 36, no. 2 (April 1974): 270, and citing McWilliams, "On Violence and Legitimacy," *Yale Law Journal* 79, no. 4 (March 1970): 623-46; "Civil Disobedience and Contemporary Constitutionalism: The American Case," *Comparative Politics* 1, no. 2 (January 1969): 211-27. See also McWilliams, "Political Arts and Political Sciences," in *Power and Community: Dissenting Essays in Political Science*, ed. Philip Green and Sanford Levinson (New York: Pantheon, 1970), 357–82. The "New Left" and the "Berkeley political theory" of his teachers, John Schaar and Sheldon Wolin, represent major (although hardly exclusive) influences on McWilliams's intellectual

development. See McWilliams, "Politics," 21 (declaring that "the New Left pioneered" the revival of emphasis on political participation). On Berkeley political theory, see Young, *Reconsidering American Liberalism*, 294–306. However, McWilliams's relationship to Berkeley political theory is beyond our scope here.

60. McWilliams, "Two-Tier Politics," 275. See also "Tocqueville and Responsible Parties," 195.

61. McWilliams, "Anti-Federalists," 36 n. 128, quoting Walter Dean Burnham, *Critical Elections and the Mainsprings of American Politics* (New York: Norton, 1970), 133; "Tocqueville and Responsible Parties," 191 ("parties as more inclusive and more genuinely public"); "Civic Associations," 51–55. For a similar discussion of parties' populist and civic roles, see David E. Price, *Bringing Back the Parties* (Washington, D.C.: Congressional Quarterly Press, 1984), 109–14.

62. Sandel, *Democracy's Discontent*, 3. Ironically, the best "Sandelian moment" in American political history coincides with the emergence of the first party system. This was Jefferson and Madison's adoption during the 1790s of a "country" opposition to Treasury Secretary Hamilton's "court" program of debt financing and mercantilism. "The argument that *brought the Republican party into being*," Sandel notes without further comment, "was that Hamilton's political economy would corrupt the morality of citizens and undermine the social conditions essential to republican government [italics added]." *Democracy's Discontent*, 135–36. During this post-Federalist period, Madison expressed in a series of *National Gazette* essays the kind of egalitarian and "populist" sentiments usually associated with Jefferson. See Hofstadter, *The Idea of a Party System: The Rise of Legitimate Opposition in the United States, 1780–1840* (Berkeley and Los Angeles: University of California Press, 1972); Douglas W. Jaenicke, "Madison v. Madison: The Party Essays v. *The Federalist Papers*," in *Reflections on the Constitution: The American Constitution After Two Hundred Years*, ed. Richard Maidment and John Zvesper (Manchester: Manchester University Press, 1989).

63. Galston, "Representation, Deliberation and Presidential Nominations: Improving the Performance of American Political Parties," in *American Political Parties*, ed. Peter W. Schramm and Bradford P. Wilson (Lanham, Md.: Rowman & Littlefield, 1993), 65; see also "The Constitutional Role of American Political Parties," in *Constitutionalism in Perspective: The United States Constitution in Twentieth Century Politics* (Lanham, Md.: University Press of America, 1988).

64. McWilliams, "Tocqueville and Responsible Parties," 192; *Fraternity in America*, 25.

65. McWilliams, "American Pluralism" 294; McWilliams and Hale, "Constitutional Convention," 17–18 (John Winthrop and the Puritans promoted the "ancient teaching" expressed through "the idea of the covenant . . . that political society is fundamentally a bond between persons, not an alliance for limited purposes"). Perry Miller, *Errand into the Wilderness* (New York: Harper & Row, 1956): 48–98. On the historical origins of the covenant idea, see Daniel J. Elazar, *Covenant and Commonwealth: From Christian Separation through the Protestant Reformation* (New Brunswick, N.J.: Transaction Publishers, 1996), and H. Richard Niebuhr, "The Idea of Covenant and American Democracy," *Church History* 23 (June 1954): 129.

66. McWilliams, *Fraternity in America*, 125-26, and "Anti-Federalists," 26 ("Christian teaching insisted on a recognition of human equality, at least in principle.")

67. Sandel quoted in Paul T. Stallsworth, "The Story of an Encounter," *Reinhold Niebuhr Today*, ed. Richard J. Neuhaus (Grand Rapids, Mich.: William B. Eerdmans, 1989): 83–84. Here, as on certain other occasions, Sandel seems to verge on embracing religious perspectives in formulating his viewpoint. Similarly, in contrast to his treatment in *Democracy's Discontent* (see text accompanying note 37), Sandel's review of Rawls's *Political Liberalism* contains a far stronger affirmation of abolitionism as "rooted in evangelical Protestantism," *Harvard Law Review* 117 (May 1994): 1790. See also Richard Sennett, "Michael Sandel and Richard Rorty: Two Models of the Republic," in Allen and Regan, *Debating Democracy's Discontent* 130 ("John Winthrop's arguments in favor of a Puritan commonwealth eerily foreshadow Michael Sandel's views on democracy"); Joan Williams, "Notes of a Jewish Episcopalian: Gender as a Language of Class, Religion as a Dialect of Liberalism," in *Debating Democracy's Discontent*, 99–113.

68. Sandel, *Limits of Justice*, 180.

69. McWilliams, "Responsible Parties," 197, quoting Alexis de Tocqueville, *Democracy in America* (1835; reprint, New York: Schocken, 1961), 2:132; "Civic Associations," 51–68. As McWilliams recognizes, many nineteenth-century Yankee Republican as well as Irish Democratic sons and daughters certainly acted like "encumbered selves" in maintaining their family's party affiliations. See Robert Kelley, *The Cultural Pattern in American Politics: The First Century* (New York: Knopf, 1979). For another commentary that nicely captures the insight lacking in Sandel's view, see John Garvey, "A Tradition of Choice: What it Means to Be an American," *Commonweal* (13 August 1999): 7–8. See also Michael Walzer, "Michael Sandel's America," in Allen and Regan, *Debating Democracy's Discontent*, 177 (the importance of immigration and choice in American history).

70. Lawler, "William Galston," 147, and Galston, *Liberal Purposes*, 154, 293, 304, 329 n. 12. Less tied to formal Aristotelian theory, Etzioni moves toward plugging this hole in their moderate communitarianism by invoking the thinking of Jewish theologian Martin Buber. In such works as *I and Thou*, Buber envisioned what Etzioni calls "the complex concept of a self congenitally contextuated with a community, a view that accords full status to both individuals and their shared union." "Moderate Communitarian Proposal," 157. Etzioni keeps his use of Buber on a secular, sociological plane and mentions nothing about the I–Thou relationship stemming from Buber's covenant theology. Yet "the covenant relationship is to social and political life what Buber's I–Thou relationship is to personal life. Through covenants, humans and their institutions are enabled to enter into dialogue while maintaining their respective integrities within a shared framework." Elazar, *Covenant and Polity in Biblical Israel: Biblical Foundations and Jewish Expressions* (New Brunswick, N.J.: Transaction Publishers, 1995), 65. See also Etzioni's preface in *Civic Repentance*, ed. Amitai Etzioni (Lanham, Md.: Rowman & Littlefield), arguing for the policy relevance of "the religious concept of repentance."

71. Historian Edmund S. Morgan is probably the most preeminent proponent of this view. A number of his writings explicitly map out a positive Weberian view of Puritanism and its legacy. See Morgan's review of *Religion and Economic Action*, by Kurt Samuelsson, *William & Mary Quarterly* 20, no. 1 (January 1963): 135–40; "The Puritan Ethic and the American Revolution," *William & Mary Quarterly* 24, no. 1 (January 1967): 3–43; *American Slavery, American Freedom* (New York: Norton, 1975): 285–86 (withdrawing his Weberian thesis from application to the slave holding South). Current social history scholarship also points away from McWilliams and toward a view of the Puritans as more capitalistic. See Staloff, "Where Religion and Profit Join Together: Commerce and Piety in Puritan New England," *Reviews in American History* 27, no. 1 (March 1999): 8–13 (commenting in particular on Innes, *Creating the Commonwealth*). And from a more intellectual perspective, see John Diggins, *The Lost Soul of American Politics: Virtue, Self-Interest, and the Foundation of Liberalism* (Chicago: University of Chicago Press, 1984). See also Charles Taylor, *Sources of the Self: The Making of the Modern Identity* (Cambridge, Mass.: Harvard University Press, 1989).

72. See, Robert Bellah et al., *Habits of the Heart: Individualism and Commitment in American Life* (Berkeley: University of California Press, 1985), 28–51, 253–56, 261, 270–71, 295–96, and *The Good Society* (New York: Knopf, 1991). However, at the same time, Bellah pursues more of a "fusionist" strategy that portrays Madisonian constitutionalism as civic republicanism (like Sandel) and sees it more in harmony with the Puritanism of John Winthrop (unlike Sandel). For McWilliams's criticism of this fusionist tendency in Bellah's earlier work on American "civil religion," see "Bible," 21. Bellah has recently departed from his pursuit of locating a suitably progressive position within the American Protestant tradition and is now exploring the "common good" emphasis in Catholicism as a more usable tradition. See "Religion and the Shape of National Culture," *America* 181, no. 3 (31 July 1999): 9–14.

73. See Orlando Patterson, "The Liberal Millennium," *New Republic*, 8 November 1999, 60 ("Whether modern communitarians know it or not," the Puritan "covenant with God . . . is the origin of their desire for freedom"). For a recent tribute to Rawls's deontological liberalism, see Thomas Nagel, "Justice, Justice, Shalt Thou Pursue," *New Republic*, 25 October 1999, 36–41. For a radical rejection of the Puritan legacy, see Sacvan Bercovitch, *The American Jeremiad* (Madison: University of Wisconsin Press, 1978). For obvious reasons, African-American and feminist thinkers might choose to pursue different communitarian paths than those tracing to the Puritans or framers. See Barbara Ehrenreich, "Another Communitarianism: Liberalism and Community," *New Republic*, 9 May 1988, 21; Vincent Harding, "Toward a Darkly Radiant Vision of America's Truth. A Letter of Concern, An Invitation to a Re-Creation," in *Community in America: The Challenges of Habits of the Heart*, ed. Charles H. Reynolds and Ralph V. Norman (Berkeley and Los Angeles: University of California Press, 1988), 67–83.

74. McWilliams quoted in David E. Price, "Community and Control: Critical Democracy Theory in the Progressive Period," *American Political Science Review* 68, no. 4 (December 1974): 1678 n. 83. Tulis, "Constituting Liberty," 67–68 (citing historian Marvin Meyers' "utopian" criticism and raising his own questions

about McWilliams's soulcraft). For evidence that he regards this *praxis* criticism as a legitimate line of attack against theorists, see McWilliams, "Democracy and Power in America," 337.

75. McWilliams, "Civic Associations," 65; "Discipline of Freedom," 56–57; "Tocqueville and Responsible Parties," 205–06; in Pomper, *Election of 1996*, 260; "American Pluralism," 320 ("The demand for reformed campaign laws is only a beginning.") See Kevin Mattson, "Doing Democracy: An Exploration of Progressive-Era Reform and Its Legacy for American Politics," *National Civic Review* 87, no. 4 (Winter 1998): 337–46.

76. Etzioni, *Capital Corruption: The New Attack on American Democracy* (Orlando, Fla.: Harcourt Brace Jovanovich, 1984). For a similar listing of third-way policy proposals, see Al From, "Prepare for a Long March: Five Simple Rules All Democrats Should Follow," *New Democrat* (July-August 1998): 27–28; see also various issues of Etzioni's *Responsive Community*, the Democratic Leadership Council's (DLC's) *New Democrat* magazine, and two books of essays published by the DLC's Progressive Policy Institute think tank: *Mandate for Change*, ed. Will Marshall and Martin Schramm, (New York: Berkeley Books, 1993), and *Building the Bridge: Ten Big Ideas to Transform America*, ed. Al From and Will Marshall (Lanham, Md: Rowman & Littlefield, 1997). For a brief review of Etzioni's *The New Golden Rule*, see McWilliams, "The One and the Many," *Commonweal* 129, no. 14 (15 August 1997), characterizing Etzioni as a kindred communitarian spirit but stating without much elaboration that his policy ideas "often misfire."

77. Pomper, *Election of 1996*, 252, 254, 259, quoting Stephen Skowronek, "The Risks of 'Third-Way' Politics," *Society* 33, no. 6 (September–October 1996): 33. In citing Skowronek's work, McWilliams engages in something of an intellectual double entendre. Skowronek places Clinton's third-wayism in a sophisticated historical framework of "preemptive" presidencies (including such diverse figures as Grover Cleveland, Woodrow Wilson, Dwight Eisenhower, and Richard Nixon). These presidencies were able to exploit divisions in the otherwise majority coalition of the opposing party but were unable to establish a majority coalition for their successors. See also Skowronek, *The Politics That Presidents Make: Presidential Leadership from John Adams to George Bush* (Cambridge, Mass.: Harvard University Press, 1993, 1997).

78. McWilliams and Hale, "Constitutional Convention," 28 (shattered families); Galston, "A Liberal-Democratic Case for the Two-Parent Family," in Etzioni, *Communitarian Reader*, 146–56; McWilliams, "The Problem of Community," 127 (church and poor); Galston, "The View from the White House—Individual and Community Empowerment," in Peter L. Berger and Richard John Neuhaus, *To Empower People: From State to Civil Society*, ed. Michael Novak, 20th anniversary ed. (Washington, D.C.: AEI, 1996), 66 (faith-based and antipoverty). Not surprisingly, some cracks seem to be developing in Galston's own theoretical wall of separation from religion that he built in *Liberal Purposes*. See "Political Theory in the 1980s: Perplexity Amidst Diversity," in *Political Science: The State of the Discipline* 2, ed. Ada W. Finifter (Washington: American Political Science Association, 1993), 37 (declaring that the biblical tradition's teaching about the intrinsic alienation of human labor "deserves more theoretical consideration than it usually

receives"); see also Galston's review of James T. Kloppenberg, *The Virtues of Liberalism, American Political Service Review* 93, no. 3 (September 1999): 702–3.

79. On Galston's advocacy of populism, see Steven M. Gillon, *The Democrats' Dilemma: Walter F. Mondale and the Liberal Legacy* (New York: Columbia University Press, 1992): 325. McWilliams, *Election of 1996*, 260.

80. McWilliams, *Fraternity in America*, 74; "On Equality as the Moral Foundation for Community," in *The Moral Foundation of the American Republic*, ed. Robert H. Horwitz (Charlottesville: University Press of Virginia, 1997), 211–12.

81. See Paul M. Buhle and Edward Rice Maximin, *William Appleman Williams: The Tragedy of Empire* (New York: Routledge, 1995).

82. McWilliams, *Fraternity in America*, 550; "Two-Tier Politics," 171–72, 174.

83. Sandel, *Democracy's Discontent*, 216–21. For a more positive assessment of some communitarian elements in Progressive thinking, see Price, "Community and Control." For McWilliams's latest, and somewhat more sympathetic, assessment of Progressivism, see his "Standing at Armageddon: Morality and Religion in American Thought," in *Progressivism and the New Democracy*, ed. Sidney M Milkis and Jerome M. Mileur (Amherst: University of Massachusetts Press, 1999), 103–25.

84. Sandel, *Democracy's Discontent*, 347–48. But in *Democracy's Discontent*, Sandel never explicitly invokes the decentralizing tradition of Anti-Federalism that McWilliams embraces. After respectfully presenting their position and dismissing the notion that they were rights-oriented individualists, Sandel drops the Anti-Federalists and their legacy off the historical stage. *Democracy's Discontent*, 35–38. But see Tulis, "Constituting Liberty," 68 (indicating that in response to McWilliams's harsh critique of the framers in his "Discipline of Freedom" essay, Sandel pointed to an alternative tradition of "political thought beginning with the Anti-Federalists").

85. Jefferson to Joseph C. Cabell, Monticello, 2 February 1816, in *Thomas Jefferson, Writings*, ed. Merrill D. Peterson (New York: Library of America, 1984), 1380.

86. McWilliams, *Fraternity in America*, 220; "Parties as Civic Associations," 55, 56; *Fraternity in America*, 220; "American Pluralism," 299.

87. Hannah Arendt, *On Revolution*, (New York: Viking, 1963), 254. For a critical view of Arendt's influence, see Paul A. Rahe, "Jefferson's Machiavellian Moment" in *Reason and Republicanism: Thomas Jefferson's Legacy of Liberty*, ed. Gary L. McDowell and Sharon L. Noble (Lanham, Md: Rowman & Littlefield, 1997), 83 n. 81 (stating that "Arendt's argument has beguiled" Pocock and other students of civic republicanism). Yarbrough, *American Virtues: Thomas Jefferson on the Character of a Free People* (Lawrence: University of Kansas Press, 1998), 138.

88. Elazar, *Covenant Constitutionalism: The Great Frontier and the Matrix of Federal Democracy* (New Brunswick, N.J.: Transaction Publishers, 1998), 25. Donald S. Lutz, *The Origins of American Constitutionalism* (Baton Rouge: University of Louisiana Press, 1988). See also Barbara Allen, "Alexis de Tocqueville on the Covenantal Tradition of American Federal Democracy," *Publius: Journal of Federalism* 28, no. 2 (Spring 1978): 1–23. But see Richard L. McCormick, *The Party Period and Public Policy: American Politics from the Age of Jackson to the Progressive*

Era (New York: Oxford University Press, 1986) (Original covenant idea "decried parties" and political partisanship).

89. McWilliams, "American Pluralism," 299, 297.

90. Christopher Tomlins, "Law, Police, and the Pursuit of Happiness in the New American Republic," *Studies in American Political Development* 4 (1990): 30 n. 90, quoting Jefferson to John Tyler 26 May 1810, *The Writings of Thomas Jefferson*, vol. 11, ed. Andrew A. Lipscomb (Washington, D.C.: Thomas Jefferson Memorial Association, 1905), 143 (authors' italics). McWilliams, "American Pluralism," 95 (Jefferson on the phalanxes of New England). See also Yarbrough, *American Virtues*, 133. For the argument that this kind of "national vision" is not antithetical to the Anti-Federalist tradition, see Russell Arben Fox, "Tending and Intending a Nation: Conflicting Visions of American National Identity," *Polity* 3, no. 4 (Summer 1999): 565–73.

91. Will Marshall, "Friend or Faux," *The American Prospect*, no. 16 (Winter 1994): 10, and Robert F. Kennedy, *To Seek a Newer World* (New York: Doubleday, 1967), 57.

92. Ferrel Guillory, "Smart Start Democratic Initiative, GOP Methods," *Raleigh News and Observer*, 23 September 1994, 10A.

93. The requirement of local community consensus distinguishes the Smart Start model from "the maximum feasible participation" notions of the federal Community Action Program (CAP) during the 1960s War on Poverty. The goal of the CAP was to empower the poor and politically dispossessed through the establishment of an institutional authority separate from the local governmental status quo. For the negative view of CAP, see Daniel P. Moynihan, *Maximum Feasible Misunderstanding: Community Action in the War on Poverty* (New York: Free Press, 1969). For a more mixed assessment, see David E. Price, "Community, Mediating Structures, and Public Policy," *Soundings* 62, no. 4 (Winter 1979): 382–85 (citing other sources).

94. By "signature" issue, we mean an issue on which politicians prominently campaign to define their candidacies. The fact that Smart Start is not strictly a targeted-class, "welfare" initiative helps to explain its status as a signature issue for North Carolinian Democrats. As politically savvy progressive commentators have argued, targeted-class welfare initiatives lack the sense of "social solidarity" that universal programs like Social Security have been able to inspire across the electorate. See Robert Kuttner, *The Life of the Party: Democratic Prospects in 1988 and Beyond* (New York: Viking 1987), 171; Theda Skocpol, "A Partnership with American Families," in *The New Majority: Toward a Popular, Progressive Politics*, ed. Stanley B. Greenberg and Theda Skocpol (New Haven, Conn.: Yale University Press, 1997), 104–29. Despite its formally universal class status, North Carolina's Smart Start disproportionately benefits poorer families in need of preventive dental care, child care support, and other services. See *North Carolina Accomplishments in Early Childhood Issues*, Office of the Governor, 6 January 1999.

95. Alexis de Tocqueville, *Democracy in America*, ed. J.P. Mayer, trans. George Lawrence (1835; reprint, New York: Doubleday, 1969), 62.

96. Guillory, "Smart Start Democratic Initiative, GOP Methods."

97. Galston has described the new children's health insurance program as a

model for "our governing institutions . . . to create a new synthesis—a contemporary federalism that balances distinctive federal and state capacities." Testimony on "The State of Federalism" before the Senate Governmental Affairs Committee, 5 May 1997, *Federal News Service*.

98. Herbert Croly, *The Promise of American Life* (1909; reprint, New Brunswick, N.J.: Transaction Publishers, 1993).

13

From Community Theory to Democratic Practice

Edward A. Schwartz

In his discussion of "The American Enlightenment" in *The Idea of Fraternity in America*, Carey McWilliams argues that the "vision of national 'fraternity'" that guided America's framers was one in which all particular loyalties and local affections must be shattered and deprived of "confidence" in order to create allegiance and attachment among citizens to the country as a whole. Indeed, he suggests, the strategy for bringing this about is even set forth in *The Federalist Papers*. There, Madison et al. argue that by bringing the "individual citizen" directly into "contact with the federal regime" and making him or her "feel personally the rewards and punishments of federal policy," the country itself eventually would inspire greater loyalty than local communities and the states. McWilliams concludes that the division of powers among different levels of government constitutes "in fact a division of citizens, and it is expected that the loyalties of the divided individual will follow the path which interest indicates toward a broader affection."[1]

Fortunately, various extra-governmental institutions have provided alternative paths for bridging the gap between local loyalties and attachment to the country. Like Alexis de Tocqueville, McWilliams credits churches and voluntary associations with having played much of this role over the course of our history. Even more important, he argues, have been our political parties, which "aim at winning a generalized loyalty, at creating a bond of identification between rulers and ruled, private men and public values."[2] The success of a party, he observes, "depends on how well it forms a civic identity in its members, a coherent picture of the self in relation to the political community over and above the divisive effects of private roles and life. It lays claim, in other words, to the whole individual

272

and the partisan act requires a consolidation of reference groups, a decision as to which loyalties the individual values most."[3]

Indeed, throughout the 1960s, when political scientists largely accepted the pluralist argument of David Truman and Robert Dahl that the only common ground among disparate interest groups was respect for the "rules of the game," McWilliams continued to insist that political parties could achieve a broad consolidation of interests and goals among those who chose to take them seriously and, "through local organizations and citizen participation—be part of a new network of ties among citizens."[4]

Yet even as he argued for a renewed commitment to building party organizations, McWilliams always understood how difficult this had become. As he put it in *Fraternity*, the "task of the party was easier, its possibilities greater, when it was rooted in local communities, in societies in which the individual's loyalty already had been given a limited public dimension."[5] Even this insight considerably understates our problem today. Those hated party machines have all but disappeared from America's cities and nothing like them has emerged in the suburbs. Ironically, the closest approximation is now being built by the Christian Coalition on the Right. By using churches to build local chapters that encourage members to lobby Congress and participate in presidential primaries, the coalition has created a party within the Republican Party that, by 1996, controlled nearly half of the Republican state committees. No group within the Democratic Party was doing anything like this at the time, least of all the Democratic National Committee. The electoral results of the 1990s spoke for themselves, at least as far as Congress was concerned.

Beyond his ongoing work in political science, Professor McWilliams has been equally committed to pursue his goals through politics itself. For example, in 1973 he agreed to serve as vice president of a new organization, called the Institute for the Study of Civic Values, which I and a number of local activists in Philadelphia were creating. We sought to promote in one city a new, democratic politics that might serve as a model for how grassroots participation might be strengthened throughout the country. The formal aim of the Institute was to help citizens work together to achieve America's historic ideals. This mission soon evolved into an ongoing effort to build neighborhood-based organizations and coalitions that would share in the implementation of government programs and services in the neighborhoods and, in the process, promote citizen participation in politics. *The Idea of Fraternity in America* had advanced a theory of how community groups and party organizations had nurtured civic fraternity in the past, despite the complex processes of American politics. Our aim was to devise a new democratic practice that would preserve these values and rebuild these institutions in the future.

The Institute has now pursued this broad project for nearly twenty-five years. In Philadelphia, at least, we have been successful. A seminar that we developed in 1974 called "Building Community" created a network of activists from all parts of the city whose organizations were soon forcing public agencies and elected officials to work with them in addressing neighborhood problems. By 1976, we emerged with a citywide coalition called the Philadelphia Council of Neighborhood Organizations (PCNO), that spearheaded major campaigns for neighborhood involvement in community development, transportation planning, economic development, and education. By the late 1970s, a significant group within PCNO had emerged as committee people in the Democratic Party ward system. By 1983, I ended up running a successful citywide campaign for one of seven at-large seats on the Philadelphia City Council, using what we called the "Neighborhood Agenda" as my platform. My victory established that neighborhood groups were a political force to be reckoned with, and they have been taken seriously ever since.

To be sure, neighborhood activists in Philadelphia have benefited from the way in which the party system still operates in the city. There remain sixty-nine wards, with more than seventeen hundred voting divisions. Every four years (it used to be two), voters in each party in every one of these divisions elect two people to represent them as committee people. These committee people, in turn, select the ward leaders who then try to determine the party nominees for every office. Of course, Democrats remain as prone to disagreement today as in the past, so there are often hot contests between candidates backed by ward leaders of different persuasions. Moreover, while strong mayors and congressmen were able to use patronage to centralize control over the parties in the past, this is no longer the case. Now, individual wards can be captured by grassroots organizations prepared to—in George Washington Plunkitt's classic phrase—"see their opportunities and take them."[6] The result is that the neighborhoods movement in Philadelphia has been among the few grassroots organizing projects in the country that has chosen to work within the political party system instead of pitting community activists against the politicians, and often against politics itself. This has worked considerably to our advantage.

Indeed, given the almost singular resilience of the political party system in Philadelphia, it is not clear at all that the integration of civic and political activism in this city can be replicated elsewhere. We are painfully aware that most organizers have no comparable system that enables them to gain institutional strength in politics. Most local organizers are on their own, at least in relation to politics.

Nonetheless, the success that the Christian Coalition has had in capturing a large segment of the Republican Party suggests that this may be more possible than most groups on the Left are willing to admit. Neighborhood activism is now a major force in cities around the country. Once a community group is in a position to browbeat elected officials, it doesn't take much additional effort to start fielding candidates to replace them. The first step lies in a process of community building that encourages people to see politics as a vehicle to make government work. The second step lies in building an agenda for political action that provides a coherent platform that candidates can endorse and organizers use to encourage their constituents to vote. As part of this process, it becomes critical to help the organizers maintain contact with one another. The new communications tools available via the Internet are ideally suited to this purpose. The final step involves persuading the organizers—who by now are spending considerable time in campaigns related to specific issues and problems—that they should also see to it that their constituents are registered to vote and turn out on election day.

This is precisely what the Christian Coalition accomplished on the Right in the 1990s, as anyone who visits its Web site can see. It is also what the Institute for the Study of Civic Values is encouraging in Philadelphia, with a heavy focus on the economic problems arising as a result of welfare reform. Now, moreover, we at the Institute are able to use the Internet to encourage groups around the country to replicate what we are doing.

The Institute sponsors four relevant projects: the Social Contract Project, which helps grassroots activists set goals for governmental action within individual neighborhoods; the JOIN Agenda, which defines a new set of public initiatives needed to promote economic opportunity in the face of welfare reform; Neighborhoods Online, which is using the Internet to build a national network of neighborhood activists interested in replicating the Institute's work in their own communities; and a new Pledge to Strengthen Democracy, to identify people in every neighborhood who are willing to encourage voter registration and turnout as their ongoing contribution to expanding citizen participation and community empowerment.

SOCIAL CONTRACT PROJECT

The mechanism the Institute has used since the mid-1970s to help grassroots organizers and leaders define what they want most from government is the neighborhood social contract. Political theorists may associate the term "social contract" with the theorists who represent the beginnings of modern political thought—Thomas Hobbes, John Locke, and Jean-Jacques Rousseau—or with John Rawls, whose *A Theory of Justice* has revived interest in social contract theory today.

Yet Plunkitt put forward a social contract theory of his own. "The district leader promises," he observed, "and that makes a solemn contract. If he lives up to it, spends most of his time chasin' after places in the departments, picks up jobs from railroads and contractors for his followers, and shows himself in all ways a true statesman, then his followers are bound in honor to uphold him, just as they're bound to uphold the Constitution of the United States."[7] This is a conception of the social contract that even people who have never heard of Hobbes, Locke, Rousseau, and Rawls can relate to their own understanding of the democratic process.

With the demise of local parties, elected officials and public administrators have engaged in an almost desperate search in recent years to find new ways to connect government to citizens. The new conventional wisdom here is shaped by David Osborne and Ted Gaebler's *Reinventing Government*, which, in a chapter of the same name, tells us how "The Entrepreneurial Spirit is Transforming the Public Sector."[8] Political parties are almost nowhere to be found in *Reinventing Government*. "Voting" does not even appear in the index. Osborne and Gaebler propose to "reinvent" government by hiring public managers who will see it as a business and treat citizens as if we were simply consumers of public services. It is a telling commentary on modern democracy that through much of the 1990s, this was regarded with near reverence by a wide range of political leaders, from Vice President Al Gore down to city managers in small cities all over the country.

The neighborhood social contracts negotiated by the Institute for the Study of Civic Values over the past several years correspond far more closely to what Plunkitt had in mind. Through our Social Contract Project, we have helped leaders of grassroots organizations throughout the city—many of whom remain active in the Democratic and Republican parties—negotiate explicit agreements with public agencies defining how they will work together to make the neighborhoods clean, safe, economically viable, and decent places in which to raise children. Osborne and Gaebler may think that we can improve civic life by turning politicians into entrepreneurs skilled in the techniques of mass marketing. We prefer the old-fashioned concept of the public servant, working with organized groups of citizens to solve problems and achieve goals that isolated individuals cannot solve on their own.

Over the past five years, the Institute has worked out a specific process for developing social contracts on this basis, one that uses the Preamble to the Constitution as an explicit framework for the agreement. Once we bring a group together, we start by asking, "Who are 'we the people' of this neighborhood?" This has proven to be a powerful way to establish that all residents have equal standing, regardless of ethnic background or economic circumstances. From there, we ask, "How can we work with government to 'secure the blessings of liberty to ourselves and our posterity?" Finally, we ask, "What must government, business, community organizations, and individual citizens do to 'promote the general welfare' in achieving the goals that we have set for the neighborhood?" As members of the group come to grips with these questions, they gradually work out the provisions of the specific social contract that make sense to them.

A good example of what this process can produce is a citywide "Block Club Social Contract" that we negotiated among a cross-section of neighborhood leaders, who came to our office every two weeks for three months to put the document together. The following provisions are a representative sampling of what it includes:

Excerpts from the Philadelphia Block Club Social Contract

Neighborhood Appearance

We commit ourselves to promote the highest possible standards of appearance and cleanliness on the blocks and in the neighborhoods where we live. To this end we pledge:

To insist that neighbors handle the disposal of trash and the maintenance of blocks in compliance with city codes. We expect the Sanitation Division of the Streets Department to manage trash collection throughout the city in an efficient and effective manner. We pledge full cooperation with law enforcement agencies in identifying and prosecuting those who dump trash illegally or who conduct illegal car repair businesses on our streets.

Neighborhood Harmony and Security

To strengthen neighborhood watch programs like Town Watch. We expect all levels of government to support community crime prevention by providing the equipment needed in such programs and by supporting adequate training of police and residents in how to make them effective.

Families and Children

We will create an atmosphere of trust that strengthens families and enables all residents of all generations to work together. To this end, we will make a special effort to insure that the spirit of cooperation that we promote on our blocks extends to our young people. . . . To this end, we pledge:

To work with schools to insure student attendance and promote positive attitudes toward learning. We will identify community people and resources that can help our children perform successfully in the classroom. We expect all institutions and organizations working with young people to develop partnerships with us to promote quality education throughout the city.

Economic Opportunity and Security

To "secure the blessings of liberty" requires that all residents of Philadelphia gain economic opportunity and security for ourselves and our families. As block leaders and residents, we pledge to help one another achieve these goals. To this end, we pledge:

To provide block and neighborhood meetings with information on job opportunities available to our residents—especially those offered by area businesses and by government programs. We expect local businesses and city development agencies to supply us with this information in a timely fashion.

As these provisions suggest, the aim here is to emphasize that the achievement of public goals depends upon an active partnership between government and citizens. The social contract itself defines these goals, along with the commitments needed to achieve them. It then depends upon the block leaders, community organizations, and public officials to live up to their agreements.

Thus far, the Institute has been able to use social contracts like these to establish priorities for improvement in a broad range of individual neighborhoods in Philadelphia. In a section of South Philadelphia known as Queen Village, for example, a social contract between residents of a civic group and the leaders of a public housing development resulted in a summer day-camp for young people, an improved relationship with the police and the neighborhood school, and an adult literacy program coordinated directly by the Institute in cooperation with the local civic groups. Each of these projects established new areas of collaboration, between citizen groups, nonprofit agencies, and government, which had not existed to that point. Similarly, we helped organizations in a neighborhood known as Kensington to develop a comprehensive proposal to become one of six urban "Empowerment Zones" by helping them see the application process as negotiating a new social contract with the federal government.[9] The groups acknowledged their support for the process by including the Social Contract Project in the application (which was funded as the appropriate framework for block leadership development).

The Institute's long-range goal is to establish the Social Contract Project as the primary instrument for structuring the relationship between citizens and government throughout the city of Philadelphia. The Block Club Social Contract provides the blueprint. The Empowerment Zone block leaders' program is showing us how best to implement these provisions in practice. At this point, a number of city council representatives have expressed interest in having us use this technique in their districts. We are making real progress, and we hope that what we learn in Philadelphia can be attempted in cities and smaller communities throughout the United States.

THE JOIN AGENDA

The second step involves distilling the major concerns raised by organizations in individual neighborhoods into a public agenda or platform for change in the entire governmental system. On a national level, the obvious example in recent years was the Republican "Contract with America," which became the vehicle that conservatives used to gain control of Congress in 1994. Interestingly enough, postelection polls showed that most Americans had little idea of what the Contract with America actually proposed in relation to government spending, abortion, crime, and welfare. Activists within the conservative movement knew, however, and the Contract with America served to rally them to political action. The "Neighborhood Agenda" developed by the Institute played a similar role in attracting support to my own campaign for councilman-at-large in Philadelphia in 1983.

Since 1997, the Institute has been advancing a new agenda in Philadelphia, this time related to the economic priorities of the Block Club Social Contract especially as they relate to welfare reform. By 2002, more than 40,000 households receiving public assistance in Philadelphia could lose all cash support as they reach the five-year lifetime limit on welfare imposed by both Congress and the Pennsylvania legislature in 1996. To respond to this crisis, the Institute has put together a new coalition of neighborhood, human service, and antipoverty groups called JOIN—Jobs and Opportunity to Improve Neighborhoods—with a specific agenda that reflects what groups are now trying to do in their neighborhoods to help welfare recipients achieve self-sufficiency. The JOIN Agenda calls upon the Pennsylvania legislature to expand adult literacy and job training services to the poor, subsidize reverse commuting from inner-city neighborhoods to suburban jobs, create public service jobs for people who cannot find work in the private sector or public agencies, and make quality day care affordable for working parents at every economic level. More than sixty organizations already have endorsed the JOIN Agenda, and its major points are already acknowledged by the press and a number of leading politicians as among the city's top priorities over the next several years.

The Institute started circulating drafts of the JOIN Agenda early in 1997. It took a year to gain broad support for it from the major neighborhood and social service agencies working directly with welfare recipients. Had the Democratic Party nominated a strong candidate to challenge Republican Tom Ridge in the 1998 Pennsylvania governor's race, the JOIN Agenda would have worked well to attract neighborhood activists to the campaign. Even without a strong Democratic candidate, a number of citizen groups have embraced the major points in the agenda—along with a campaign for public education—as a vehicle for grassroots organizing and advocacy. By 1999, key points in the JOIN Agenda related to adult education and training and child care were adopted by candidates in both parties running for mayor. The priorities in the agenda are likely to remain important to Democratic Party candidates for years to come, since the issues they raise address not only welfare recipients entering the workforce, but all people at the bottom end of the job market struggling to make ends meet while giving adequate support to their children.

The JOIN Agenda represents the kind of political program that can become a rallying cry for electoral politics on the Left in any state where welfare reform forces thousands of women and children into homeless shelters and onto the streets or, also likely, into the workforce at salaries that depress the wage rates of all working people. Whether the JOIN Agenda achieves this stature will depend not merely on the crisis—witness the scattershot response to homelessness that the Left has offered over the years—but on the skill of local organizers in developing local and state and even a national public agenda defining how the country must respond.

ORGANIZING ON-LINE

Building support for the JOIN Agenda in Philadelphia and encouraging groups in other cities to develop similar economic opportunity platforms has required us to develop new ways to communicate with the leaders and organizers throughout the country. Among the greatest challenges facing any movement—especially one aimed at people who are already involved in projects of their own—is making time to meet. Until recently, moreover, the only way that groups of people could share information and ideas with one another without a time lag was through face-to-face meetings. Now, however, the Internet enables us to overcome this obstacle, at least on a limited basis. Through E-mail "listservs" (Internet mailing lists), thousands of people can communicate with one another simultaneously. It is not an absolute substitute for face-to-face contact, but it does permit collective discussion at a distance in ways never possible before. The World Wide Web, in turn, gives us fast access to information about political issues and legislative developments that citizen groups have rarely been able to access before, and never at a moment's notice. Major national organizations like the Children's Defense Fund and National Rifle Association are now using the Net to communicate with their followers around the country. More significantly, even a local organization like the Institute for the Study of Civic Values can use the Internet to connect with activists and organizations nationally in ways that would have been impossible a few short years ago. I made these points in much greater depth *in NetActivism: How Citizens Use the Internet*.[10] For all its limits, the Internet is turning out to be a great political resource.

Our recent progress organizing in Philadelphia is benefiting considerably from use of the Internet. Most of the groups that now attend monthly meetings of JOIN, as an example, participate in a local E-mail list that the Institute runs called "neighbors-online." We have even started a separate E-mail list for people working directly with welfare recipients, called FAN (Family Advocates Network). At its current rate of growth, we expect FAN to have one thousand subscribers within a year. And we are making information about JOIN available to a much broader on-line audience through a Web site on which we post platform and position papers for national distribution.

The Internet, then, provides an unparalleled opportunity for national groups to organize locally and for local groups to build national support. Conservatives were quick to seize upon these new technologies and use them to their best advantage. Now groups on the Left are catching up. The Children's Defense Fund distributes an electronic newsletter every few days to more than ten thousand supporters around the country and uses its Web site to attract people to its "Stand for Children" march on Washington every year.

And by taking leadership in what is now called "net activism," the Institute is receiving broad exposure for our other efforts to help grassroots organizations navigate the political system. Groups in cities as far away as Minneapolis and Tulsa have started developing social contracts of their own. Welfare-to-work coalitions are starting to write to us via E-mail asking how they, too, can build coalitions like JOIN. A student organization in Hong Kong even wrote to thank us for the use of our material in developing a civic education program it was developing in anticipation of the pending takeover by mainland China. All politics may be local, as Tip O'Neill observed, but the Internet now permits the global village to derive strength from what is happening in the villages themselves.

GETTING OUT THE VOTE

At this point, however, the greatest challenge facing not only the Institute, but all organizers interested in reclaiming democratic politics in neighborhoods and communities, involves being able to translate community organizing and coalition-building into getting out the vote. Progressive activists may find consolation in opinion polls that show broad public support for increased government spending in education, adult literacy and training, and community revitalization. These are all irrelevant unless representatives end up in Congress and the state legislatures prepared to carry out the program. In politics, the only polls that really matter are the ones that close at 8 P.M. on election day. The Right has understood this principle over the years and organized accordingly. The Left has not.

Consider what happened in the congressional elections of 1996, even as Bill Clinton was reclaiming the presidency by a landslide. To support the congressional representatives they had helped elect in 1994, the Christian Coalition sent four million voter guides to more than 125,000 churches for use by grassroots organizers in getting supporters to the polls. The guides were simple enough. They listed the bills in which the coalition had an interest and how individual representatives voted on them. They left it to their supporters to do the rest. The AFL-CIO, by contrast, invested $35 million in media ads, in a number of "swing" districts, attacking incumbents for their votes on health care. The ads stopped by October. No grassroots organizing in these target districts followed them. The result? The Christian Coalition held on to most of the seats it had targeted; the labor movement didn't win a single one.

At least the labor movement is still trying to influence electoral politics; many of the nation's leading community organizers take pride in flaunting it. Ernesto Cortes, a spokesman for the Industrial Areas Foundation (IAF) created years ago by the late Saul Alinsky to train local organizers, asserts that, "voting, elections, turnout" are the "least important elements of political action," and to focus on them "trivializes our citizens by disconnecting them from the real debate and real power of public life. . . . If there is to be genuine participatory politics in this country, there must be opportunities for ordinary people to initiate action about matters that are important to their interests."[11] How, then, does the Industrial Areas Foundation define these opportunities? As the leader of an IAF project in Philadelphia explained in an informal discussion on organizing at the Institute: "We consider ourselves successful when we can bring one thousand people into a room to push for their demands." In other words, persuading a local community development administrator to support a neighborhood project using federal Community Development Block Grant funds represents real power, whereas electing a representative who fights for the Community Development Block Grant program in Congress does not. With a conception of political power like this operating on the Left, the Right wins by default.

The real challenge involves helping community activists see the connection between federal actions and local results as the basis for translating local organizing into electoral power in national politics. The conservative activists who picket abortion clinics can also be counted on to send faxes to Washington to block federal funding of these clinics. By contrast, most people now volunteering in soup kitchens seem to have no idea what is happening with the food stamp program in Congress, even though it feeds more needy families than all the soup kitchens put together. We appear to be developing a conception of service in America in which political involvement plays no part. This does, indeed, trivialize our citizens by disconnecting them from the real debate and power of public life, in Cortes's formulation of the problem. Unlike the IAF, however, most volunteers have no fixed position on the matter; they just want to help. What is necessary is a coherent strategy to involve citizens at every stage of the political process, and not just at the trough long after the legislative battles over funding are won or lost.

To address this problem, then, the Institute is about to undertake a new initiative, first in Philadelphia, and then around the country. The aim is to define voter registration and turnout campaigns as a legitimate activity for volunteers, even a new dimension of volunteerism. We have even developed a "Pledge to Strengthen Democracy" for the campaign. It reads: "[T]o fulfill America's promise of democracy—government 'of the people, by the people, and for the people'—I pledge to work actively on my block, in my community, at my workplace, and in our schools to insure that all Americans are registered to vote and participate in every election." Moreover, like the Christian Coalition voter guides, this Pledge to Strengthen Democracy can be implemented on a nonpartisan basis, since it focuses on getting people to the polls and not on specific candidates or campaigns. Like the coalition, we are confident that when people do decide to vote, they are more than capable of figuring out where their interests lie.

There has been no more dangerous proposition advanced in American politics, especially among those who seek support from government, than the principle that says that voting "trivializes" citizens. Voting *empowers* citizens. Active citizenship may involve more than mere voting, but it requires no less. Politicians don't care how loud you shout at them if you don't vote, but they'll strain to hear you if you do. If there is to be a revival of democracy in America, it must be built on this basic understanding of how the system works.

FROM DISAPPOINTMENT TO HOPE

In 1973, the Institute for the Study of Civic Values emerged in the city of Philadelphia as a champion of what now would be called civic engagement. We led citizen seminars on "building community." We pushed for the city to encourage the creation of community development corporations addressing neighborhood housing and economic needs. We helped grassroots activists understand the city budget and how they themselves could improve city services through programs like recycling and Town Watch. All of this was part of a Neighborhood Agenda that has guided the relationship between city departments and community organizations ever since.

Yet, a primary aim of all these initiatives was not merely to improve neighborhoods, but to revitalize democratic politics by encouraging citizens to participate actively in community politics. Once we did start organizing neighborhoods in Philadelphia, it didn't take long before a grassroots army emerged seeking positions as committee people and ward leaders. Many of Philadelphia's strongest political leaders today got their start through this process, people like Congressman Chaka Fattah and Dwight Evans, a well-known state legislator who serves as chairman of the House Appropriations Committee. At a time when money and media dominate politics, these representatives won their seats the old-fashioned way: they organized.

The projects the Institute has initiated in the 1990s aim at carrying this process forward in Philadelphia and outward to other communities and cities around the country. The Social Contract Project provides a means for citizens and elected officials to work together in addressing the problems facing individual neighborhoods. The JOIN Agenda provides candidates a platform that addresses the major economic, educational, and social crises that are bound to develop, as millions of single parents now receiving support from Temporary Assistance to Needy Families (TANF) must leave their children at home unattended in order to work, as now required in every state. We are using the Internet to help activists connect with one another and to convey their demands to elected officials and the press. The Pledge to Strengthen Democracy represents a new approach to expanding the electorate by making voter registration and participation a legitimate mission for volunteers.

"The doubt that politics makes, or can make, more than a trivial difference to our lives," Carey McWilliams observes in *The Politics of Disappointment,* "calls into question the possibility of self-governance and hence the basis of the American republic."[12] At its core, the Institute for the Study of Civic Values has existed to strengthen the possibility of self-governance as the basis of the American republic. This is where the theory of community developed by Professor McWilliams in *The Idea of Fraternity in America* led us, as we contemplated what the "long march through existing institutions" would require. We are honored to be working with him in shaping the democratic practice that his theory has inspired.

NOTES

1. Wilson Carey McWilliams, *The Idea of Fraternity in America* (Berkeley and Los Angeles: University of California Press, 1973), 191 (hereafter cited as *Fraternity in America*).

2. Ibid., 71.

3. Ibid.

4. McWilliams, *The Politics of Disappointment* (Chatham, N.J.: Chatham House, 1995), 33, and 31–34.

5. McWilliams, *Fraternity in America*, 72.

6. William L. Riordon, *Plunkitt of Tammany Hall* (New York: Meridian, 1963), 5.

7. Ibid., 36.

8. David Osborne and Ted Gaebler, *Reinventing Government* (New York: Penguin, 1993).

9. Empowerment Zones were the distressed urban areas singled out by the Clinton administration for business tax incentives and sizable federal grants awarded competitively to cities that put forward imaginative comprehensive plans for revitalization.

10. Edward Schwartz, *NetActivism: How Citizens Use the Internet* (Cambridge, Mass.: O'Reilly and Associates, 1996).

11. Ernesto Cortes Jr., "Reweaving the Fabric: The Iron Rule and the IAF Strategy for Power and Politics." *Citizen Practices Network Web Site* <www.cpn.org>. Reprinted with permission from *Interwoven Destinies: Cities and the Nation*, ed. Henry G. Cisneros (New York: W. W. Norton, 1993) 295–319.

12. McWilliams, *The Politics of Disappointment*, 124.

Conclusion
(Virtue and Democracy)

14

Majority Tyranny in Aristotle and Tocqueville

Harvey C. Mansfield

To compare Aristotle and Alexis de Tocqueville may not seem appropriate because Tocqueville does not seem to address Aristotle directly. He did not read Aristotle every day as he said he read Pascal, Montesquieu, and Rousseau. The latter are modern philosophers living in the midst of modernity who, unlike the early philosophers on the front line of modernity, such as Machiavelli, Bacon, and Hobbes, did not have to confront the ancients, above all Aristotle. Tocqueville does not mention Aristotle in *Democracy in America*, and his most prominent possible reference to him dismisses a key notion of his political science, the mixed regime: "The government called mixed has always seemed to me a chimera" (I 2.7, 289).[1]

Yet, that dismissal begins to reveal an interesting comparison. For Tocqueville, the political world, the modern world, is irreversibly democratic; that is a "providential fact" (*DA*, introduction, 7). Aristocracy is in the past; so one cannot attempt to mix it with democracy as did Aristotle. But although aristocracy is irrevocably in the past for Tocqueville, it is not lost to view. Even as the world becomes ever more democratic, he brings the contrast between democracy and aristocracy constantly before his readers, and always illuminates one with the other. In this he resembles Aristotle more than the democratic theorists of our day, who care for nothing but democracy and never even imagine a legitimate alternative.

Both Aristotle and Tocqueville speak of the distinction between the few and the many, but differently: Aristotle as a dispute and a choice, Tocqueville as historical succession. Both also speak of majority tyranny but, again, differently: Aristotle in the context of the disputed claims of the few and the many, Tocqueville in the absence of any legitimate claim openly maintaining the viewpoint of the few. In the modern democracy Tocqueville studies, majority tyranny comes with special force because the many do not face opposition from the few. The few lose their legitimacy as such; they are reduced to the status of a minority, which is the many without a majority, a lesser number when there is no argument but that of the greater number.[2] To consider what happens when the few are reduced to a minority of individuals, let us begin with Aristotle.

Aristotle's discussion of the few and the many occurs mostly in books three and four of the *Politics*. I shall mention only a few points from the text without attempting a long interpretation that would show how Aristotle develops his argument. The main point clearly emerging from the text is that politics is a dispute—a dispute taking the form of an interactive debate—between the few and the many. Whereas in modern democracies the majority is often accused of ignoring the minority, in Aristotle's politics, the few and the many take account of, and argue with, one another. Aristotle as political philosopher listens to their debate and intervenes inconspicuously on each side to point out difficulties, suggest improvements, and propose prudent concessions to the other side. Tocqueville, too, works through the parties he sees rather than from above them: "I undertook to see not otherwise but further than the parties" (*DA*, introduction, 18). Neither of them asserts, in the manner of Plato, the right of the philosopher to rule; instead, they make themselves unassertive commentators on the assertions of others, of political men.

Aristotle calls attention to the importance of assertiveness in politics from the beginning of book three in considering the citizen and the regime. Who is a citizen is often in dispute, Aristotle notes, and bringing to the fore the distinction between the many and the few, he adds that a citizen in a democracy is often not one in an oligarchy (*Pol.* 1275a4).[3] The citizen (*politēs*) participates in rule, and thus is relative to the regime (*politeia*), and since there are several regimes, the good man (who is above regimes) is not the same as the best citizen (who is not). Vulgar persons who perform necessary services such as manual labor are sometimes not citizens because citizenship, as ruling, is considered to be an honor (1278a38). It is an honor to which all lay claim as their just due. But in doing so, they judge badly because most persons are bad judges concerning their own things (1280a14). Here Aristotle introduces partisanship over justice, and and he narrows the partisans to those who think justice is equality and those who think it is inequality. Both judge badly by supposing that a part of justice—the part they like, appreciate, and set forth—is the whole. These partisans are clearly either democratic or oligarchical, and just as clearly Aristotle undertakes to show that they are parts of a whole, thus partly wrong and partly right. That is the interaction between the few and the many.

Next, Aristotle makes clear that what might seem—especially to us modern democrats—a difference in number between the few and the many is actually a difference in quality. The many are the poor, the have-nots; the few are the rich, the haves. The dispute between them is essentially between poor and rich, only accidentally between many and few. The many (*hoi polloi*) are not just isolated individuals, again as we modern democrats suppose, but are united into a multitude (*To plēthos*) by some common or collective quality in which they take pride; and since one cannot take pride in being poor, in merely suffering from a want, the many come to claim to rule on account of, and for the sake of, their freedom, a quality in virtue of which all can be equal. At one point, Aristotle seems to conclude in favor of rule by the multitude, or a certain multitude (1281b21, 1282a37); this passage has been much cited and sometimes improved by Aristotle's friends today, who wish he were more democratic than he is. Aristotle here does not abolish the few or deny their claim as such, and he provisionally approves the rule of the multitude on the ground of its virtue, that is, on the aristocratic ground.

The few, however, do not need to be taught that they actually advance a virtue, for they immediately stand up for virtue without prompting. The few think that they are better than the many by virtue of their virtue, which they are eager to advance. They claim to rule because they are better than the ordinary average sort, on whom they do not hesitate to pass an adverse judgment. A certain virtue will be found in both democracy and oligarchy, indeed in any regime, but to claim virtue is most characteristic of oligarchy, which calls itself aristocracy, because a claim of virtue is a claim of superiority, a claim that distinguishes the virtuous few from the undistinguished many. Even the commoner virtues, such as courage and moderation, will be turned to the account of a virtuous few who can claim to practice them to an uncommon degree.

Now a claim of human excellence is also a claim of the excellence of humans, stating what distinguishes human beings from beasts (1281b20). To be human is not only to be democratically a member of the human race but also to be oligarchically superior to the rest of nonintelligent nature, for humanity is an aristocracy within nature. The few, asserting themselves superior to the many in politics, also represent the many in claiming the virtue that raises men above beasts. Virtue is latent in nature because nature makes men capable of virtue, but men have to act on their own and assert their virtue if they are to receive their due. At the end of Shakespeare's *Julius Caesar*, Antony says of Brutus:

> His life was gentle, and the elements
> So mix'd in him that Nature might stand up
> And say to all the world: "This was a man!"

Unfortunately nature does not speak, and the few who are lovers of honor, like Antony, must speak up and claim the honor due to men. Ordinary men are indebted to extraordinary men for the honor that extraordinary virtue lends to ordinary virtue. Brutus shows us what a man, that is, a perfect man, can be; he fills out to the full the meaning of the lesser virtue we have. By this completion, which is not just an excess, he explains what we are by what we yearn for, or ought to yearn for.

At the same time, it is not enough for the few merely to assert their superior virtue over that of the many. They must prove the assertion by showing that virtue is possible, or in accordance with nature (*kata physin*) if not by nature (*physei*). Politically, the proof requires a showing that the virtue of the few can be reconciled with the freedom of the many. Whereas the few have their superior souls, the many have their recalcitrant bodies, and human nature somehow comprises both. As the few bring virtue to the many, the many bring nature to the few. Aristotle's political argument reminds us that human nature is both above the rest of nature and within it.

Aristotle for the most part discusses tyranny as the usurpation or the unjust rule of one man. But he also brings up majority tyranny when it is directed against the few or one man. In showing that claims of justice arise from certain groups, that the *what* of justice is involved with the *who*, he mentions that the majority (*hoi pleious*, strictly, the more) may attempt to distribute among itself the things of the minority (*hoi elattous*, strictly, the less; 1281a18), an action manifestly unjust, he says, because it will destroy the city. This follows an instance in which the poor despoil the rich and justify themselves with an oath to Zeus. So, when you consider that the majority is not necessarily poor, and you take away the misleading invocation of Zeus, the action is revealed to be unjust, as would be that of a tyrant using force. In order to see itself as unjust, the majority needs to imagine itself as suffering under a tyrant. The attempt to redistribute everything to the majority is necessarily unjust because human qualities are concentrated in a few, the noble. The nobility of a multitude resides in its most noble members, its leaders. To redistribute nobility to all destroys it, and that is unjust, Aristotle concludes, thus identifying the just and the noble (1281a2–10).

Another reference to majority tyranny occurs when Aristotle discusses the democratic practice of ostracism. He mentions the advice that Periander gave silently to Thrasyboulos, as one tyrant to another, when, in front of the messenger sent to him, he lopped off the prominent stalks in a cornfield (1284a27; cf. 1311a19). Aristotle likens this tyrannical behavior toward outstanding citizens not only to the democratic practice of ostracizing them but even to the discomfort of any regime containing a member out of proportion to the rest, a superstar to whom the rest of the team cannot adjust. After attacking majority tyranny, he partly justifies it. Aristotle has a tempered appreciation of the work done in politics by the few on behalf of humanity.

For Tocqueville, the situation is altogether different because the few can no longer claim to rule in their own name. Modern democracy lives, as we have seen, in an "equality of conditions" that results from "a gradual development" and continues as "a great revolution" (*DA*, introduction, 4, 6). Tocqueville considers this "a social movement"; he avoids discussing the origins of this change in political philosophy, from Machiavelli's sardonic remark that "the few [*i pochi*] were always ministers of the few" (*Discourses on Livy*, I 49.3) to the equality of men posited in Thomas Hobbes's state of nature. Tocqueville does allude to equalizing doctrine in the introduction to *Democracy in America* when he denounces the "intellectual miseries" of his time. Somehow the theories such as Hobbes's whose chief purpose was to create a legitimate government have failed to do that, but instead have produced degraded souls (*DA*, introduction, 9–10). Whether because the theorists could not explain convincingly how inalienable rights in the individual could ever be alienated to the sovereign, or because the simplifications of these theorists gave rise to contrary simplifications in reaction, the consequence is that theories have not created legitimacy for the democratic revolution, and yet practice has left no alternative. The moral force of the majority, being unopposed, is now irresistible, and Tocqueville devotes a chapter to a chilling description of its "omnipotence" (I 2.7).

Majority will is omnipotent in democratic America, because it extends to thought. Absolute sovereigns in Europe have not been able to prevent certain thoughts hostile to their authority from circulating, but the empire of the democratic majority reaches into the soul, and Tocqueville concludes that "there is no liberty of the mind in America" (I 2.7, 294). It is worse (he says) than the Spanish Inquisition. This "moral empire" is based on an idea, Tocqueville notes, making a limited exception to his policy of ignoring the philosophical origins of democracy. The idea is that "there is more enlightenment and wisdom in many men gathered together than in one alone," which he calls "the theory of equality applied to intellects" (I 2.7, 284). That doctrine "attacks the pride of man in its last refuge," and it is also false according to Tocqueville, as we know from his repeated references to the "intellectual inequality" that comes directly from God (I 1.3, 57; II 2.13, 651).

Tocqueville says nothing about the enlightenment and wisdom that might be lacking in the majority, but speaks instead of the doctrine's attack on pride. Prompted by Aristotle, we can see the effect here of the

absence of the few in American political argument. It is not so much philosophers (or intellectuals) who suffer from majority tyranny over thought
in America as the proud few with worldly ambition, and their suppres-
sion affects the ordinary man as well. So in listing the effects of that power,
Tocqueville emphasizes loss of independence rather than ignorance, particularly the lack of men who show "that virile candor, that manly independence of thought" (I 2.7, 296) that had once characterized some Americans and that always distinguishes great characters.

It seems, then, that the majority, by denying all intellectual inequality,
ends up depriving itself of a forceful sense of independence. It is often
remarked that Tocqueville seems to change his tune from the first volume
of _Democracy in America_, published in 1835, in which his main anxiety is
majority tyranny, to the second volume published five years later, in which
it is democratic apathy and "mild despotism" (II 4.6, and note A, p. 862).
I do not say that the two volumes can be entirely reconciled. But the connection between them is in the action of the majority on itself, as tyranny
over the intellect becomes tyranny over pride. In the first volume,
Tocqueville compares those who speak to the people to the courtiers who
used to flatter Louis XIV. He remarks that in absolute monarchies, the king
often had great virtues whereas the courtiers were always vile. But suppose that no one has great virtues, and the way is open to the "individualism" and apathy that Tocqueville deplores in his second volume.

Tocqueville discusses the tyranny of one as well as majority tyranny,
but the latter is his concern. Like Aristotle, he says that the majority, taken
collectively, is only one individual opposed to another individual that is
named the minority (I 2.7, 288). Why, then, put so much stock in the majority if it can, contrary to the theory of intellectual equality, have all the
defects and passions of a single mind? And in reference to Europe, he
describes a new despotism of "one alone" much worse than that of kings
because now, in democratic conditions, there is no nobility to check him.
The disappearance of the nobility leaves a mass of confused and impotent individuals incapable of offering resistance to one alone. "One alone"
(_un seul_) reminds us of _uno solo_, the Machiavellian prince. But the Machiavellian prince was set down among a people vigorous enough to hate the
few; he was a master over those who do not want to be mastered.
Tocqueville's despot dominates an apathetic people, and his description
cries out for the name of Napoleon (I 2.9, 362–66).

What can be done about majority tyranny? Tocqueville is never one to
counsel despair, and he says that the force of the majority is only _almost_
irresistible (I 2.7, 299; cf. 282). Indeed, his remedies are well known, but
not so well appreciated is their aristocratic character. Tocqueville rejects
mixed government, to be sure, but by "mixed" he appears to mean equally

mixed, an eventuality Aristotle too thought hardly likely (I 2.7, 289). Tocqueville appears to follow Montesquieu in saying that, instead of mixing social powers, one must accept one of them as superior and then place obstacles before it. But Tocqueville does not in fact rely merely on obstacles to the majority will. In the chapter on the omnipotence of the majority, he criticizes the state constitutions in America for increasing rather than checking majority power, while leaving it to be inferred that the federal Constitution does constitute an obstacle to majority will (I 2.7, 282n, 290).

Other apparent obstacles, however, are mixtures of an Aristotelian kind. Tocqueville says that any particular majority is like a jury representing the human race; and one could appeal from that majority to the universal human majority. By extending the moral argument for majority rule, Tocqueville reduces the moral force of a particular majority, but increases the moral force of all majorities, or of the majority as such. Will not particular majorities learn to claim they represent humanity? We have seen such claims in the twentieth century, the Communists (or Bolsheviks, the majority) asserting that they represent the proletariat, the universal class; and the Nazis maintaining that the German people will purify the human race.

Tocqueville also brings up religion as a check on the majority. But religion appeals to human dissatisfaction with the material and the temporal, to sentiments more characteristic of an aristocratic age than a democratic one. That is why religion in democracy is probably, in most cases, more democratic than religious, hence often not an effectual obstacle to democracy. Tocqueville offers the right of association expressly as a limit on the omnipotence of the majority. That right undermines the moral authority of any present majority by appealing to a possible future majority, the one to be formed by a new association. Again, the majority principle is used to check itself. But like all the rights Tocqueville mentions, this one, according to him, has an aristocratic origin and an aristocratic function if not character. It comes from aristocratic England and it substitutes an artificial association of equals, one that must be constructed by art or science, for the natural association provided in an aristocratic hierarchy. In sum, the few must not appear as themselves, as a party of aristocrats. They will be tolerated in the exercise of rights also available to the majority, as one among many. And as individuals, they may even be welcomed as well as envied when they are more successful than the many. What they must not do is assert the right of the few against the many. They must accept democracy, but they must work within it to remedy its defects.

A recovery of Aristotle's perspective on politics, with its distinction between the few and the many, would surely be a benefit to our political science. Without that distinction political science today suffers from using substitutes for it, such as concepts of minority or elite, which presuppose the adequacy of the standpoint of the many solely. A certain false consciousness is the result, characterized by formal respect for the universality of equality and actual attention to the stubborn fact of ambition among the few. But this fact cannot be well understood unless political science comes to terms with the desire of a few to be few, to seek distinction from the many, and to rule on the basis of such distinction for the benefit of the whole. This desire is not the only political outlook or the only correct one, yet it needs to be seen in competition with the outlook of the many and not simply suppressed by it. Tocqueville attempted to retain this competition between the few and the many, despite the assured dominance of democracy for the foreseeable future, by constantly comparing the new regime of democracy with the old one of aristocracy. The comparison enriches his description of democracy by bringing its features into relief and enabling him to conclude that we have democracy now. Although our democracy is always democratizing itself further, it is nonetheless democracy; we do not have to wait to find it over the horizon.

Yet one cannot, of course, speak simply of the few and the many. There are several fews and any number of multitudes. The few can be the few rich or the few ambitious, the few honor-lovers who are always so political, so important for politics. Perhaps Aristotle and Tocqueville would agree that the true few are those who exceed others in intellect, the wise. But Aristotle indicates that it is not wise for the wise to appear in public and to advance their claim to rule (if they wanted to rule). The wise are few but *too* few; in order to gain power they would have to ally with others, thus diluting their wisdom. In the end their alliance might bring no improvement or actually make things worse (*Pol.* 1301a39–1301b1; 1304b3–5).

In modern times, the rule of the wise appears particularly unwise. Modern regimes are, for reasons we do not need to go into, infected by intellectuals and professors. Any claim on behalf of the few that tended in the direction of the rule of the wise might easily be appropriated by professors less forbearing about grasping for power, less fastidious in the use of it, less modest in sharing it, than the philosophers with whom Aristotle was acquainted. One gags at the thought that such characters might be the chief beneficiaries of the classical principle of the rule of the wise. At no time does democracy seem more attractive than when it is seen to exclude the rule of professors and intellectuals. When I think of this powerful argument for democracy, I think of Mark Twain. And when I think of Twain, I think of the man whose hero is Twain, whom this volume honors, Carey McWilliams.

NOTES

1. Page references are to the French text in Alexis de Tocqueville, *De la démocratie en Amérique*, vol. 2 of *Oeuvres, Édition Pléiade* (Paris: Gallimard, 1992), I 2.7., 289 (hereafter cited as *DA*).

2. "The few, the brave, the Marines!" Here is a recruiting slogan strange to modern ears, yet apparently it works for a few. Consider how its force would be diminished if "the few" were replaced by "a minority."

3. All references to the *Politics* (hereafter cited as *Pol.*), are to the standard section numbers.

Index

Aaron, Daniel, 235
accident, Bible on, 17–18
Achilles, 214–16, 218
Adams, Henry, 125
Adams-Jefferson correspondence, 67–79
Adams, John, 67–79, 81
Adams, John Quincy, 83, 94, 177–78, 180
Addams, Jane, 130–48
Alien and Sedition Acts, 92, 176
Alinsky, Saul, 282
ancients: on friendship, 49–57; on nature, 4–5
Anouilh, Jean, 215
Anti-Federalism, 171–74, 239
Aquinas, Thomas, Saint, 39n23, 41n31–32
Arendt, Hannah, 254
aristocracy: Adams-Jefferson correspondence on, 70–71, 73–75; Aristotle on, 290–92; and citizenship, 155–58; Thoreau on, 128; Tocqueville on, 172
Aristotle: on citizenship, 157; on civic education, 6, 166; on friendship, 48–49, 52–57, 67; on political community, 156; on responsibility, 33; on tyranny of

majority, 289–97
art, Tocqueville on, 103–5
associations, 6; McWilliams on, 272. *See also* institutions
Augustine, Saint, 26, 40n31, 41n34, 43n42

Baldwin, James, 240
Banning, Lance, 188n21
Barber, Benjamin R., 62
Bell, Daniel, 262n45
Bellah, Robert, 267n72
Benton, Thomas Hart, 184
Bible, 193, 212n48, 214; Addams on, 131–32; McWilliams on, 13; political theory and, 13–43; Spinoza on, 31
Bourne, Randolph, 145n34
Boyce, Donald, 220
Brand, Donald, 173
Brecht, Bertolt, 215
Brooke, Dorothea, 218–19
Brown, Pat, 2
Buber, Martin, 266n70
Budd, Billy, 218–19
Burke, Edmund, 193, 209

Calhoun, John C., 83, 91, 183
campaign finance reform, 251–52

299

About the Contributors

Dennis Bathory writes about Saint Augustine, Alexis de Tocqueville, and William Shakespeare and teaches political theory at Rutgers University where he has been a colleague of Wilson Carey McWilliams for nearly thirty years. Like several in this volume, he is a graduate of Oberlin College where he met McWilliams in 1961.

Patrick J. Deneen is assistant professor of politics at Princeton University. He is the author of *The Odyssey of Political Theory: The Politics of Departure and Return,* as well as articles on ancient and American political thought. He has been a student and friend of McWilliams since 1982.

Dennis Hale earned a B.A. in government at Oberlin College in 1966, and a Ph.D. in political science at City University of New York in 1977. Since 1978 he has been a member of the political science department at Boston College and served as department chair from 1989 to 1997. He is the co-editor, with Marc Landy, of *The Nature of Politics: Selected Essays of Bertrand de Jouvenel* and *The Good Life: Essays in Political Economy* by Bertrand de Jouvenel. He has published essays on American citizenship, local government, property taxation, and public administration, and is at work on a study of the jury system.

Norman Jacobson is professor emeritus at the University of California, specializing in modern European and American political thought. Since his retirement from Berkeley, he has been visiting professor at Stanford University. His most recent publication is "The Strange Case of Hobbesian Man."

Marc Landy is professor of political science at Boston College. With Sidney Milkis, he wrote *Presidential Greatness*. He also wrote *The Environmental Protection Agency from Nixon to Clinton: Asking the Wrong Questions* and is an editor of *The New Politics of Public Policy*. His recent articles include: "Local Government and Environmental Policy," in *Dilemmas of Scale in American Federal Democracy* (edited by Martha Derthick) and, with Kyle Dell, "The Politics of Risk Reform," in *The Duke Environmental Law and Policy Forum*.

Harvey C. Mansfield is William R. Kenan, Jr. Professor of Government at Harvard University. He has written on Edmund Burke, Niccolò Machiavelli, executive power, liberalism, and American constitutionalism. In 1960–62, he taught at the University of California, Berkeley, where he had the great and enduring pleasure of meeting McWilliams.

Mac McCorkle is president of McCorkle Policy Consulting in Durham, North Carolina. He has written on Charles Beard's reading of the Constitution in *The American Journal of Legal History* and the new Republican South in *Southern Cultures*, as well as other articles on American politics.

Sidney M. Milkis is professor of government and senior scholar at the Miller Center of Public Affairs, University of Virginia. He is the author of *The President and the Parties: The Transformation of the American Party System Since the New Deal* and *Political Parties and Constitutional Government: Remaking American Democracy*, and coauthor, with Marc Landy, of *Presidential Greatness*. He is deeply indebted to McWilliams, the preeminent interpreter of the American political experience of our time, for his generous tutorials and unfailing friendship.

Thomas L. Pangle is professor of political science at the University of Toronto, and a Fellow of the Royal Society of Canada. He is the author of *The Ennobling of Democracy* and *The Spirit of Modern Republicanism*, among other writings.

Gerald M. Pomper is Board of Governors Professor of Political Science at Rutgers University. He is the author of *Passions and Interests*, and has edited a quadrennial series on United States elections from 1976 to 2000, which includes contributions by him, McWilliams, and others. His essay in this book will be the basis of a fuller study to be published by Yale University Press.

David E. Price is Fourth District congressman from North Carolina and a former professor of political science and public policy at Duke University. He has written *Bringing Back the Parties, The Congressional Experience,* and several articles on American political thought, ethics and public policy, and Congress.

Joseph Romance is assistant professor of political science at Drew University and a coauthor of *A Republic of Parties?* His research, as befitting a student of McWilliams, concerns American political thought and the American founding.

Edward Schwartz is president of the Institute for the Study of Civic Values. He has served as a city councilman-at-large and director of Philadelphia's Office of Housing and Community Development. He is the author of *NetActivism: How Citizens Use the Internet.*

Nancy L. Schwartz is professor of government at Wesleyan University. She has written *The Blue Guitar: Political Representation and Community* and articles on Karl Marx, Max Weber, equality, and elections in Israel. She is working on a project on women and courage in Greek and Jewish thought. At Oberlin College in the 1960s, she was introduced to the study of international relations by McWilliams and George A. Lanyi.

Tracy B. Strong is professor of political science at the University of California, San Diego. He is the author of many articles and several books, including *Friedrich Nietzsche and the Politics of Transfiguration, Jean-Jacques Rousseau: The Politics of the Ordinary,* and, with Marcel Hénaff, the forthcoming *Public Space and Democracy.* From 1990 until 1999, he was the editor of *Political Theory.* He was introduced to the study of political theory and politics at Oberlin College in the early 1960s by McWilliams and John D. Lewis.

Bob Pepperman Taylor is associate professor of political science and the director of the John Dewey Honors Program at the University of Vermont. He is the author of *Our Limits Transgressed: Environmental Political Thought in America* and *America's Bachelor Uncle: Thoreau and the American Polity.*

Jean M. Yarbrough is professor of government and legal studies at Bowdoin College. She is the author of *American Virtues: Thomas Jefferson on the Character of a Free People,* in a series edited by McWilliams and Lance Banning, as well as numerous articles on American political thought. She and McWilliams have been friends for twenty-five years.